WRONGFUL DISMISSAL HANDBOOK

John R. Sproat
LL.B. (Western), LL.M. (Harvard)

CARSWELL
Thomson Professional Publishing

The paper used in this publication meets the minimum requirements of the American National Standard for Information Sciences — Permanence of Paper for Printed Library Materials, ANSI Z39.48-1984.

Canadian Cataloguing in Publication Data

Sproat, John R., 1952—
Wrongful dismissal handbook

Includes index.
ISBN 0-459-55991-5

1. Employees — Dismissal of — Law and legislation — Ontario. I. Title.

KE0658.S77 1995 344.713'012596 C95-932289-2
KF3471.S77 1995

CARSWELL
Thomson Professional Publishing

One Corporate Plaza, 2075 Kennedy Road, Scarborough, Ontario M1T 3V4
Customer Service:
Toronto 1-416-609-3800
Elsewhere in Canada/U.S. 1-800-387-5164
Fax 1-416-298-5094

TABLE OF CONTENTS

WRONGFUL DISMISSAL

TABLE OF CONTENTS

TABLE OF CASES

All references are to headings of the text.

TABLE OF STATUTES

References are to headings in the text, except for references to Appendices, which indicate that the text of an Act or regulation is reproduced in an Appendix at the end of the book.

CANADA

NEW BRUNSWICK

ONTARIO

Part II — Wrongful Dismissal

2
INTRODUCTION

The principles of law pertaining to wrongful dismissal generally incline in favour of the employee. This is stated as a fact and not as a criticism. The generally greater sophistication and resources of the employer and the relative vulnerability of the employee justify this result.

A consideration throughout this Part is that if the parties do not agree with the common law legal principles that have been developed, it is within their power to, in effect, change the law. The parties to an employment contract enjoy freedom of contract and, subject to compliance with any applicable statutes, are free to agree on whatever contractual terms they see fit. For the purposes of certainty, contractual terms should be documented in an employment contract.

The point should also be made that employment contracts are desirable for employees at all levels. Since an employee's entitlement on termination depends primarily on age, position and length of service, it makes no sense to reserve employment contracts for only those with more senior positions. An employment contract need not be lengthy or complex. Many employment contracts are not more than one or two pages.

Having ascertained the applicable legal principles, whether at common law or pursuant to an employment contract, it is of overriding significance to consider the facts of the particular case. The sympathies of the Court also generally incline in favour of the employee. Again, this is stated as a fact and not as a criticism.

The Court tends to view the employment relationship as resting somewhere between a family type of relationship and an arm's length commercial relationship. Thus, for reasons that are both understandable and reasonable, the Court tends to view particular conduct of an employee in the context of overall service to the employer and takes into account, to some extent, personal difficulties and idiosyncrasies of the employee. Thus, the Court is much more prepared to consider extenuating circumstances in judging particular conduct against an applicable legal standard than it would be in any other commercial context.

It must also be remembered that judges are not omniscient and their findings are not infallible. In making findings of fact, on a balance of probabilities, the Court may find that the employer, having greater resources and sophistication than the employee, bears a special responsibility to record the terms of the employment contract and the events that transpire during the course of employment. If the employer fails to do so, this will often incline the Court in favour of the evidence tendered by an employee on a particular point.

In summary, in considering any employment law problem legal counsel, and their clients, should be careful to consider the general context. The legal advice that would be appropriate given a recitation of a particular set of facts, on a particular date, may be quite inappropriate when considered in the broader context of the entire employment history and the circumstances of the employee.

3
THE CONTRACT OF EMPLOYMENT

3.1 GENERAL PRINCIPLES

The law of wrongful dismissal is, quite simply, the law of contract applied to persons in an employment relationship. Each and every employee has an employment contract. While it is quite common to hear employers and employees state that they do not have a contract, an accurate statement is that they do not have a specific written employment agreement. The very agreement of the employee to do certain work, and the agreement of the employer to pay for that work, constitutes a contract.

A contract is, for the most part, a creation of the parties. The most fundamental principle throughout this Part is that the parties have freedom to contract as they choose and for that reason the central question is, "What did the parties agree to?" In the absence of a comprehensive written employment contract it is often very difficult to ascertain precisely what the parties have agreed to. Further, the determination of precisely what was agreed to is most important after the relationship has terminated, when the parties are often in an antagonistic, adversarial relationship. This leaves the Court in the position of having to piece together the terms of the contract from findings of fact as to pre-employment representations, written and unwritten employer policies and practices, communications between employer and employee and the conduct of the parties over the course of the employment relationship. This would be a difficult exercise at the best of times. It becomes much more difficult, however, when the recollection of the parties is coloured by ill will.

In determining what the parties have agreed to, the courts will generally resolve any ambiguity or doubt in favour of the contractual interpretation advanced by the employee. In broad terms, the fact that the employer has greater economic resources, legal sophistication and opportunity to document the contractual terms supports the logic of what amounts to a presumption in favour of the employee.

The second fundamental principle underlying this Part is that once you have determined what the parties have agreed to, one or the other of the parties cannot effect fundamental, adverse changes to the agreement without providing reasonable advance notice of such change. To implement a fundamental adverse change without reasonable advance notice will generally constitute a breach of contract. The most important example of this principle is the requirement that in the absence of "just cause" for dismissal, or an agreement to the contrary, the employer must provide the employee with reasonable advance notice of termination. A similar requirement exists for many other types of fundamental changes and the implementation of a fundamental change without proper notice may constitute a constructive termination of the employment relationship (see Chapter 4).

As stated above, this Part is concerned with the contract created by the parties. Parts III and IV, which deal with the *Human Rights Code* and the *Employment Standards Act*, address the extent to which the agreement of the parties is supplemented, or perhaps overridden, by statutes enacted to achieve certain public policy objectives.

3.2 WRITTEN CONTRACTS

(a) Enforceability of Written Contracts

The traditional approach to employment contracts, insofar as they purport to limit the period of notice to which the employee is entitled on dismissal, is demonstrated by the trial decision of the Supreme Court of Ontario in *Wallace v. Toronto Dominion Bank* (1981), 39 O.R. (2d) 350, 81 C.L.L.C. 14,122 (H.C.), reversed in part (1983), 41 O.R. (2d) 161, 83 C.L.L.C. 14,031, 145 D.L.R. (3d) 431 (C.A.). In this case, the plaintiff had signed an employment agreement in January 1970, some three months after commencing employment, providing that the bank might terminate the plaintiff's employment at any time upon four weeks' notice or payment in lieu hereof. In January 1976, the bank unilaterally amended the agreement to provide for eight weeks' notice. This amendment was prompted by certain amendments to the *Canada Labour Code*. As set out in the Court of Appeal reasons, the contractual entitlement to termination pay was, at all times, greater than the entitlement under the *Canada Labour Code*.

Although Wallace's annual salary increased from $17,500 in 1974 to $37,050 in 1978, it was felt that he did not fit the corporate mould. In July 1978, the bank determined that it would place Wallace on probation for three months and, in any event, reduce his salary by $6,100 at the conclusion of the probationary period. Wallace's performance during the probationary period was satisfactory. At the conclusion of the probationary period, however, a dispute arose as to whether the fact of the probation would be deleted from his record. When the bank refused to delete this notation from his record, Wallace left his employment. Mr. Justice Osborne, the trial Judge, found that the actions of the bank constituted an act of constructive dismissal. He then considered whether the agreement providing for eight weeks' pay on termination was binding.

Mr. Justice Osborne found that the stipulation for eight weeks' pay in lieu of notice was "unfair" and "unenforceable". In support of this conclusion he cited the following passage from the reasons of Lord Denning in *Lloyds Bank Ltd. v. Bundy* (1974), [1975] 1 Q.B. 326 at 339 (C.A.):

> Gathering all together, I would suggest that through all these instances there runs a single thread. They rest on "inequality of bargaining power." By virtue of it, the English law gives relief to one who, without independent advice, enters into a contract upon terms which are very unfair or transfers property for a consideration which is grossly inadequate, when his bargaining power is grievously impaired by reason of his own needs or desires, or by his own ignorance or infirmity, coupled with undue influences or pressures brought to bear on him by or for the benefit of the other. When I use the word "undue" I do not mean to suggest that the principle depends on proof of any wrongdoing. The one who stipulates for an unfair advantage may be moved solely by his own self-interest, unconscious of the distress he is bringing to the other. (at p. 362)

The Ontario Court of Appeal, however, allowed the bank's appeal, holding that the agreement providing for eight weeks' pay on termination was binding. Mr. Justice Robins first noted that no issue of unconscionability or unenforceability had been pleaded by the plaintiff, and that there was virtually no evidence as to the circumstances of the hiring. His Lordship, for a majority of the Court, then addressed the legal issues in fairly broad terms, stating:

> Here, the terms were not hidden in a maze of fine print but were set forth clearly and understandably; on the evidence, there was no attempt to take advantage of the plaintiff or to exert influence over him so as to procure a contract that

> otherwise would not have been made; and nothing that transpired can be treated as being oppressive of him or as constituting the type of coercion that may vitiate consent.
>
> . . . .
>
> Certainly, there are readily imaginable cases where an employee's level of responsibility and corresponding status has escalated so significantly during his period of employment that it can be concluded that the substratum of an employment contract entered into at the time of his original hiring has disappeared or it can be implied that that contract could not have been intended to apply to the position in the company ultimately occupied by him. But that is not this case. Here, the plaintiff, as already indicated, did not attain a level of senior responsibility and his position on leaving the bank commanded a lower rating on the bank's scale than the position he held on entering its employ. In addition, the staff declaration and personnel manual made clear throughout that the termination provisions agreed to continued in effect and remained applicable to persons of the plaintiff's status. In the circumstances of this employment relationship, passage of time cannot, of itself, afford a basis for vitiating the contract. (at pp. 180-181)

In dissent, however, Mr. Justice Houlden adopted the following summary of the law:

> In his text, *Fraud in Equity* (London, 1957), Sheridan sums up the relevant law in these words (at p. 73):
>
> > The cases in which equity has relieved from a bargain where there is no misrepresentation, no fiduciary relation, no mistake or undue influence or duress, and no question of a party being an expectant heir or the like, are difficult to classify. Probably the only safe generalisation is that the court considers each case on its individual merits to see whether one party has taken advantage of the weakness or necessity of the other to an extent which strikes the judge as being a greater advantage than the current morality of the ordinary run of business men allows. (at pp. 169-170)

Mr. Justice Houlden found that Wallace should be relieved of the consequence of the termination provision. In support of his conclusion he referred to the fact that the initial hiring was not conditional upon executing an employment agreement, the employment agreement was not signed until the expiry of the probationary period (at which time Wallace was no doubt anxious to continue his employment) and the fact that the termination clause was never explained to Wallace.

Jobber v. Addressograph Multigraph of Can. Ltd. (1980), 10 B.L.R. 278 (Ont. H.C.), reversed (1980), 1 C.C.E.L. 87 (Ont. C.A.), is a case decided before *Wallace, supra,* but which was not reported until after *Wallace*, and as such has received less attention. In *Jobber*, the plaintiff had been employed by the defendant for 18 years, pursuant to identical written contracts of employment entered into with each change in job position. At the time of termination in 1978, the plaintiff occupied the second most important position in the company.

The written contract contained the following provision under the heading "Termination":

> This contract may be terminated at any time and without cause by AM or by you. In the event of termination, AM will give you at least thirty days advance notice of termination plus any additional notice that may be required by any applicable legislation and similarly, you shall give AM a minimum of thirty days notice if you voluntarily terminate this Agreement. (at p. 90)

A unanimous Ontario Court of Appeal upheld the contractual term limiting notice, stating:

> There is no suggestion that the parties were not at arms' length at the time of entering into the agreement, nor is there any suggestion that there was any coercion or improper influence of any kind forcing the respondent to accept this term. In our view the clause is clear and unambiguous and states the measurement of the required length of notice when either party decided to terminate the employment without cause. The fact that no notice was given does not thereby eliminate the provisions of the termination clause from consideration. (at p. 91)

In the years since the *Wallace* decision, numerous cases have upheld clearly drafted employment contracts which have been fairly presented to, and accepted by, the employee. An example is the case of *Hine v. Susan Shoe Industries Ltd.* (1989), 28 C.C.E.L. 179, 71 O.R. (2d) 438 (H.C.), affirmed (1994), 3 C.C.E.L. (2d) 119, 18 O.R. (3d) 255 (C.A.). In this case the employee had been given an opportunity to "write his own ticket," and had drafted the employment contract. The Court upheld the contractual notice provision even though it was by that time 24 years old. The Court held that as the fundamental terms of the contract had been applied for the 24-year term of the employment, and the contract was not unconscionable or otherwise unenforceable, the Court was bound to enforce its terms.

As hereinafter set out, the pre-*Wallace* reluctance to uphold employment contracts will assert itself if the contract is unclear or if the continuing agreement of the employee to be bound by the contract was obtained improperly.

(b) Circumstances Rendering Written Contracts Unenforceable

The general principles of contract law apply to employment contracts. It is beyond the scope of this work to discuss all of the general contract law principles which may lead to invalidity or unenforceability. In practical terms, however, employment contracts will most often be argued to be unenforceable, or invalid, on the basis that:

1. There is in fact no agreement between the parties, applicable at the relevant time (usually at the time of termination), with respect to the term in issue. This would include the question of whether or not a term had simply been stipulated unilaterally, or had been agreed to. In the alternative, the issue could be whether a term that had been agreed to continued to govern at the relevant time.

2. The agreement, although proven in evidence, was not voluntarily entered into in that the agreement was secured by duress or undue influence, or was otherwise unconscionable.

The following cases provide typical examples of the types of situation in which a court may find an alleged contractual term to be unenforceable.

In *Nardocchio v. Cdn. Imperial Bank of Commerce* (1979), 41 N.S.R. (2d) 26, 76 A.P.R. 26 (T.D.), a written employment contract was found to be unenforceable. The plaintiff had been employed by the bank for approximately 12 years, beginning as a teller and rising through the ranks to the position of an assistant accountant. The termination was effected by a letter which simply recited the fact of termination and indicated that three months' salary was being given in lieu of notice.

The bank defended on the basis of a document signed by the plaintiff which provided in part:

> (4) that after the expiration of my probationary period as aforesaid my employment may be terminated by me upon giving three months' prior notice in writing to the Bank or by the Bank upon giving to me three months' prior notice in writing or paying to me an amount equivalent to three months' salary in lieu of such notice . . . . (at pp. 30-31)

The plaintiff's evidence was that although it was her signature on the document, ''she was not aware of the existence of the document or its contents at any time during her employment with the bank''. (at p. 34)

The Court concluded that:

> I am not at all satisfied that Miss Nardocchio knew what she was signing or understood all the terms and conditions of the form. In those circumstances I find it difficult to conclude that there was a meeting of minds on all the terms of the agreement and that there was a mutually agreed upon contract with respect to the termination of employment clauses.
>
> It seems to me that the defendant bank would have been wise to clarify all the terms and conditions of employment to the plaintiff upon her advancement to a management position in 1975. At the very least this would have made it impossible for the plaintiff to plead lack of knowledge of the termination provisions.
>
> I also bear in mind that Miss Nardocchio had never at any stage of her employment been referred to the so-called contract of employment, Exhibit 1, and I accept her evidence that she was not aware of its existence. In these circumstances I consider that the three month notice provision contained in numbered paragraph 4 of Exhibit 1 if applied would be a harsh term and in my opinion that term of the contract is not enforceable. (at p. 41)

O'Shaughnessy v. Drake International Inc. (1986), 14 C.C.E.L. 192 (Ont. H.C.), provides a further example of a situation in which an employment contract was found to be unenforceable. In this case O'Shaughnessy orally agreed to accept employment as a sales representative. It was only after he had commenced his employment that he was presented with a package of documents, one of which was a ''Memorandum of Agreement'' which limited the notice period to which he would be entitled on termination. Approximately ten months after commencing employment, O'Shaughnessy was promoted to the position of branch manager. There was evidence that it was the practice of Drake to provide branch managers with a new employment agreement, different from the employment agreement applicable to sales representatives.

The Court commented on the significance of the failure to provide O'Shaughnessy with a new employment agreement upon his promotion to branch manager, as follows:

> I accept the evidence of the plaintiff that when he was promoted to branch manager of the Ottawa operation he was to obtain from his employer a new contract for his execution. That contract never arrived, but the plaintiff commenced and continued performing his new duties until he was dismissed in November 1982.
>
> The defence relies heavily on the first clause of the agreement which states:
>
> The Employee shall serve the Employer in such capacity as may from time to time be determined by the Employer.
>
> That provision, says Drake, constitutes an agreement that the terms of the memorandum of agreement continue in force regardless of the type of work the manager is required to perform. That could be the case in a situation where no new agreement was contemplated. However, I am satisfied on the evidence of the plaintiff and of one of his former superiors, Walter Roy Fitzgerald, who was vice-president, Security Services of Drake for North America, that there was to be a new written contract setting out the terms of O'Shaughnessy's new position. At the time the new oral agreement was entered into and Mr. O'Shaughnessy commenced his new duties, the former written contract came to an end. The fact that the new terms of employment were apparently never reduced to writing is irrelevant. (at p. 194)

Singh v. Valley Forge Automotive of Can. Ltd. (1989), 27 C.C.E.L. 181 (Ont. Dist. Ct.), demonstrates the difficulty in relying upon terms that are stipulated by the employer after hiring. In that case the plaintiff was hired by the defendant and thereafter signed several documents of a routine nature and a further document that contained the words "I understand and agree that my employment is for no definite term and may, regardless of the date of payment of my wages and salary, be terminated at any time without any previous notice." The plaintiff was subsequently dismissed with one week's notice. The defendant conceded that the plaintiff had not been dismissed for cause but argued that the document quoted above should govern.

The Court allowed the action, stating that at the time of hiring the plaintiff had entered into an employment contract for an indefinite term. On the evidence, the Court found that the contract entered into when the plaintiff was hired was not varied by the subsequent signing of the document since there was no evidence of a mutual intention to vary the original contractual terms. Furthermore, as the parties had not intended that the plaintiff could or would be terminated without notice, the implied term requiring reasonable notice of termination applied.

(c) Statutory Invalidation of Employment Contracts

Before discussing this subject, some words of explanation are in order because the title is somewhat misleading. As previously stated, statutory enactments generally prevail over the terms of an employment contract, whether written or oral. Thus, in a sense, virtually the whole of the *Human Rights Code* and the *Employment Standards Act* ("*E.S.A.*") could be viewed as statutory enactments invalidating employment contracts that are inconsistent with the statute.

Most written employment contracts, however, contain a provision which limits the compensation to which an employee is entitled to in the event of termination. The termination provision is usually the most important reason, and often the *raison d'être,* for having a written employment agreement. It seems, therefore, to be appropriate to discuss under this heading the effect of the *E.S.A.* on termination provisions that may be included in written employment contracts.

The *E.S.A.* contains the following provisions:

> **3.** Subject to section 4, no employer, employee, employers' organization or employees' organization shall contract out of or waive an employment standard, and any such contracting out or waiver is null and void. [R.S.O. 1990, c. E.14]
>
> . . . .
>
> **6.**-(1) No civil remedy of an employee against his or her employer is suspended or affected by this Act. [R.S.O. 1990, c. E.14]

In *Machtinger v. HOJ Industries Ltd.* (10 April 1987), Toronto 5340/84, 5341/85 (Ont. H.C.), reversed (1988), 23 C.C.E.L. 77, 66 O.R. (2d) 545, 55 D.L.R. (4th) 401, (*sub nom. Machtinger v. HOJ Industries Ltd.; Lefebvre v. HOJ Industries Ltd.*) 31 O.A.C. 1 (C.A.), reversed 40 C.C.E.L. 1, 7 O.R (3d) 480 (note), [1992] 1 S.C.R. 986, 92 C.L.L.C. 14,022, 91 D.L.R. (4th) 491, (*sub nom. Lefebvre v. HOJ Industries Ltd.; Machtinger v. HOJ Indutries Ltd.*) 136 N.R. 40, 53 O.A.C. 200, the Court considered the situation of two employees who had signed a series of employment contracts which, at the time of termination, provided for a period of notice less than the minimum standard prescribed by the *E.S.A.* In the case of one employee the contract provided for two weeks' notice, or pay in lieu of notice, and in the case of the other employee, for no notice, or pay in lieu of notice. At trial, the Court held that the contractual provisions respecting notice were rendered null and void by virtue of section 3 of the *E.S.A.* The Court then simply proceeded to award each of the employees the period of notice appropriate at common law, which in the case of one employee was seven months' notice, and in the case of the other employee, seven and one-half months' notice. At trial it had been admitted that the contracts of employment were valid and binding apart from the *E.S.A.*

The Court of Appeal, however, allowed the appeal and found that the employees were not entitled to recover any amount in addition to the minimum provided by the *E.S.A.* The Supreme Court of Canada allowed a further appeal and restored the judgment at trial.

Mr. Justice Iacobucci, for the Court, started with the proposition that there is a presumption that reasonable advance notice of termination of an employment contract is required, which presumption can be rebutted only if the contract of employment clearly specifies some other period of notice. Iacobucci J., however, concluded that since the contractual provisions respecting notice were null and void they were "null and void for all purposes, and cannot be used as evidence of the party's intention". While that reasoning was sufficient to dispose of the appeal, Iacobucci J. went on to make some very general comments as to the policy considerations and the nature of the employment contract as follows:

> The harm which the Act seeks to remedy is that individual employees, and in particular non-unionized employees, are often in an unequal bargaining position in relation to their employers. As stated by Swinton, supra, at p. 363:
>
> > [T]he terms of the employment contract rarely result from an exercise of free bargaining power in the way that the paradigm commercial exchange between two traders does. Individual employees on the whole lack both the bargaining power and the information necessary to achieve more favourable contract provisions than those offered by the employer, particularly with regard to tenure.
>
> Accordingly, an interpretation of the Act which encourages employers to comply with the minimum requirements of the Act, and so extends its protections to as many employees as possible, is to be favoured over one that does not. In this regard, the fact that many individual employees may be unaware of their statutory and common law rights in the employment context is of fundamental importance. As Brian Etherington suggests in "The Enforcement of Harsh Termination Provisions in Personal Employment Contracts: The Rebirth of Freedom of Contract in Ontario" (1990) McGill L.J. 459, at p. 468, "the majority of unorganized employees would not even expect reasonable notice prior to dismissal and many would be surprised to learn they are not employed at the employer's discretion."
>
> If the only sanction which employers potentially face for failure to comply with the minimum notice periods prescribed by the Act is an order that they minimally comply with the Act, employers will have little incentive to make contracts with their employees that comply with the Act. As Swinton and Etherington suggest, most individual employees are unaware of their legal rights, or unwilling or unable to go to the trouble and expense of having them vindicated. Employers can rely on the fact that many employees will not challenge contractual notice provisions which are in fact contrary to employment standards legislation. Employers such as the present respondent can contract with their employees for notice periods below the statutory minimum, knowing that only those individual employees who take legal action after they are dismissed will in fact receive the protection of the minimum statutory notice provisions. (at pp. 17-18)

It is, however, interesting to note that the bargaining power of Lefebvre was such that in 1985, at age 29, he had a compensation package that paid him approximately $75,000 per annum. Further, the conclusion that "most individual employees are unaware of their legal rights, or unwilling or unable to go to the trouble and expense of having them vindicated" is not consistent with the experience of human resources professionals and employment law lawyers.

(d) Significance of Documents Outside the Contract

Certain documents may be specifically referred to in the written employment contract, and as such should properly be read with, and regarded as part of, the employment contract. There are, however, numerous other documents which may be argued to be part of the employment contract, or to affect the terms that might otherwise be implied into the particular contract of employment, whether oral or written. By way of example, a company may issue general statements of policy. For a small company these policy statements may simply be notices posted on an irregular basis. For larger companies there may be lengthy policy and procedure manuals that attempt to provide a comprehensive statement of the respective rights and obligations of employer and employee.

There may also be documents directed to the position of particular employees. Thus, a memorandum from a person in authority indicating that a particular person will not have to work on the weekends, or will not be subject to a transfer to a new geographic location, may be argued to be part of the employment contract. If one recalls that the contract is nothing more than the agreement of the parties, virtually any document created by a person in authority, and having the effect of benefiting an employee, may be argued to be part of the contract.

In the case of company documents which benefit the employee, the employee will always have a good argument that he or she continued employment after publication of the document in reliance upon it, and for that reason it should be considered as part of the employment contract. On the other hand, since all contractual terms must expressly or impliedly be agreed to by the parties, an employee generally has a strong argument that any employer publication which is to the detriment of the employee, has not been agreed to, notwithstanding the fact of continued employment. This is particularly the case when the employer publication, suggesting conditions to the detriment of the employee, has been instituted without advance notice to the employee, or when the employer attempts to rely upon it within a relatively short period of time after publication.

In *King v. Gulf Canada Ltd.* (1992), 45 C.C.E.L. 238, 60 O.A.C. 139 (C.A.), leave to appeal to S.C.C. refused (June 17, 1993), Doc. 23440 (S.C.C.), the Court considered whether a letter sent to the employee by the president of the company, after approximately nine years of employment, and four years prior to termination, constituted part of the contract of employment. This letter addressed the operating and business principles of Gulf Canada and stated that the principles constituted a condition of continued employment.

The Court, however, rejected the argument advanced by the employee that the business principles were contractual terms of employment stating as follows:

> In relying on the July 1978 letter as contractual, counsel for the appellant points to two specific provisions in the document – first, a clause under the "Basic Business Principles" part, which reads, ". . . the following specific principles represent the policy of the Company *and are binding on all employees*" [emphasis added]; and second, a clause under the "Application" part, which reads, "Strict compliance with the guidelines contained in the foregoing Business Principles *is a condition of continued employment for all employees.*" [Emphasis added.]
>
> In his reasons the trial judge treated the July 1978 letter as part of the employment contract between the parties. On page 11 of his reasons he states:
>
> > It is the position of the plaintiff that it [the letter] formed part of and was a term of his [Mr. King's] continued employment. This was not seriously disputed by the defendant and for the purposes of these reasons I shall assume that it does.
>
> This issue may not have been disputed seriously at trial, but it certainly was on appeal. The respondent argues that Mr. King did nothing to change his position in reliance on this document, and therefore it does not constitute a binding argeement between the parties. This is a reasonable position given the evidence referred to on the appeal. In his evidence, Mr. King acknowledged the letter to be a statement of the principles under which the company had operated in the past, and he stated that it gave him some comfort; however, we were referred to no evidence that it changed in any way his relationship with, or his work on behalf of the company.
>
> In addition, I am of the view that the words of the letter which have a contractual flavour, do not have the effect of rendering the letter a legally binding contract. They are contained in the parts of the letter which outline broadly the "Basic Business Principles of Gulf Canada" and their "Application". The "Basic Business Principles" are very broadly framed motherhood type statements, and although they are stated to be "binding on all employees", we are referred to no evidence indicating that either party intended these statements to constitute words of contract between the parties. I take a similar view of the apparently contractual words contained in the "Application" part of the letter. (at p. 241)

In *Lyonde v. Cdn. Acceptance Corp.* (1983), 3 C.C.E.L. 220 (Ont. H.C.), the Court addressed the significance of a company policy document that was published in 1979, in considering the 1981 termination of the vice-president of administration after 24 years of service. The Court discussed the significance of the company policy stating:

> The second point taken by the defendant is that provision 2452 of the defendant's management and personnel procedures is a contract or part of a contract of employment between these parties. That document was prepared in the year 1979 and sets out the company's policy with respect to separation pay allowances and, applied to someone of the plaintiff's time with the company,

> indicates that the company's policy is to pay about six months' salary in lieu of notice.
>
> It is contended that, because the plaintiff admittedly knew of that document and was part of the management team at the time it was adopted as company policy, it is, in fact, a contract between the defendant and himself, or that it ought to be implied to be a part of the contract of employment between the plaintiff and the defendant.
>
> I find it somewhat difficult in theory to comprehend how the policy of one party to a contract can become binding upon the other party to the contract simply because it has been adopted as policy. As a factual matter, I find it difficult to accept that an employee who, at that time, had been with the company for over 21 years, would be expected to resign if a company adopted a policy which, so far as he knew at that time, probably had no relation to him whatsoever. At that time, I have no doubt that he thought that he would work till his normal retirement age of 65 and, particularly in the light of the letter which he had received from the executive vice-president of the parent company, he would have reason to expect that he was continuing in his position for the rest of his working life. He certainly did not specifically accept or reject the company policy. I think all that that is, is company policy; it is nothing more or less. (at pp. 223-224)

In his decision Mr. Justice Galligan left open the question of whether an employer could introduce the terms of an employment policy into the employment contract, by providing the employee with reasonable advance notice that after a certain date their employment would continue pursuant to terms and conditions set out in the employment policy. In this regard Mr. Justice Galligan stated:

> It would remain for the Court to determine in an individual case whether the company policy constituted reasonable notice in law, or whether it did not. This is not a case where he specifically accepted company policy as binding upon him, nor do I think it is a case in which his conduct must necessarily be taken as constituting acceptance of the company policy. (at p. 224)

Thus, a mere statement of policy is not a part of the employment contract. The further question, concerning the right of the employer to give advance notice that employment will continue on specified terms, thereby rendering continued service after the passage of a reasonable notice period an acceptance of the specified terms, is discussed in Chapter 27.2.

(e) Conclusions

The lesson of the foregoing cases is that a properly worded and clear contractual provision limiting notice will be upheld. With the encouragement of the decision in *Wallace* (see heading 3.2(a), above), it is strongly recommended that employers consider employment contracts that specify and limit the period of notice. As a practical matter, the spirit of optimism that pervades the hiring process will mean that few employees will balk at agreeing to a contractually limited notice period. In the event that the employee does resist agreeing to a limited period of notice, then it is always open to the employer to amend or waive the provision as part of the pre-hiring negotiating process.

The cardinal rule with written employment contracts is to secure the agreement of the employee to the employment agreement, in its entirety, at the outset. In other words, the employer should not conclude an oral employment agreement consisting of an agreement as to position and salary, and then attempt to impose the additional terms of the written agreement after the fact. Instead, the initial offer of employment should specify that employment will be pursuant to a written employment agreement, and a copy of the agreement should be provided to the prospective employee at that time. While the Court in *Wallace* upheld the agreement, notwithstanding the manner of execution, other courts, or even an Ontario court on slightly different facts, may well come to the opposite conclusion.

If an employer wishes to contractually limit the period of notice, a sliding scale period of notice which augments any statutory entitlement is preferable. An example of this might be a provision which provides for one week of notice for each year of service in addition to any statutory entitlement.

It is also desirable to have a system whereby the employee acts to affirm the contract from time to time during the course of employment. This affirmation could be evidenced by executing a new employment agreement every time the employee changes position or receives a salary increase. It would probably be sufficient, however, if the employer, on making changes in position or salary, simply confirmed in writing the change and the agreement of the parties that, except for the change, employment would continue pursuant to the terms of the original agreement. Such a system, and a sliding scale of notice period, blunts the argument that changes in the employee's responsibility and status have caused the substratum of the original employment contract to disappear or that there is an implied term that the original contractual term was not intended to apply in the event of a later termination from a significantly elevated position.

While this discussion has focused on employment contracts as a means of defining entitlement in the event of termination, employment contracts can address other aspects of the employment contract. By way of example, an employment agreement can alter what would otherwise be the common law position as to the level of competence required of the employee, the standard of "just cause" for dismissal, or the obligation of the employer to pay employees during periods of illness.

Sample provisions for employment contracts are found at Chapter 32.3 and a sample letter affirming an employment contract is found at Chapter 32.4.

3.3 UNWRITTEN CONTRACTS

If there is no written contract or, as will often be the case, if the written contract is not comprehensive, the Court will piece together the contractual obligations of the parties having regard to:

1. Any terms that have been agreed to orally by the parties.
2. Terms that the Court will imply on the basis that the term is so basic or necessary that if the parties had addressed their minds to the issue they would have been in agreement as to the term.
3. Terms that have became so customary that the Court will imply them, even though there is reason to doubt that both parties would have been in agreement as to the term, unless there is clear evidence to the contrary.
4. Any representations by the parties (most often by the employer) which have been relied upon to the detriment of the person receiving the representation, whether or not the representation was the subject of an oral agreement.

In practical terms, the necessity to determine the precise contractual terms almost always arises in the adversarial context of a wrongful dismissal action. In the face of conflicting evidence as to a contractual term the Court will most often adopt the interpretation advanced by the employee. There are two principal reasons for favouring the employee in this regard:

1. The employer is the "expert" in personnel matters, often employing personnel specialists including legal counsel. As such the employer is properly regarded as the author of the contract in whatever form it may be, and any ambiguities should be resolved against the employer.
2. In practical terms, and particularly at other than the senior management level, it might well be considered presumptuous or offensive for the employee to take the initiative with a superior to document discussions and submit them to management as forming part of the employment contract.

3.4 FIXED OR INDEFINITE TERM CONTRACTS

The Court will be inclined, in employment situations, to find an indefinite term contract rather than a fixed term contract. There are two principal reasons for this:

1. The employer position that a contract is for a fixed term is usually advanced to support the position that the employee can be terminated, at the end of the fixed term, with no advance notice. Termination without advance notice is generally perceived to be unfair and the Court is, therefore, inclined against such a finding.
2. The finding of a fixed term contract can also present difficulties when the parties continue a contractual relationship after the fixed term and without further agreement. These difficulties are avoided by finding an indefinite term contract.

As the following cases demonstrate, however, in appropriate circumstances the Court will find a fixed term contract. The duty of the employee to mitigate damages upon termination of a fixed term contract is discussed in Chapter 6.3(b).

In the case of *Hubler v. Geneva Cosmetics Inc.* (1984), 4 C.C.E.L. 318 (Ont. Co. Ct.), the employee was hired as a marketing director. A document confirming the appointment stated that her duties were to prepare a marketing plan, in collaboration with two other employees, by October 1, 1982 and to prepare a marketing budget by November 1, 1982. The employer terminated the employee on December 31, 1982 and alleged that she had been hired on a fixed term basis, the fixed term being that stipulated for the aforementioned tasks. On the issue of whether the employee was hired for an indefinite period, the Court held that:

> [t]he plaintiff, who was unemployed at the time, accepted the invitation to apply for this position. She was interviewed by the president and hired. Her duties are set out in tab 10, the position description which she obtained from the president's secretary. That document refers to the position of director of marketing, which was the exact position indicated in tab 7 for which the plaintiff had been hired. The duties are set out under 13 headings, and, as far as I know, the plaintiff, in addition to anything else that she may have done, did in fact embark on the performance of those duties. In fact she was treated as a regular employee in every way. A credit card was issued to her, and she represented the company at an association meeting. I am completely satisfied on the evidence that she was hired as a permanent employee for an indefinite period. (at p. 320)

Thus, even though the document alluded to certain time frames, the Court held that the employee was hired for an indefinite period and was entitled to reasonable notice.

In the case of *Pelletier v. Caisse Populaire Lasalle Sudbury Ltée.* (1984), 5 C.C.E.L. 1 (Ont. H.C.), affirmed (1986), 56 O.R. (2d) 784 (C.A.), the employee was hired as branch manager. The employment contract provided as follows:

> 1) CONDITIONS
>
> . . .
>
> (b) The appointment and agreement shall have effect until the employee shall have reached the age of 65 years, subject to prior cancellation as indicated below.
>
> . . .
>
> (d) The manager may not be dismissed save for just cause, such as explicit insubordination against the authority of the Caisse or his inability to renew the Fidelity Bond. The question of the justness of the cause shall be decided by a Sudbury District judge. (at p. 4)

The employee was dismissed without "just cause". The Court was of the opinion that these clauses entitled the employee to employment from the time of hiring until age 65. The fact that there was no clause for dismissal upon reasonable notice led the Court to conclude that it was a fixed term contract. The Court held that:

> [u]nder the 1977 contract, the plaintiff would remain an employee until he reached the age of 65 years, because there was no cause for his dismissal. I find that no implied term of reasonable notice for dismissal can be read into the contract. Unlike the facts in *Cooke v. CKOY Ltd.*, [1963] 2 O.R. 257, 39 D.L.R. (2d) 209 (H.C.), the plaintiff was subject to the direction of the board and he was therefore a servant. The Master and Servant Act, R.S.O. 1980, c. 257, s. 2, provides that a contract of service is binding for no longer than nine years from the date thereof. In the present case, the contract is not binding after September 30, 1986. The fact that the Master and Servant Act was not pleaded is irrelevant because it is substantive law which must be applied. (at p. 9)

Thus, even though the contract was for a fixed term until age 65, the *Master and Servant Act*, R.S.O. 1980, c. 257 [renamed the *Employers and Employees Act*, R.S.O. 1990, c. E.12] limited the notice period to the 36½ months left, until the ninth anniversary of the contract. If not for the *Master and Servant Act,* the employee would have been entitled to damages on account of the approximately 22 years left to run on the contract, subject to the obligation of the employee to attempt to mitigate damages.

In the case of *Krewenchuk v. Lewis Construction Ltd.* (1985), 8 C.C.E.L. 206 (B.C.S.C.), the Court was concerned with the termination of an employee who had always been subject to lay-offs because of the nature of his employment as a finishing carpenter. All the work was assigned on a job-to-job basis. Often the employee would be laid off between jobs. He had, except for a brief period, worked for the employer for 23 years. Because of his length of service, the Court found that he was entitled to reasonable notice of termination, even though the work had always been assigned on a job-to-job basis. The Court held that:

> On the evidence, the defendant has failed to satisfy me that there is a custom and usage in the non-union construction industry that long term employees can be terminated without notice and without severance pay. The evidence clearly establishes that short term employees can be laid off between projects without notice or severance pay, but that is not the case here. (at p. 211)

Thus, although the work was not continuous, the Court found the employee to be hired for an indefinite period.

In the case of *Riddell v. Vancouver (City)* (1985), 11 C.C.E.L. 288 (B.C.C.A.), affirming (1984), 5 C.C.E.L. 55 (B.C.S.C.), the employee had responded to an advertisement for the position of industrial park manager. The advertisement stated that the position would last for three years, and could go on for as long as five years. The employee was not told at the time of hiring that the position was unionized, nor was any mention made of the collective agreement or the Vancouver Charter. The Vancouver Charter provided that employees "engaged on a monthly or longer basis" were entitled to 30 days' notice of termination. Similarly, under the collective agreement, employees were entitled to 30 days' notice. The Court, however, held that the employee was not subject to the collective agreement and also held that the Vancouver Charter did not apply. The trial Judge stated that:

> It is my finding on the evidence adduced before me at the trial that the plaintiff had a valid oral contract of employment for a definite term of three years. The defendant argued that if I found that the plaintiff had such a contract he was "engaged on a monthly or longer basis" and was subject to termination

(*Continued on page 3-15*)

> upon one month's notice in writing. I do not agree. I consider that the words "or longer basis" should be read ejusdem generis with "monthly" and should be confined to contracts of indefinite duration and should not be extended to contracts of a fixed term. . . . (at p. 59)

The British Columbia Court of Appeal upheld this decision.

In the case of *Paddon v. Phillips Barratt Kaiser Engineering Ltd.* (1987), 18 B.C.L.R. (2d) 170 (S.C.), the employer had entered into a contract with the government of Zaire to manage two copper mines. The contract with Zaire was for three years, with a possible extension of a further two years. The government of Zaire was able to bring the contract to an end prematurely upon four months' notice. The employee was hired as a result of the contract with Zaire. The employment contract made reference to Zaire's ability to end the contract after four months' notice. Clause 13 of the employment contract extended this notice period to all employees if the contract were ended. Clause 14 of the employment contract was the termination provision, which stated:

> In the event of termination of this agreement between yourself and PBK, for whatever reason, your expenses will be paid back to your point of origin, and your salary will be paid to the time of your termination in Zaire, plus an allowance for travel time to your point of origin by the shortest route. (at p. 175)

The Court interpreted clause 14 to apply only to terminations for cause and held that:

> I have here in mind the fixed term on the agreement being for approximately three years, with a bonus hanging on the successful completion of that three years by the employee, on the one side. On the other, I have in mind the interpretation of cl. 14, which is urged on behalf of the defendant, that being that it is an unfettered right to let the employee go for any reason. The basic intention of that agreement which I have found is that it was for three years of employment, approximately three years of employment, to the end of November 1986. To give cl. 14 the interpretation urged by the defendant would, in my view, run so contrary to this being a fixed-term contract as to, in effect, be repugnant to it. This is not to say that the parties cannot enter into a contract for a fixed term and then give one side or the other absolute discretion to put [it] into that contract in the interim, but there is little logic to that, and I find no logic to that here. I also find that it was not explained to Mr. Paddon that that could occur here. That he could be let go for cause was clear and is in harmony with an interpretation available to cl. 14. That he could be let go because of the ending of the head contract with Zaire is clear because of cl. 13. But to suggest that there is an absolutely unfettered right, in my view, runs contrary to what I find to be the basic intention of that agreement. (at p. 178)

The foregoing cases illustrate the considerations which a court will take into account in deciding whether a contract is for a fixed term. Each case will turn on its own facts. While the courts may incline against finding a fixed term contract, they will do so on proper evidence.

It is also necessary to consider the application of the *Statute of Frauds*, R.S.O. 1990, c. S.19, to fixed term contracts having a term of one year or more. In *Brendon v. Kellogg Salada Can. Inc.* (1989), 24 C.C.E.L. 179 (Ont. Dist. Ct.), the Court considered a situation in which the parties had agreed to a fixed one-year term of employment but had failed to document the agreement in writing. After seven months of employment the plaintiff was terminated without notice or cause. His Honour Judge Gautreau found that the *Statute of Frauds* did apply, reasoning as follows:

> Section 4 of the *Statute of Frauds* says, quite simply that:
>
> > No action shall be brought . . . upon any agreement that is not to be performed within the space of one year from the making thereof, unless the agreement upon which the action is brought, or some memorandum or note thereof is in writing and signed by the party to be charged therewith or some person thereunto by him lawfully authorized.
>
> Although I am satisfied that the parties clearly intended that the plaintiff would be kept on for [a] year unless he clearly "bombed out", and, although I am satisfied that this was the agreement, I am confronted by the *Statute of Frauds* which says that the plaintiff can't enforce it without a memorandum or note in writing.
>
> The plaintiff's position in relation to this is that to apply the *Statute of Frauds* would be unfair. I agree. But unfairness has been the history of the *Statute of Frauds,* and Courts have been consistently trying to get around it, and in many cases they have, for many many years. I acknowledge that the *Statute of Frauds* has been the subject of much criticism. And in this connection, a brief reference to Fridman on *The Law of Contract in Canada,* 2d ed. (Toronto: Carswell, 1986) at 219 will demonstrate this.
>
> Despite this, I am nevertheless confronted by two decisions. One is *Britain v. Rossiter,* a decision of the English Court of Appeal (1879), 11 Q.B.D. 123. The headnote briefly reads as follows, and I think it is an accurate representation of the decision:
>
> > A contract to serve for one year, the service to commence on the second day after that on which the contract is made, is a contract not to be performed within a year within the meaning of the Statute of Frauds, s. 4.
>
> And a further paragraph:
>
> > The doctrine as to part performance, whereby a contract not enforceable by an action at law, owing to the provisions of the Statute of Frauds, s. 4, was rendered enforceable in equity, was confined to suits as to the sale of interests in land, and its operation has not been extended by the provisions of the Supreme Court of Judicature Act, 1873.
>
> Then there is a decision of our own Court of Appeal, *Ackerman v. Thomson & McKinnon, Auchincloss, Kohlmeyer Inc.* (1974), 4 O.R. (2d) 240, 47 D.L.R. (3d) 524. And again I read from the headnote which says:
>
> > A written memorandum of an alleged two-year contract of employment, though signed by the employer, is insufficient to satisfy the requirements of

the Statute of Frauds . . . if it omits any reference to the duration of the contract sought to be enforced.

In the text of the reasons at p. 525, it is stated:

It is my view that because this memorandum makes no mention of the duration of the appointment of the respondent to the institutional sales

(*Continued on page 17*)

> department, it is defective in that it thereby omits reference to this material term of the alleged contract.

And then further on:

> At this point I perhaps should also note that the equitable doctrine of part performance has no application to this contract, being a contract of hiring. Accordingly, the two-year agreement in my view is unenforceable. (at pp. 183-184)

The Court proceeded to consider the rights of the plaintiff on the basis that the fixed term contract was unenforceable, stating:

> It is acknowledged by all that, despite the fact that the contract is unenforceable, nevertheless reasonable notice is still required to terminate the employment. The question that faces me is what is reasonable notice in these circumstances. What is fair? Is the fact that the defendant takes advantage of a technical defence a factor that goes into the equation of determining what is fair and what is reasonable? And when I say this, I have to acknowledge that the technical defence that the defendant is utilizing is perfectly legal and is expressly provided for by the Legislature.
>
> It is my opinion that all the circumstances must be looked at when determining what is reasonable notice. What is reasonable and fair is the test. And reasonableness and fairness cannot be decided in a vacuum. The circumstances here must include the fact that there was a contract for 1 year. The fact that the contract is unenforceable doesn't mean that the contract is void, and it does not mean that the Court cannot recognize the reality of its existence. The *Statute of Frauds* deals with enforceability of a contract and not with the validity of the transaction. In other words, the Statute deals with procedural matters and not substantive matters.
>
> In this case, we have a valued employee who has been employed for the past 7 months on what was intended to be a 1 year contract, and he had been employed for 6 previous summers with the defendant, admittedly not in high skill jobs, but, nevertheless, he was so employed. I recognize that it is not appropriate to base the term of notice on periods of broken service, but, nevertheless, this is still a fact or circumstance in this case.
>
> The company led him to believe that he was to be employed for a period of 1 year, and it was the common expectation of the parties that this would be so. This expectation is a real thing, and it must be recognized, even though it might not be enforceable. In the circumstances of this case, I think that a reasonable and fair period of notice is 3 months. I can't enforce the contract, but I think the defendant is estopped from saying that the period of notice should be that which is applied to a straight temporary employee, which might well be 2 weeks. I do not feel that the defendant can create a joint expectation and then hide behind the Statute. (at pp. 185-186)

3.5 EMPLOYEES AND INDEPENDENT CONTRACTORS

(a) Distinguishing Employees from Independent Contractors

In certain cases it may be necessary to distinguish between employees and independent contractors. While both employees and independent contractors can stipulate for whatever contractual rights they choose, in the absence of an express agreement an independent contractor will generally enjoy fewer, and more limited, legal rights than an employee.

In *Doyle v. London Life Insurance Co.* (1985), 68 B.C.L.R. 285, 23 D.L.R. (4th) 443 (C.A.), leave to appeal to Supreme Court of Canada refused (1986), 64 N.R. 318n (S.C.C.), the Court affirmed the trial judgment which, in considering the status of a commission sales agent, identified the general principles used to distinguish independent contractors, as follows:

> From my review of all of the foregoing cases I take the following to be tests which can appropriately be applied in attempting to determine the true status of a commission sales agent:
>
> 1. Whether or not the agent was limited exclusively to the service of the principal;
> 2. Whether or not the agent is subject to the control of the principal, not only as to the product sold, but also as to when, where and how it is sold;
> 3. Whether or not the agent has an investment or interest in what are characterized as the "tools" relating to his service;
> 4. Whether or not the agent has undertaken any risk in the business sense or, alternatively, has any expectation of profit associated with the delivery of his service as distinct from a fixed commission;
> 5. Whether or not the activity of the agent is part of the business organization of the principal for which he works. In other words, whose business is it?
>
> There are many more subsidiary tests that could be distilled from the authorities above-noted, but the foregoing would appear to be the criteria of major importance. It is also clear from the authorities that these tests are mutually exclusive. As a consequence they provide at best a set of guidelines which may be of assistance after an exhaustive review of the facts in each case. (at pp. 8-9, unreported reasons for judgment, B.C.S.C., Wood J., March 28, 1984)

On the facts of this case the Court found that a life insurance commission salesman was an employee.

A similar conclusion, in a different context, was reached in *Jaremko v. A.E. LePage Real Estate Services Ltd.* (1987), 17 C.C.E.L. 262, 59 O.R. (2d) 757, 39 D.L.R. (4th) 252 (H.C.), affirmed (1989), 69 O.R. (2d) 323, 60 D.L.R. (4th) 762 (C.A.). In this case the employee was a real estate agent who, for income tax purposes, characterized his status as "self-employed". It was held that this self-characterization was not determinative and the Court discussed the issue as follows:

> The defendant argues that Mr. Jaremko, not being in a master-and-servant relationship with A.E. LePage, is not entitled to reasonable notice of termination. Certainly some salesmen operating on pure commission cannot be said to have a master-and-servant relationship with their principals. In this case the main facts relied on by the defendant are that Mr. Jaremko's remuneration was based on commission rather than on salary; that he had considerable freedom to operate on his own with few time constraints; and that after he obtained his real estate broker's licence in 1981, his subsequent income tax returns indicated that he was

in business on his own behalf, allowing him to deduct some business expenses for tax purposes. The method of calculating income, and deductions therefrom, for tax purposes is certainly not a definitive argument. No evidence was adduced by either side to indicate the normal method of treating income for tax purposes by real estate agents. Mr. Jaremko's evidence was that the returns were prepared by his accountant, and the method of declaring income and deductions therefrom was also that recommended by his accountant. While Mr. Jaremko had substantial freedom to operate from the point of view of arranging his time, substantial control was exercised by A.E. LePage over his operations. He made use of A.E. LePage office space and secretarial assistance; he was subject to company policy and company discipline; he received memoranda material from A.E. LePage referring to him as one of a group of "salespeople . . . employed by our Company"; he was permitted to, and did in fact apply for a promotion within the company; and he was included in the company bonus and profit-sharing plan. On the facts of his case I have no doubt that a master-and-servant relationship did in fact and law exist between Mr. Jaremko and A.E. LePage. (at pp. 263-264)

(b) Significance of Independent Contractor Status

On the same basis that the Court will tend to resolve ambiguities in employment contracts against employers (see Chapter 3.3), the Court will also tend to find employee status, in preference to finding independent contractor status. In addition, as hereinafter set out, even if the Court finds independent contractor status, the Court is not precluded from finding that the independent contractor is entitled to reasonable advance notice of the termination of the contract or compensation in lieu of notice.

In the case of *Aldo Ippolito & Co. v. Can. Packers Inc.* (1986), 14 C.C.E.L. 76, 57 O.R. (2d) 65, 32 D.L.R. (4th) 440, 17 O.A.C. 180 (C.A.), additional reasons at (1986), 14 C.C.E.L. 76 at 89, varying (1984), 29 B.L.R. 167 (Ont. H.C.), the Court was concerned with the issue of reasonable notice. Ippolito provided sales representative services through his corporation to a variety of manufacturers. Ippolito's corporation entered into a contractual relationship with Canada Packers for the provision of sales representative services for its nut products. Canada Packers maintained this contractual relationship with Ippolito for 13 years before terminating the contract without notice.

The majority of the Court of Appeal held that Ippolito's corporation was entitled to notice of termination, which they found to be 30 days since the contract provided for a minimum of 30 days' notice. In dissent, Mr. Justice Goodman was of the opinion that the trial Judge was correct in his interpretation of the termination provision as being only the minimum notice required and that other circumstances could be taken into account in determining reasonable notice. As the nature of the services provided was cyclical, the trial Judge had awarded one year's notice. Mr. Justice Goodman limited the notice period to six months, because at the end of six months the cycle in which the termination occurred would be completed, and Ippolito's corporation would obtain the commission for which it had rendered its services. Both the majority and dissenting decisions proceeded on the basis that an independent contractor was entitled to reasonable notice of the termination of the contract, absent an express agreement as to the appropriate period of notice.

Further, in *Paper Sales Corp. v. Miller Brothers, Co. (1962)* (1975), 7 O.R. (2d) 460 at 461 (H.C.), affirmed 7 O.R. (2d) 460, 55 D.L.R. (3d) 492 (C.A.), Paper Sales had been the exclusive sales agent for Miller Brothers for over 34 years. Miller Brothers terminated the contract with three months' notice. There was no express notice provision in the contract between Paper Sales and Miller Brothers. The trial Judge, after examining the relationship and deciding that it was one of exclusive sales agency, concluded that the contract could only be terminated upon reasonable notice. In determining what would be the extent of a reasonable notice period the trial Judge was of the opinion that:

> [e]ach case must depend upon its own circumstances and upon the general nature of the situation. Where a company has engaged staff and incurred every obligation in order to fulfil the terms of its contract with its principal, then the notice must be sufficient to enable it to properly cope with the new situation created by the termination. (at p. 464)

The trial Judge found one year's notice to be reasonable. This award was upheld by the Court of Appeal.

In conclusion, independent contractors are entitled to reasonable notice of termination of the contract or compensation in lieu of notice. The Court will examine the circumstances of the contractual relationship to determine what is reasonable notice in the absence of an express provision addressing the issue of the period of notice required for termination.

3.6 SIGNIFICANCE OF A COLLECTIVE AGREEMENT

In many instances an employment relationship will be governed not by an individual employment contract, but rather by a collective agreement to which the employer and the union are parties. This agreement binds the employees who fall within its scope. The leading case in support of the proposition that an employee who is subject to a collective agreement is not entitled to bring an action for wrongful dismissal at common law is the Supreme Court of Canada decision in *McGavin Toastmaster Ltd. v. Ainscough,* [1976] 1 S.C.R. 718, [1975] 5 W.W.R. 444, 75 C.L.L.C. 14,277, 54 D.L.R. (3d) 1, 4 N.R. 618. The following passage from the judgment of Chief Justice Laskin is frequently quoted:

> I do not think that in the face of labour relations legislation such as existed at the material time in British Columbia, in the face of the certification of the union, of which the plaintiffs were members, as bargaining agent of a specified unit of employees of the company and in the face of the collective agreement in force between the union and the appellant company, it is possible to speak of individual contracts of employment and to treat the collective agreement as a mere appendage of individual relationships. . . .
>
> The common law as it applies to individual employment contracts is no longer relevant to employer-employee relations governed by a collective agree-

> ment which, as the one involved here, deals with discharge, termination of employment, severance pay and a host of other matters that have been negotiated between union and company as the principal parties thereto. (at pp. 724-725)

Subsequent decisions have varied as to whether the Chief Justice meant that collective agreements oust all wrongful dismissal remedies available to a grievor at common law, or whether the common law retained jurisdiction when the claim asserted was not covered, directly or by implication, in the agreement. The Court dealt with these questions in *Bourne v. Otis Elevator Co.* (1984), 4 C.C.E.L. 1, 45 O.R. (2d) 321, 42 C.P.C. 12, 6 D.L.R. (4th) 560 (H.C.). Mr. Justice Southey stated at the outset that:

> the *McGavin* decision is not binding authority that an employee covered by a collective agreement cannot sue his employer on a contract relating to aspects of employment not covered by the collective agreement. (at pp. 5-6)

The trial court decision in *Bourne,* in the face of conflicting authorities, had been that the common law retained some residual jurisdiction unless specifically ousted by the agreement. Mr. Justice Southey, however, reached the following conclusion:

> With great respect to the learned County Court Judge, I think the weight of the authorities . . . supports the company's position that the collective agreement supersedes all individual contracts of employment, so that they cannot thereafter be the basis of an action for wrongful dismissal by a member of the bargaining unit.
>
> . . . .
>
> In any event, the appeal must be allowed in this case, because, in my view, the collective agreement covering the plaintiff and the company dealt with the matters in issue, although not in specific terms. (at p. 7)

Thus, Mr. Justice Southey concluded:

> . . . it is not necessary for the collective agreement to deal specifically with an issue to oust the jurisdiction of the Court, if it deals with the issue by clear implication. (at p. 8)

Also noteworthy is *Lawn v. Algonquin College of Applied Arts & Technology* (1982), 39 O.R. (2d) 377, 139 D.L.R. (3d) 120 (H.C.), in which Mr. Justice Grange stated:

> I do not believe there has been a definitive determination binding on me of the effect of a failure to grieve a dismissal allegedly without cause to a board of arbitrators when the matter is as here covered by a collective agreement. (at p. 383)

Mr. Justice Grange noted a number of cases in which the issue was resolved differently. In the end he decided to follow the reasoning of Chief

Justice Laskin in *McGavin Toastmaster Ltd., supra.* His conclusion refers to the *McGavin* decision as follows:

> The action concerned a claim for severance pay resulting from a closure of the defendant's plant and did not directly concern jurisdiction. Indeed, the Chief Justice specifically left open the precise question which was not raised in argument (see p. 721 S.C.R.) but the principles enunciated *supra* seem inevitably to lead to the conclusion that claims arising out of dismissal in circumstances such as those in the case at bar are governed by arbitration and arbitration proceedings and are not governed by the courts under the common law. (at p. 384)

The reasoning in *McGavin Toastmaster Ltd. v. Ainscough* and *Lawn v. Algonquin College* was followed in *Hooper v. Wellington (County) Bd. of Education* (1984), 4 C.C.E.L. 310, 46 O.R. (2d) 680, 10 D.L.R. (4th) 281, 40 O.A.C. 93 (Div. Ct.).

The issue, however, has not been definitively resolved. In particular, courts have been reluctant to deny common law jurisdiction where to do so would leave the complainant without any avenue to pursue a remedy. Reference may be made, for example, to *McHugh v. Carleton University* (1983), 2 C.C.E.L. 109 (Ont. H.C.), where probationers had been excluded from the grievance procedure provided in the collective agreement but were found to be entitled to look to the common law for a remedy; and *Audet v. Hornepayne Community Hospital* (14 December 1988), Algoma 5000/88 (Ont. Dist. Ct.), in which an employee who had been hired and dismissed within the interval between certification of the union and the conclusion of the collective agreement was permitted to pursue his action in court.

Different considerations apply, however, when the rights asserted arose prior to, and apart from, the collective agreement. In the case of *Roberts v. Dresser Industries Canada Ltd.* (1990), 28 C.C.E.L. 221, 75 O.R. (2d) 609, 90 C.L.L.C. 14,038, (*sub nom. Johnston v. Dresser Industries Canada Ltd.*) 36 O.A.C. 371 (C.A.), the Ontario Court of Appeal considered the effect of a representation, found to form part of an initial employment contract, in light of a subsequent collective agreement that limited the amount of notice required. The facts and the conclusions of the trial judge were set out in the decision of the Court of Appeal as follows:

> i) during the interviews in England, Dresser's representatives made representations to the respondents of security of employment for a reasonable period of time, not less than 2 years;
> ii) the respondents relied upon such representations in deciding to accept the jobs offered to them and to emigrate to Canada;
> iii) none of the respondents was advised by Dresser's representatives that there was a collective agreement in existence between Dresser and the union that set out certain terms of employment and was binding upon all members of the union;
> iv) no copy of the collective agreement was made available to any of the respondents until they had completed their probationary period; and

v) the representations regarding security of employment for at least 2 years were intended by the parties, and constituted, a term of the contract between them.

And he reached the following conclusions:

vi) that individual contracts of employment cannot co-exist with a collective agreement where the individual contracts address, expressly or by clear implication, the same matters dealt with in the collective agreement;
vii) that a claim for damages arising out of rights created by a collective agreement must be pursued in accordance with the remedy contemplated in the collective agreement rather than by Court action;
viii) that recourse may be had to Court action in the present case, where the respondents became subject to the terms of the collective agreement well after the formation of the individual contracts between them and Dresser; and
ix) that Dresser had in each instance breached those contracts by terminating the employment of the respondents prior to 2 years from the date of commencement of their employment. (at pp. 223-224)

On appeal, counsel for Dresser argued that individuals could not apply to a court to assert rights under a contract of employment once those individuals became subject to a collective agreement. The Court of Appeal reviewed the cases relied upon by counsel for Dresser as follows:

> *Zambri* [*Cdn. Pacific Railway Co. v. Zambri*, [1962] S.C.R. 609, 62 C.L.L.C. 15,407, 34 D.L.R. (2d) 654], supra, concerned the disposition of charges laid against an employer for alleged violations of a provincial labour relations statute by the termination of employment of a number of employees following a lawful strike. *McGavin* [*McGavin Toastmaster Ltd. v. Ainscough*, [1976] 1 S.C.R. 718, [1975] 5 W.W.R. 444, 4 N.R. 618, 75 C.L.L.C. 14,277, 54 D.L.R. (3d) 1], supra, concerned the entitlement of employees to severance pay, pursuant to the terms of a collective agreement, after an employer closed its plant following an illegal strike. *St. Anne Nackawic* [*St. Anne Nackawic Pulp and Paper Co. v. C.P.U., Loc. 219*, [1986] 1 S.C.R. 704, 86 C.L.L.C. 14,037, 28 D.L.R. (4th) [1], 68 N.R. 112, 73 N.B.R. (2d) 236, 184 A.P.R. 236], supra, concerned the right of an employer to sue a union for damages by reason of a strike which was illegal under a provincial labour relations statute and was a breach of the collective agreement between the employer and the union.
>
> With respect to *Zambri*, the trial Judge in the present case found support for his disposition of the claims of the six respondents in the observation of Judson J. (at p. 624, S.C.R.; at p. 666, D.L.R.) that:
>
>> [W]hen there is a collective agreement in effect, it is difficult to see how there can be anything left outside, *except possibly the act of hiring*. (Trial Judge's emphasis).
>
> The *McGavin* and *St. Anne Nackawic* cases were considered in a decision of the British Columbia Court of Appeal in *Wainwright v. Vancouver Shipyards Co.* (1987), 14 B.C.L.R. (2d) 247, 38 D.L.R. (4th) 760. Leave to appeal to S.C.C. refused (1987), 86 N.R. 237 (note). That decision, which was reported after the

present case was argued at trial, dealt with a remarkably similar fact situation. In *Wainwright*, the defendant had a contract to build an ice-breaker and required skilled employees for that purpose. It advertised for prospective employees in New Brunswick. At their interviews, the plaintiffs expressed reservations about travelling from New Brunswick to Vancouver, and were assured of "several years" (found by the trial Judge to be not less than 3 years) full employment without lay-off if they made the move. They did but, after a year and a half, were laid off due to a work shortage. The plaintiffs were required to become members of a union which had a closed shop agreement with the defendant and, pursuant to the collective agreement, were the first to be laid off. Their action for damages succeeded at trial, and the employer appealed.

On the appeal, the employer contended that the employees' contracts of employment were governed by the terms of the collective agreement and that the Court had no jurisdiction to entertain a claim for damages for breach of such contracts. In support, its counsel relied, among other cases, upon *McGavin* and *St. Anne Nackawic*. The employees contended that the discussions which brought them from New Brunswick to Vancouver resulted in "pre-employment contracts" for breach of which they could properly bring action.

The appeal was dismissed. Hinkson J.A., who delivered the judgment of the Court, adverted to *McGavin* and *St. Anne Nackawic* and concluded as follows (at pp. 762-763, D.L.R.; at p. 250, B.C.L.R.):

> In the *McGavin* case, Chief Justice Laskin said at p. 6 D.L.R., p. 725 S.C.R., in dealing with the question of the relationship between parties who become master and servant or employer and employee, the following:
>
> "The reality is, and has been for many years now throughout Canada, that individual relationships as between employer and employee have meaning only at the hiring stage and even then there are qualifications which arise by reason of union security clauses in collective agreements."
>
> That passage was cited with approval by Mr. Justice Estey in the *St. Anne* case. At p. 12 D.L.R., p. 718 S.C.R., in the *St. Anne* case Mr. Justice Estey said:
>
> "The collective agreement establishes the broad parameters of the relationship between the employer and his employees. This relationship is properly regulated through arbitration and it would, in general, subvert both the relationship and the statutory scheme under which it arises to hold that matters addressed and governed by the collective agreement may nevertheless be the subject of actions in the courts at common law."
>
> It is upon the basis of that reasoning that the appellant contends that the court here had no jurisdiction.
>
> In my opinion, *if the claims of the plaintiffs in these proceedings were that because of the pre-employment contracts, they could not be laid off pursuant to the terms of the collective agreement, clearly that would be a matter for arbitration, but those are not the claims advanced here. The trial judge found upon the basis of the evidence of the plaintiffs that they were given to understand that they would not be laid off for three years. That finding supports a conclusion that there were pre-employment contracts. These claims do not arise out of the collective agreement. They are claims arising out of a contract*

governed by common law principles. In my opinion, the court did have jurisdiction. I think that this is clear from what was said by Chief Justice Laskin in the *McGavin* case and approved, by Mr. Justice Estey in the *St. Anne* case." (Emphasis added.)

I respectfully agree with the view expressed by Hinkson J.A. which is, in essence, the basis upon which the trial Judge in the present case found in favour of the respondents and is, in my opinion, fatal to the position advanced by Dresser in support of these appeals. (at pp. 225-227)

3.7 GOVERNMENT EMPLOYEES

(a) Employment at Pleasure or Entitlement to Reasonable Notice

The traditional position regarding government employees is that an employee of the Crown is employed at the pleasure of the Crown. This means that the employee can be dismissed without cause or notice. The rapid expansion of the public service, coupled with the fundamental unfairness of a dismissal without cause or notice, has caused the courts to incline against finding employment at pleasure unless it is plain that this was the intent of the governing statute.

The judicial attitude in such cases is represented by the decision of the Supreme Court of Canada in *Nicholson v. Haldimand-Norfolk Commissioners of Police* (1978), [1979] 1 S.C.R. 311, 78 C.L.L.C. 14,181, 88 D.L.R. (3d) 671, 23 N.R. 410. The issue in that case was whether a regulation under the *Police Act* was equivalent to being employed at pleasure. Nicholson, at the time he was dismissed, was a junior constable who had been with the police force for 14 months. The regulation in question allegedly permitted the Board to terminate Nicholson's employment without a hearing. The opinion of the Board was that this was equivalent to being employed at pleasure.

The Court held that Nicholson was not employed at pleasure but was an office holder under statute. Chief Justice Laskin stated that:

> [t]he assimilation by the Ontario Court of Appeal of the position of a constable under s. 27(*b*) to that of a constable at common law holding office at pleasure involved importing the term "at pleasure", with its connotation of peremptory power of dismissal without need to give notice or reason before or after, into s. 27(*b*). The words "at pleasure" which at one time governed the appointment of all members of a police force in a municipality having a Board (see *The Police Act*, R.S.O. 1950, c. 279, s. 13) were removed by 1951 (Ont.), c. 66, s. 1 and, thereafter, regulations were promulgated along the lines of those still in force and applicable here. I wish to emphasize here that the frame of the Act and regulations thereunder has left the words "at pleasure" behind as relics of Crown law which no longer governs the relations of police and Boards or Municipal Councils. (at p. 320)
>
> . . . .
>
> I would observe here that the old common law rule, deriving much of its force from Crown law, that a person engaged as an office holder at pleasure may

> be put out without reason or prior notice ought itself to be re-examined. It has an anachronistic flavour in light of collective agreements, which are pervasive in both public and private employment, and which offer broad protection against arbitrary dismissal in the case of employees who cannot claim the status of office holders. . . . (at pp. 322-323)

The Supreme Court of Canada affirmed the reasoning in *Nicholson* in *Wilson v. Nova Scotia (Civil Service Comm.)* (1981), 81 C.L.L.C. 14,109, 119 D.L.R. (3d) 1, 35 N.R. 103, 43 N.S.R. (2d) 631, 81 A.P.R. 631. This case dealt with the question of whether employees who were covered by the collective agreement were entitled to have a dismissal grievance submitted to arbitration, or whether the Crown could legally insist that it retained an unimpaired power to dismiss at pleasure. The Court held that the Crown's right is subject to modification such as by means of a collective agreement. The Court was of the opinion that, by agreement,

> [t]he law in Canada, in Canadian provinces, as well as in other common law jurisdictions has gone far down the road to establishing a relative equality of legal position as between the Crown and those with whom it deals, too far in my opinion to warrant a reversion to an anachronism. (at (D.L.R.) p. 9)

In the case of *Wuorinen v. Worker's Compensation Board* (1983), 1 C.C.E.L. 29 (B.C.S.C.), the Court held that the common law rule could also be abridged by individual employment contracts. Wuorinen had been promoted from a position which was within the collective agreement to a position outside of the collective agreement. At the time of his promotion Wuorinen was assured that his treatment would be no less favourable than treatment under the collective agreement. Wuorinen's position was eliminated and he was dismissed with only 24 hours' notice. The Court held that, even though the Board possessed the right to dismiss at pleasure, its actions in this case were in breach of the term of his employment contract that he would be no less favourably treated than under the collective agreement.

It is beyond the scope of this book to attempt to survey the legal rights of all government employees. In each case it is necessary to consider the terms of the governing statute and the terms of the particular employment contract. In many cases, however, the statute will be silent and the Court will imply a contractual term requiring that termination can only be for "just cause" or upon reasonable notice.

(b) Right to Procedural Fairness in Relation to Discharge

In *Nicholson v. Haldimand-Norfolk Commissioners of Police* (1978), [1979] 1 S.C.R. 311, 78 C.L.L.C. 14,181, 88 D.L.R. (3d) 671, 23 N.R. 410, the Supreme Court of Canada held that Nicholson was entitled to fair treatment in his dismissal. This right to procedural fairness was examined in *Evershed v. Ontario* (1984), 3 C.C.E.L. 81, 44 O.R. (2d) 763, 6 Admin. L.R. 103, 5 D.L.R. (4th) 340, (*sub nom. Evershed v. Ministry of Education*) 1 O.A.C. 333 (Div. Ct.), affirmed (1985), 50 O.R. (2d) 198, 11 Admin. L.R. 164, 17 D.L.R. (4th)

168, 7 O.A.C. 307 (C.A.). Evershed, an elementary school teacher, had pleaded guilty to charges of possession of unlawfully imported pornography and possession of marijuana. The School Board sent a transcript of the Court proceedings to the Minister of Education with a recommendation that Evershed be dismissed. Evershed was never made aware of the School Board's recommendation nor was he given any opportunity to present his own case. The Minister cancelled Evershed's teacher's certificate. The Court, in finding for Evershed, stated that:

> [t]here is no doubt that the offence charged and the admission of facts made at the time when the applicant pleaded guilty show a very serious matter which could well go to the moral issue to which the Minister must address herself. However, the consequences of terminating a teacher's certificate are drastic and the applicant is entitled to procedural fairness. In the present case, he was never made aware that his certificate might be terminated. The board had indicated that it was considering applying to obtain permission to immediately terminate his contract but that is a far different thing from what, in fact, happened. The Minister could easily have sent a letter to the applicant that she was considering the cancellation of his certificate and give him an opportunity to at least reply in writing so that his point of view would be before her, before the decision was made. She did not do so. (at p. 84)

As a result, Evershed was found to be entitled to have his side of the case presented to the Minister.

In the case of *Deighton v. Vancouver (City) Police Bd.* (1986), 15 C.C.E.L. 215 (B.C.S.C.), Deighton was a probationary constable with the City of Vancouver police. While off duty he became involved in an incident at a cabaret which included drunkenness, sexual assault of a female patron, assault of an employee of the cabaret and other charges. Deighton was served notice of disciplinary action under the Police (Discipline) Regulations. The Board, however, instead of following the Regulations, proceeded to terminate Deighton, as a probationary employee, under a provision of the collective agreement which did not entitle Deighton to a hearing.

The Court was of the opinion that this was an improper procedure and that the Board should have proceeded under the Regulations. The Court also stated that:

> Even if Deighton were not entitled to be dealt with under the Police (Discipline) Regulations, he would be entitled to be dealt with fairly. At the very least such fairness would require that he be informed of the substance of the complaints against him *and* that he be afforded some opportunity to respond, either orally or in writing. . . . (at p. 221)

The rights of the holder of an office, appointed pursuant to a statute, were also considered at length in *Knight v. Indian Head School Division No. 19*, 30 C.C.E.L. 237, [1990] 1 S.C.R. 653, 43 Admin. L.R. 157, [1990] 3 W.W.R. 289, 90 C.L.L.C. 14,010, 69 D.L.R. (4th) 489, 106 N.R. 17, 83 Sask. R. 81 (S.C.C.).

This case provides a useful starting point for persons interested in a detailed analysis of this subject.

Government employees, and other employees appointed pursuant to statutory authority, are generally entitled to the protection of procedural fairness in connection with a decision to terminate their employment. It is beyond the scope of this book to consider what is due process in each case, as much depends upon the particular situation and the governing statute. In every situation, however, the Court will be interested in whether the employee had an opportunity to be heard, either orally or in writing.

3.8 CONCLUSION

Chapter 3 has described the various elements taken into account in determining the terms of the contract between the parties. Both employer and employee have an interest in assuring a mutual and verifiable understanding with respect to the terms of the contract. This mutual and verifiable understanding can be most readily achieved by the use of written employment contracts.

Having determined the contractual terms it is then possible to determine what will constitute a breach of the contractual terms. Chapter 4 considers those breaches of the employment contract that are so serious that they are regarded as providing "just cause" for the termination of the employment contract.

4

JUST CAUSE FOR DISMISSAL

4.1 GENERAL PRINCIPLE

If "just cause" in law exists for termination, then the employer, subject to the possible requirement to meet minimum statutory requirements, is entitled to terminate the employee forthwith and without further obligation. It must be emphasized that the words "just cause" are used as a legal term of art to denote a situation which justifies summary termination of the employment contract. If just cause does not exist, then the employer has an obligation to give reasonable advance notice of termination or compensate the employee in lieu thereof. As the consequence of a finding of just cause is harsh, it is very difficult to prove. It is not every act of misconduct or impropriety on the part of the employee that will constitute just cause, just as it is not every breach of a commercial contract that will permit the innocent party to bring the contract to an end. In order to constitute just cause for dismissal, the acts of the employee must constitute a repudiation of the employment relationship which the employer may accept by terminating the contract. As it is the employer who alleges just cause, it is the employer who has the onus of proof in this regard.

The parties have freedom to contract on virtually any terms and the corollary of this is that there can be no exhaustive definition of what will constitute just cause. In practical terms, however, almost all allegations of just cause will fall into one of the categories set out below.

Before considering whether certain specific acts of misconduct or impropriety constitute just cause, there are three matters which may vitiate what would otherwise constitute just cause. These are:

(a) Condonation
(b) Failure to Warn
(c) Failure to Afford a Fair Hearing

4.2 PRELIMINARY CONSIDERATIONS

(a) Condonation

(i) *General Principle*

In the typical case, condonation occurs during the course of employment when the employer elects to ignore or forgive unacceptable conduct by the employee. There is also some authority for the proposition that the acts of the employer, at and after termination, may operate to condone behaviour prior to termination. While it is submitted that an employer's conduct at termination cannot constitute condonation, condonation during employment and condonation at the time of termination are discussed under separate headings.

(ii) *Condonation During the Course of Employment*

The case of *Nossal v. Better Business Bureau of Metropolitan Toronto Inc.* (1985), 12 C.C.E.L. 85, 51 O.R. (2d) 279, 19 D.L.R. (4th) 547, 9 O.A.C. 184 (C.A.), presents an interesting set of circumstances and a comprehensive statement of the law. In this case there had been a number of different types of complaints about the performance of the plaintiff. The first complaint was punctuality, the evidence being that the plaintiff had been late 90 times in 1982, and had been further warned concerning lateness in February of 1983. The second complaint was that in February 1983, during a heated exchange over her assignment to a new position, the plaintiff threatened to use confidential information to embarrass her supervisor. The third complaint, which culminated in her dismissal, was that on April 8, 1983 the plaintiff absented herself from the office at a critical time, as a result of which a promotional magazine was not published on time.

The trial Judge found that the various complaints could not be viewed cumulatively and as a result found that the plaintiff had been wrongfully dismissed.

The Court of Appeal, however, reversed the trial decision, finding that the Court was entitled to consider all of the complaints together. In this regard the Court of Appeal stated:

> Almost 100 years ago, this Court dealt with the issue of the use of accumulated past conduct by employees. In *McIntyre v. Hockin* (1889), 16 O.A.R. 498, Maclennan J.A., speaking for the Court, said at pp. 501-02:
>
>> It may be proper, however, to add a few words on the subject of condonation. When an employer becomes aware of misconduct on the part of his servant, sufficient to justify dismissal, he may adopt either of two courses. He may dismiss, or he may overlook the fault. But he cannot retain the servant in his employment, and afterwards at any distance of time turn him away. It would be most unjust if he could do that, for one of the consequences of dismissal for good cause is, that the servant can recover nothing for his services beyond the last pay day, whether his engagement be by the year or otherwise: Smiths Law of Master and Servant, 4th ed., p. 220; *Boston Deep Sea Fishing Co. v. Ansell*, 39 Ch. D. 339. If he retains the servant in his employment for any considerable time after discovering his fault, that is condonation, and he cannot afterwards dismiss for that fault without anything new. No doubt the employer ought to have a reasonable time to determine what to do, to consider whether he will dismiss or not, or to look for another servant. So, also, he must have full knowledge of the nature and extent of the fault, for he cannot forgive or condone matters of which he is not fully informed. Further, condonation is subject to an implied condition of future good conduct, and whenever any new misconduct occurs, the old offences may be invoked and may be put in the scale against the offender as cause for dismissal.
>
> . . . .
>
> In any event, the case at hand presents even stronger reason for placing past misconduct in the scale. The trial Judge found that the earlier misconduct did not amount to sufficient cause for discharge. How, then, could it be said that the failure to discharge prevents the employer from using the past misconduct as a part of the accumulation?
>
> In my respectful view, past misconduct of an employee, whether sufficient to amount to just cause for discharge or not, can be used or put in the scale with subsequent misconduct to determine if the accumulation amounts to just cause.
>
> The learned trial Judge appears to have been of the view that past misconduct would have to be of the same kind as the subsequent misconduct before it became significant. I do not agree. The critical question remains, whether or not the accumulated misconduct, composed of similar and dissimilar misconduct, amounts to just cause. (For an example of the accumulation of dissimilar acts of

> misconduct, see *Atkinson v. Boyd, Phillips & Co.* (1979), 9 B.C.L.R. 255 (B.C. C.A.) [leave to appeal to S.C.C. dismissed 28 N.R. 139 (S.C.C.)].
>
> Applying those principles to the case at hand, it is my view that the earlier pattern of lateness, the threats to Mr. Tuz and the wrongful absence at a critical time, taken together amount to just cause and the Bureau was entitled to terminate the plaintiff's employment. (at pp. 89-91)

A strict reading of the foregoing statement of the law might suggest that condonation need be of little concern to the employer. In this regard, the fact that an employer can condone certain conduct, and then later rely upon that conduct should there be further misconduct, even if unrelated, suggests that an employer does not suffer any continuing prejudice from an act of condonation. In practical terms, however, this is seldom the case. Any condonation of conduct may suggest to the Court that that type of conduct is not serious and may undercut the credibility of later complaints concerning similar conduct. Further, and again as a practical matter, the greater the history of condonation, the greater the obligation of the employer to give very specific and definite warnings prior to termination.

(iii) *Condonation at the Time of Termination*

As stated, there are cases which suggest that actions of the employer coincident with the termination, or indeed after the termination, may be construed as a condonation of the actions of the employee and so preclude reliance on just cause.

In *Tracey v. Swansea Construction Co.* (1964), [1965] 1 O.R. 203, 47 D.L.R. (2d) 295 (H.C.), affirmed without written reasons, [1965] 2 O.R. 182 (note), 50 D.L.R. (2d) 130 (note) (C.A.), Mr. Justice Thompson regarded the granting of advance notice of termination, or a tender of payment in lieu thereof, as a bar to reliance upon just cause. His Lordship stated:

> The simple position appears to me to be this. The defendant desired to dismiss the plaintiff. If there was misconduct or default sufficient to justify discharge it had one of two courses open to it. It could have summarily dismissed for cause or it could have decided to overlook, waive or condone the misconduct and terminate upon notice, or payment in lieu of notice, in accordance with the provision of the contract for termination implied by law. It could not do both, for one would operate as a repudiation of the contract for a breach thereof, and the other, conversely, would operate as an affirmation of the contract and the adoption of its provisions for termination. The fact that the defendant was in error as to the length of, or sufficiency of, the notice given could in no way alter the effect of its intention as expressed by its conduct. (at p. 220)

On similar facts, however, the opposite conclusion was reached in *Matheson v. Matheson International Trucks Ltd.* (1984), 4 C.C.E.L. 271 (Ont. H.C.). In this case Associate Chief Justice Parker dealt with a situation in which the company terminated its president. While the Court found that the plaintiff "knew or ought to have known that there were serious problems with his performance," no reasons were given for the termination and the plaintiff was offered one month's severance pay. The Court found that the offer of such payment did not preclude reliance upon just cause. In this regard His Lordship stated:

> In my opinion, the giving of one month's pay by the employer was an act of generosity, as opposed to one of condonation. In support of this approach, I rely upon *Empey v. Coastal Towing Co.*, [1977] 1 W.W.R. 673, 31 C.P.R. (2d) 157 (B.C. S.C.), and *Castell v. Gardiner etc. & Ass.* (1972), 30 D.L.R. (3d) 506 (B.C. S.C.). If it were the law that an employer who gives some pay to an employee whom he has a right to dismiss for cause loses that right, employers would simply never give any severance pay when terminating an employee for what they perceive as just cause. (at p. 275)

Associate Chief Justice Parker commented on *Tracy v. Swansea Construction Co., supra*, as follows:

> In *Tracey v. Swansea Const. Co.*, supra, the employer dismissed the plaintiff-employee for cause but gave one week's notice. The employer relied upon the defence of just cause. The Court looked at the entire pattern of events, beginning with the first acts of alleged misconduct and the employer's forbearance from acting on that information, and ending at the moment of dismissal with one week's notice. The giving of a week's notice at the moment of termination was treated as evidence of condonation because it was given after a period of time when the employer could have acted upon the events which in themselves would have given rise to just cause for dismissal. (at p. 274)

While it is submitted that a payment or any other conciliatory gesture, at the time of termination, should not be construed as an election that the employer is terminating without cause, and should not estop the employer from alleging just cause, the employee will no doubt take a contrary position. Thus, the employer should be very wary of any words or deeds at the time of termination which may be viewed as inconsistent with an allegation of just cause (see Chapter 30.2(c) and (d)).

(b) Failure to Warn

The cases concerning the obligation of the employer to warn an employee prior to termination must be read in conjunction with those concerning condonation. Thus, where the employee's performance is substandard, or there is some other breach of the employment contract such as lateness or absenteeism, it may be that the employer's silence (itself a failure to warn) constitutes the act of condonation.

The notion that employers should warn employees that poor performance or misconduct will not be tolerated is rooted in common sense. No employee, or employer, is perfect. To the extent that the employee falls short of that ideal, it is natural to expect that the employer will criticize, or ultimately warn, the employee with a view to correcting the problem and improving performance. When common sense calls for the employer to make a statement, but silence prevails, it is reasonable for the employee to conclude that the conduct being displayed is something which the employer expects or tolerates as part of the contract of employment.

It has been suggested that, in some circumstances, the employer has an absolute obligation to provide a warning. In *Rajakaruna v. Peel (Regional Municipality)* (1981), 10 A.C.W.S. (2d) 522 (Ont. Co. Ct.), the plaintiff had been dismissed for insubordination, consisting of a refusal to work overtime when ordered to do so by a superior. The Court found that dismissal was not justified in that the plaintiff had a reasonable excuse for disobeying the order. In *obiter*, however, the Court stated, "Before an employee can be summarily dismissed for failure to carry out his duties, it must be shown that the employee was given appropriate warning that the employment is in jeopardy" (at p. 10, unreported reasons for judgment (25 September 1981)). In other cases, the Court has suggested that the failure to give a warning where incompetence is alleged can lead to the finding that just cause does not exist. See *Manning v. Surrey Memorial Hospital Society,* [1975] 54 D.L.R. (3d) 312 (B.C.S.C.); and *David v. Eastend Union Hospital Bd.* (1979), 99 D.L.R. (3d) 73 (Sask. Q.B.). The consequences of a breach of this implied obligation to give a warning can, therefore, be very serious.

It is submitted, however, that the preferable view is that expressed by Mr. Justice Steele in *Fonceca v. McDonnell Douglas Can. Ltd.* (1983), 1 C.C.E.L. 51 (Ont. H.C.). In this case the plaintiff, a professional engineer, was found to be a disruptive force in the workplace. Steele J. described the plaintiff as follows:

> I find that the plaintiff constantly, in public, belittled those whom he considered not to be his superiors. He was loud and rude to such people to the extent that the morale in the department was deteriorating badly. Several specific instances were given in evidence, showing his poor relations with those with whom he worked or whom he considered to be inferior to him. . . .
>
> The plaintiff was a disruptive force in the department, particularly after the early part of December 1980, when a group grievance was filed against him by six employees under the union collective bargaining agreement. The union accepted the company's position that it had spoken to the plaintiff and advised him of the provisions of the collective agreement but stated its intention to object if further incidents occurred. This was the only known group grievance that had ever been filed in this large company against a person in supervisory status. Many other specific incidents referred to were trivial and would probably not have amounted to anything if he had apologized or dealt with them in a reasonable way. However, he did not. When added together, they show a proud but overbearing, discourteous person who did not know how to apologize or to get on with people. (at p. 54)
>
> . . . .
>
> I find that at no time was the plaintiff specifically warned that, if his conduct did not improve, his job would be at risk. However, he was advised on numerous occasions that he should try to work with the company rather than against it, and that he should co-operate with and treat fellow employees courteously, and on at least three occasions was asked to apologize to fellow employees. However, the

> plaintiff did not do so and in fact adamantly took the position that there was nothing to apologize for. In other words, the plaintiff was not and appears still not to be aware of this serious defect in his character. (at p. 56)

In upholding the discharge of the plaintiff for just cause, it is respectfully submitted that Steele J. concisely and accurately stated the law with respect to the significance of warnings, as follows:

> Clearly, an employer is entitled to dismiss an employee who has been warned from time to time that he has an incompatible personality conflict but refuses or is unable to improve or correct his relationships and similar incidents occur later. Where the incidents complained of are trivial, but annoying, then warnings are necessary before termination for cause is justified. However, where incidents, each in themselves, are serious, even though not sufficient to justify dismissal at the time, then a warning is not essential. In the present case, though no written or oral warning was given, any reasonable person having had three union grievances filed against him and having been told consistently by his employer to try to work and co-operate with people, should know that if such conduct continued he would be liable to dismissal. Unfortunately, the plaintiff is not the normal, reasonable man. Even so, he was aware of the disposition of the second union grievance to the effect that similar conduct would not be tolerated in the future. Notwithstanding that, the plaintiff did not change his ways and, when the last grievance was filed, he was properly dismissed. In my opinion, a specific warning to the plaintiff would have had no effect upon him whatsoever. (at pp. 57-58)

If the conduct in question is not so serious that the employer wishes to consider dismissal, it is still advisable to issue a warning. If, however, the conduct is such that the employer wishes to consider termination, the employer should withhold judgment and seek advice quickly. In such a case the danger is that by issuing a warning the employee could argue, based on the logic of *Tracey v. Swansea Construction Co.* (1964), [1965] 1 O.R. 203, 47 (2d) 295 (H.C.), affirmed without written reasons, [1965] 2 O.R. 182 (note), 50 D.L.R. (2d) 130 (note) (C.A.), that the employer had elected to waive any right to terminate due to the misconduct by electing to warn instead. It is, however, advisable for the employer to move as quickly as possible to prevent the further argument that the delay in acting constitutes condonation.

The failure of the employer to give a warning concerning poor performance may also be a factor relied upon by the employee in support of a claim for mental distress damages (see Chapter 6.5(b)(iv)).

(c) Failure to Afford a Fair Hearing

It is a fundamental principle of justice that interested persons must be given an opportunity to be heard prior to the making of a judicial or quasi-judicial decision that will affect them adversely. Certain cases have raised the question of whether this obligation to provide a hearing should be imported into employer and employee relations.

This issue was considered in *Robarts v. Cdn. National Railway* (1980), 2

C.C.E.L. 168 (Ont. H.C.). The plaintiff, Robarts, was employed as an equipment supervisor. The defendant had a number of complaints with the plaintiff's performance, including a complaint regarding an incident in which a C.N.R. crane toppled, causing injury to its operator and $14,000 damage to the crane. This incident occurred approximately two weeks prior to termination and the defendant received a verbal report from the crane operator during that two-week period, which blamed the plaintiff for the accident. The defendant "seized" on the crane incident as a reason to demote the plaintiff. At no time was the plaintiff advised of the verbal report by the operator, or that the crane incident was considered by the defendant in deciding to demote the plaintiff. The demotion was ultimately found to be a constructive dismissal. Mr. Justice Steele, without citing authority for the proposition, stated:

> With respect to the crane incident I find that it was incompetence on the part of the plaintiff but, in view of the fact that he was denied natural justice in that it was not brought to his attention until August 29, 1978, and that he was not told of the verbal report of the crane operator and therefore was not given an opportunity to defend himself, I find that the employer did not act fairly or reasonably and cannot rely on it as grounds for dismissal for cause. (at pp. 173-174)

In *Reilly v. Steelcase Can. Ltd.* (1979), 26 O.R. (2d) 725, 103 D.L.R. (3d) 704 (H.C.), Mr. Justice Keith of the Supreme Court of Ontario did cite authority for the proposition that an employee being terminated must be afforded natural justice, failing which the termination is nullified. In this case, there was a denial of the opportunity to be heard with respect to allegations that the plaintiff had an adulterous relationship with the wife of a fellow employee and that the plaintiff had acted in an indiscreet and unbecoming manner in the presence of customers. The court cited *Fisher v. Keane* (1878), 11 Ch. D. 353, in which Jessel M.R. issued an injunction having the effect of setting aside the decision of a private club to expel a member. After quoting from *Fisher v. Keane*, Keith J. stated:

> It seems to me that if a man's social reputation is not to be adversely affected by a decision of a club committee taken in the member's absence and without giving him an opportunity to be heard, will not be tolerated by the Court, *a fortiori*, a decision taken in like manner, to dismiss an employee holding a responsible position, ought not to stand. (at p. 735)

Keith J. also proceeded, with apparent approval, to cite the headnote in *Tracey v. Swansea Construction Co.* (1964), [1965] 1 O.R. 203, 47 D.L.R. (2d) 295 (H.C.), affirmed without written reasons, [1965] 2 O.R. 182 (note), 50 D.L.R. (2d) 130 (note) (C.A.), as follows:

> An employer who dismisses an employee for cause need not state the grounds of dismissal, and if good ground existed in fact, it is immaterial whether or not it was known to the employer at the time, and he may justify the dismissal by proof of facts ascertained subsequent thereto even if different from those alleged or given at the time. However, where the facts relied on were known to the employer for some time and he retains the employee after the lapse of a reasona-

> ble time within which he could be expected to act upon the grounds for dismissal, he must be taken to have condoned the misconduct and cannot subsequently rely upon it to support dismissal. (at p. 735)

While his reference to the right to a hearing was *obiter*, it appears that Keith J. was prepared to restrict the propositions stated in *Tracey v. Swansea* to cases in which the employer wished to rely on knowledge acquired after termination.

In *GTE Sylvania Ltd. v. Pulsifer* (1983), 1 C.C.E.L. 62 at 67, 56 N.S.R. (2d) 424, 117 A.P.R. 424 (C.A.), reversing 1 C.C.E.L. 62 at 64, 51 N.S.R. (2d) 298, 102 A.P.R. 298 (T.D.), however, the Nova Scotia Court of Appeal firmly rejected the notion that the principles of natural justice apply to the dismissal of a person, except perhaps a person employed or dismissed pursuant to some statutory authority. The plaintiff in this case was a salesman with access to sample lighting fixtures which were to be used for demonstration purposes or given away to customers. In fact it was alleged that the plaintiff requested, and was given, a camera lens in return for a sample lighting fixture, which constituted a personal benefit to the plaintiff in breach of his employment contract.

At the termination interview, the plaintiff's superior questioned the plaintiff regarding the circumstances under which the particular sample fixture was given away. The supervisor deliberately refrained from making any mention of the camera lens. Instead the plaintiff was asked to provide a satisfactory explanation for the transaction, failing which he would be terminated. A satisfactory explanation was not forthcoming and the plaintiff was terminated.

In support of its conclusion that the plaintiff had no right to be confronted with the allegation, the Court cited the judgment of the Supreme Court of Canada in *Lake Ont. Portland Cement Co. v. Groner*, [1961] S.C.R. 553 at 564, 28 D.L.R. (2d) 589 at 598, which quoted Halsbury's *Laws of England*, 2d ed., vol. 22 at p. 155, as follows:

> It is not necessary that the master, dismissing a servant for good cause, should state the ground for such dismissal; and, provided good ground existed in fact, it is immaterial whether or not it was known to the employer at the time of the dismissal. Justification of dismissal can accordingly be shown by proof of facts ascertained subsequently to the dismissal, or on grounds differing from those alleged at the time. (at p. 77)

The Court, in *G.T.E. Sylvania*, also cited Batt's *Law of Master and Servant* (5th ed., 1967, at p. 100), as follows:

> It appears that a master, dismissing his servant summarily for a good cause, need not state the grounds of his dismissal. It is sufficient if, when the servant sues him, he satisfies the court that he was justified in terminating the service and, indeed, although one reason was given at the time of dismissal which was unjustifiable therefor, another reason, even unknown to the employer at the time of dismissal may be pleaded in a subsequent action for wrongful dismissal. (at p. 78)

In cases such as *Reilly v. Steelcase Can. Ltd., supra*, where allegations relate to isolated incidents, and especially in cases in which previous warnings have not been given, it would seem prudent to afford an opportunity to be heard. If the employee offers an explanation, the employer may determine that there is no reason to terminate the services of a valued employee. If the employee has no explanation, the employer will be more secure in the decision to terminate. Thus, apart from the legal considerations, it is probably a sound management practice to afford the employee an opportunity to be heard.

It is submitted, however, that as a matter of law the position of the Nova Scotia Court of Appeal in *G.T.E. Sylvania, supra*, should be adopted. To award damages to an employee who has breached and repudiated the contract makes no sense in terms of the law of contract. To find that the employer is not entitled to rely upon just cause by virtue of a failure to afford a hearing relieves the employee from the consequences of his or her own breach and repudiation and shifts the burden of such conduct to the employer.

4.3 WHAT CONSTITUTES JUST CAUSE FOR DISMISSAL

(a) Incompetence

(i) *General Principles*

The general legal principles were canvassed by Associate Chief Justice Parker in *Matheson v. Matheson International Trucks Ltd.* (1984), 4 C.C.E.L. 271 (Ont. H.C.), the facts of which case are discussed below in greater detail. In this case Associate Chief Justice Parker stated:

> The plaintiff focuses on the words "best of his ability" and says that the test of competency should be determined by the employee's capacity. I reject that argument because it runs counter to the proposition that all employees are engaged subject to an implied warranty that they are reasonably competent for the work for which they are employed. To accept the plaintiff's argument would lead to the absurd result that a well-intentioned but wholly incompetent employee would be immune from termination of his employment.
>
> Counsel for the plaintiff further argues that the employer must prove gross incompetency. He relies upon the following comment by Wilson J. in *Erlund v. Quality Communication Prods. Ltd.* (1972), 29 D.L.R. (3d) 476 at 481 (Man. Q.B.):
>
>> Incompetence, of course, is a cause for dismissal, but hardly without notice, unless the incompetence be gross to the point where it merges with other factors of greater severity, which I do not find here.
>
> In my opinion, it would be necessary for the employer to prove gross incompetence only if the firing had been abrupt. The evidence discloses that Mr. Matheson had many prior warnings indicating that his level of performance was unsatisfactory. (at p. 276)

This statement of the law, however, may suggest that employers have a greater latitude to dismiss for incompetence than may, as a practical matter, exist. Thus, while there may be an implied warranty of reasonable competence by the employee, the interviewing and hiring process demonstrates that the employer has also reached the conclusion that the employee has the required competence. It is, therefore, very difficult to persuade a court that the sole issue in a case is competence. In fact, in almost all cases the allegations of incompetence will "merge with other factors of greater severity." Further, as the reported cases demonstrate, a finding of just cause for incompetence is exceedingly rare.

(ii) *The Difficulty in Defining Competence*

In order to define incompetence it is first necessary to consider the standard of competence required by the contract of employment. Pre-employment representations made by the employer concerning the requirements of the position, and by the employee concerning his or her qualifications and ability to meet those requirements, are additional relevant considerations. As well, the extent to which those representations form part of the contract of employment must be considered.

Manners v. Fraser Surrey Docks Ltd. (1981), 9 A.C.W.S. (2d) 155 [Docket No. Vancouver C803159] (B.C.S.C.), provides an example of such a pre-employment representation. The plaintiff had represented to the defendant employer that "he was aware of the duties and responsibilities of a dock superintendent and he was able and competent to perform those duties" (at p. 7, unreported reasons for judgment (11 May 1981)). The plaintiff was hired as a dock superintendent. It quickly became apparent that he could not handle the job and his employment was terminated after less than two weeks' service. In the result, the Supreme Court of British Columbia found just cause for dismissal, consisting of incompetence, even though the Court was prepared to find that the plaintiff, in time, could have learned the job of dock superintendent. *Manners* was an unusual case in that the contract defined the acceptable level of competence in specific terms, namely, being able to discharge the specialized function of a dock superintendent. *Manners* may be analogous, for example, to an applicant for a position as a computer programmer misrepresenting his ability to work with the necessary computer language.

In most cases, however, there will be no precise contractual definition of competence. In the real world, employers often judge competency in terms of results. Leaving aside the situation of a professional golfer or tennis player, there are few occupations in which the results achieved will not be the product of a broad range of factors extraneous to the individual employee, and perhaps extraneous to the employer as well.

Thus, the salesman who is not achieving sales quotas will, fairly or unfairly, implicate the manufacturing department for defective manufacture or late delivery, the marketing department for poor promotion, the service department for dealer resistance, his largest customer for being the subject of a takeover and the Bank of Canada for raising interest rates. To decide whether, and to what degree, these various factors affected sales results in a particular territory would require the wisdom of Solomon. When you recall that the employer has the onus of proving just cause, take into account the natural sympathy and concern of the Court for a terminated employee and the consequence of a finding of just cause, these extraneous factors can make it next to impossible to persuade a court that acts of incompetence constitute just cause for dismissal.

Thus, while the general principles of law concerning competence can be readily stated, the difficulty is in applying the principles to particular cases. It seems, therefore, most instructive to review a number of cases in which the Court has, or has not, upheld a termination on the ground of incompetence.

(iii) *Incompetence Constituting Just Cause for Dismissal*

In *Matheson v. Matheson International Trucks Ltd.* (1984), 4 C.C.E.L. 271 (Ont. H.C.), the plaintiff had been employed by International Harvester for 30 years prior to deciding to acquire his own dealership. Pursuant to an agreement with International Harvester, the defendant was incorporated, with the plaintiff contributing $75,000 to capital and International Harvester contributing $665,000. The plaintiff was named president and general manager of the defendant. As the particulars of incompetence are important, it is necessary to refer to them at some length. In discussing the allegations of incompetence Associate Chief Justice Parker stated:

> The first fiscal year of the defendant consisted of the months of September and October 1979. The defendant made a profit in that period and Mr. Matheson's share was used to increase his equity in the company from $75,000 to $91,000. Problems began the second year. Although none of the incidents complained of amounted to serious misconduct, they did indicate that Mr. Matheson was not carrying out his responsibilities. He failed to submit reports and financial statements on time. When information was requested, he could not supply it. He ignored correspondence sent to him by the directors and failed to carry out their requests. He was referred to an Achievement Valuation of himself as company president made in 1979 by Mr. Revell dated April 12, 1979. There are five levels of achievement in every category. The lowest, F, is defined as "Fails to meet minimum position accountabilities". Mr. Matheson was graded F in all categories. The completed report was signed by the plaintiff. Although he stated in evidence that he disagreed with the evaluation, he did not suggest to anyone at the time that it was incorrect. When Mr. Matheson was questioned about various matters complained of, many of his answers were vague and uncertain. He implied that the problems were beyond his control.
>
> . . . .
>
> By February of 1980, the letters to Mr. Matheson were becoming more ominous. A letter from Mr. Day listed ten matters of concern, one of which read, "Continuing under current management". Mr. Matheson was asked what he thought was meant by this and he said, "I didn't think about it". On cross-examination he was asked did he not think this referred to him and he stated "no". I cannot accept his evidence on this point. (at p. 277)
>
> . . . .

> Mr. Day testified that each dealer was given an audit package from which the accountants prepared the final audited statements. In 1978 and 1979 the accountants were unable to prepare financial statements for the defendant because supporting documents were not available to them. Mr. Day testified that in the first quarter of 1980 he was unable to secure financial statements from the accountants or even get unaudited monthly financial statements from Mr. Matheson. When he failed to submit financial statements, letters would be written to him but he did not reply.
>
> Mr. Matheson submitted one budget eight months after the year end; by that point it was not of much help to anyone. An estimate of future sales made after the period had passed could hardly be relied on. A statement that sales exceeded sales estimates means nothing if the estimates were not given until after the sales were made.
>
> The president of each dealer company was responsible for submitting a management plan the first month of each fiscal year setting out the budget for the coming year. Correspondence indicates that Mr. Day pressed Mr. Matheson for his plan in February but did not receive it until June when only four months were left in the fiscal year. By then the plan was useless.
>
> Mr. Day testified that Mr. Matheson was unwilling to accept suggestions and did not carry out directives from the board. While he seemed to accept criticism, he took no corrective action to solve the problem discussed. Even when he promised corrective action, promises were never kept. Mr. Matheson did not know what was going on within his company. Mr. Matheson's sole concern was increasing sales; however, the company's more pressing problems were in the areas of management and accounting. By tying up too much money in vehicle inventory, parts and accounts receivables, the company had no cash to operate.
>
> The defendant has satisfied me that Mr. Matheson was incompetent and that his discharge was justified. (at pp. 279-280)

In *Matheson* the allegation of just cause succeeded because the Court had objective, uncontradicted evidence, namely, the failure of the employee to answer correspondence and submit reports in a timely fashion. Despite the fact that the Court characterized the termination as being for incompetence, it could be argued that the failure to respond to requests constituted wilful neglect and/or insubordination. In other words, presumably the employee was competent to respond to correspondence and to prepare reports. Thus, the failure to do so was the result of a deliberate decision of the employee that he would not do so. The position of the employer would have been much more difficult had the employee decided to give at least the appearance of competence and diligence, by responding in a timely fashion. The employer would have faced a virtually insurmountable hurdle in trying to establish just cause based on the financial results and the quality of the correspondence and reports submitted.

LaRose v. T. Eaton Co. (1980), 3 C.C.E.L. 51 (Ont. Co. Ct.), provides a further example of a case in which the Court found that incompetence was just cause for dismissal, albeit on the ground that the incompetence really merged with a refusal to follow orders bordering on wilful neglect of duty. The plaintiff had been employed for 17 years in a clerical capacity dealing with customers' accounts. With one exception the plaintiff's rating on annual performance reviews was never above satisfactory. After a number of warnings that his poor performance could result in dismissal, and after temporary improvements, the plaintiff's performance again deteriorated and he was terminated. In finding that there was just cause for dismissal, the Court stated:

> What have to be weighed in this case are the respective duties owed by the employee to his employer and, in turn, by the employer to its employee. After 17 years of service one would not expect to see an employee dismissed out of hand or dismissed even after some brief and unreasonable warning. On the other hand, an employee who has muddled along for 17 years without having had his potential seriously tested has no valid complaint if, after being given a reasonable opportunity, his failure to measure up to reasonable requirements which are within his demonstrated ability results in his dismissal. (at pp. 55-56)

(iv) *Incompetence Not Constituting Just Cause for Dismissal*

Allegations of just cause and particularly allegations of incompetence, will be viewed in light of the overall service of the employee and the pressure of the job. In *Robinson v. Cdn. Acceptance Corp.* (1973), 43 D.L.R. (3d) 301 (N.S.T.D.), affirmed (1974), 9 N.S.R. (2d) 226, 47 D.L.R. (3d) 417 (C.A.), the Nova Scotia Supreme Court found that just cause did not exist, notwithstanding that it also found that, at the time of termination, the plaintiff could no longer function in his job. In his reasons Mr. Justice Hart stated:

> Between September of 1972 and March of 1973, the plaintiff began to experience difficulties. He became emotionally involved in an extra-marital affair, with which he was unable to cope. As a result, he sought refuge, firstly, in excessive drinking and, finally, in emotional collapse. His problem reflected itself in his periodic absences from where he was expected to be in connection with his employment and, finally, in the necessity for hospitalization to recover from an extreme emotional breakdown.
>
> During this period immediately before the plaintiff's dismissal, which was short compared to his 10 years of service with the company, there is no evidence that he wilfully intended to disobey the dictates of his superiors or to neglect his work. The company's statistics show on the contrary that the branches under his supervision were performing in a normal manner, even though for a short time he was not able to give them the attention they required. The plaintiff was going through the type of experience which many executives encounter some time during their business career, and for which many companies make allowance through their personnel policies. There cannot be many executives who work under years of constant pressure who do not at some time go through a period of emotional upset, during which they cease to function as efficiently as they would at normal times. (at p. 309)

In a similar vein, in *Olson v. Motor Coach Industries Ltd.*, [1977] 4 W.W.R. 634 (Man. Q.B.), affirmed [1978] 1 W.W.R. 726, 81 D.L.R. (3d) 132 (Man. C.A.), the plaintiff had progressed through the ranks of the company from labourer to general foreman in charge of 140 to 160 manufacturing employees. The plaintiff was employed as foreman for approximately 17 months prior to termination. At trial it was agreed between the parties that the plaintiff "was not satisfactorily performing his duties as a general foreman but attempted to perform those duties to the best of his ability and talents." In rejecting the contention that there was just cause, Mr. Justice Wright stated:

> Unquestionably, defendant had the right to dismiss plaintiff if it was unhappy with plaintiff's performance in his job but unless plaintiff was guilty of misconduct or other justifiable cause "going to show (in effect) that he is repudiating the contract with his employer" defendant was not entitled to dismiss him without reasonable notice. The evidence falls far short of reaching this standard. (at pp. 637-638)

In *Babcock v. C. & R. Weickert Enterprises Ltd.* (1993), 50 C.C.E.L. 1, (*sub nom. Babcock v. Weickert (C. & R.) Enterprises Ltd.*) 126 N.S.R. (2d) 170, 352 A.P.R. 170 (C.A.), the Court found that the failure to provide the employee with reasonable time to correct the deficiencies in his performance, of which he had been warned, precluded a finding of just cause for dismissal.

(v) *Conclusions*

In practical terms it is usually futile to try to establish just cause based solely upon allegations of incompetence. In this regard, it may be helpful to recite the litany of comments typically made by judges at pre-trial conferences when allegations of incompetence are relied upon. These are as follows:

1. Your client hired this person and obviously made the judgment that he or she could do the job — what has really happened since that time to change your client's view?
2. Your client elected to hire the employee without a probationary period (or even worse, the employee successfully completed the probationary period). Again, what has really changed that would now entitle your client to inflict the "capital punishment" of the employment world?
3. If your client wanted to be able to terminate employees, without what it views as an inordinate cost, then why didn't you ask the employee to agree to an employment contract?

While some of these comments may not address the stated legal test for finding incompetence amounting to just cause for dismissal, they should be kept in mind when considering a termination by reason of incompetence.

In addition, one must consider that incompetence is rarely the sole factor that leads to termination. Employees who have been employed for any length of time have usually demonstrated that they are capable of competent performance. Further, employees generally want to do a good job and to continue, or advance, in their employment. Thus, when an employee is doing a poor job it is often a result of other contributing causes such as a personality conflict with management or perhaps poor health. As a general rule, the greater the number of factors at work the greater the difficulty of the employer in proving just cause for dismissal.

(b) Insubordination

(i) *General Principle*

Insubordination, as hereinafter discussed, includes any refusal of an employee to follow instructions, and any other conduct of the employee that constitutes a challenge to persons in authority or their policies.

In *Codner v. Joint Construction Ltd.* (1989), 27 C.C.E.L. 144, 74 Nfld. & P.E.I.R. 219, 231 A.P.R. 219 (Nfld. T.D.), the Court found that an isolated incident involving intemperate language was sufficient to establish just cause for dismissal. The plaintiff was a seasonal employee and alleged that he was wrongfully dismissed and that the defendant had made false allegations that the plaintiff was responsible for the theft of gasoline by using the company credit card for personal gas purchases. The Court focused upon the language used by the plaintiff, stating:

> There is an additional factor involved here and that is the language of the plaintiff when Ronald Walsh senior the owner and president of the defendant, was discussing the use of the said card with the plaintiff namely "you're a f... liar". Although an isolated incident, the words were destructive of the employment relationship between the plaintiff and the defendant particularly in view of the evidence and notwithstanding the words were not said in the presence of any other employees, I find they did constitute just cause for dismissal. (at p. 154)

(ii) *Wilful Disobedience*

In *Laws v. London Chronicle (Indicator Newspapers) Ltd.*, [1959] 2 All E.R. 285 (C.A.), Lord Evershed summarized the law as follows:

> It is, no doubt, therefore, generally true that wilful disobedience of an order will justify summary dismissal, since wilful disobedience of a lawful and reasonable order shows a disregard — a complete disregard — of a condition essential to the contract of service, namely, the condition that the servant must obey the proper orders of the master and that, unless he does so, the relationship is, so to speak, struck at fundamentally.
>
> . . . .
>
> . . . I think that it is not right to say that one act of disobedience, to justify dismissal, must be of a grave and serious character. I do, however, think (following the passages which I have already cited) that one act of disobedience or misconduct can justify dismissal only if it is of a nature which goes to show (in effect) that the servant is repudiating the contract, or one of its essential conditions; and for that reason, therefore, I think that one finds in the passages which I have read that the disobedience must at least have the quality that it is "wilful": it does (in other words) connote a deliberate flouting of the essential contractual conditions. (at pp. 287-288)

In *Holden v. Metro Transit Operating Co.* (1983), 1 C.C.E.L. 159 (B.C.S.C.), the Court applied the *Laws* case in finding just cause for dismissal on the basis of insubordination. The plaintiff was employed as manager of the finance division of the defendant. A position became available in the finance division and a dispute arose between the plaintiff who favoured recruiting a person from outside the defendant, and his superiors who favoured transferring an existing employee named Woof to the available position. When his superiors decided that the existing employee should be offered the available position, the plaintiff undertook a running battle to undermine and counter-

(*Continued on page 4-17*)

mand this decision. In this regard the plaintiff refused to sign the requisite transfer form and by memorandum notified his superiors that:

> As I advised you verbally, I will be unable to sign the "Employee Change of Status" form to authorize the appointment of Mr. D. Woof as Manager, Corporate Reporting.
>
> As you are aware from our previous discussions and as pointed out in my memo of March 2, 1981, I do not agree with this appointment and in order to maintain my professional integrity as well as my credibility within the organization, I cannot support it.
>
> The form is therefore being returned, herewith, for whatever action you deem necessary. (at p. 164)

In upholding the dismissal for just cause, the Court commented that:

> There is no question that Patton had the authority to appoint Woof and the authority to direct the plaintiff to appoint Woof. The plaintiff could not hire but only recommend. The plaintiff acknowledged that he refused to appoint as ordered and refused to recognize the appointment. This conduct persisted over a period of weeks. He determined to follow a course of conduct which was in conflict with the instructions of his superiors because he wrongly perceived that his power as finance division manager was being diminished or limited by upper management's failure to allow him to appoint his own underlings.
>
> The plaintiff wilfully and deliberately disregarded the essential conditions of his employment contract by refusing to comply with the orders of his superior, not only once but on numerous occasions over a protracted period of time. The plaintiff knew that his refusal to comply with the direct orders of his superior could result in summary dismissal. He said as much when he indicated that he would seek legal advice. It was a flagrant act of insubordination and consequently the defendant was entitled to dismiss the plaintiff summarily. (at p. 165)

Another interesting case in which the Court upheld a dismissal for just cause on the basis of insubordination is *Ogle v. Cdn. Newspapers Co.* (1984), 5 C.C.E.L. 162 (Alta. Q.B.). In this case the plaintiff, who was the city editor of the newspaper, adopted a negative and unhelpful posture with respect to certain changes in the format of the newspaper that the newly appointed managing director was attempting to implement.

The Court summarized the evidence and, in oral reasons, stated its conclusion as follows:

> On the evidence I have received, I have concluded that Mr. Ogle, a long-term employee, and at least to a point, a formerly good employee, didn't agree with the changes and didn't want to adjust to the changes and to use the vernacular, dragged his feet with respect to implementing those changes. I'm also satisfied that the conduct of Mr. Ogle, in essence, and to some significant degree, undermined Mr. Farrington's efforts to make the changes. That he showed a lack of co-operation, and a negative attitude. It also appears to me from the evidence that Mr. Farrington gave a fair degree of encouragement in urging Mr. Ogle to do these things and in giving him time to do these things and in encouraging him to

do these things so that I do not think that Mr. Farrington's efforts in that regard were unreasonable.

A term of every contract of employment that will be implied is that an employee will serve honestly and faithfully. The employee must accept proper orders that are given to him. He must implement them, that is a duty upon him. That duty, if anything, is heavier when, as here, Mr. Ogle was in a management position. The actions of Mr. Ogle, in my view, were not in good faith in attempting to implement the required changes, he spoke negatively about them, he disparaged them, and to a degree he didn't do them. He allowed a hostility to build between himself and Mr. Farrington and with respect to that, of course there is no supreme law that says we will each get along with the other or that employees will necessarily get along with their superiors. But I'm satisfied that he became quite upset by what was happening as evidenced I think by his telephone calls to Mr. Pohle, as evidenced by the rumour in the back room of the 14th to the 15th that he was going to be quitting as an experienced journalist. Perhaps he just found that he could not agree with these changes and, as I say, it's not for this Court to pass judgment on whether those changes are good or poor with respect to a newspaper's format. He was given many chances, really, I believe on the evidence, to improve his performance.

This takes us, then, back to the meeting of the 14th and 15th of December. I accept Mr. Farrington's evidence that he asked for and that he earnestly wished to obtain Mr. Ogle's support. He did not get that commitment in the context of those conversations; of course he did not take Ex. 6 as such a commitment. I think Mr. Farrington came to the conclusion that he would not have the support of Mr. Ogle and that in that regard Mr. Ogle would not properly do his job as city editor, which in turn gave rise to the offer of other employment. The evidence before me certainly does not reveal any commitment by Mr. Ogle to co-operate and to implement.

That being so, I consider that there was a fundamental breach of the contract of employment by Mr. Ogle. At that time he made it clear that he would not change his ways, that he would not co-operate, that he would not implement, because he had not been, and when asked for a commitment, it was certainly not given. What has happened here was a repudiation by Mr. Ogle of a fundamental term of his employment contract, that is to say that he co-operate and implement proper directives and procedures, that he not undermine the proper directives and procedures. Mr. Ogle's repudiation of his contract of employment was the cause of his termination. (at pp. 171-172)

Insubordination will constitute just cause notwithstanding that the insubordinate behaviour of the employee arises from philosophical and ethical differences with the employer. In *Bell v. Society for the Promotion of Education & Activities for Children in the Home* (1984), 6 C.C.E.L. 156, 34 Sask. R. 203 (Q.B.), affirmed (1986), 47 Sask. R. 290 (C.A.), the employee, who held a doctorate in psychology, was the executive director of a society providing in-home services to mentally retarded persons. While in this position he learned that the parents of a severely disabled girl had made the necessary arrangements for her to have a partial hysterectomy. The employee, who was opposed to such surgery on ethical and philosophical grounds, voiced objections to the surgery and was instructed by the president of the defendant that he should take no further steps until the board of the defendant could consider the matter. Contrary to that instruction, the employee set about to prevent the surgery as follows:

1. He telephoned government and private agencies to determine if such surgery could constitute child abuse, so that a complaint could be registered.
2. He met with the admissions committee of the defendant, which committee included board members, to discuss the girl in question but did not disclose his knowledge of the proposed surgery or his steps in connection therewith.
3. He disclosed the name of the girl's paediatrician to interested third parties, who in turn notified the Deputy Minister of Health, who in turn contacted the hospital where the proposed surgery was to take place.

As a consequence of the steps taken, the doctor who was to perform the operation became concerned that by performing the operation he could be subject to some form of discipline or sanction. As a result the operation was cancelled. In upholding the discharge on the basis of just cause, the Court stated:

> It is a fundamental of a person's professional standing that his professional duty to the client/patient and to himself exceeds any responsibility he might have to aboard or to a person from whom he would otherwise take direction.
>
> But justification must be judged with a level eye. He went too far, and he overstates his justification. He had made up his mind to frustrate the desires of the family; he was determined to bypass the board and its potential interference.
>
> To turn the defendant's goals and policies against itself is a reversal of the roles. His mandate was to carry out the objectives and goals which had been set by the board. Being aware that the board had no policy, and having received directions from the president not to take steps without the direction of the board, it was less than straightforward to undertake the flurry of activity in defiance of her directions. To suggest that the board, and not Marilyn Heiber, is his employer is a truth which emphasizes his determination in this case to accept no interference. (at p. 161)
>
> . . . .
>
> Nonetheless, the plaintiff had the right to consider this question and, having regard to his professional ethics, to make further inquiry. Having done so, and having been informed that this was not considered child abuse, it was not his duty to pursue the matter with the zeal which he followed.
>
> His lack of candour with the board or to the president represents the kind of conduct which the board could no longer accept. The board did not dismiss him abruptly, without further consideration, limiting its consideration only to this incident. Rather, the board soberly and carefully examined various other matters of complaint.

. . . .

> The board bases its decision to dismiss squarely on the conduct of the plaintiff in the major incident noted above. In my view, the plaintiff's persistence beyond what was required of him professionally, and his failure to deal frankly with the board rendered intolerable his continued employment.
>
> Under the circumstances, the board was justified in dismissing him for cause without notice. (at p. 162)

A further case which is concerned with insubordination, but is potentially of broad significance to employers, is *Gracia v. Sears Can. Inc.* (1986), 16 C.C.E.L. 1 (B.C. Co. Ct.). An employee, who had been off work claiming a compensable accident, was determined by the Workers' Compensation Board to be ineligible for benefits. Faced with the inconsistency between the employee's claim for disability, and the determination of the Board, the defendant offered the plaintiff three options:

1. return to work; or
2. take a 3-month leave of absence without pay; or
3. provide a doctor's letter confirming disability.

The plaintiff failed to elect any of the options and, as a consequence, was terminated. In discussing the claim the Court addressed the issue in a common sense manner, and in plain terms stated:

> The question is: Have the employer and the employee acted within the terms of the employment contract? Here those terms are not set out in writing but only as a matter of practice and so the question must be answered in terms of what is reasonable within this relationship.
>
> In this case Sears acted reasonably. It had medical advice on file from Mr. Gracia's family doctor and from the Worker's Compensation Board which indicated that Mr. Gracia was fit. Mr. Gracia knew of that information. Sears also had the information received in the phone call to Dr. Zack's office. If there was an error in the doctor's letter and telephone call, that cannot be held against Sears.
>
> My impression was that Sears was doing its best to be fair. The company accepted that Mr. Gracia did not feel able to return to his job. Sears was prepared to provide sick benefit pay if medical verification was supplied. Sears was prepared in any event to wait 3 months or longer, if Mr. Gracia's claim could be supported by a doctor's letter.
>
> That request was not unreasonable. When it was not met, the termination could not be said to be wrongful. The employee had failed to carry out the reasonable direction of his employer.
>
> The termination here was far from summary. It could have been avoided by Mr. Gracia obeying a simple but essential condition: come back to work or let us have medical assurance that you can't.
>
> The claim is dismissed. (at pp. 7-8)

In the case of *Bratti v. F & W Wholesale Ltd.* (1989), 28 C.C.E.L. 142 (B.C. Co. Ct.), the employee, Bratti, was a baker who had been employed for eighteen years. The employer instituted a procedure to ensure that its employees took their vacations at non-conflicting times. Bratti attempted to book the same vacation time booked by another employee and the employer denied this request due to an unexpected increase in business. Bratti, after being warned that he would be terminated if he took his vacation as planned, took his vacation and was terminated. The Court held:

> I have no doubt that in this case the disobedience of Bratti to the reasonable requirement of Perri that he not go for vacation, at that particular time, was wilful disobedience and a deliberate flouting of an essential contractual condition, that is: that Bratti, being an essential employee, not take his holidays at a time extremely inconvenient to F & W's operations.
>
> Although, in hindsight, the operations of F & W were not prejudiced to the extent that they had to be discontinued or curtailed, the potential for that to happen was present throughout all of the deliberations between Bratti and Perri and, I find, it was only due to good fortune that Perri was able to obtain another baker from another operation of the principals of the company to cover for Bratti during his absence. His unilateral decision, therefore, to take his vacation when he did was to the prejudice of the proper conduct of F & W's business and had the potential for putting the whole operation of the company considerably at risk. (at p. 150)

(iii) *Disregard of Proper Procedures*

Another aspect of insubordination is the failure to follow established corporate procedures. In *Bell v. Cessna Aircraft Co.* (1980), 19 B.C.L.R. 252, 10 B.L.R. 31 (S.C.), reversed (1982), 33 B.C.L.R. 181, 82 C.L.L.C. 14,169, 131 D.L.R. (3d) 551 (C.A.), leave to appeal to Supreme Court of Canada refused (1982), 43 N.R. 167 (note) (S.C.C.) the plaintiff was the district sales manager of the Canadian division of the defendant and, as such, the plaintiff reported to G, who was the Canadian sales manager, who in turn reported to J, who was the zone manager, who in turn reported to N in the United States. In 1979 the plaintiff formed the opinion that his sales quota had been raised to an unreasonably high level and that J and G were conspiring against him. The plaintiff became convinced that he was to be terminated and, therefore, bypassed the Canadian management and sought an appointment with N in the United States. N listened and then left the matter for Canadian management to deal with. G felt that the plaintiff's conduct demonstrated that he would not in future be amenable to any criticism, constructive or not, and that the example of an employee bypassing Canadian management to rectify perceived wrongs would be a "disastrous" example. As a result, the plaintiff's employment was terminated.

In the British Columbia Supreme Court, Mr. Justice Locke found that there was just cause on the ground that the plaintiff "struck at the root of his own contract of employment" by challenging the internal reporting structure of the defendant. On appeal, however, the British Columbia Court of Appeal took a more charitable view of the conduct of the plaintiff. The Court reasoned as follows:

> In my opinion, the learned trial judge erred in law in holding that the only ground for bypassing middle management was to expose a fraud or a malevolent conspiracy likely to affect the operations of the company. While it may be wrong to

> go over the head of one's immediate supervisors for the purpose of criticizing business or administrative decisions made by middle management and thus afford grounds for immediate dismissal, different considerations apply where an employee's job is at stake. In my view, simple justice requires that where a junior executive on reasonable grounds and acting in good faith believes that he is about to be discharged he should have the opportunity to present his side of the case to top management. I am unable to understand how such action on the part of a junior executive can constitute a repudiation by him of his contract of employment. While it may be that the employee's conduct in presenting his case to top management will cause his immediate superiors to lose confidence in him and make his continued employment impossible, such conduct does not constitute cause for dismissal. In such circumstances the employer may terminate the employment contract but only upon giving reasonable notice of termination. (at p. 188)

The broad distinction, therefore, is drawn between the permissible bypassing of management to expose a fraud or to protect one's job and the impermissible bypassing of supervisors for the mere purpose of criticizing management decisions. The obvious difficulty is in drawing the line in intermediate cases.

In *Rock v. Canadian Red Cross Society* (1994), 5 C.C.E.L. (2d) 231, 94 C.L.L.C. 14,048 (Ont. Gen. Div.), additional reasons at (1994), 7 C.C.E.L. (2d) 146 (Ont. Gen. Div.), the plaintiff was the director of the Red Cross blood transfusion centre in Ottawa. The plaintiff was an eminent scientist involved in various research projects involving third-party funding.

Contrary to Red Cross policy, the plaintiff established a separate bank account to accept donations. Funds in the account were primarily used for research and scientific purposes, although some money was used for staff social events. This included events at which alcohol was served contrary to Red Cross policy.

Problems arose when interest accrued in the account and the plaintiff and a subordinate agreed that the subordinate would report the interest as personal income and be reimbursed for the additional tax he incurred.

The plaintiff was given a number of reasons for termination, some of which were unfounded, culminating in what the Red Cross referred to as a loss of "all confidence and trust".

The Court, however, concluded that there was not just cause for dismissal stating:

> There is no question that an employee such as Dr. Rock has a duty to be frank and honest with her employer and not to conceal relevant information from them. In this particular case there is no concealment of information, because there was no report required as to all of the activities of the centre.
>
> . . . .
>
> There was no question that Dr. Rock breached the policy of the Canadian Red Cross in maintaining separate accounts and in charging alcohol to these accounts, both clearly contrary to the established policy of the Red Cross. The question is whether these breaches, although serious, justified termination. The facts in this case can be distinguished from those in *Donaldson v. Philippine Airlines* [(1985), 7 C.C.E.L. 229 (Ont.C.A.)] as in that case, the district manager withheld the true state

of affairs from the company by concealing the information. He deliberately withheld essential information from the company and placed the company in financial jeopardy. In Dr. Rock's case, she did not withhold or conceal any information. She did not derive any personal benefit and did not expose the Canadian Red Cross to any financial loss.

Granted, the Canadian Red Cross did lose the benefit of the interest on monies generated from the research and contracts. However, this is offset by the amount of monies generated by Dr. Rock during her tenure.

In view of Dr. Rock's position and extensive contribution to the Canadian Red Cross in scientific research, the breach of policy by Dr. Rock could have been dealt with by other forms of discipline rather than by immediate termination. (at 5 C.C.E.L. (2d), pp. 254-255)

(iv) *Conclusions*

An allegation of insubordination is more likely to succeed in establishing just cause than an allegation of incompetence. Firstly, insubordinate conduct is more readily identifiable and hence more easily proven. In contrast, incompetent performance may have to be viewed cumulatively over a period of time, and compared to the performance of other employees, to be meaningful. Secondly, in a results-oriented context, such as the business world, incompetence must usually be substantiated by poor statistical results which may be affected by many extraneous factors. By way of example, one could not readily conclude that a sales manager was incompetent, even if he clearly lacked certain managerial skills, if for some intangible reason sales results were favourable. There is no comparable necessity to judge insubordinate behaviour on the basis of the results of such behaviour.

(c) Absenteeism and Lateness

Absence from work without valid reason constitutes a serious breach of the contract of employment. In the case of salaried employees who are paid notwithstanding occasional absences, to absent oneself without valid reason borders on misrepresentation and dishonesty. Absenteeism, as discussed under this heading, means occasional absences from work, which are not the product of a specific, serious illness. In other words, the type of absence which the employee generally can justify by a telephone call indicating the employee will not be reporting for work, or a simple statement by the employee that he or she is not feeling well.

In *Chantler v. Applied Power* (1982), 1 C.C.E.L. 141 (Ont. H.C.), rather blatant and persistent lateness and absenteeism were not found to amount to just cause for dismissal. The plaintiff had full-time employment with the defendant, and also had active farming and accounting businesses as additional sources of income. The trial Judge made the following findings:

1. that on July 5, 1979 the plaintiff, notwithstanding that he had a business meeting scheduled with a company official from the United States from 10:00 a.m., occupied himself in selling his farm produce such that he arrived at work at 11:30 a.m., and even then did not make any effort to contact the company official;

2. that the evidence of the plaintiff that he was sick in bed on July 9, 1979, and so did not report for work, could not be believed. It appeared to the Court that the plaintiff simply absented himself so that he could assist with the harvesting of strawberries at his farm;
3. that the plaintiff was habitually late, and had received at least one warning because of that.

Despite these findings the Court did not find just cause for dismissal. As the plaintiff was not terminated until September 27, 1979, it may be that the Court was influenced by the extent to which the plaintiff's conduct was condoned, or due to the defendant's failure to warn. Absent the factor of condonation, it is respectfully submitted that the employee richly deserved summary termination and that just cause should have been found.

Nossal v. Better Business Bureau of Metropolitan Toronto Inc. (1985), 12 C.C.E.L. 85, 51 O.R. (2d) 279, 19 D.L.R. (4th) 547, 9 O.A.C. 184 (C.A.), is a case in which the employer condoned the fact that the employee was late a startling 90 times in one calendar year. However, the Court found that later misconduct on the part of the employee entitled the employer, and the Court, to consider the lateness together with the later misconduct, and so uphold dismissal for just cause. In dealing with lateness, it is necessary for the employer to be diligent in warning employees that lateness will not be tolerated, and in acting on such warning should the conduct continue. It is difficult to imagine any valid excuse for persistent lateness, and a series of explicit warnings, coupled with a continuation of late reporting, should amount to just cause for dismissal.

The case of absenteeism is much more difficult. Some individuals enjoy good health, while others may have a weaker constitution and be subject to all manner of illnesses which result in frequent temporary absences. Thus, it is of little or no probative value to show that a particular individual is absent significantly more days than the average employee.

From the employer's point of view, an additional difficulty is securing reliable information concerning the malady suffered by the employee. It would be unreasonable to attempt to require that employees consult a doctor

(*Continued on page 4-23*)

for even the slightest ailment. In the absence of some medical evidence, it will be exceedingly difficult for an employer to convince a court that the employee did not, in fact, suffer from the illness claimed. In the typical case, where the employee claims to have remained home, as a result of some illness, it is virtually impossible to contradict the employee.

It remains, however, that an employer has some latitude in an employment contract to require medical information from an employee. While it would be unreasonable to request medical information with respect to any and all absences, it would seem a reasonable condition to require medical evidence with respect to absences of a certain duration, and perhaps even a shorter absence if there is a specific, and unusually high, incidence of absence by the employee. Further, the case of *Gracia v. Sears Can. Inc.* (1986), 16 C.C.E.L. 1 (B.C. Co. Ct.), provides some authority for the employer to insist upon being provided with medical information. While the situation in *Gracia* was one of a disability extending over several months, the case could be argued to stand for the general proposition that an employer, called upon to pay an employee during a period of absence, is entitled to insist upon reasonable medical information to justify such absence.

An employer may also consider stipulating, in an employment contract, that the employer will not pay absent employees or will not pay employees who are absent for greater than a prescribed number of days in a given period. In the absence of such a contractual term the common law position is that an employer must continue to pay an employee during periods of absence, other than absence brought about by a permanent disability (see *Dartmouth Ferry Comm. v. Marks* (1903), 34 S.C.R. 366 at 374-375, discussed in Chapter 4.3(d)).

In considering whether absenteeism or illness constitute just cause for dismissal, and the enforceability of a contractual provision denying pay to absent employees, it is also necessary to consider the implications of the Ontario *Human Rights Code* provisions regarding handicap (see Chapter 13.9).

(d) Permanent Disability

Absenteeism may also result from serious illness. The leading case on point is the decision of the Supreme Court of Canada in *Dartmouth Ferry Comm. v. Marks* (1903), 34 S.C.R. 366. In this case, a ferry captain became ill and was off work for several months. Despite the fact that his physician believed that he was recovering, it was determined just prior to his death that he suffered from an incurable disease. The widow, as executrix of her husband's estate, sought to recover her husband's wages for the period of his illness. Writing for a majority of the Court, Mr. Justice Davies stated:

> That truth is now admitted and is beyond controversy that on and after the 15th of December, when Captain Marks ceased working, he was permanently disabled from doing his work he had contracted to do. In law, this disablement is termed

> the act of God. It not only, in my opinion, justified the Commission in formally determining the contract, if they had chosen to take that course, but by rendering it impossible that he could ever afterwards discharge his duties under his contract, the permanent disablement determined and ended the contract. . . There is no analogy between such permanent disablement and temporary sickness. The law permits the latter on the ground of common humanity to be offered as an excuse for not discharging duty temporarily and suffers the disabled party to recover wages for the time he is temporarily away from his work. But while releasing the permanently disabled workman from damages for the non-performance of his contract, it does not permit him to recover wages without doing work. (at pp. 374-375)

Mr. Justice Killam, concurring in the result, stated:

> As the employee does not warrant the continuance of his physical ability to work, he does not contract absolutely and at all events to do so. Disability due to illness excuses him. And since his promise is so qualified, strict and full performance of service is not a condition precedent to the right to wages. The wages are payable for such service as he can reasonably be called upon to give and for such only. (at p. 383)

Another leading case is *Yeager v. R. J. Hastings Agencies Ltd.* (1984), 5 C.C.E.L. 266, [1985] 1 W.W.R. 218 (B.C. S.C.). The plaintiff had been employed for some 30 years prior to his termination in 1982. He had commenced employment as a warehouseman, and proceeded through the ranks to become the number two person in the organization, and a significant, although minority, shareholder. For a substantial period of his service he spent up to 40 weeks each year "on the road."

In or about 1980 the plaintiff began exhibiting a number of unusual symptoms, including poor co-ordination, involuntary facial mannerisms, a poor memory, and an irritable and unpleasant disposition. In the latter part of 1981 the plaintiff was diagnosed incorrectly as suffering from an incurable form of organic brain disease.

The Judge commented on the mental state and job performance of the plaintiff, as follows:

> I have already described how, for 10 to 15 years from 1955 onward, the plaintiff spent many weeks each year travelling in pursuit of the defendant's business. The resulting long absences from home inevitably took their toll on his marriage. In 1972 and, again, in 1975, he sought the assistance of marriage counselling and for that purpose was given psychiatric referrals by his family doctor. His need for psychiatric counselling at this point demonstrates that as early as five years before the first circumstance relied upon by the defendant as justification for summary dismissal, the plaintiff had begun to suffer from what I conclude eventually became a serious mental illness. (at p. 280)
>
> . . . .
>
> . . .The plaintiff, after 27 years of exemplary service to the defendant company, began, in 1979, to exhibit signs of reduced performance on the job. This circumstance was the direct result of a mental illness from which he was then suffering. Over the course of the next three years that illness increased in its

severity. As that happened, there was a corresponding increase in its interference with and negative impact upon his ability to perform his job. By 1981, the illness was severe enough that the plaintiff's ability to perform his job was significantly impaired. By the beginning of 1982, as the result of the progressive development of that illness, the plaintiff was occupationally disabled. The illness itself proved to be of a temporary nature. The plaintiff's mental condition has improved steadily since the end of 1982 to the point where, by the time of trial, he was in a better emotional condition than he had been at any time since 1972, long before any troubles arose on the job. (at p. 283)

The Court then considered the law, as it applied to the facts of this case. In this regard the Court held as follows:

Two years is a long period of disability. However, as noted above, the length of the period of disability alone is not determinative of the issue. In *Warburton v. Co-op Wholesale Soc. Ltd.*, supra, an absence from work of 13 months due to injury on the job was characterized by all members of the Court of Appeal as a "temporary illness".

In *Marshall v. Harland & Wolff Ltd.*, [1972] 1 W.L.R. 899, [1972] 2 All E.R. 715, [1972] I.C.R. 101, the Court suggested some guidelines that could be used in determining whether an illness should be considered temporary or permanent in the case of a contract of employment for an indefinite period terminable by notice. There, an employee became disabled due to illness during his 23rd year on the job. After an absence of 18 months he was terminated. In speaking for the Court, which held that his termination was wrongful, Sir John Donaldson said, at p. 101 [I.C.R., pp. 718-19 All E.R.]:

In the context of incapacity due to sickness, the question of whether or not the relationship has come to an end by frustration sounds more difficult than it is. The tribunal must ask itself: was the employee's incapacity, looked at before the purported dismissal, of such a nature, or did it appear likely to continue for such a period, that further performance of his obligations in the future would either be impossible or would be a thing radically different from that undertaken by him and agreed to be accepted by the employer under the agreed terms of his employment? In considering the answer to this question, the tribunal should take account of:

(a) The terms of the contract, including the provisions as to sickness pay - The whole basis of weekly employment may be destroyed more quickly than that of monthly employment and that in turn more quickly than annual employment. When the contract provides for sick pay, it is plain that the contract cannot be frustrated so long as the employee returns to work, or appears likely to return to work, within the period during which such sick pay is payable. But the converse is not necessarily true, for the right to sick pay may expire before the incapacity has gone on, or appears likely to go on, for so long as to make a return to work impossible or radically different from the obligations undertaken under the contract of employment.

(b) How long the employment was likely to last in the absence of sickness - The relationship is less likely to survive if the employment was inherently temporary in its nature or for the duration of a particular job, than if it was expected to be long term or even life long.

> (c) The nature of the employment - Where the employee is one of many in the same category, the relationship is more likely to survive the period of incapacity than if he occupies a key post which must be filled and filled on a permanent basis if his absence is prolonged.
>
> (d) The nature of the illness or injury and how long it has already continued and the prospects of recovery - The greater the degree of incapacity and the longer the period over which it has persisted and is likely to persist, the more likely it is that the relationship has been destroyed.
>
> (e) The period of past employment - A relationship which is of long standing is not so easily destroyed as one which has but a short history. This is good sense and, we think, no less good law, even if it involves some implied and scarcely detectable change in the contract of employment year by year as the duration of the relationship lengthens. The legal basis is that over a long period of service the parties must be assumed to have contemplated a longer period or periods of sickness than over a shorter period.
>
> These factors are interrelated and cumulative, but are not necessarily exhaustive of those which have to be taken into account. (at pp. 288-290)

Applying the law to the facts of the case, the Court found that the disability could not be regarded as permanent. In this regard the Court said:

> He was 55 years of age at the time of his dismissal. Subject to the usual contingencies, he had ten years of continued service to look forward to before reaching normal retirement age.
>
> On the basis of these circumstances alone, I hold that the plaintiff's disability due to illness for a period of two years, followed as it would have been by his return to work with normal job performance thereafter, was not an incapacity of such a nature that it frustrated the contract of employment between these parties and entitled the defendant company to treat that contract as at an end.
>
> I am also of the view that this conclusion is not affected by the erroneous diagnosis of permanent organic brain disease which was current at the time of the plaintiff's dismissal. In the *Dartmouth Ferry Commission* case [*Dartmouth Ferry Comm. v. Marks* (1903), 34 S.C.R. 366], supra, Davies J. suggested that the characterization of a disabling illness as either temporary or permanent is to be determined on the basis of its ultimate outcome and not by the state of knowledge existing at the time of the termination. At [S.C.R.] p. 375 he said:
>
> > The belief of the employee or his medical adviser that the former's disability was only temporary cannot affect the question in the light of the subsequent knowledge which revealed its permanency. The excuse for not working for a short time, which a temporary illness would justify, cannot apply to absence from work caused by permanent disability. (at pp. 290-291)

A further example of the judicial attitude in cases of this nature is the case of *Zelisko v. "99" Truck Parts & Equipment Ltd.* (1985), 8 C.C.E.L. 201 (B.C. S.C.). The plaintiff was a mechanic and service manager for a company engaged in rebuilding truck components. At the time of termination the plaintiff was 34 years of age, had been employed for 14 years, and had been disabled for 20 months. The Court referred to the *Yeager* case, *supra*, and held that this period of disability could not, in the overall context of the employment, be regarded as a permanent disability.

In conclusion, the determination of the Supreme Court of Canada in *Dartmouth Ferry Comm. v. Marks* (1903), 34 S.C.R. 366, that the central issue of whether a disability is temporary or permanent is to be judged on the basis of the "ultimate outcome and not by the state of knowledge at the time of termination" presents considerable difficulty and uncertainty to both parties. If anything, this difficulty is compounded by the fact that the Court stated that regardless of whether the employer took any affirmative steps to terminate employment, "the permanent disablement determined and ended the contract."

It is respectfully submitted that the preferable principle would be to find that, in the absence of an agreement to the contrary, the obligation of the employer should be to compensate a permanently disabled employee for a reasonable period of time after the onset of the permanent disability. The period of reasonable notice would be the same period as would otherwise be found appropriate in the event of termination (see Chapter 6.1).

As the authority on point, however, is by the Supreme Court of Canada, any change must be implemented by that Court, the legislature or by agreement of the parties. It is, therefore, strongly suggested that the entitlement of employees in the event of permanent disability should be addressed in employment contracts or employer policies.

(e) Intoxication and Addiction

(i) *Differentiating Intoxication from Addiction*

As a matter of law a distinction must be drawn between those instances of intoxication resulting from an addiction to drugs or alcohol, and those instances unrelated to addiction. See Chapter 4.3(e)(iv) for an expert discussion of the nature of an addiction and the medical validity of this distinction.

If an employee is intoxicated while at work, this is a serious breach of the employment contract. Not only is the employee unfit to perform the duties of the employment contract, the employee is often a disruptive or demoralizing influence in the workplace, and an embarrassment to the employer if in contact with the public. There are a number of cases upholding terminations for just cause based upon the intoxication of the employee, although the facts of each case must be carefully scrutinized to assess the magnitude of the breach of the particular contract of employment. Thus, the intoxication of a journalist while in the office would not be as serious a breach of contract as comparable intoxication on the part of a construction supervisor on the job site.

If the employee does not take the position that the intoxication is the product of an addiction the legal principles applicable to other instances of deliberate misconduct apply. Depending upon the situation, one incident of intoxication may provide just cause for dismissal. In the alternative, a warning or warnings may be necessary to justify a termination for just cause.

The complexion of the case changes, however, if the employee takes the position that the intoxication was the manifestation of an illness, namely, alcoholism or drug addiction. If an addiction is established (which is virtually certain given the fact of an incident or incidents of intoxication and the plea of the employee that an addiction is the cause), then the legal principles that will apply are those relating to permanent disability. Cases dealing with intoxication and addiction are, therefore, hereinafter discussed under separate headings.

(ii) *Intoxication*

In *MacDonald v. Azar* (1947), [1948] 1 D.L.R. 854 (N.S.S.C.), the Court dealt with a serious case of intoxication. The evidence of intoxication was as follows:

> The plaintiff entered upon his duties under this agreement on the date thereof and continued in defendant's employ until November 23, 1946 when the defendant dismissed the plaintiff. The matter of this dismissal is one of the questions raised in this action. The plaintiff alleges that the dismissal was "without any just cause" and the defendant says that the dismissal was justified by the plaintiff's misconduct.
>
> The misconduct alleged as sufficient cause for the dismissal may be summarized as follows:
>
> 1. Persistent and wilful disobedience to orders;
> 2. Intoxication which prevented plaintiff from attending to his duties and which would be likely to prejudice defendant's business;
> 3. Lack of attention to business.
>
> The disobedience to orders in so far as it was persistent consists of personal use of a show car or demonstration car which was ordered to be available for show purposes all the time and always to be left in the garage at nights. I have no doubt that such were defendant's instructions and that the plaintiff deliberately paid no attention to them. He used the car for his private purposes to an unreasonable extent during defendant's absence from the city and seldom left it in the garage at night. He also disconnected the speedometer of this car and when instructed to connect it and leave it connected, again disconnected it. This could only be for the purpose of deceiving someone, either the defendant or a customer and is a matter of some seriousness.
>
> The matter of intoxication was what finally brought about plaintiff's dismissal. The evidence in this regard has been given by the plaintiff himself. Put in a few words, it is as follows: He left his work on November 9, 1946, took the demonstration car with him and got intoxicated, visiting one place after another where liquor could be got. He was some nights away from his home and some nights at home until he finally landed in the hospital on November 17th. He was in the hospital until the 22nd. On that day he came to the defendant's place of business apparently not yet sober; he told defendant that he was weak and would come back next day. Next day the defendant dismissed him. In the meantime, defendant had seen him driving apparently intoxicated, and had found the car on the street at an early hour parked 5 or 6 ft. from the curb with the doors unlocked and partly open and had taken it to the garage. There were empty liquor bottles in the car. (at pp. 856-857)

In reaching its conclusion the Court stated:

> Intoxication as a ground for dismissal depends upon circumstances and is a question of fact. Sir Wm. Young in *The "Bella Mudge"* (1878), Young's Adm. Dec. 222, expressed the opinion that the intemperate habits of the captain of a ship did not constitute sufficient ground for dismissing him. He followed a case of *The "Atlantic"* (1862), Lush. 566, 167 E.R. 257, where Dr. Lushington refused to forfeit the wages of a captain on the ground of an occasional intoxication but the author of Labatt on Master & Servant, 2nd ed., vol. 1, p. 928 adds this note: "But these decisions were based on considerations deduced from the peculiar circumstances of maritime service, and are not authorities as to the obligations of a servant on land."
>
> In *Bass Furnace Co. v. Glasscock* (1886), 82 Ala. 452, the Court said (pp. 454-5): "We do not doubt that public drunkenness of any employee, while in the service of the employer, and manifesting itself in boisterous and disorderly conduct, either towards the employer or third persons, is such misconduct as to constitute a violation of the stipulation, implied in every contract of service, that the employee will conduct himself with such decency and politeness of deportment as not to work injury to the business of the employer."
>
> I think that the standard to be applied to the manager of an automobile business should be a reasonably high one. A manager who is away from business for two weeks at a time, on a drunken spree cannot exercise efficient supervision over other employees. To drive a car while intoxicated is a serious offence in itself, and would possibly cause serious consequences to defendant's car insurance. The evidence may not prove that the plaintiff was intoxicated while driving the car, but empty bottles were found in it and it was left open and improperly parked and certainly this was inconsistent with the duty of a man who was manager of a large automobile business.
>
> The question of whether or not the drunkenness in question was justification for the dismissal was held to be a question of fact in *Clouston & Co. v. Corry*, [1906] A.C. 122, and I therefore consider the circumstances and find that the dismissal was justified. (at pp. 857-858)

Marystown Shipyard Ltd. v. Rose (1985), 6 C.C.E.L. 220, 52 Nfld. & P.E.I.R. 144, 153 A.P.R. 144 (Nfld. C.A.), is an example of a more recent case in which the Court found that one instance of intoxication constituted just cause for dismissal. The employee held the position of "rigger-foreman," and on the day in question was working the night shift and responsible for the work of five riggers.

The Court summarized the law, and the significant facts, as follows:

> The law is clear that an employer can discharge his employee for cause. This Court, speaking through Morgan J.A. in *Anstey v. C.N.R.* (1980), 27 Nfld. & P.E.I.R. 95, 74 A.P.R. 95 (Nfld. C.A.), has said that:
>
> > It is well settled that a master can discharge his servant for cause. It is equally well settled that, while there is no fixed rule defining the degree of misconduct which will justify dismissal, drunkenness during the performance of one's duty may constitute cause for summary dismissal - particularly where attended by the possibility of serious consequences. The extent of the

> condition of intoxication which will establish a justification for dismissal is difficult of determination and depends on the particular circumstances.
>
> I think it is equally clear that the facts of the case at Bar warranted the respondent's summary dismissal from his employment. Although he denied it, the evidence as a whole establishes without doubt that he was intoxicated and severely impaired by alcohol while he was supposed to be carrying out a supervisory job of considerable responsibility. The company had a policy (and in fact it is expressly stated in the collective agreement with its union) that drinking on the job was an offence punishable by dismissal. In his position, part of which was the recommending of disciplinary action under the collective agreement, the respondent must be taken to have been aware of this policy, and he knowingly disobeyed the rule. In my view, the appellant had no choice but to dismiss him. (at p. 222)

The conduct in question need not be in the actual course of employment in order to justify a finding of just cause for dismissal. In *Bell v. General Motors of Can.* (1989), 27 C.C.E.L. 110 (Ont. H.C.), the plaintiff was employed by General Motors of Canada for over twenty years. For two years prior to his discharge, the plaintiff had a romantic relationship with a secretary in his department. The plaintiff was also drinking "at least a forty ounce bottle" of alcohol per day. The evidence showed that he often drank before going to work, at mealtimes, and in the evening. He did not feel it impaired his ability at work and he was never reprimanded at work, nor was any mention of his drinking ever made to him by his superiors.

In the final incident before discharge, the plaintiff had consumed ten to twelve bottles of beer and a quart of rye by the time the secretary came to his apartment to review some work-related material and to have dinner. The plaintiff thereupon assaulted the secretary by punching and kicking her. The employer terminated for just cause on the basis that the plaintiff's conduct in assaulting a subordinate employee was completely unacceptable. Although the conduct was off company premises, the assault was partly work-related, and prejudicial to employee morale.

The Court, in dismissing the action, relied upon the principles in *Lake Ont. Portland Cement Co. v. Groner*, [1961] S.C.R. 553, 28 D.L.R. (2d) 589. The Court believed that the principles discussed by Mr. Justice Ritchie, albeit in that case referring to a dishonest employee, had application. The Court, relying upon this decision, quoted Ritchie J. (at D.L.R. p. 598):

> It may be, as Mr. Justice Morden says in the course of his judgment in the Court of Appeal, that the respondent's misconduct "was not incompatible with the proper discharge of the duties to which he was employed", but in my view it is not so much the conduct itself as the fact that he was capable of it which justifies the respondent's dismissal. . . . As was said by Lord Atkinson in *Federal Supply & Cold Storage Co. of South Africa v. Angehrn & Piel* (1910), 103 L.T. 150 at p. 151, "it is the revelation of character which justifies the dismissal". (at p. 116)

Relying upon this passage, the Court felt that it was the revelation of the plaintiff's character that constituted just cause for dismissal. His conduct in assaulting a fellow employee was inconsistent with the duties of a supervisor, or indeed with the respect owed by one employee to another.

Robinson v. Cdn. Acceptance Corp. (1973), 43 D.L.R. (3d) 301 (N.S. T.D.), affirmed (1974), 47 D.L.R. (3d) 417, 9 N.S.R. (2d) 226 (C.A.), suggests that, absent safety considerations, where emotional or personal problems lead to a bout of drunkenness and a relatively brief period of unsatisfactory performance, just cause for dismissal does not exist. In this case, the trial Court stated:

> After considering the many decided cases and the facts in issue, I do not believe that the defendant was justified in discharging the plaintiff as it did. Apart from one isolated incident in Truro, no complaint was found with the plaintiff's conduct or ability to carry out his work until the fall of 1972. For 10 years the plaintiff had performed satisfactorily and had obviously rendered a benefit to the company.
>
> Between September of 1972 and March of 1973, the plaintiff began to experience difficulties. He became emotionally involved in an extra-marital affair, with which he was unable to cope. As a result, he sought refuge, firstly, in excessive drinking and, finally, in emotional collapse. His problem reflected itself in his periodic absences from where he was expected to be in connection with his employment and, finally, in the necessity for hospitalization to recover from an extreme emotional breakdown.
>
> During this period immediately before the plaintiff's dismissal, which was short compared to his 10 years of service with the company, there is no evidence that he wilfully intended to disobey the dictates of his superiors or to neglect his work. The company's statistics show on the contrary that the branches under his supervision were performing in a normal manner, even though for a short time he was not able to give them the attention they required. The plaintiff was going through the type of experience which many executives encounter some time during their business career, and for which many companies make allowance through their personnel policies. There cannot be many executives who work under years of constant pressure who do not at some time go through a period of emotional upset, during which they cease to function as efficiently as they would at normal times. (at p. 309)

The mere fact, however, that an employee exhibits signs of alcohol consumption does not constitute a breach of contract. In *Johnston v. Algoma Steel Corp.* (1989), 24 C.C.E.L. 1, 89 C.L.L.C. 14,012 (Ont. H.C.), Mr. Justice Granger stated:

> If . . . Algoma was purporting to fire Johnston for having the smell of alcohol on his breath while on duty, such conduct would not justify termination for cause, unless the consumption of alcohol affected his ability to perform his job: *MacDonald v. Azar*, [1948] 1 D.L.R. 854 (N.S. S.C.); and *Armstrong v. Tyndall Quarry Co.* (1910), 20 Man. R. 254, 16 W.W.R. 111 (K.B.). All of the evidence which I have accepted indicates that Johnston was always capable of carrying out his duties in a satisfactory manner. (at pp. 9-10)

It should, however, be noted that each case will depend upon the terms of the particular contract of employment. Thus, the parties may expressly agree, or the facts may give rise to an implication, that an employee is to refrain from consuming alcohol before and during work hours so that at no time would the employee evidence any signs of the consumption of alcohol.

Extrapolating from the relatively few reported cases, it is suggested that the courts will consider the following criteria in determining whether an employer is justified in dismissing an intoxicated employee:

1. the potential for physical injury to the intoxicated employee and others;
2. the injury, or potential injury, to the employer's interest or reputation caused by the employee during his period of intoxication;
3. the length and quality of the past service provided by the employee;
4. any circumstances personal to the employee which may have given rise to the inappropriate conduct; and
5. the extent to which intoxication was accepted or condoned by the employer, particularly in those cases in which alcohol and entertaining are a normal part of the working day.

In determining whether just cause for dismissal exists the employer must weigh the actual or potential prejudice it has suffered against any mitigating circumstances which the employee may be able to prove in court.

(iii) *Addiction*

As stated, in the case of an addiction, the Court will apply the general principles applicable to a permanent disability (see Chapter 4.3(d)). It may be instructive, however, to consider a number of cases specifically dealing with an addiction causing poor performance that would otherwise constitute just cause for dismissal. In *McDougal v. Van Allen Co.* (1909), 19 O.L.R. 351 (K.B.), the Court considered an unusual situation in which the employee developed a drug addiction. The plaintiff in this case had used "Agnew's Catarrh Cure," which contained cocaine, to treat a cold. After using the drug for over a year the plaintiff was physically and mentally incapable of doing his job as a salesman, and was admitted to a sanatorium for treatment of his addiction. The defendant then terminated the plaintiff's employment.

The Court found that the plaintiff had been wrongfully dismissed stating:

> Nor, as I think, does the fact that the sickness of the plaintiff was brought on to a great extent, if not wholly, by his own folly, make a sufficient difference. It is true that many of the cases seem to assume that a sickness caused by the plaintiff's own fault will be upon a different foundation from one not so occasioned. See (*e.g.*) the head note in *Cuckson v. Stones*, 1 E. & E. 248; Campbell's edition of Fraser's Master and Servant, p. 140; and the Imperial statute 57 & 58 Vict. ch. 60, sec. 160, makes a distinction also. The only case actually decided that I have seen is *K-- v. Raschen*, 38 L.T. 38, in which the servant suffered from a disease which he certainly could not have had but for his own act; and it was held that that made no difference. It is true that the act there had been committed before the engagement and may have been a single isolated act, while here the sickness resulted from a series of foolish acts committed after the engagement.

> Cleasby, B., says, 38 L.T. at p. 40: "*Primâ facie*, illness is to be attributed to the act of God, and we are not justified in going back for any length of time, and entering into an investigation as to what may have been the cause of it." I do not think that this sickness of a nervous subject, allowing himself to be overcome by a seductive drug which sapped his powers of self-control as well as his physical strength, can fairly be taken out of the category "act of God." A man differently constituted might have escaped serious injury; the plaintiff's constitution afforded a suitable and prepared *nidus* for the operation of the poison. (at pp. 357-358)

Thus, in the case of alcohol or drug addiction the legal principles enunciated with respect to absenteeism due to illness will probably be applied. As well, recent grievance arbitration cases suggest that alcoholism is an illness and does not constitute cause for discipline. See, for example, *Cdn. Union of United Brewery, Flour, Cereal, Soft Drink & Distillery Workers, Local 304 v. Molson's Brewery (Ont.) Ltd.* (1979), 23 L.A.C. (2d) 392 (Ont.). In reviewing an arbitration award, the Appellate Division of the Nova Scotia Supreme Court accepted this view in *Cdn. General Electric Co. v. Oil, Chemical & Atomic Workers International Union, Local 9-832* (1975), 56 D.L.R. (3d) 745, 11 N.S.R. (2d) 550 (C.A.).

While the fact of alcoholism may constitute an illness, which in and of itself does not constitute cause for discipline, alcoholism may result in persistent improper behaviour and provide just cause for dismissal. In *Visentin v. Shell Canada Ltd.* (1989), 29 C.C.E.L. 65, 100 A.R. 155 (Q.B.), the plaintiff was employed as a field operator at a gas field. He was an alcoholic who enrolled for counselling in an Employee Assistance Program offered by the employer, however, the plaintiff failed to successfully complete the program and failed to stop drinking. Further, the plaintiff was involved in a series of incidents in which his behaviour was erratic and showed disregard for safety-related procedures.

In dismissing the action, the Court made the following comments with respect to the alcoholism of the plaintiff:

> In addition, the plaintiff is an alcoholic. The evidence established that alcoholism is a disease for which there is no medical cure and viewed in that way it is a permanent illness. However, it is treatable and can be controlled, but relapses may occur. The plaintiff first turned to the E.A.P. Program for assistance in May 1986. According to Dr. William Csokonay, a specialist in community medicine and medical consultant to the defendant's E.A.P. Program, the plaintiff did not have his alcoholism under control as of June 28, 1987 because of a lack of commitment by him. Furthermore, in his view, a further period of treatment extending over a 2-year period would be required in order to bring his malady under control, provided that the plaintiff gave his full cooperation.
>
> There was no evidence that the plaintiff was under the influence of alcohol when he was working. However, his alcoholism, his failure to persevere in a course of treatment, and the cumulative effect of the incidents described rendered the plaintiff unfit for employment in a gas field where safety procedures had to be strictly observed. Thus the defendant had the right to dismiss the plaintiff

for cause: *Atkinson v. Boyd Phillips & Co.* (1979), 9 B.C.L.R. 255 (C.A.), leave to appeal to S.C.C. refused (1979), 28 N.R. 139 (S.C.C.); *Jupiter General Insurance Co. v. Shroff,* [1937] 3 All E.R. 67 (P.C.). (at pp. 70-71).

In considering whether an addiction constitutes just cause for dismissal it is also necessary to consider the implications of the Ontario *Human Rights Code* (see Chapter 13.9).

An employer policy, commented upon favourably by the Canadian Human Rights Tribunal in *Niles v. Canadian National Railway* (1991), 37 C.C.E.L. 58, 91 C.L.L.C. 17,018, 14 C.H.R.R. D/327, reversed (1992), 92 C.L.L.C. 17,031 (Fed. C.A.), is reproduced in Chapter 13.9.

(iv) *The Prevention and Treatment of Substance Abuse: A Contemporary Perspective*

THE PREVENTION AND TREATMENT OF SUBSTANCE ABUSE: A CONTEMPORARY PERSPECTIVE

David A. Korn, M.D., D.T.P.H., D.T.M.&H.
Paul D. Nichols, B.A., D.H.A., C.H.E.

The task of developing a chapter on substance abuse in this volume dedicated to issues of employment law initially seemed quite straightforward. Substance abuse is a major issue confronting employers, employees, trade unions, and the courts and others involved in workplace matters. The task became a little more complex as we contemplated imparting an understanding of substance abuse to the reader.

(*Continued on page 4-33*)

Before attempting to do so, we thought it might be useful to consider substance abuse in relation to the workplace. First of all, it is important to note that we are not talking only about alcohol, the most widely abused drug, but also prescription drugs, illicit drugs such as cocaine and heroin and over-the-counter drugs. Their impact is staggering. The Addiction Research Foundation estimates that in Canada 5 to 10 percent of all employees have an alcohol or drug problem. As well, excessive drinking or drug use among employees is estimated to cost Canadian employers over one billion dollars a year. Almost one-half the accidents in mining, railway and forestry are thought to be alcohol-related. Clearly an employee who abuses alcohol and drugs can cause employers problems with corporate productivity through declining work performance. Associated problems include safety, corporate morale and costs through absenteeism. It is estimated that chemically dependent people are one-third less productive than non-abusers, miss ten times as much work, are three times more likely to injure themselves or others, are late three times as often and are five times more likely to file worker's compensation claims (EAP Digest, 1986).

While there is little doubt about the importance of substance abuse as an employment-related issue, there is not as much general agreement about the nature of substance abuse itself. This is undoubtedly related to the many ways in which society has attempted to understand substance abuse over the years. Let us consider a few of those in an attempt to shed some light on our current understanding of substance abuse problems. Before doing so, it is important to note that much of what we today understand regarding substance abuse, really grew out of our understanding of alcohol abuse, the substance that has been most widely researched and arguably the best understood substance of abuse.

Possibly one of the longest standing views about alcohol abuse is one rooted in morality. That is, individuals are seen as rational and those who are using substances in problematic ways are doing so even though other options were available. Many religions have long viewed intoxication as sinful and there are other groups that see alcohol problems as spiritual deficiencies within individuals.

A closely related view of alcohol problems was epitomized in the Temperance movement of the late nineteenth and early twentieth centuries. Its core doctrine was a belief in abstinence, or at least moderation, given the inherently hazardous nature of the substance alcohol. That is, alcohol problems were caused by alcohol, a drug so dangerous that it should be used extremely cautiously, if at all.

A very powerful view of alcohol problems, the disease model, emerged in the 1930s and has grown in acceptance over the succeeding decades. The disease model holds that the use of alcohol in harmful quantities is a chronic disease with a predictable progression to death if unchecked. The disease is viewed as incurable but capable of being controlled or arrested through abstinence from alcohol. Persons suffering from the disease are typically viewed as ill, lacking control over both their use and ability to stop drinking once started. There is currently considerable interest in the study of a genetic link to substance abuse and this may shed some light on the heritability of the problem.

This view of alcohol problems did a great deal to minimize the stigma associated with alcohol problems, by in effect removing the belief that an individual was responsible for his or her problems. It led to more understanding treatment of alcohol problems and was the model most frequently adopted by physicians involved in the treatment of alcohol problems.

Ironically, it was probably the absolution of personal responsibility for the condition that resulted in a growing popularity of other ways of looking at alcohol problems. That is, a core feature of other models is a belief that the individual does have some responsibility for his condition and as a result has the basic resources to change. Depending on the particular model, it is believed that the change can be aided by education, through principles of conditioning, alterations in a person's interaction with his environment or working through issues of a dysfunctional childhood.

Throughout the history of interest in alcohol problems, there have been proponents of each of the major beliefs who were often at odds with each other in an attempt to understand, prevent and treat the consequence of alcohol abuse. The importance of the model as one moves to consider attempts to prevent and treat abuse is quite striking. For example, those who support the temperance view would likely see attempts to control the supply of alcohol as a positive step in the prevention of problems. Proponents of the disease model, on the other hand, while perhaps acknowledging the positive potential in supply side control, might not see this as a preventive measure based upon their belief that the cause of the problem is not a function of alcohol alone.

While there is both popular and empirical support for at least parts of all the models and views we have discussed, none alone is sufficient to understand or intervene with alcohol problems. Recently, there have been attempts to integrate some of the key competing concepts of these models. One particular approach of promise has been articulated by community health professionals who consider the complex interaction of three main variables in understanding and dealing with any particular disease. These factors are the substance, the individual or the personal risk factors, e.g., biological, genetic, that bear on one's susceptibility to diseases and the aspect of the environment, i.e., family, employer, community, that, in this case, contribute to alcohol abuse. As mentioned, a key feature of this model is the integration of heretofore competing concepts related to alcohol abuse. This goes beyond the traditional one best way of explaining or understanding alcohol abuse toward a broader concept that recognizes the interaction of many factors.

From the discussion of a number of ways of understanding substance abuse, one can see how certain components of some, if not all, of the models have made lasting impressions and to some extent, probably colour our understanding of substance abuse. Consider, for example, terms like "demon rum" and "evil brew" that sprang from the moralistic model to the legally significant concept of a permanent disability that comes out of the disease model. This is to suggest that this multiplicity of understandings has undoubtedly led us as individuals to adopt a set of beliefs and values about substance abuse that allow us to differentiate between non-pathological substance use and substance abuse. Perhaps one of the most objective approaches to this is the set of characteristics of substance abuse disorders as described by the American Psychiatric Association in the Diagnostic and Statistical Manual III. These are as follows:

1. A pattern of pathological drug abuse manifested by intoxication throughout the day.
2. Inability to reduce or stop use.
3. Repeated attempts to control use with periods of temporary abstinence or restriction of use to certain times of the day.
4. Continuation of substance abuse despite a serious physical disorder aggravated by the use of the substance.
5. The need for regular use of the substance for adequate functioning.
6. An episode of complication as a result of intoxication.

While there are today a variety of objective measures of the existence and extent of a substance abuse problem, most authorities will generally acknowledge a problem when the individual is experiencing emotional, mental, physical, spiritual, family or employment problems as a direct result of the use of a chemical. In short, a substance abuse problem is deemed to exist when chemical use impairs or interferes with an important dimension of life and living.

Much of the interest historically in alcohol abuse related to attempts to not only understand it, but to deal with it. Recently, in more enlightened times, the focus has been on help for the affected individual, in other words, treatment. Not surprisingly, there is a wide range of opinion about what constitutes treatment, what is the most effective form of treatment, who should deliver it or be responsible and so on.

Miller and Hester, in their book, *Alcoholism Treatment Approaches*, dispel as simplistic three classical myths of treatment, namely, that there is one best approach to treatment, that nothing works and that everything works. Acknowledging that this is a new frontier, these authors advance three assumptions along the road towards what they term an "informed eclecticism." These are:

1. There is no single best treatment approach that will work for everyone.
2. There are different types of individuals who will respond to different treatment approaches.

3. Individuals can be matched to optimal treatments to increase treatment effectiveness.

While these may not seem like revolutionary concepts, they do represent state of the art thought in a field where convictions about the most effective form of treatment are extremely deeply ingrained. It is also important to realize that substance abuse treatment is a relatively new field that lacks not only the range of treatment alternatives necessary for effective matching but also the objective criteria required to do this.

In spite of the conclusion that there is no simple best treatment approach, many treatment programs share common elements. One of Canada's leading treatment centres, The Donwood Institute in Toronto, is a case in point. Established in 1967, The Donwood is Ontario's only public hospital for the treatment of drug and alcohol addiction. The Donwood has 47 beds that are occupied by clients in the four-week residential program. In addition to this program, The Donwood offers a 15-day, 3-week day program for those clients less seriously impaired. As well, an evening program is intended to accommodate clients who are employed through sessions offered two evenings a week over a period of three months. All programs are followed by an aftercare program intended to facilitate community reintegration. The programs support individuals in their recoveries from alcohol and drug abuse. Abstinence is the goal and most realistic for those with severe problems. Individual support is given through assessment, medically supervised detoxification and an education program that consists of group therapy, relaxation and a wide range of counselling and other activities designed to support healthful lifestyles free of drugs and alcohol.

The Donwood has studied treatment outcomes as early as 1988. In that year, 81% of a sample of 542 alcohol dependent clients showed significant improvement one year after treatment. In a 1989 outcome study of 100 clients, 56% of those abusing alcohol, 29% of cross-addicted clients and 15% of those abusing drugs other than alcohol were abstinent one year after treatment. Those success rates compare favourably with the best in the field.

Implicit in many treatment programs is the notion of providing help and assistance to individuals who are experiencing problems with substance abuse. Treatment is compassionate and non-judgmental in that individuals are not held morally, spiritually or intellectually responsible for their compulsive patterns of destructive behaviour. Many programs appear even tacitly if not overtly to follow disease theory precepts that substance abusers are not responsible for the symptoms of their disease. However, they are responsible for their program of recovery.

There have been many critics of this model when applied to addiction. A full examination of the advantages and disadvantages of the disease model is beyond the scope of this chapter. However, it is interesting to note that while the disease model may have had a benefit in terms of facilitating humane treatment for a large population of substance abusers, it does not hold the same potential for advancing efforts designed to prevent substance abuse. Zinberg, writing in *Addictive Disease: Concept to Controversy* (1981), noted that the disease model diverts attention from appropriate social action to overly simplified organic explanations and narrowly conceived biological research quests. Stated another way, a major challenge in the substance abuse field, indeed in the entire health field, lies in disease prevention and health promotion. Much of the effort to date has focused on treatment of the few, relatively speaking, who are substance abusers rather than on the many who may be at risk of substance abuse or affected by it in other ways.

In Ontario, the Ministry of Health, in a document titled "*A Framework for the Response to Alcohol and Drug Problems in Ontario*" (1988), has recognized the concept of a continuum of risk. This risk continuum equates the average level of consumption in terms of number of drinks per week to a risk category in the following way:

Risk Category	Consumption
No Risk	No alcohol consumption
Low Risk	1-14 drinks per week
Moderate Risk	15-34 drinks per week
Medium Risk	35 drinks or more per week

As the document points out, the range of problems associated with consumption is broad and includes psycho-social problems, such as deterioration in important relationships, legal problems (such as impaired driving or drug charges) and health problems ranging from alcohol-related accidents to chronic diseases associated with high levels of consumption over a long period of time.

As a treatment centre, The Donwood has traditionally dealt with people in the High Risk category by providing them with access to comprehensive assessments, matching them to appropriate services including aftercare.

The Donwood Institute has begun planning and structuring some of its programs and services based upon the concept of well-being or wellness as it is known. Essentially, using a wellness framework, health can be viewed as a continuum from illness or lost health on the left of centre, to a state of being well at the mid-point and on to a higher level wellness on the right. In terms of substance abuse, many treatment approaches help individuals move from an area of lost health to health regained, that is, the mid-point, but are not directed to moving the individual past this mid-point.

We now know that recovery involves more than stopping the use of drugs. While abstinence is the most commonly accepted goal of treatment, recovery needs to be seen in this broader context of health recovery. Given the far reaching implications of addiction, one must consider recovery in terms of family, community and work relationships and above all a sense of self-worth.

The challenge for the future is to move individuals affected by substance abuse through mechanisms of health promotion and disease prevention towards high level wellness embodying personal responsibility for health, development of a supportive environment, integrated and balanced healthful lifestyles, high self-esteem and a conscious commitment to excellence.

David Korn is the President and Chief Executive Officer, and Paul Nichols is the Vice-President, of the renowned Donwood Institute, Toronto, a facility for the prevention and treatment of substance abuse.

(v) *Conclusions*

The employer's legal obligation in dealing with an employee who is an alcoholic or drug addict may be quite onerous. The nature of these illnesses is such that there may not be a clear path to a cure and the employer may have to suffer through several relapses of the employee before it can be said that the illness is permanent in nature, thereby ending the contract of employment.

Further, particularly in those cases in which the addiction was caused or contributed to by job-related stress, the courts may well expect the employer to adopt an active role in assisting the employee. To take the extreme example of a senior executive who has devoted his life to the employer, to the exclusion of family and other activities, and who becomes an alcoholic, a court may very well expect the employer to take the initiative to arrange for counselling and treatment. The addiction itself may inhibit or preclude the employee from being able to deal rationally with obtaining assistance and the employer who shrinks from providing needed assistance may find it difficult to persuade a court that the situation was hopeless and the illness permanent.

(f) Dishonesty

(i) *General Principle*

Dishonesty, as hereinafter discussed, encompasses not only theft or fraud, but any type of untrustworthy conduct. Dishonesty is relevant not only when it occurs in the course of employment. In certain circumstances, dishonesty prior to commencing employment, or dishonesty during the time of employment but in relation to matters unconnected with the employment, may also be relied upon as constituting just cause for dismissal. These various types of dishonesty are discussed separately.

Dishonesty is a particular type of deliberate improper conduct. Other types of deliberate improper conduct are discussed under the headings of ''Sexual Harassment'' (Chapter 4.3(g)) and ''Other Criminal, Immoral or Improper Conduct'' (Chapter 4.3(h)). In general terms, the approach of the courts in considering all of these cases will be similar. In most cases the judicial analysis will focus on the extent to which the conduct in question is connected with the employment relationship, and the extent to which the conduct may be indicative of the future reliability of the employee.

In *Kong v. Oshawa Group Ltd.* (1993), 46 C.C.E.L. 181 (Ont. Gen. Div.), the Court considered a case in which the plaintiff had been acquitted of theft at a criminal trial and a just cause defence based upon theft was asserted as a defence to a wrongful dismissal claim. The Court discussed the question of whether the criminal verdict was relevant, and the standard of proof, as follows:

> The fact that Mr. Kong's criminal trial resulted in an acquittal is irrelevant to the civil issue before me. See *Murphy v. Canadian Tire Corp.* (1991), 39 C.C.E.L. 205. In this case, Matheson J. of the Ontario Court (General Division), on facts parallel to the facts before me, found that the outcome of the criminal adjudication was irrelevant to the issues before him. See also *Hughes v. R.T. Holman Ltd.* (1982), 40 Nfld. & P.E.I.R. 190 (P.E.I.S.C.).
>
> Notwithstanding the outcome of the criminal trial, it is my task to look at all of the evidence and consider it carefully with a view to determining whether or not on the balance of probabilities theft actually occurred. I find that theft occurred on the balance of probabilities, and that Oshawa was justified in its dismissal on this ground alone. Even one isolated act of theft is cause for dismissal. See *Ball v. MacMillan Bloedel Ltd.* (1989), 29 C.C.E.L. 99 (B.C.S.C.). It is also clearly established in the case law that an employer needs to establish the theft on the balance of probabilities and not beyond a reasonable doubt. In my view, the employer, Oshawa, has established the theft on the balance of probabilities. See *Housepian v. Work Wear Corp. of Canada* (1981), 33 O.R. (2d) 575 at 581. (at p. 185)

The Court went on to consider whether reasonable suspicion could constitute just cause for dismissal stating:

> I note also that in the authorities, it is established that an employee can be dismissed on the mere suspicion of theft if the facts of the case reasonably support the suspicion. See *LeBlanc v. Cartier Co-operative Ltd.* (1980), 31 N.B.R. (2d) 284 (N.B.Q.B.) and see *Gleed v. Edmonton (City)* (1982), 18 A.C.W.S. [(2d)] at 257. (at p. 185)

It is, however, respectfully submitted that this latter proposition is not correct. Surely there is no implied term of a contract which holds that, as between employee and employer, the employee is to bear all of the risk in the event that a situation arises in which the employee, although innocent, is the subject of reasonable suspicion. If the employer has reasonable suspicion this may be a valid business reason to terminate, however, there is no reason why the employer should not compensate the employee who, although suspected, is on the evidence innocent of any wrongdoing.

(ii) *Dishonesty Prior to Employment*

Dishonesty on the part of an employee prior to the actual commencement of employment can justify dismissal. In *Pliniussen v. University of*

(*Continued on page 4-39*)

Western Ont. (1983), 2 C.C.E.L. 1, 83 C.L.L.C. 14,068 (Ont. Co. Ct.), the plaintiff was hired as a part-time lecturer in the defendant's School of Business Administration. His employment was to commence the following September. Prior to the opening of school, however, the university administration discovered that the plaintiff had been charged in connection with certain fraudulent insurance claims. The plaintiff confessed his guilt to a university official and his contract was terminated. The Court found that there was potential for damage to the reputation of the school if the fraudulent conduct of the plaintiff became public knowledge. The Court held that the dean of the school had "acted very properly in removing a source of damage to, or potential damage to the reputation of the school for which he had charge. In the Court's view, he had no other alternative than to dismiss the plaintiff" (at p. 6).

In *Pliniussen*, the potential effect of the plaintiff's conduct on the reputation of the school and on its students was an important factor in the Court's finding that there was just cause. These considerations would probably be of less importance in a case involving a lower profile or less influential employee.

The failure of an employee to disclose relevant facts prior to entering into a contract of employment will normally not justify dismissal. Where, however, the contract is found by the Court to be one requiring the "utmost good faith," the potential employee will be required to disclose all personal information that is relevant to the position. In *Courtright v. Cdn. Pacific Ltd.* (1983), 4 C.C.E.L. 152, 45 O.R. (2d) 52, 26 B.L.R. 17, 5 D.L.R. (4th) 488 (H.C.), affirmed (1985), 50 O.R. (2d) 560, 18 D.L.R. (4th) 639 (C.A.), the plaintiff, a solicitor, had obtained a position in the defendant's legal department. In that position, he would have been required to work closely with government agencies. Courtright failed to disclose that, at the time of his hiring, he was under police investigation for alleged influence peddling. After the defendant offered him a position, he was arrested by the police. Upon learning of the situation, the defendant terminated its contract with the plaintiff. The Ontario Supreme Court held that the defendant was justified in taking this action even though the plaintiff was found not guilty in criminal proceedings which concluded prior to the civil trial. The Court stated:

> In other words it is my view that the highest fiduciary relationship exists between a solicitor and a potential client when he discusses whether a contract of employment shall be entered into and this obliges complete disclosure by the solicitor of any pertinent matter which would or could have a direct relationship to the effective performance of the duties which are clearly set out to the solicitor in which he would be involved in the performance of such contract or retainer. (at p. 165)

While the situation in *Courtright* was somewhat unusual, the decision might be relevant in situations where employees hold positions of a fiduciary nature, or other senior positions in which their behaviour and character would reflect directly and significantly on the employer.

In *Cornell v. Rogers Cablesystems Inc.* (1987), 17 C.C.E.L. 232, 87 C.L.L.C. 14,054 (Ont. Dist. Ct.), the dishonesty, while prior to employment, was in an effort to gain employment. In this case, an application for employment submitted by the plaintiff contained numerous blatant falsehoods. Prior to joining Rogers the plaintiff had been employed by Philips Electronics Limited. However, he suffered health problems and his employment with Philips was ultimately terminated. In applying for employment with Rogers, the plaintiff made the following misrepresentations:

1. He applied for the position using Philips stationery, implying he still worked for Philips.
2. He gave as the reason for seeking new employment the fact that Philips wanted him to relocate in Vancouver.
3. He indicated that he had studied business management at the University of Toronto.
4. He indicated that in order to assume employment he would have to give Philips two weeks' notice of his resignation.

In this case the plaintiff was a probationary employee. The Court clearly felt that the misrepresentations would also have constituted just cause for the dismissal of a non-probationary employee. After referring to the misrepresentations in the initial application, the Court stated:

> The conclusion is irresistible that in the event the resume had been truthful Cornell would not have been engaged for the position with the defendant; he would not even have been interviewed. I recognize the subjective views of Mr. Cornell that the truth would inhibit him in his job search and that he was justified in avoiding the truth in order to "get his foot in the door". In my opinion the misrepresentations were most material. The comments of Mr. Justice Power in the recent Alberta case of *Schafer v. Pan Matrix Informatics Ltd.* [(1987), (*sub nom. Schafer v. Computer Career Institute*) 80 A.R. 378 (Q.B.)] which was referred to me by Mr. Levitt are most appropriate:
>
>> In my opinion, there was justification for the dismissal of the plaintiff for cause by the defendant corporation. The plaintiff fraudulently misstated his qualifications when negotiating his position and terms of employment with the defendant corporation. In addition, the plaintiff falsely stated that he had a secure and senior position of employment with the DeVry Institute.
>>
>> The evidence establishes that the defendant corporation would not have offered a position of employment to the plaintiff had they known the truth about the behaviour, reputation and performance of the plaintiff at the DeVry Institute.
>
> It is not necessary to refer to the case law to conclude that an employer has the right to expect honesty and integrity from an employee in a supervisory position. I hasten to add that the standard is not one of perfection and I do not attempt to define what is or is not acceptable. However, I cannot accept that such deceit was "innocent", as Mr. Cornell characterized the lies. Notwithstanding that the misrepresentations were not discovered until after the termination, they

> were of such a character that they went to the very root of Mr. Cornell's qualifications for the position. (at pp. 237-238)

Cornell is also referred to in Chapter 4.4, "Dismissal of Probationary Employees."

(iii) *Dishonesty During the Period of Employment But Other Than in the Course of Employment*

It is fairly rare that events other than in the course of employment will be relied on as providing just cause for termination and as such there are relatively few cases. Since the conduct is outside of the course of employment there is usually no direct impact on the employer. In such cases, however, the Court will often view the incident as revealing the true character of the employee. The significance of a revelation of character is indicated by the words of Mr. Justice Ritchie in *Lake Ont. Portland Cement Co. v. Groner*, [1961] S.C.R. 553, 28 D.L.R. (2d) 589:

> [I]n my view it is not so much the misconduct itself as the fact that he was capable of it which justifies the respondent's dismissal. (at p. 564)

In *Cdn. Imperial Bank of Commerce v. Rifou*, 13 C.C.E.L. 293, [1986] 3 F.C. 486, 86 C.L.L.C. 14,046, 25 C.R.R. 164, 72 N.R. 12 (C.A.), the Court considered an application to quash the decision of an adjudicator, who had ordered the reinstatement of a loans officer who had been convicted of shoplifting. The employee had served the bank for approximately 17 years, and the adjudicator concluded that it was appropriate that the employee be reinstated. (It should be noted that the power to reinstate is a statutory power set out in the *Canada Labour Code* and that the courts have no comparable power of reinstatement). In this regard the adjudicator stated:

> I conclude that the theft was an aberration, for which there may not be an explanation known to the Complainant, and that, given the event of criminal conviction and suspension from employment, which may be much more reliable conditioners than an excuse which may be contrived or an expression of remorse that may be fabricated, the aberration is a much less plausible base for projecting future conduct than the Complainant's long and commendable work record. I note also that her job function is clerical, and does not involve handling money or like property. I note also that the theft was not work related and occurred off duty and off the employer's premises. I accept the Complainant's explanation for the incorrect and cryptic statements in the Unemployment Insurance events. The explanations are credible and I believe them.
>
> I conclude, therefore, that the facts do not establish a case for an uncompromising response from the Employer to the Complainant's culpable behaviour. That conclusion lets in the Complainant's case for mitigation, mainly her work record, the complex severity of the consequences of termination, and the distance between what she did and her duties and opportunities at work. (at pp. 298-299)

The Federal Court of Appeal, however, concluded that the adjudicator had erred in finding that the job function of the employee did not involve handling money or like property. In this regard, a performance review document specified that one of the duties of the employee included selling travellers' cheques, drafts and money orders.

In the result, the Court quashed the order of the adjudicator, and referred the matter back to the adjudicator for reconsideration. Upon reconsideration the adjudicator, however, came to the same conclusion that the employee should be reinstated (*Rifou v. Cdn. Imperial Bank of Commerce* (1986), 15 C.C.E.L. 67 (Adjud. under the *Canada Labour Code*)).

In *Black v. FCA International Ltd./FCA Internationale Ltée* (1989), 27 C.C.E.L. 277 (B.C. S.C.), the plaintiff was a branch manager with seven years' service. The plaintiff was told to be on time for a company seminar that was to be held in the evening after a one-hour dinner break. On this particular day, he had plans to have dinner with a friend whom he had not seen for many years and who was in town for only one day. When leaving for dinner the plaintiff was asked where he was going and explained that he had a dentist's appointment. The plaintiff was 30 minutes late for the evening seminar and the employer discovered the following day that the plaintiff had not had a dental appointment and immediately dismissed the plaintiff for lying.

The Court found that the employee's statement was not a premeditated lie but one "blurted out" in response to a question that the employer had no right to ask since the plaintiff was free to do as he pleased on his dinner break. The Court concluded that the burden of proving just cause rests with the employer and it was not satisfied that the "lie" either taken alone or in conjunction with the plaintiff's performance warranted his dismissal without cause.

An unusual instance of dishonesty arose in the case of *Carrick v. Cooper Can. Ltd.* (1983), 2 C.C.E.L. 87 (Ont. H.C.). The plaintiff was employed as vice-president of operations for a sporting goods company. The defendant had a facility in the Barbados and the plaintiff told his wife that he would be away for a week in the Barbados, on a business trip, with the president and a vice-president of the defendant. In fact, the plaintiff was vacationing in Bermuda with a woman other than his wife. The situation came to light when the defendant attempted to contact the plaintiff during his vacation, and was advised by his wife that he was in the Barbados on business with senior officers of the defendant.

The position of the defendant was that news of the plaintiff's infidelity, and the circumstances, became generally known in the company with the result that comments were made such as, "Bill did not know the difference between Barbados and Bermuda." Discussions took place between the plaintiff and defendant, with the defendant claiming that the plaintiff had resigned and the plaintiff contending that he had been dismissed. The Court ultimately sided with the plaintiff, found that he had been dismissed, and found that there was no just cause for dismissal. In this regard the Court held:

> In all of the circumstances, it may be said that the plaintiff could have handled the situation of notice to his employers in a more efficient manner. The moral aspect of his conduct may be judged in different ways by different people. It is unimportant to the issues in this case as his conduct did not, in a material way, directly or indirectly affect the operations and management of the defendant or the plaintiff's credibility. (at p. 95)

The Court also cited *Reilly v. Steelcase Can. Ltd.* (1979), 26 O.R. (2d) 725, 103 D.L.R. (3d) 704 (H.C.), discussed at Chapter 4.3(i), in which adultery, committed with the spouse of a fellow employee, was found to not constitute just cause for dismissal.

While not disagreeing with the result reached by the Court in *Carrick*, it is submitted that the plaintiff came perilously close to a situation which would have constituted just cause. The instance of adultery is not as significant as the fact that, in order to cover his tracks, the plaintiff fabricated a story involving his employer and its senior executives. This put the defendant, and its employees, in the invidious position of either having to lie for the plaintiff, or indicate to the plaintiff's wife that her husband was a liar.

(iv) *Dishonesty in the Course of Employment*

Dishonest conduct in the course of employment will, absent significant and mitigating circumstances, provide just cause for dismissal. In cases such as theft from the employer, the act itself constitutes a clear breach and repudiation of the employment contract.

As will be seen, most of the reported cases do not involve any direct financial benefit to the employee or loss to the employer. The reason for this is that dishonesty resulting in financial benefit to an employee at the expense of the employer so clearly constitutes just cause for dismissal that such a case is unlikely to be litigated.

A good summary of the law is set out in *Beyea v. Irving Oil Ltd.* (1985), 8 C.C.E.L. 128, 63 N.B.R. (2d) 243, 164 A.P.R. 243 (Q.B.), affirmed (1986), 14 C.C.E.L. 67, 70 N.B.R. (2d) 1, 179 A.P.R. 1 (C.A.). The plaintiff was a 47-year-old plant foreman who had been employed for 28 years. The plaintiff was dismissed for having arranged to deliver waste oil to a neighbour, rather than having it disposed of by an associated company. The oil was apparently used by the neighbour to keep down dust on a roadway, and approximately 24 drums of oil were diverted for that purpose. Upon being confronted with these facts the plaintiff first denied the story, and then admitted the facts but took the position that the oil was of no value, and that his disposal of it had been authorized by a superior. The Court found that there was no such approval and that the removal of oil was contrary to the express policy of the defendant. It would also appear that at least some of the drums contained oil that did have some value. In upholding the termination for just cause the Court provided a helpful discussion of the standard of proof required in a case where a criminal act is alleged, and as to the general principles of law applicable, stating:

The defendant has alleged dishonesty and alleges theft. I do not feel that had the plaintiff been charged criminally with theft with respect to this matter that there would have been a conviction. Nevertheless, I would characterize his behaviour, both with respect to the manner in which he sent the product off the premises and his actions subsequent thereto, as being deceitful.

It is urged on behalf of the plaintiff that where criminality or a criminal act is alleged, such must be proved with more certainty than the ordinary balance of probabilities. The test remains the balance of probability, but in finding what is reasonably probable, due regard must be had to the gravity of the suggestion with respect to the acts which are alleged to have been committed: *Hanes v. Wawanesa Mut. Ins. Co.*, [1963] S.C.R. 154, [1963] 1 C.C.C. 321, 36 D.L.R. (2d) 718 (S.C.C.). On the evidence before me and having due regard to the seriousness of the allegations, although I do not hold that there was criminal intent, I do find that the evidence discloses circumstances as I have described, and that these amount to deceit on the part of the plaintiff.

The next question is whether or not this is cause. In considering whether or not it constitutes cause for dismissal without notice, one must have regard to the position held by the plaintiff. He was the plant foreman and as such exercised authority over a substantial number of the employees. His actions would be noted by the employees who were under him and would tend to set the standard for their own behaviour. It would be important, from the defendant's point of view, that there be no question with respect to the honesty of his conduct.

It is not relevant that the defendant may not have suffered an actual financial loss, nor is the extent of the financial loss particularly relevant. In considering misconduct such as this, it is the capability of the employee to conduct himself in such manner that particularly justifies his dismissal. See *LeFurgey v. Royal Bank of Can.* (1984), 56 N.B.R. (2d) 286, 146 A.P.R. 286 (N.B. Q.B.), and the excerpts referred to therein at pp. 303-04:

> It is not relevant that the bank may not have suffered an actual loss in this particular transaction nor is it relevant that the bank representatives may not have been aware for example of the Russell matter before termination of employment. See *Lake Ontario Portland Cement Company Limited v. Groner*, [1961] S.C.R. 553, Ritchie, J., at p. 563:
>
> "The fact that the appellant did not know of the respondent's dishonest conduct at the time when he was dismissed, and that it was first pleaded by way of an amendment to its defence at the trial does not, in my opinion, detract from its validity as a ground for dispensing with his services. The law in this regard is accurately summarized in Halsbury's Laws of England (2nd Ed.), vol. 22, p. 155, where it is said:
>
> 'It is not necessary that the master, dismissing a servant for good cause, should state the ground for such dismissal; and, provided good ground existed in fact, it is immaterial whether or not it was known to the employer at the time of the dismissal. Justification of dismissal can accordingly be shown by proof of facts ascertained subsequently to the dismissal, or on grounds differing from those alleged at the time.'
>
> It may be, as Mr. Justice Morden says in the course of his judgment in the Court of Appeal, that the respondent's misconduct "was not incompatible with the proper discharge of the duties for which he was employed", but in

> my view it is not so much the misconduct itself as the fact that he was capable of it which justifies the respondent's dismissal ... As was said by Lord Atkinson in *Federal Supply & Cold Storage Company of South Africa v. Angehrn and Piel* ((1910), 103 L.T. 150, at 151, 80 L.J.P.C. 1) "it is the revelation of character which justifies the dismissal."
>
> Deceitful conduct is incompatible with the plaintiff's proper discharge of his duties, particularly in his capacity of employment as plant foreman and, in my view, constitutes misconduct which justifies his dismissal without notice. (at pp. 140-142)

A conflict of interest, while not generally criminal in nature, is nevertheless the sort of untrustworthy conduct to be discussed under the rubric of "dishonesty."

An employee who has placed himself in a position in which his or her personal interests directly conflict with the interests of the employer is often the subject of dismissal. An example of such a conflict of interest is an employee operating a business which competes with the business of the employer. In the case of *Duguay v. Maritime Welding & Rentals Ltd.* (1989), 28 C.C.E.L. 126, 100 N.B.R. (2d) 212, 252 A.P.R. 212 (Q.B.), Duguay was the directing mind of his employer. Due to his position he came to know of a contract which was being tendered by Brunswick Mining and Smelting Company. Duguay, with an employee of a competitor who possessed the special knowledge necessary for the completion of the contract, formed a new company to bid on the contract. When making representations to Brunswick, Duguay at no time informed them that he was acting for himself and not for his employer. Duguay's company was awarded the contract. The employer found out about the conflict of interest and confronted Duguay. While Duguay agreed to end his involvement with the new company he was, nevertheless, terminated. Deschênes J. held that the conduct of Duguay provided just cause for dismissal stating:

> It is clear, therefore, that what is of importance is not the fact that an actual conflict of interest existed or that an employer actually suffered a prejudice as a result of an employee's disloyal conduct.
>
> What justifies the dismissal is the loss of trust and confidence in an employee who has shown disloyalty and infidelity toward his employer (see: *Tom Servinis Enterprises Ltd. v. Smerling Import Can. Ltd.*, [1982] 14 A.C.W.S. (2d) 416 (Ont. H.C.)). (at p. 131)

In *Jewitt v. Prism Resources Ltd* (1980), 110 D.L.R. (3d) 713 (B.C. S.C.), affirmed (1981), 30 B.C.L.R. 43, 14 B.L.R. 288, 127 D.L.R. (3d) 190 (C.A.), the plaintiff had been employed as president of a public company. Approximately six months after being hired, the plaintiff instructed his executive assistant to "trace" the signature of a director of the defendant on to the audited financial statements of the company prior to circulation to the shareholders. Although the financial statements were accurate, and the plaintiff had caused the signature to be traced as a matter of convenience, the plaintiff was dismissed.

In finding that the company had just cause for dismissal, the Court held that:

> In my respectful view, honesty is still important; and perhaps the more senior and responsible the position held, the more that honesty must be not only inherent, but patent. Here, in my opinion, there were reasonable grounds for the defendant to see, in what the plaintiff did, a revelation of character which justified his dismissal. (at p. 715)

Altschul v. Tom Davis Management Ltd. (1985), 6 C.C.E.L. 180 (Ont. Dist. Ct.), is another case in which the Court upheld dismissal on the basis that the employee's conduct revealed a character trait which justified summary dismissal. The plaintiff had been employed for approximately five months as a comtroller and financial adviser. In the course of his employment the plaintiff advised another employee of the company to pay bribes if that would help in gaining contracts for the defendant. In reaching its conclusion that this constituted just cause for dismissal, the Court stated:

> I concur with the defendant's arguments for, in this instance, the person fully in charge of the financial management of the company, counselled the doing of an illegal act to a new employee. The revelation of character of such a senior employee and officer of the company should not have to be countenanced by responsible business. Mr. Davis, in evidence, stated that if word got around in the business community that his company was party to illegal acts, such as bribes, that his chances of expanding a new line and the business itself would be severely handicapped. There was no specific evidence to support this, but I have no hesitation in accepting his opinion. In my view, the conduct of Mr. Altschul, in counselling the offering of bribes and his support for same, demonstrated a character so flawed as to be no longer worthy of trust by his employer. (at p. 183)

Ivanore v. Cdn. Imperial Bank of Commerce (1983), 3 C.C.E.L. 26 (Adjud. under the *Canada Labour Code*), is a further example of a situation in which just cause on the basis of dishonesty was upheld, notwithstanding that the employee acted without the possibility of personal gain. In this case the employee had falsified a number of statements on customer applications. In one instance, a "popular branch customer" applied for a $1,700 loan in order to pay the arrears on another loan his girlfriend had with the Bank. With respect to that loan the employee showed the purpose of the loan as "furniture." She conducted what was referred to as a "sloppy" investigation of the customer, neglecting to obtain particulars such as the correct employment and residence history of the customer, and failing to detect the fact that he had a prior bankruptcy. In upholding discharge the adjudicator stated:

> I do not propose to state any sweeping principle on dishonesty and the appropriate disciplinary response in the banking industry. As in other employment contexts, dishonesty is viewed seriously. The principles of corrective discipline must be brought to it as to other employment offences in appropriate cases. But I think they are few; pilfering office supplies or lies associated with other correctable problems like tardiness may be two examples.

> Generally I consider the standards of honesty and integrity the community expects in its dealings with a bank must be reflected in bank employees' behaviour with customers and the handling of customer funds and those the bank uses for profitable purposes. That standard is a strict one. A serious deviation from it causing loss of trust could properly be treated as just cause for dismissal. (at p. 49)
>
> . . . .
>
> I have seriously considered if Mrs. Ivanore's action should properly be characterized as a performance problem rather than an honesty or loyalty issue. I have concluded it cannot. I am satisfied she was not lulled into errant practices by a general climate of deception or that she was the victim of training that condoned a wink and nod attitude to operating procedures.
>
> The inescapable conclusion is that she simply chose dishonesty as an expediency. While that might be said in the context of this employment to be equated to work performance, I find it is more properly characterized as a disregard for truth and the trust placed in her independent judgment and responsibility. That trust is basic to her function and authority as a loans officer. She was well aware of her expected behaviour and trust. Whether for personal convenience or branch statistics she simply chose to deceive. (at p. 50)

If the employee has been dishonest, or has otherwise been guilty of misconduct resulting in criminal charges, the employer does not need to await the outcome of the criminal charges before discharging the employee. In the case of *Dennis v. Northwest Territories (Commissioner)* (1989), 28 C.C.E.L. 54, [1989] N.W.T.R. 269 (S.C.), the employee was the supervisor of the Yellowknife Correctional Centre and had misused the inmates' welfare fund, of which he was a trustee, for his own benefit. He had also entered into personal contracts with the inmates for their services as skilled native carvers, contrary to directives in that regard, and had purchased carvings by the native inmates and sold them at a profit.

The employer originally intended to await the outcome of the criminal proceedings before deciding to discipline the employee. Pursuant to provisions in the *Public Service Act*, the employer suspended the employee for six months and then extended that suspension for a further six months. At the end of that year the employer decided to conduct its own investigation into the misconduct. During the investigation the employee was invited to make a presentation to the investigative committee but declined to do so in view of the pending criminal proceedings. The investigative committee found that the employee had misused his position. As a result the employee was dismissed. After setting out the applicable provisions of the *Public Service Act* of the Northwest Territories, Richard J. held that the procedure followed by the employer was correct and accorded with the intention of the legislation. This result is consistent with the general principle that criminal and civil proceedings are separate. Further, while a criminal conviction would provide *prima facie* proof of just cause, a finding of not guilty in a criminal proceeding would not be relevant to a civil proceeding. An accused in a criminal proceeding is entitled to be found not guilty based upon a reasonable doubt as to guilt, while proof in a civil proceeding is on the balance of probabilities.

It is not, however, every act of dishonesty on the part of an employee that will constitute just cause for dismissal. In *Pilato v. Hamilton Place Convention Centre Inc.* (1984), 3 C.C.E.L. 241, 45 O.R. (2d) 652, 84 C.L.L.C. 14,039, 7 D.L.R. (4th) 342 (H.C.), the plaintiff had been employed as the general manager of the municipally owned centre. He permitted a pornographic videotape to be shown in his office at the centre. Two members of the centre's board of directors had been in attendance. In response to questions put to him at a joint meeting of the city council and the board of directors, the plaintiff denied that the directors had been present. Despite a vote of confidence by the board, the plaintiff was later dismissed on the alleged basis that he had "lied" to the board and the council. The trial Judge, however, found that the lies in question were not of such a "kind or degree" as to provide just cause for dismissal (at p. 242).

(v) *Conclusions*

This discussion with respect to the law regarding dishonesty has dealt with the law under headings which differentiate cases based upon the time at which the dishonesty occurred, or the context in which the dishonesty occurred. While it is hoped this will be helpful in understanding the principles, and locating helpful cases, it should not obscure the fact that there is, in essence, one governing principle. In all cases of dishonesty the Court is concerned with whether the conduct of the employee reveals a character which justifies dismissal, in that the employee cannot be trusted or relied upon in the future. When the dishonesty occurs prior to employment, or outside the course of employment, it is less likely that a court will find the revelation of character inherent in the conduct to be a reliable indicator of trustworthiness or reliability in the future. The central concern of the Court is to ascertain whether the employee is able to do the job in future.

(g) Sexual Harassment

Sexual harassment of an employee is not only reprehensible conduct, it constitutes a breach of trust and abuse of authority. Entirely apart from any statutory provisions, sexual harassment is the type of deliberate, improper conduct which would readily give rise to a finding of just cause for dismissal. In addition, most provinces have enacted human rights legislation which, explicitly or implicitly, prohibits sexual harassment. The Ontario *Human Rights Code,* provides as follows:

> 7(2) Every person who is an employee has a right to freedom from harassment in the workplace because of sex by his or her employer or agent of the employer or by another employee.

> (3) Every person has a right to be free from,
>
> (*a*) a sexual solicitation or advance made by a person in a position to confer, grant or deny a benefit or advancement to the person where the person making the solicitation or advance knows or ought reasonably to know that it is unwelcome; or
>
> (*b*) a reprisal or a threat of reprisal for the rejection of a sexual solicitation or advance where the reprisal is made or threatened by a person in a position to confer, grant or deny a benefit or advancement to the person.

Section 10(1) defines "harassment" to mean:

> engaging in a course of vexatious comment or conduct that is known or ought reasonably to be known to be unwelcome.

The *Code* also makes it an offence, punishable by a fine of up to $25,000 (section 44), to contravene section 9. Thus, there would seem to be a strong consensus that sexual harassment will not be tolerated.

In *Himmelman v. King's Edgehill School* (1985), 7 C.C.E.L. 16, 67 N.S.R. (2d) 358, 115 A.P.R. 358 (T.D.), the Court had no difficulty in finding that the sexual harassment complained of constituted just cause for dismissal. The plaintiff was employed as the bursar of a private, co-educational boarding school and his conduct was particularly egregious. The Court summarized the evidence as follows:

> The evidence revealed the following series of incidents. One morning soon after Mrs. Romans began work at the school, the photocopier ran out of paper. Mrs. Romans sought help from Mr. Himmelman to insert new paper into the machine. As he was standing beside her in the act of assisting her, he either grabbed or brushed her right breast. She reacted instantly and struck Mr. Himmelman, whose sole reaction was to laugh. She warned him never to do that again.
>
> On two or three other occasions, Mr. Himmelman in passing paper to her while she was seated at her desk, brushed Mrs. Romans' breasts. Finally, she asked him whether he had a problem with his hands. His reaction was to grin and say "No, why?".
>
> On at least one occasion and probably more, Mr. Himmelman inquired while in the office behind closed doors about Mrs. Romans' weekend activities with her husband and how they acted together in bed. He said that he himself believed in an "open" marriage and that he had a very "square" wife. Mrs. Romans told Mr. Himmelman that if he felt that way, he should never have married.
>
> On other occasions, Mr. Himmelman would comment to Mrs. Romans about certain sexual activities he or others had observed among the students.
>
> At another time, Mr. Himmelman told Mrs. Romans what a nice backside she had. She told him to keep his eyes off her backside and thereafter she only wore slacks to work.
>
> At another time, while Mr. Himmelman was standing beside her desk, Mrs. Romans remarked that she needed something or other. Following this remark,

> Mr. Himmelman grabbed himself through his trousers and said "you need some of this". She told him he was sick and needed help. He just laughed and went on with his work and she left abruptly for the washroom.
>
> Finally, Mrs. Romans told of an incident which occurred on September 22, 1983, and which finally led her to complain to the Human Rights Commission. She was going for coffee and met Mr. Himmelman in a stairwell. She had just entered the stairwell and was going down to the kitchen. Mr. Himmelman was coming up from the kitchen. He said "Ha, ha, I've got you now" and advanced toward her. He held out his hand as if to grab her. She was frightened and warned him not to touch her. He just grinned and she escaped by running down the stairs past him. Shortly thereafter Mrs. Romans complained to the Human Rights Commission. (at pp. 23-24)

The Court used plain and strong language in denouncing the conduct of the plaintiff, stating that:

> The acts complained of here are offensive in themselves and should occasion strong and meaningful rebuke. Whatever may have been permitted or accepted by society in the past, society accepts no longer the sexual harassment of women such as occurred in this case. Mr. Himmelman's actions were brutish, offensively sexual, and completely reprehensible.
>
> The question, however, is whether these actions amount to just cause for the school, which was the employer of both of Mr. Himmelman and Mrs. Romans, to dismiss Mr. Himmelman from its employ.
>
> In my view the acts themselves if known to the employer (and they were in this case) constitute grounds for summary dismissal in today's climate of equality between the sexes and human rights.
>
> Clearly, however, the harassment in this case comes well within the "undue familiarities" referred to by Christie, above, to the point that Mrs. Romans, another employee, considered quitting and, in fact, took action through the Human Rights Commission that could only eventually result in her leaving the school.
>
> Additionally, it should be recognized that King's-Edgehill School is a coeducational, private boarding school charged with responsibility for the moral and educational upbringing of the boys and girls entrusted to its care. To permit the conduct complained of by Mrs. Romans within the offices of the school would be to sanction moral degradation and seriously and adversely affect the reputation of the school.
>
> I find that the acts complained of by Gail Romans did in fact occur, that these actions constituted sexual harassment of Mrs. Romans by Mr. Himmelman, and that they constituted adequate and proper grounds for King's Edgehill School to summarily dismiss Mr. Himmelman from its employ. (at pp. 25-26)

A further example of a sexual harassment constituting just cause for dismissal is contained in *Tellier v. Bank of Montreal* (1987), 17 C.C.E.L. 1 (Ont. Dist. Ct.). It is notable that the plaintiff was a member of senior management and had 18 years of service with the bank. The Judge described the plaintiff as having "a work record of unqualified success." Nevertheless, and it is submitted, quite properly, the Court found that the flagrant and persistent conduct of the plaintiff justified immediate termination. The Court summarized the conduct of the plaintiff as follows:

> 1. While the department was still located on the 19th floor of First Canadian Place, Mr. Tellier frequently placed his hand on Miss Holloway's posterior as he walked past her during working hours. These incidents occurred in the presence of other departmental employees.
>
> 2. At a cocktail party held by Uniglobe Travel last winter, Miss Holloway stated that Mr. Tellier placed his hand on her breast under the pretext of assisting her to adjust a name tag. Miss Holloway identified another Corporate Training employee who witnessed this incident; Mr. Houston has spoken with this individual who states that she recalls seeing Mr. Tellier "put his hand on Linda's chest."
>
> 3. At the time of Mr. M.G. Davies' transfer from Corporate Training to C.H.R.A. (Corporate Human Resources Administration) this spring, Mr. Davies and his wife took Miss Holloway and two or three other Corporate Training employees to lunch; Mr. Tellier was in attendance, and while seated beside Miss Holloway at the table repeatedly put his hand on her leg. We have spoken with Mr. Davies about this incident, and while he cannot specifically recall seeing the gesture described by Miss Holloway on that particular occasion, he has witnessed similar incidents at other times.
>
> 4. About two months ago, during working hours, Miss Holloway was seated alone in the "terminal room" at the Institute; she was sitting down, working at a terminal, and she states that Mr. Tellier came into the room, stood beside her chair and pressed the lower part of his body against her shoulder. No one else was present on that occasion. (at pp. 3-4)

The Court accepted that the complaints aforesaid were substantiated, and concluded as follows:

> The Bank of Montreal had no other reasonable alternative under the circumstances but to terminate the employment of Mr. Tellier, considering especially the senior position he held. The bank obviously had a heavy responsibility to protect its employees. If the bank did not take positive action against Mr. Tellier, it could leave itself open to a charge under the *Canadian Human Rights Act*, S.C. 1976-77, c. 33. (at p. 12)

Inappropriate touching and conduct will not, however, in every case provide just cause for dismissal. In *Hewes v. Etobicoke (City)* (1993), 93 C.L.L.C. 14,042 (Ont. C.A.), leave to appeal to Supreme Court of Canada refused (1993), 65 O.A.C. 79 (note), 158 N.R. 319 (note) (S.C.C.), the trial judge concluded that the evidence against the plaintiff did not provide just cause. The Court of Appeal summarized the evidence against the plaintiff as follows:

> Allegations against the respondent which were believed by the trial judge consisted of the following:

(i) There was one incident involving a female employee who was described as having a tomboy personality, where the accepted evidence was that the respondent "grabbed her bum for a couple of seconds". The trial judge found, in the context of the event, that this incident was "only marginally, if at all, of a sexual nature". He did not consider this behaviour to provide grounds for dismissal for cause.

(ii) Southey J. accepted evidence that the respondent favoured the same employee by arranging favourable shifts for her, giving her extra overtime, helping her to obtain a licence to drive city vehicles, and permitting her to be absent from the workplace. The allegation that these matters constituted preferential treatment in return for sexual favours was not made out on the evidence. As stated by the trial judge, any complaints of other employees arising from these facts could have been dealt with appropriately through the union grievance procedure.

(iii) The trial judge accepted evidence that the respondent did sometimes touch female employees — poking them in the ribs, rubbing their necks or shoulders, and leaning over them "to reach the microphone at their desks when it was unnecessary to do so, thereby pressing his body against theirs". However, he found that, "Any unwanted touching of the female employees by the plaintiff . . . was not of a sexual nature, was of no great significance to the persons involved, and was stopped when requested or objected to." (at pp. 12,262-12,263)

In finding that there was no just cause for dismissal, it appears that the Court was strongly influenced by the evidence of a female employee that the plaintiff was "a physical man" and that "there was nothing sexual in his touching" (at p. 12,262). It is, however, somewhat difficult to understand how a course of conduct which is targeted at women and is calculated to result in unnecessary and inappropriate touching can be construed as not being sexual. It may well be that the result was influenced by the fact that the plaintiff was a long service employee such that it would be appropriate that even serious misconduct be dealt with first by way of warning. It is, however, respectfully submitted that conduct of the nature described in *Hewes* will, in most circumstances, result in a finding of just cause for dismissal.

The cases just discussed both involve situations in which sexual harassment involved an actual touching of the employee, and the other acts of harassment were flagrant and persistent. It is, however, submitted that a sexual harassment that does not involve touching, and in which the nature and quality of the acts might be less offensive than the cases discussed, will nevertheless result in a finding of just cause for dismissal. By way of example, the persistent inquiry into an employee's sexual activities, or with respect to an employee's physical attributes, after being advised that such comments are unwelcome, could result in a finding of just cause for dismissal.

An example of a situation of abusive conduct without physical touching is *Brick v. Bell Communications Systems Inc.* (1989), 27 C.C.E.L. 118 (Ont. H.C.). The plaintiff was a long-term employee with exemplary performance reviews who had been dismissed, allegedly for just cause, based on his treatment of a female technician under his supervision.

The behaviour of the plaintiff was sexually oriented and highly unprofessional. The incidents relied upon by the employer to justify the termination included the following:

1. that the plaintiff paged the female employee just a few minutes after she had been in his presence, stating that he missed her and that he wanted to hear her voice;
2. that in a bistro, in front of her girlfriend, the plaintiff kept repeating that he wanted a relationship with the female employee until she told him she was not interested;
3. that in the presence of a customer the plaintiff said the female employee was cold in bed;
4. that when the female employee returned from a trip to Hawaii the plaintiff said that she had gone all the way to Hawaii to ''get laid'';
5. that on the job the plaintiff yelled at the female employee and another employee: ''Are you working or having sex?'';
6. that when the female employee asked how much car allowance she would get on a certain assignment the plaintiff told her that all she would get was a big kiss.

There was conflict on the evidence as to whether the plaintiff, while at the premises of a customer, told a female employee of the customer that ''Your ass looks great in the dress you are wearing'' and later, while alone with the employee, made ''some comment as to how she would look with her clothes off.'' While the Court accepted the plaintiff's evidence that such comments had not been made, the Court proceeded to express the view that even if such comments were made, they would not constitute just cause for dismissal, stating:

> Even if Brick had made the two comments Gaudet testified he made, it would still be my view that BCSI was not justified in dismissing him. The comments Gaudet testified he made were not so obscene or disgusting that any offence given by them could not be cured by an apology. While such comments would be impertinent and would show lack of respect, they would be intended to flatter not give insult.
>
> An employer is not justified in dismissing an employee just because a customer takes serious exception to his off-colour remark. The words spoken and the context in which they were spoken would have to be examined to determine whether the violent reaction of the customer was justified. If a customer took offence at the rather mild comments here alleged, he or she could be expected to object to such comments having been made. If in spite of such object[ion] like

(*Continued on page 4-52.1*)

comments were repeated then that might be grounds for dismissal. (at pp. 130-131)

The Court also noted that the technician herself used off-colour language and, generally speaking, repaid the plaintiff's comments in kind. For instance, the Court found evidence that more than once, in front of fellow employees, she indicated that the plaintiff would only interest her if the plaintiff were much younger and more "sexually endowed." The Court concluded that the technician was not disturbed by the plaintiff's remarks, noting that she continued to socialize with him until he decided it was unwise to do so and that she did not complain about his remarks until she was disciplined.

The Court summarized its conclusion about the plaintiff stating:

> There is simply no suggestion in the evidence that Brick was a man that could not control his sexual desires and that women generally or some women, in particular, were not safe in his presence. Nor, is there any suggestion that generally speaking he did not respect women, and that he treated them only as sexual objects. Expect for the incidents that I have described there is no evidence that women generally felt uncomfortable in his presence, or that he made lascivious remarks to women that offended them. I conclude that if any [woman] made it clear to Brick that his words or conduct offended her he would immediately change his ways. (at p. 130)

The Court concluded that the plaintiff was wrongfully dismissed and entitled to six months' notice.

It is respectfully submitted that the result in this case is questionable having regard to the public policy expressed in the *Human Rights Code* and affirmed in *Cuff v. Gypsy Restaurant* (1987), 8 C.H.R.R. D/3972, 87 C.L.L.C. 17,015 (Ont. Bd. of Inquiry). It is further respectfully submitted that the *obiter* statement suggesting that vulgar comments to a customer would not provide just cause for dismissal is simply wrong.

It is fundamental to the employment contract that the employee is to act in the best interests of the employer. The fact that a subordinate employee may or may not have taken offence to certain comments is of little significance. By making the comments, at a minimum, the plaintiff disabled himself from being perceived as fair and objective in dealing with his own employees. Further, the plaintiff's vulgar comments to a customer were of a type that might jeopardize or destroy a commercial relationship. This is precisely the sort of deliberate misconduct that should constitute just cause for dismissal.

Chapter 15.2 considers at greater length the prohibition against sexual harassment contained in the Ontario *Human Rights Code.*

(h) Other Criminal, Immoral or Improper Conduct

As stated, dishonesty and sexual harassment are particular examples of offensive conduct. In considering other types of criminal, immoral or improper conduct, the courts adopt an approach similar to the approach in cases of dishonesty and sexual harassment.

In *Rhodes v. Zehrmart Ltd.* (1986), 15 C.C.E.L. 137 (Ont. Div. Ct.), the Court considered the case of a part-time grocery clerk, who was terminated after five years of employment, after admitting that he had purchased marijuana from a senior employee. The plaintiff had purchased the marijuana on two occasions away from his place of employment. There was no evidence that he ever had the drug at his place of employment or that he was under the influence of drugs while working. At trial the Court upheld the termination on the basis that it had become public knowledge that persons in the employ of the defendant were engaged in selling marijuana, and that this would bring the reputation of the defendant into disrepute. On appeal, however, the Court disagreed, finding that there was no evidence to support the finding that the conduct of the plaintiff had been prejudicial to the reputation of the defendant. As a result damages were awarded to the plaintiff.

Gilson v. Fort Vermilion School Division No. 52 (1985), 12 C.C.E.L. 72, 61 A.R. 225 (Alta. Bd. of Reference under the School Act), is concerned with a criminal act committed in the course of employment. In this case a teacher of some 23 years, and who enjoyed a good reputation as a teacher, became involved in two incidents involving a student in his Grade Three class. The Judge, who constituted the statutory Board of Reference appointed to consider the validity of a resignation submitted by the teacher, described the incidents as follows:

> In the first of these, the appellant placed a jacket which the child had left in an inappropriate place into the wastepaper basket. The student went home without his jacket. His parents complained to the principal who retrieved the jacket from the school's garbage disposal and returned it to the child. Apparently, the appellant had intended to return the jacket to the child before the end of the school day. A janitor had, however, removed the garbage from the classroom while the class was in the gym. The appellant did not attempt to find the jacket and let the student go home without it.
>
> . . . .
>
> The second incident involving Duane Lambert occurred on the 5th of October, 1984. It appears that Duane Lambert had taken the top off a pencil sharpener. The appellant admits that he then held Duane by the hair, that he rubbed the pencil shavings into his face and that he pushed or touched him on the seat with his shoe. In evidence before me the appellant stated that he did not believe that such conduct was an inappropriate form of discipline for a Grade III student or that he had overreacted to the situation. (at p. 77)

Faced with these facts the deputy superintendent of schools advised the plaintiff that there were four possible solutions:

1. resolution of the difficulty after discussion with the boy's parents;
2. transfer of the plaintiff to another school with a notation on the plaintiff's personnel file regarding these incidents;
3. a resignation, in which case the incidents would not be referred to on his employment record; and

4. a recommendation for the termination of the plaintiff's employment.

It proved impossible to resolve matters with the parents through discussion, and in fact the parents repeatedly threatened to lay criminal charges. This left three options. Faced with these alternatives the plaintiff was given one day to consider his options, and the following day he delivered a written resignation to the Board. After submitting his resignation, and acting on advice from the Alberta Teachers' Association, the plaintiff purported to revoke his resignation. The Court upheld the resignation as voluntary, stating as follows:

> I am satisfied that the appellant had some real options and that he was not being forced to resign. Winsor gave the appellant a day to think about the alternative and to discuss the matter with his wife, the A.T.A. and/or counsel. The appellant did discuss the matter with his wife who suggested that they accept the transfer to Rainbow Lake. The appellant chose not to discuss the matter with anyone else.
>
> While the appellant indicated that he felt the atmosphere was threatening and that he felt under some pressure, he admitted that the discussion was serious, calm and that there was no shouting and that there were not raised voices. If the appellant felt threatened it was because of his own attitude and not because of anything done by Winsor or Campbell.
>
> If the appellant had chosen not to resign, Winsor was still left with the option of either recommending a forced transfer or of recommending the termination of the contract. In either case the appellant would then have had the opportunity of airing his position before the school board in the hopes of convincing the board that he had done nothing wrong or that the transfer or termination was not justified.
>
> In my view the appellant resigned voluntarily after he was given several options to consider. He was not forced to resign and was not acting under duress. The appellant's appeal is dismissed. (at pp. 83-84)

It seems implicit in the finding of the Court that it viewed the conduct of the plaintiff as constituting just cause for dismissal. Had the conduct not constituted just cause for dismissal, then the options put to the plaintiff would have constituted a constructive dismissal (see Chapter 5), and the plaintiff would not have had an obligation to consider the options.

This case is also somewhat unusual in that the Court does not appear to have given the plaintiff proper credit for some 23 years of good service as a teacher. To that extent the case is anomalous when compared with other cases in which the courts have excused periods of drunkenness or non-performance, on the ground that the employee has a generally good record. The explanation for the rather harsh result in this case, however, may be that the plaintiff did not take the position that the conduct in question was an aberration or that the conduct was the product of any physical or mental difficulties which he was suffering at the time. On the contrary, the plaintiff apparently testified that he could see nothing wrong with the forms of discipline imposed. Thus, it may be the evidence of the plaintiff in this regard, and the revelation of character that it entailed, that led to the conclusion of the Court.

In *Kucey v. Gelfant* (1993), 48 C.C.E.L. 121, 93 C.L.L.C. 14,060 (B.C.S.C.), the plaintiff was a dental specialist who practiced with the defendants. The Court observed that there is an implied term in an employment contract that the employee will "faithfully, honestly and diligently serve his employer".

The Court found that the plaintiff had stated to his dental assistant, laboratory technicians employed by the defendants, and in the presence of patients, that one of the defendants was "not up to par" and not as good as the plaintiff and other comments generally disparaging the defendants. The Court found that these comments constituted a breach of the employment contract and constituted just cause for dismissal.

The conduct in question need not be in the actual course of employment in order to justify a finding of just cause for dismissal. In *Bell v. General Motors of Can.* (1989), 27 C.C.E.L. 110 (Ont. H.C.), the plaintiff was employed by General Motors of Canada for over twenty years. For two years prior to his discharge, the plaintiff had a romantic relationship with a secretary in his department. The plaintiff was also drinking "at least a forty ounce bottle" of alcohol per day. The evidence showed that he often drank before going to work, at mealtimes, and in the evening. He did not feel it impaired his ability at work and he was never reprimanded at work, nor was any mention of his drinking ever made to him by his superiors.

In the final incident before discharge, the plaintiff had consumed ten to twelve bottles of beer and a quart of rye by the time the secretary came to his apartment to review some work-related material and to have dinner. The plaintiff thereupon assaulted the secretary by punching and kicking her. The employer terminated for just cause on the basis that the plaintiff's conduct in assaulting a subordinate employee was completely unacceptable. Although the conduct was off company premises, the assault was partly work-related, and prejudicial to employee morale.

The Court, in dismissing the action, relied upon the principles in *Lake Ont. Portland Cement Co. v. Groner*, [1961] S.C.R. 553, 28 D.L.R. (2d) 589. The Court believed that the principles discussed by Mr. Justice Ritchie, albeit in that case referring to a dishonest employee, had application. The Court, relying upon this decision, quoted Ritchie J. (at D.L.R. p. 598):

> It may be, as Mr. Justice Morden says in the course of his judgment in the Court of Appeal, that the respondent's misconduct "was not incompatible with the proper discharge of the duties to which he was employed", but in my view it is not so much the conduct itself as the fact that he was capable of it which justifies the respondent's dismissal. . . . As was said by Lord Atkinson in *Federal Supply & Cold Storage Co. of South Africa v. Angehrn & Piel* (1910), 103 L.T. 150 at p. 151, "it is the revelation of character which justifies the dismissal". (at p. 116)

Relying upon this passage, the Court felt that it was the revelation of the plaintiff's character that constituted just cause for dismissal. His conduct in assaulting a fellow employee was inconsistent with the duties of a supervisor, or indeed with the respect owed by one employee to another.

(i) Other Conduct Incompatible with Continued Employment

As has been stated throughout this section, the principal focus in considering an allegation of just cause is the impact of the impugned conduct on the employer and/or the ability of the employee to carry out the responsibilities of the position in future. Thus, the cases to be discussed under this heading are somewhat anomalous. In general terms they involve employee conduct which is not intrinsically unlawful or improper but which may be incompatible with maintenance of the employment relationship.

An interesting and unusual situation arose in *Cdn. Imperial Bank of Commerce v. Boisvert*, 13 C.C.E.L. 264, [1986] 2 F.C. 431, 68 N.R. 355 (C.A.), leave to appeal to Supreme Court of Canada refused (1986), (*sub nom. C.I.B.C. v. Chayer*) 72 N.R. 367 (note) (S.C.C.), in which the Court upheld the termination of a bank employee notwithstanding the fact that there was no proof of any blameworthy conduct on her part. As stated, however, the facts were highly unusual. The employee commenced employment in 1974 and was employed in a managerial capacity. In 1976 she began cohabiting with one Beaulieu and became engaged to him in 1977. Such cohabitation was interrupted by the imprisonment of Beaulieu for a period in 1978-1979 for offences including robbery. In early 1982, two robberies occurred at the same branch of the Bank, one being an armed robbery in which two bank employees suffered gunshot wounds. Within minutes of the second robbery Beaulieu was arrested at the apartment of the bank employee. Three days thereafter the bank advised the employee to resign, or she would be dismissed. An adjudicator

(*Continued on page 4-53*)

appointed under the *Canada Labour Code* ordered that the employee be reinstated, on the basis that her dismissal was unjust in the absence of any evidence suggesting that she had knowledge or responsibility for the robberies that had been committed.

The Federal Court of Appeal, however, disagreed with the decision of the adjudicator, and upheld the dismissal. The Court found it significant that the employee had signed an employment contract, which stated, in relevant part:

> In consideration of my being hired by the Canadian Imperial Bank of Commerce (the "Bank"), I do hereby solemnly promise, undertake and agree:
>
> 1. to act with honesty and loyalty . . .
>
> 2. to preserve the most absolute secrecy regarding all the operations and affairs of the Bank . . .
>
> . . .
>
> 8. that my employment may be terminated:
>
> . . .
>
> (d) by the Bank at any time during or after my probation, without prior notice or salary in view thereof, for any good and sufficient reason including, but without limiting the generality of the foregoing, conduct prejudicial to the interests and reputation of the Bank . . (at pp. 279-280)

The Court then discussed the evidence and stated its conclusion, as hereinafter set out:

> Whether or not the respondent knew in advance of the robberies against her own Bank (and the adjudicator has found that there is no evidence that she did), Beaulieu's blatant use of their joint premises as a centre of operations would indicate that he was making small attempt to keep her uninvolved. In any event, at least by February 1980, her continued cohabitation with Beaulieu placed her in a situation of incompatibility with her duties to her employer. Even if never carried out against her own Bank, Beaulieu's illegal activities were of such a nature as to constitute a standing threat to all financial institutions, her own included. As a key employee, she had direct knowledge of her own Bank's security arrangements and indirect knowledge of those of other banks. In such a close association she might even unwittingly let slip a detail helpful to an alert criminal mind.
>
> The adjudicator's interpretation that Beaulieu was until 1980 a rehabilitated criminal ("who had served a prison term, and had thus paid his debt to society") who then suddenly turned from Dr. Jekyll into Mr. Hyde ("who suddenly began committing bank robberies") is simply not credible. His criminality must be deemed to have been clearly visible to her, and it was only the adjudicator's idée fixe that conflict of interest requires an act *contrary to law* on the employee's part that prevented him from seeing the situation as it was. She betrayed her duty to her employer by continuing to associate with a person so apparently dedicated to playing Robin Hood for his own benefit. Nothing more is required for incompatibility with the interests of her employer.
>
> This conclusion is above all established by the respondent's obligations under the contract of employment itself: according to Lord James in *Clouston & Co. v. Corry*, [1906] A.C. 122 at 129 (P.C.):

> [M]isconduct inconsistent with the fulfilment of the express or implied conditions of service will justify dismissal.
>
> In the case at Bar, she undertook to act with honesty and loyalty and to avoid any conduct prejudicial to the interests and reputation of the Bank. We have already seen that her conduct was prejudicial to the interests of the Bank; that it was prejudicial to the Bank's reputation requires no proof. In these circumstances the Bank also had, under the contract, a right to terminate her employment without notice. (at pp. 284-285)

Another instructive, albeit unusual, case is *Fraser v. Canada (Treasury Bd.) (Department of National Revenue)*, 9 C.C.E.L. 233, (*sub nom. Fraser v. P.S.S.R.B.*) [1985] 2 S.C.R. 455, 18 Admin. L.R. 72, 86 C.L.L.C. 14,003, 19 C.R.R. 152, 23 D.L.R. (4th) 122, 63 N.R. 161. A supervisor employed by Revenue Canada undertook a campaign of persistent and virulent criticism of the federal government, and in particular its policies with respect to metrification and the entrenchment of the *Charter of Rights*. The following extracts from the Supreme Court of Canada decision indicate the lengths to which the employee carried his crusade:

> The substantive criticism was of two major and, at the time, divisive policies — the metric conversion program and the Charter. In form, the criticism was prolonged and, as the national media focused its attention on Mr. Fraser, increasingly derogatory in tone. As events developed, his criticism went beyond the two policies mentioned above. He began to impugn and attack the character of the Prime Minister and the integrity of the Government. He did this on a local, then a national, and finally an international basis. He said in Kingston:
>
> > We have sold the rights of English-speaking Quebecers down the drain.
> >
> > The Federal Government never had any mandate from the people.
> >
> > We are not killing Jews as they did in Nazi Germany, but Canadians are up against that same insidious mentality today from their government.
>
> He telexed Sir Francis Pym, leader of the British House of Commons:
>
> > You are dealing with a federal government that has a record of broken promises to the Canadian people. (at pp. 248-249)

The Court then commented on the general obligation owed by employees to their employers, and the type of evidence which would suffice to show impairment of the ability of the employee to do his job properly. In this regard the Court stated:

> As a general rule, federal public servants should be loyal to their employer, the Government of Canada. The loyalty owed is to the Government of Canada, not the political party in power at any one time. A public servant need not vote for the governing party. Nor need he or she publicly espouse its policies. And indeed, in some circumstances, a public servant may actively and publicly express opposition to the policies of a government. This would be appropriate if, for example, the Government were engaged in illegal acts, or if its policies jeopardized the life, health or safety of the public servant or others, or if the public servant's criticism

had no impact on his or her ability to perform effectively the duties of a public servant or on the public perception of that ability. But, having stated these qualifications (and there may be others), it is my view that a public servant must not engage, as the appellant did in the present case, in sustained and highly visible attacks on major Government policies. In conducting himself in this way the appellant, in my view, displayed a lack of loyalty to the Government that was inconsistent with his duties as an employee of the Government. (at p. 246)

. . . .

In spite of this the Adjudicator concluded that Mr. Fraser's activities were job-related in that they led to "impairment" of his ability to do his job properly. Indeed he found impairment in two senses: first, impairment to perform effectively the specific job because of the inferred effect on clients; secondly, and in a wider sense, impairment to be a public servant because of the special and important characteristics of that occupation.

I do not think the Adjudicator erred on either count. As to impairment to perform the specific job, I think the general rule should be that direct evidence of impairment is required. However, this rule is not absolute. When, as here, the nature of the public servant's occupation is both important and sensitive and when, as here, the substance, form and context of the public servant's criticism is extreme, then an inference of impairment can be drawn. In this case the inference drawn by the Adjudicator, namely that Mr. Fraser's conduct could or would give rise to public concern, unease and distrust of his ability to perform his employment duties, was not an unreasonable one for him to make.

Turning to impairment in the wider sense, I am of opinion that direct evidence is not necessarily required. The traditions and contemporary standards of the public service can be matters of direct evidence. But they can also be matters of study, of written and oral argument, of general knowledge on the part of experienced public sector adjudicators, and ultimately, of reasonable inference by those adjudicators. It is open to an adjudicator to infer impairment on the whole of the evidence if there is evidence of a pattern of behaviour which an adjudicator could reasonably conclude would impair the usefulness of the public servant. Was there such evidence of behaviour in this case? In order to answer that question it becomes relevant to consider the substance, form and context of Mr. Fraser's criticism of government policy.

. . . .

When one examines the substance of the criticisms (two major government policies and the character and integrity of the Prime Minister and Government), the context of those criticisms (prolonged, virtually full-time, in public meetings, on radio, on television, in newspapers, local, national, international), and the form of the criticisms (initially restrained, but increasingly vitriolic and vituperative) the Adjudicator's conclusion that Mr. Fraser's ability to perform his own job and his suitability to remain in the public service were both impaired was a fair conclusion. Though no direct evidence of the fact of impairment of capacity is required, here the evidence clearly established circumstances from which the inference of impairment is clearly irresistible. Put simply, although there is not an absolute prohibition against public servants criticizing government policies, Mr. Fraser in this case went much too far. (at pp. 248-249)

In *Cashin v. Cdn. Broadcasting Corp.*, 20 C.C.E.L. 23, [1988] 3 F.C. 494, 86 N.R. 24, 88 C.L.L.C. 17,019, 9 C.H.R.R. D/5343 (C.A.), the Court had occasion to consider the application of the reasoning in the *Fraser* case. Cashin was a writer and radio broadcaster employed by the CBC in Newfoundland. Her husband, who was a prominent figure in Newfoundland, was appointed to the board of directors of Petro-Canada and the response of the CBC was to terminate her employment, on the principal ground that she could no longer be perceived as objective. The case came before the Federal Court of Appeal after a Review Tribunal under the *Canadian Human Rights Act* had applied the reasoning in the *Fraser* case, and had found that the termination was justified and did not constitute discrimination on the basis of marital status. The Court reversed this finding and placed considerable emphasis on the fact that the CBC acknowledged that it would have dealt with the situation differently had Cashin used a surname different from her husband's, or if she had been associated with him in a non-spousal relationship. The Court distinguished *Fraser* on the basis that Fraser was terminated because of his own conduct, and that conduct was found to be criticism of the government which was inconsistent with the obligations of a public servant. In the case of Cashin there was no criticism of her actual work, but only an unsubstantiated judgment that she would not be perceived as being objective. In delivering concurring reasons Mr. Justice Mahoney made the point that there were a number of comparable situations, of prominent persons being associated with reporters, in which the CBC had not taken the position that there was a perceived lack of objectivity. The examples given, and the comments of Mahoney J., are as follows:

> Perhaps actuated by reluctance to publicly record the personal relationships of other media personalities and potential news subjects or sources, neither the Tribunal nor the Review Tribunal referred to that undisputed evidence which, in my opinion, supports both the conclusion that the discrimination here was based on her marital status and not simply on the fact that Rosann Cashin was married to a particular person and also the Tribunal's conclusion, reversed by the Review Tribunal, that the CBC's version of perceived objectivity did not meet the test established by the Supreme Court of Canada in the *Etobicoke* case, *Ont. Human Rights Comm. v. Etobicoke (Borough)*, [1982] 1 S.C.R. 202, 82 C.L.L.C. 17,005, 3 C.H.R.R. D/781, 132 D.L.R. (3d) 14, 40 N.R. 159, for a bona fide occupational requirement. I propose to do this by simply describing situations which the CBC tolerated without naming the persons concerned but providing references to the record should another Court have occasion to review this judgment. I shall also refer only to the relationships involving persons employed by the CBC in news broadcasting and not to those employed to express opinions nor to employees of other news organizations. All references are to the record of the Tribunal, App. I to the case.
>
> A co-host of a national television news program is described as the "regular date" of "a key Tory backroom strategist", in fact a recent national director of the party, vol. 7, p. 1157. A national affairs reporter is the wife of "a well known political activist" and leader of a radical element in the New Democratic Party,

> vol. 3, p. 457. The wife of a radio national affairs correspondent and Parliamentary bureau chief is communications director for a Leader of the Opposition, vol. 3, pp. 458, 497; vol. 8, p. 1323. A reporter/producer for a nationally televised news program is married to a Prime Minister's press secretary, vol. 3, p. 501; vol. 8, p. 1329. Prior to that marriage, the press secretary had a relationship with another television news reporter, vol. 8, p. 1334. A senior television news correspondent has a relationship with a Prime Minister's legislative assistant, vol. 3, p. 502; vol. 8, p. 1329.
>
> All of these relationships were well known to the CBC's management. They demonstrate that the requirement of perceived objectivity was, in fact, invoked in the entirely subjective fashion described by Donna Logan, the senior CBC management person to testify. Mr. Justice MacGuigan has quoted the gist of her evidence on the point.
>
> Common to all of those relationships, married or not, the parties did not share surnames. The mass of its audience was unlikely to be aware of the relationship and, therefore, by CBC standards, the perception of the objectivity of its on air news personnel was not called into question even though the job titles of at least some of their partners suggest an active interest, perhaps duty, to influence the content and presentation of the news. (at pp. 221-222)

This is not to say that a termination might not be upheld in a situation in which a journalist was married to, or had a close personal relationship with, a person whose job it was to influence the media to a certain point of view. It is clear, however, that the CBC had disabled itself from putting the termination on this basis, due to the fact that there was a widespread and well-known practice at the CBC of continuing the employment of journalists having such relationships.

In *Reilly v. Steelcase Can. Ltd.* (1979), 26 O.R. (2d) 725, 103 D.L.R. (3d) 704 (H.C.), the Court was concerned with whether the fact of an adulterous, "serious" relationship between an employee and the wife of a fellow employee constituted just cause for dismissal. The Court noted that while there were precedent cases in 1910 and 1918 which upheld the dismissal of a farm hand, and a City of Toronto fireman, on the basis of the fact that they had both boasted of adulterous affairs, there had been substantial changes in social values since that time. In this regard the Court, after reviewing the precedent cases, stated:

> Approaching the problem so objectively and having regard to the contemporary mores, the Courts established the principles of law by which each case should be determined and did not blindly accept the views of the individual employer.
>
> This becomes very important because between 1886, for example, when *Pearce v. Foster* [(1886), 17 Q.B.D. 536] was decided and 1918, for example, when *McPherson v. City of Toronto* [(1918), 43 O.L.R. 326, 43 D.L.R. 604] was decided and 1979 when the present case must be decided, there has been a social revolution of enormous proportions. One need only to look at the *Divorce Act*, 1968 (Can.), c. 24, and the *Family Law Reform Act*, 1978 (Ont.), c. 2, to realize the gulf that separates current thinking with respect to personal and social relationships that are acceptable today with those that were acceptable in the society of 60 to 100 years ago.
>
> The principles of law set out in the cases I have quoted from are indeed as sound as when they were enunciated, but when applied, they must be relevant to present society. Lord Esher in *Pearce v. Foster* recognized that each case would have to be assessed on its own merits when he said:

> What circumstances will put a servant into the position of not being able to perform, in a due manner, his duties, or of not being able to perform his duty in a faithful manner, it is impossible to enumerate. Innumerable circumstances have actually occurred which fall within that proposition, and innumerable other circumstances which never have yet occurred, will occur, which also will fall within the proposition.

> As I apprehend this statement, it means that each case must be looked at objectively, in the light of all the facts, and as related to the test of current social acceptability. (at pp. 739-740)

In the result, the Court found that just cause for dismissal did not exist.

Dooley v. C.N. Weber Ltd. (1994), 3 C.C.E.L. (2d) 95 (Ont. Gen. Div.) is a variation of *Reilly, supra*, in which the sexual conduct complained of was more closely related to employment. In *Dooley*, the plaintiff was a member of the Management Operating Committee. He had a sexual relationship with a subordinate employee while employed in Kitchener. This became known to the President of the company and when the plaintiff was later transferred to Toronto he was specifically warned that if he had a sexual relationship with any other subordinate employees the company would consider it grounds for immediate dismissal. The plaintiff did have a sexual relationship with a subordinate employee in Toronto and was terminated. The Court concluded that the company did not have just cause for dismissal stating:

> In my view, the version of the law as enunciated by Keith J. in *Reilly* in 1979 is still the law of the province of Ontario at this time.
>
> Applying the law as enunciated in *Reilly* by Keith J. to this case, I have no hesitation in concluding that the company has not satisfied, on all the evidence before me, and based on the balance of probabilities, the onus that they had "just cause" to dismiss Dooley.
>
> The company failed to satisfy this onus because the order given by Jack to Dooley was not reasonable in today's world, particularly where there is no evidence before me that the company suffered in any manner whatsoever, either financially or otherwise, arising out of the conduct of Dooley while employed at the Toronto location. In addition, the circumstances of this case clearly indicate that the order given by Jack to Dooley relating to his association with women subordinates in Toronto was not within the scope of his employment with the company. (at p. 100)

In *Thomas v. Lafleche Union Hospital Board* (1989), 27 C.C.E.L. 156, 82 Sask. R. 70 (Q.B.), affirmed 36 C.C.E.L. 251, [1991] 5 W.W.R. 209, 91 C.L.L.C. 14,042, 93 Sask. R. 150, 4 W.A.C. 150 (C.A.), there was a statutory requirement that the position held by the plaintiff be held by a registered nurse. The plaintiff nurse was found guilty of professional misconduct and professional incompetence resulting in loss of registration.

The Court held that the contract of employment was frustrated when the plaintiff lost his registered nurse status and the parties were, therefore, excused from further performance of their obligations under it. Accordingly, the defendant was not obligated to provide the plaintiff with notice of termination, nor was it obligated to compensate him for salary and benefits during a notice period. In any event, the Court found that there was just cause for dismissal on the basis that a person cannot be retained in a managerial/supervisory position having been found guilty of professional misconduct and professional incompetence.

In *Backman v. Hyundai Auto Canada Inc.* (1990), 33 C.C.E.L. 300, 100 N.S.R. (2d) 24, 272 A.P.R. 24 (T.D.), the Court found that the mere fact that criminal charges had been laid did not constitute just cause for dismissal. Backman had approximately two years of service with Hyundai and had recently been promoted to the position of regional sales manager at the time he was charged with trafficking in narcotics. Backman's name was linked to Hyundai in the media. Hyundai had recently been the subject of exposure in the media during a well-publicized inquiry and was sensitive about its public image. Hyundai terminated Backman after the charge was laid, to avoid publicity adverse to its business, and despite the fact it believed him to be innocent. Backman was ultimately acquitted at trial.

Davison J. considered whether criminal charges could form the basis for just cause for dismissal, stating:

> Did the defendant's concern about the bad publicity, coupled with the belief of its officers that the plaintiff was innocent of the charges, amount to just cause for dismissal?
>
> The onus is on the defendant to prove just cause. There is no evidence of any misconduct on the part of the plaintiff. I reject the suggestion that a meeting in his office with a person with a criminal record and who was subsequently convicted of an offence which related to the offence with which Backman was charged constituted just cause for dismissal.
>
> Mr. Justice Cooper of the Appeal division of the Supreme Court of Nova Scotia considered the term "just cause" in *Walker v. Keating* (1973), 6 N.S.R. (2d) 1 (C.A.). He stated that p. 11:
>
> In the first place I think 'just cause' as used in s. 76(5)(b)(i) of the *Education Act* must mean such cause as would justify a master in summarily dismissing a servant. Whether or not just cause for dismissal exists has been held to be a question of mixed fact and law — see, *Re United Steelworkers of America, Local 7085 and East Coast Smelting & Chemical Co. Ltd.* (1972), 21 D.L.R. (3d) 23. MacDonald, J., in the *Canadian Gypsum* case, supra, at p. 314 refers to the legal requirement for justifiable dismissal without notice as being that set out in 25 *Halsbury* (3rd Ed.), p. 485, namely:
>
> 'Misconduct, inconsistent with the due and faithful discharge by the servant of the duties for which he was engaged, is good cause for his dismissal.'
>
> And in the leading case of *Clouston & Co. v. Corry*, [1906] A.C. at 129, it was said that 'misconduct inconsistent with the fulfilment of the express or implied conditions of service will justify dismissal'. (Cf. *Laws v. London Chronicle (Indicator Newspapers) Ltd.* (1959), 2 A.E.R. 285.)
>
> I refer also to what was said by Schroeder, J.A., in his dissenting judgment approved by the Supreme Court in *Regina v. Arthurs; Ex parte Port Arthur Shipbuilding Co.*, [1947] 2 O.R. 49, at p. 55:
>
> 'If an employee has been guilty of serious misconduct, habitual neglect of duty, incompetence, or conduct incompatible with his duties, or prejudicial to the

employer's business, or if he has been guilty of wilful disobedience to the employer's orders in a matter of substance, the law recognizes the employer's right summarily to dismiss the delinquent employee.'

Schroeder, J.A.'s judgment was approved in the Supreme Court of Canada, [1969] S.C.R. 85.

When the officers of the defendant learned of the charges, they made no independent inquiries or investigation as to the conduct of the plaintiff which may have contributed to the charges. Possibly this inaction stemmed from the belief in Backman's innocence.

There was no evidence the defendant suffered harm because of the reference to it in the media. Dealers testified at trial that there was no evidence the publicity affected the defendant's business.

There was no evidence of misconduct, incompetence, or neglect of duty on the part of Backman. There was no evidence to suggest the employer had reasonable grounds to believe that there was fear of substantial adverse affects on its business as a result of the charges. The defendant has not met the onus of showing, on the balance of probabilities, it had just cause to dismiss the plaintiff. (at pp. 312-314)

In *Hulme v. Cadillac Fairview Corp.* (1993), 1 C.C.E.L. (2d) 94 (Ont. Gen. Div.), the plaintiff was a development officer who worked on major real estate development projects. He was removed from a particular project and was told that he would be kept on salary until another suitable project was found. No such project was found for several months and the plaintiff, therefore, commenced an action for wrongful dismissal alleging that he had been constructively dismissed. Mr. Justice Montgomery concluded that the plaintiff had not been constructively dismissed and that the defendant had just cause to terminate the relationship having regard to the fact that "[i]t is inconsistent with an employment relationship for an employee to be suing a company for wrongful dismissal" (at pp. 101-102).

(j) Frustration of the Employment Contract

Frustration of an employment contract is not, strictly speaking, a head of just cause. It is comparable, however, in that it is a situation in which an employment contract is brought to an end without further obligation on the part of the employer. It therefore seems most appropriate to discuss the subject of frustration in association with the various just cause defences.

A helpful summary of the general principles is set out in *St. John v. TNT Canada Inc.* (1991), 38 C.C.E.L. 55, 56 B.C.L.R. (2d) 311, in which the Court considered whether a strike that led to the employer discontinuing its operations in western Canada served to frustrate the employment contracts of its non-union employees. The Court cited a number of Supreme Court of Canada decisions as follows:

In *Peter Kiewit Sons' Co. of Canada v. Eakins Construction Ltd.*, [1960] S.C.R. 361, 22 D.L.R. (2d) 465, Judson J., speaking for the majority of the Supreme Court of Canada (Locke, Abbott, Martland JJ. concurring), defined this principle, at p. 483 [D.L.R.]:

> I take the statement of the principle from p. 729 [A.C.] of the *Fareham* case [*Davis Contractors Ltd. v. Fareham Urban District Council*, [1956] A.C. 696, [1956] 2 All E.R. 145 (H.L.)]: "Frustration occurs whenever the law recognizes that without default of either party a contractual obligation has become incapable of being performed because the circumstances in which performance is called for would render it a thing radically different from that which was undertaken by the contract. *Non haec in foedera veni.* It was not this that I promised to do . . . *It is not hardship or inconvenience or material loss itself which calls the principle of frustration into play.* There must be as well such a change in the significance of the obligation that the thing undertaken would, if performed, be a different thing from that contracted for. (at pp. 59-60) [Emphasis added.]
>
> . . . .

In *Canadian Government Merchant Marine Ltd. v. Canadian Trading Co.*, 64 S.C.R. 106, [1922] 3 W.W.R. 197, 68 D.L.R. 544, the appellants undertook to carry cargo on a ship near completion. Due to labour problems, the vessels were delayed and the voyage could not be made. The appellants claimed frustration as a defence for not fulfilling their obligation. This defence was unanimously rejected by the court. Each of the five judges sitting on the appeal wrote a separate judgment. The decision of the court suggests that the allocation of risk approach discussed previously is applicable in such cases.

Idington J. stated, at pp. 545-546 [D.L.R.]:

> A further pretence is set up that a strike, or threatened strike, was to blame in part for the delay.
>
> Resting upon this failure of the contractor the appellant invokes the doctrine of impossibility upon which the case of *Taylor v. Caldwell* [citations omitted] was decided.
>
> I do not think that can be made applicable herein unless we are to so extend the operation of the doctrine as to render almost any and every conceivable contract of little value.

Duff J. stated, at pp. 547-548:

> For the purpose of deciding whether a particular case falls within the principle you must consider the nature of the contract and the circumstances in which it was made in order to see from the nature of the contract whether the parties must have made their bargain on the footing that a particular thing or state of facts should be in existence when the time for performance should occur . . . and if reasonable persons situated as the parties were must have agreed that the promissor's contractual obligations should come to an end if that state of circumstances should not exist then a term to that effect may be implied . . . . *But it is most important to remember that no such term should be implied when it is possible to hold that reasonable men could have contemplated the taking the risk of the circumstances being what they, in fact, proved to be when the time for performance arrived.*
>
> . . . .
>
> Real impossibility of performance, arising from destruction of the ships by fire,

> for example, would have presented a different case .... Impossibility arising from such causes is not the impossibility contemplated by the case of *Taylor v. Caldwell*. (at pp. 61-62) [Citations omitted, emphasis added.]

Having adopted these statements of the general principle, the Court had little difficulty in concluding that a strike did not frustrate the employment contracts:

> Applying these principles to the case at bar, it is clear that the occurrence of a strike is a foreseeable event. Further, it is also foreseeable that one party to a labour negotiation may not be able to impose its terms on the other party. TNT clearly assumed the risk of the consequences of its negotiations with the Teamsters Union. Further, TNT did not provide for this provision in its contract with St. John, and accordingly it chose to assume this risk.
>
> Based on the nature and circumstances of the contract between TNT and St. John, it is not evident that the parties contemplated ending their relationship if there was a strike at TNT. If fact, a contrary intent was indicated. TNT had experienced at least one strike by the same union previously. There is no evidence to indicate that this event resulted in the frustration of all contracts by TNT. Accordingly, such a term ought not to be implied since reasonable persons would conclude that TNT assumed the risk of imposing its terms on the Teamsters Union during collective bargaining. (at pp. 62-63)

Thomas v. Lafleche Union Hospital Board (1989), 27 C.C.E.L. 156, 82 Sask. R. 70 (Q.B.), affirmed 36 C.C.E.L. 251, [1991] 5 W.W.R. 209, 91 C.L.L.C. 14,042, 93 Sask. R. 150, 4 W.A.C. 150 (C.A.), is a case in which an employment contract was frustrated. In this case there was a statutory requirement that the employee be a registered nurse. Subsequently, the employee was found guilty of professional misconduct and incompetence and lost his registration. The Court found that the contract was frustrated and the parties were, therefore, excused from further performance of their obligations.

The Court also found just cause for dismissal on the basis that a person cannot be retained in a managerial/supervisory position having been found guilty of professional misconduct and professional incompetence.

A situation in which frustration of the employment contract was not found is *Crossman v. Scotia Textiles Ltd.* (1989), 27 C.C.E.L. 302, 2 C.O.H.S.C. 1, 98 N.B.R. (2d) 248, 248 A.P.R. 248 (Q.B.), varied (1990), 30 C.C.E.L. 318, 2 C.O.H.S.C. 169, 105 N.B.R. (2d) 91, 264 A.P.R. 91 (C.A.). In *Crossman*, the plaintiff was employed by the defendant for seven years. The plaintiff subsequently began to experience respiratory problems and was frequently absent from work. The plaintiff informed the employer that he had received medical advice that the fumes in the workplace aggravated his bronchial problem. Since no suitable form of employment was available, the defendant terminated the plaintiff's employment. The defendant argued that the employment contract was frustrated by reason of the plaintiff's inability to continue in his employment.

The Court, however, found that the plaintiff had been wrongfully dismissed due to the failure of the employer to comply with certain provisions of the *Occupational Health and Safety Act*, S.N.B. 1983, c. O-0.2. The Court found that the plaintiff had reasonable grounds for believing that to perform his job in the existing environment of his workplace was likely to endanger his health. Therefore, the Court turned its mind to section 20 of the *Act*, which sets out the procedure to be followed in that situation.

The Court found that the provisions of the *Act* constituted a ''statutory term'' of the employment and, having found an employer breach of the statutory term, proceeded to make a finding of wrongful dismissal. It is, however, respectfully submitted that the Court should have considered what, if any, damages flowed from the breach of the statutory term. If, in fact, through no fault of the employer, the employee could no longer work, it is respectfully submitted that the contract was frustrated. In the alternative, if the illness of the employee was occasioned by fault on the part of the employer, then the employer was in breach of contract and properly liable for the damages flowing from such breach.

(k) Conflict of Interest

In *Connolly v. General Motors of Canada Ltd.* (1993), 50 C.C.E.L. 247 (Ont. Gen. Div.), the Court considered a case in which a maintenance supervisor had borrowed money from one of his employer's suppliers.

The General Motors policy respecting conflict of interest is useful as a precedent and for that reason the principal elements of the policy are set out at length, as follows:

> CONFLICT OF INTEREST
>
> The basic underlying principle in conflict of interest is that employees should avoid any activity, investment or interest that might reflect unfavourably upon the integrity or good name of themselves or of General Motors. A conflict of interest is an obligation to or relationship with any person or organization which competes or does business with General Motors that *could effect an employee's judgment in fulfilling his or her responsibilities to General Motors.*
>
> . . .
>
> *An unbiased judgment and decision is what General Motors expects — and disclosure of all the facts is essential.*
>
> . . .
>
> *Disclosure is the Keystone*
>
> Many questions relating to conflict of interest in government and industry can be avoided by timely and adequate disclosure of the facts. As an example, the Corporation may consent to an employees' being in a situation that may appear to present a conflict of interest. It can only do so, however, if the facts are known and no unethical or criminal conduct is involved.
>
> . . .
>
> A seemingly harmless investment or activity which is entered into without unethical intent on the part of the employee can easily raise suspicion in the mind of a third party who is unfamiliar with all of the facts. Often, such suspicion can result in

injury to the reputation and character of the employee and General Motors. As part of its commitment to all of its employees, shareholders, customers and suppliers to maintain the highest possible reputation, General Motors expects all employees to disclose immediately, or in advance if possible, any situation in which they are involved which *could result in a conflict of interest or otherwise violate Corporation policies.*

. . .

INTERESTS IN OTHER BUSINESSES

A special aspect of conflict of interest relates to interests or investment in other businesses. Employees and members of their household should not have any interest or investment in any supplier, customer or competitor of General Motors Corporation which could create a conflict of interest. This means that employees should avoid personal interests and investments which would influence the objectivity and independence of their judgment or conduct in carrying out their duties and responsibilities to the Corporation.

As noted earlier, certain employees are canvassed periodically regarding *potential conflicts of interest.* In responding, they *should disclose any ''material interest''* [a ''material interest'' is defined as: '' . . . 2. Any interest in (including a loan to or from) a business which is not publicly owned.''] *in a supplier, customer or competitor. Any such employee who is about to acquire a material interest or investment which he or she would be required to disclose should report such proposed action in a Questionnaire.*

DEALING WITH SUPPLIERS

It is the policy of General Motors to select suppliers in a completely impartial manner on the basis of price, quality, performance and suitability of the product or service. Each employee is expected to avoid doing anything which could imply selection of a supplier on any basis other than the best interests of General Motors or which could give any supplier an improper advantage over another.

. . .

GIFTS, GRATUTIES AND PAYMENTS
United States

For many years, General Motors has had a formalized policy with regard to the giving of business gifts to employees as well as to business associates. The Corporation policy with regard to the giving or receipt of gifts and gratuities by employees provides that:

> No Corporation representative or member of his or her immediate family will give or accept any cash, gifts, special accommodations, favours or use of property or facilities to or from anyone with whom the representative does business or is negotiating business on behalf of the Corporation.

The intent of this policy is that the giving or accepting of anything of value by General Motors employees to or from any of its suppliers, dealers or customers is prohibited. Such conduct may be criminal under certain laws if done to influence an employee in the performance of his or her responsibilities. The policy, however, does not preclude gifts of items of nominal value. Such business gifts to an individual (and the individual's spouse), whether outside or Corporation personnel, shall be limited to a total cost of $25 for a year. Gifts bearing a logo, which are distributed generally and cost no more than $4, may be excluded from the $25 annual limitation.

. . .

Employees and members of their immediate families may not accept a loan or other service from a financial institution or any discount on personal purchases of products from a company which does business with General Motors, if such a situation could be construed as being offered to influence the General Motors business relationship. Any discounts or loans or other financial institution services which are made available to all General Motors employees as a general practice may be accepted. [Emphasis in original.] (at pp. 250-252)

Mr. Justice Ferguson had little difficulty in concluding that there was just cause for dismissal, reasoning as follows:

There is no doubt in my mind that the plaintiff's conduct put him in a position of conflict of interest both in the context of the employer's guidelines and under common law. There is also no doubt in my mind that this conduct was sufficient cause for dismissal. The courts have consistently treated conflict of interest as a serious matter [see *Durand v. Quaker Oats Co. of Canada Ltd.* (1990), 45 B.C.L.R. (2d) 354 (C.A.); *Syndmiller v. Dome Petroleum Ltd.* (1986), 43 Alta. L.R. (2d) 392 (C.A.); *Ennis v. C.I.B.C.* (1986), 13 C.C.E.L. 25 (B.C.S.C.); *Snider v. N.B. Telephone Co.* (1987), 78 N.B.R. (2d) 266 (C.A.)].

However, because the plaintiff contested this characterization so vigorously I shall comment briefly on some of the evidence he relied on.

He claimed that he didn't think there was anything wrong with what he had done. I find that his understanding or recognition of what constituted a conflict is not determinative. The conduct should be viewed objectively [see *Snider v. N.B. Telephone Co., supra*]. It may be that in some circumstances the employee's understanding could be a mitigating factor but not in this case because I find that he did understand the impropriety of his conduct even though he may not have appreciated its gravity.

While there is no proof that the conflict resulted in the conferral of any benefit on G & R or in a quantifiable loss to GM, this is irrelevant [see *Marks v. Addison On Bay Ltd.* (1991), 38 C.C.E.L. 291 (Ont. Gen. Div.); *Duguay v. Maritime Welding & Rentals Ltd.* (1989), 28 C.C.E.L. 126 (N.B.Q.B.); *Laverty v. Cooper Plating Inc.* (1987), 17 C.C.E.L. 44 (Ont. Dist. Ct.)]. Dismissal is justified because the employee's conduct constitutes disloyalty and infidelity sufficient to warrant a loss of trust and confidence by the employer [see *Durand v. Quaker Oats Co. of Canada Ltd., supra*]. As the guidelines make clear, even the appearance of impropriety of this kind is to be avoided.

. . . .

The plaintiff contended that he had no influence over what GM ordered from G & R and therefore he could not be in a "real" conflict. There are two issues here. First, I find on the evidence that the plaintiff was in a position to directly or indirectly influence the timing, the quantity and the choice of products supplied by G & R. Second, the extent of his influence is not material [see *Duguay v. Maritime Welding*

& Rentals Ltd. (1989), 28 C.C.E.L. 126 (N.B.Q.B.) at p. 131]. Even if he had no such potential influence his conduct would justify dismissal. (at pp. 254-255)

It is, however, always important to have regard to the facts of the particular case. In *Atkins v. Windsor Star (The)* (1994), 2 C.C.E.L. (2d) 229 (Ont. Gen. Div.), the employee had been employed for nine years selling advertising space for The Windsor Star. The plaintiff's hobby was bass fishing and he and his brother created the ''Professional Bass Fisherman Association'' and circulated a publication which contained advertising. All of the work by the plaintiff was done after hours and potential advertisers were identified from the Yellow Pages.

There was clearly a conflict of interest to the extent that certain of the advertisers in the plaintiff's publication were also advertisers in The Windsor Star and were serviced by the plaintiff. The plaintiff acknowledged that his contact with these advertisers on behalf of The Windsor Star facilitated his solicitations for his own publication. Further, the plaintiff was aware that The Windsor Star published a supplement every spring dealing with recreational activities including fishing, with a view to attracting additional advertising revenue. The plaintiff received approximately $12,000 in advertising revenue and distributed 50,000 copies of the publication in the City of Windsor. In comparison, the plaintiff's annual advertising sales on behalf of The Windsor Star were $600,000, and the annual advertising revenue of The Windsor Star was in the range of $30 million.

The advertising director of The Windsor Star received a copy of the plaintiff's publication at his home and the plaintiff was terminated.

The Court rejected the defence of ''just cause'' holding that:

> I can find nothing dishonest in Mr. Atkins' activities. In his view he was simply promoting a recreational activity or recreational organization, and was carefully doing it on his own time without using or interfering with any of the resources of the employer. I have no evidence that the ads Atkins obtained reduced or interfered with the advertising revenue of the Star. Even if a conclusion could be reached, that some of the advertising revenue received by Atkins would have, without his efforts, gone to the Star, nevertheless in comparison with the total revenues of the Star, such amounts would have been trifling or inconsequential.
>
> In my view, seen objectively, if publication of this tabloid had continued on a regular recurring basis, there was a potential for meaningful revenue loss to the Star, and thus for conflict. Further, there was a potential for other employees to follow Atkins' lead. However, it was totally unnecessary, and perhaps counterproductive, for the Star to attempt to stem such competition by discharging Mr. Atkins. Surely if he had been told, in no uncertain terms, that a recurrence would result in his termination, the threat would have been removed. (at p. 235)

4.4 DISMISSAL OF PROBATIONARY EMPLOYEES

(a) Meaning of Probationary Employee and Probationary Period

When a probationary period is stipulated, it is almost always a requirement imposed upon new employees. A question may arise, however, with respect to whether a probationary period may be imposed upon regular employees, after a period of non-probationary employment, due to some shortcoming in their performance. The question of putting regular employees on probation is discussed separately in Chapter 4.4(d), and the discussion in Chapter 4.4(a) and (b) is concerned only with new employees.

In *Mitchell v. R.* (1979), 23 O.R. (2d) 65 (H.C.), Madame Justice Van Camp offered the following definition of a probationary employee:

> [T]he term is well understood in business and industry as an employee who is being tested to enable the employer to ascertain the suitability of the employee for its purposes. Probation is a period when the employee may prove that he is suitable for regular employment as a permanent employee and will meet the standards set by the employer. . . . (at p. 83)

This definition was adopted by Mr. Justice Noble in *Ritchie v. Intercontinental Packers Ltd.* (1982), 2 C.C.E.L. 147, 16 B.L.R. 74, 14 Sask. R. 206 (Q.B.), hereinafter discussed in some detail.

The related term, "probationary period", was defined in *Roy v. Beresford, Nigadoo, Petit-Rocher & Pointe-Verte Regional Police Comm.* (1986), 15 C.C.E.L. 167, 72 N.B.R. (2d) 19, 183 A.P.R. 19 (Q.B.), as follows:

> At the root of the matter lies the question: what is meant by probationary period? Is it not a stated period of hiring during which a candidate to a particular vacancy is tested by an employer in order to assess his ability to meet the requirements of that position? (at p. 173)

The precise duties and obligations during the probationary period depend upon what has actually been agreed to by the parties. One aspect of the probationary period that should be addressed is whether the employee is to be allowed all, or a substantial part, of the probationary period to demonstrate his or her worth. In the alternative, the employer can reserve the right to dismiss at any time during the probationary period without notice or pay in lieu thereof, subject to having just cause for the dismissal.

Stephens v. Morris Rod Weeder Co. (1989), 27 C.C.E.L. 92, 76 Sask. R. 20 (Q.B.), is an example of a situation in which the Court found that the contractual term relating to the probationary period contemplated that the plaintiff would be entitled to all, or virtually all, of the probationary period to demonstrate his capability. In *Stephens*, the plaintiff had received several verbal and written warnings concerning his lateness and absenteeism. As a result, the defendant demoted the plaintiff and placed him on three months' probation. While the Court questioned whether the defendant had the right to unilaterally impose a probationary period, it found that the plaintiff accepted the demotion. The employer's policy manual, however, provided that in the event of a transfer, an employee was to be given a 90-day trial period "to prove his ability to perform the job." One month into the probationary period, the plaintiff was terminated on the grounds that his attitude to his work had not improved.

The Court reasoned as follows:

> In my judgment, fairness dictated that whatever the manner the 3-month term was put into place, the plaintiff could expect to be given a reasonable time to show that he could meet the requirements of his new assignment. A probationary employee is one who is being tested to enable the employer to ascertain the suitability of the employee for its purposes. Probation is a period when the employee may prove that he is suitable for regular employment as a permanent employee and will meet the standards as set by the employer: *Mitchell v. R.*, 23 O.R. (2d) 65, [1979] 1 A.C.W.S. 227 (H.C.). I have already given my assessment of the two incidents given by Tornberg as the main reason for terminating the plaintiff. In my view, the defendant did not have reasonable and probable grounds to conclude after but 1 month into the term of probation that the plaintiff would in fact be unable to perform the work in the position to which he was transferred. Indeed, the plaintiff was told on December 3, 1985, ''you will be on a 3 months probation period, during which time your performance will be reviewed.
>
> So the plaintiff was entitled to the whole of the probationary period — 3 months in any event — to show that he was capable of doing the job. (at p. 100)

The standard of just cause for the dismissal of a probationary employee is discussed in the following section.

(b) Just Cause for Dismissal of Probationary Employees

His Honour Judge Fanjoy, in *Cornell v. Rogers Cablesystems Inc.* (1987), 17 C.C.E.L. 232, 87 C.L.L.C. 14,054 (Ont. Dist. Ct.), summarized the law as follows:

> What is the duty of an employer to a probationary employee in the circumstances? This has been referred to in many reported cases; however, a good summary is contained in the judgment of Jewers Co. Ct. J. in *Kirby v. Motor Coach Industries Ltd.* (1980), 6 Man. R. (2d) 395 (Man. Co. Ct.) [reversed (1981), 10 Man. R. (2d) 36, 81 C.L.L.C. 14,138 (*sub nom. Motor Coach Industries Ltd. v. Kirby* (Man. C.A.)] when he says at p. 404-5:
>
> 1. The onus is upon an employer to show that it has ''just cause'' to discharge even a probationary employee;
> 2. ''Just cause'' may be that the employee is, in the opinion of the employer, unsuitable for a job;
> 3. The unsuitability which would justify the termination of a probationary employee may go beyond those grounds which might support the discharge of a regular employee, and may include such considerations as character, compatibility, as well as ability to meet the present and future production standards expected by the employer. (See *Brown and Beatty* (*supra*) page 391);
> 4. Where a probationer has been terminated for unsuitability, the employer's judgment and discretion in the matter cannot be questioned, . . .
> 5. All of the foregoing is subject to the requirement of the employer showing that the discharge was in the bona fide exercise of the employer's discretion and judgment that the employee was not suitable and not for some other reason or improper motive which would not justify a dismissal.
>
> I would add that the employer must act fairly and with reasonable diligence in determining the employee's suitability. In this case, the November 8 memo from

> Mr. Pickles to the plaintiff was a frank warning with respect to the plaintiff's deficiencies and was given for the purpose of assisting the plaintiff in making the adjustment necessary to perform the duties for the position. It was not "out of the blue"; continual suggestions, advice and assistance had been given throughout by Mr. Pickles. (at pp. 236-237)

Reference may also be made to the case of *Ritchie v. Intercontinental Packers Ltd.* (1982), 2 C.C.E.L. 147, 16 B.L.R. 74, 14 Sask. R. 206 (Q.B.). The plaintiff was hired as a "manager of human resource services" in the defendant's plant. His responsibilities included the determination of personnel policies, settlement of union grievances and the motivation of staff. He was one of three people, in a plant of over 800 employees, who reported directly to the president.

The plaintiff understood that he was hired subject to a six-month probationary period. During this time he was found to be unsuitable for permanent employment because of complaints that he was arrogant, abrasive and had acted unilaterally without consulting his supervisors. Mr. Justice Noble noted that, traditionally,

> [t]he common law gave a probationary employee little or no rights to recover damages if dismissed by his employer during or at the end of the period of probation. (at p. 150)

Mr. Justice Noble observed that, more recently,

> the law governing the subject appears to have entered a discernable state of flux away from the unfettered discretion of the employer towards an attitude of greater fairness in dismissing the probationary employee. (at p. 150)

Noble J. rejected the defence submission that an employer was entitled to dismiss a probationer without notice or cause except if it be shown that the employer acted on an improper motive (*Markey v. Port Weller Dry Docks Ltd.*, (1974), 4 O.R. (2d) 12 (Co. Ct.)).

Noting that there was little judicial discussion directly on point, Noble J. found support in the Supreme Court of Canada judgments in *Nicholson v. Haldimand-Norfolk Commissioners of Police*, [1979] 1 S.C.R. 311, 78 C.L.L.C. 14,181, 88 D.L.R. (3d) 671, 23 N.R. 410, and *A.G. Can. v. Public Service Staff Relations Bd.*, (*sub nom. Jacmain v. A.G. Can.*) [1987] 2 S.C.R. 15, 78 C.L.L.C. 14,117, 81 D.L.R. (3d) 1, 18 N.R. 361. While recognizing that these decisions involved public service employees governed by statute, Noble J. stressed the Supreme Court's inclusion of probationary employees among those persons to whom fairness is owed.

In dismissing the action, Noble J. summarized the employer's discretion, in dealing with probationary employees, as follows:

> . . . Thus where such an employee is fired, it seems to me that the only onus that rests on an employer to justify the dismissal, is that he show the Court he acted fairly and with reasonable diligence in determining whether or not the proposed employee was suitable in the job for which he was being tested. So long as the probationary employee is given a reasonable opportunity to demonstrate his ability

to meet the standards the employer sets out when he is hired, including not only a testing of his skills, but also his ability to work in harmony with others, his potential usefulness to the employer in the future, and such other factors as the employer deems essential to the viable performance of the position, then he has no complaint. As for the employer, he cannot be held liable if his assessment

(*Continued on page 4-61*)

of the probationary employees' suitability for the job is based on such criteria and a fair and reasonable determination of the question. In my opinion the law does not require the employer to do anything more. (at p. 153)

(c) Entitlement to Notice in the Event of Termination Without Just Cause

In *Roy v. Beresford, Nigadoo, Petit-Rocher & Pointe-Verte Regional Police Comm.* (1986), 15 C.C.E.L. 167, 72 N.B.R. (2d) 19, 183 A.P.R. 19 (Q.B.), the Court stated that:

> Whether the label used is "wrongful dismissal" or "wrongful refusal", the end result is the same: effectively, employment is terminated. In both instances, the measure of damages which flows therefrom should be based on compensation in lieu of notice. (at p. 175)

Mr. Justice Huband, however, in *Kirby v. Motor Coach Industries Ltd.* (1981), 1 C.C.E.L. 260, 81 C.L.L.C. 14,138, 10 Man. R. (2d) 36 (C.A.), held that probationary status must be considered in assessing the period of reasonable notice:

> At the very least the plaintiff's probationary status has an effect on the length of notice. What constitutes reasonable notice for a probationary employee may well be insufficient for a regular employee. In the instant case, probationary status is reflected in the magnitude of compensation in lieu of notice. Probationary status is one of the circumstances to take into account in assessing appropriate compensation. (at pp. 265-266)

It is, however, submitted that probationary status should be given little, if any, weight in determining the period of reasonable notice. An employer can discharge a probationary employee by meeting a minimal just cause requirement. If, however, an employer cannot establish just cause, this often means that the employer did not even make a good faith effort to assess the suitability of the employee or allowed an improper motive to taint the decision. In such a case it does not seem to make sense to further reduce what is already a relatively slight notice entitlement by reason only of the fact that the employee was terminated during a probationary period.

(d) Placing Permanent Employees on Probation

As already noted, probationary status is most commonly imposed on new employees. *Buckle v. Mother Parker's Foods Ltd.* (1985), 7 C.C.E.L. 119 (Ont. Dist. Ct.), affirmed (1986), 11 C.C.E.L. 299, 8 C.P.C. (2d) 265, 15 O.A.C. 116 (Div. Ct.), however, dealt with a situation in which a permanent employee was placed on probation. In this case, the plaintiff began having increasing trouble performing the work required of him. The plaintiff accepted the imposition of probationary status and understood that if his performance did not improve his position would be terminated in three months. The plaintiff, however, was terminated before the expiry of the three-month period.

Mr. Justice Trotter of the Ontario District Court found that the plaintiff's employment "was terminated without just cause or proper motive and without reasonable notice" (at p. 124) and awarded damages for wrongful dismissal.

An appeal to the Divisional Court was dismissed, with the Court stating that:

> In accepting the probation, he accepted its terms, but was entitled to rely on having the opportunity to show during the 3-month period that he was capable of doing the job. When he was terminated before the expiration of the 3-month period, because he asked for a vacation, he was denied that opportunity. This denial constituted a breach of the terms of the probationary employment, and the employee was then entitled to at least the same period of notice as that to which he would have been entitled if he had treated the relegation to probationary status as a constructive dismissal. (at p. 300)

In summary, it is submitted that:

1. The parties are generally free to contract on whatever terms they choose. As a result, it is open to a regular employee, as in *Buckle*, to agree to revert to a probationary status, or to accept probationary status as being incidental to the acceptance of a new position.
2. In the absence of agreement by the employee, the employer has no right to unilaterally cause a regular employee to revert to probationary status. In this regard it is difficult enough to define just cause for regular and probationary employees. It seems pointless to attempt a further definition of cause that would justify the relegation of a regular employee to probationary status. Further, to permit an employer to relegate a regular employee to probationary status, based on grounds that would be less stringent than just cause for the dismissal of a regular employee, allows the employer to accomplish indirectly what cannot be done directly. Once the employee is relegated to probationary status it is relatively easy to meet the just cause standard for probationary employees. In simple terms, the regular employee would be out the door, without further obligation on the part of the employer, without the appropriate just cause standard for a regular employee ever having been met. In conclusion, therefore, the unilateral imposition of a probationary term by the employer should generally be regarded as an act of constructive dismissal. (See Chapter 5.1(a), "Constructive Dismissal – General Principles").
3. Having regard to the foregoing, an employer should not attempt to relegate regular employees to probationary status. Very few employees will agree to accept probationary status since it is clearly against their interests to do so. Even those who appear to agree may argue, after they have been terminated, that their apparent agreement was involuntary. The better course for an employer is to issue an explicit warning to unsatisfactory employees that their employment will be terminated within a certain period if their performance does not improve. The employer must, however, still meet the just cause standard for a regular employee.

5
CONSTRUCTIVE DISMISSAL

5.1 GENERAL PRINCIPLES

There are circumstances in which the employer, although not acting explicitly to terminate a person's employment, acts unilaterally to alter the employment terms and conditions such that the employee is entitled to regard the employer's conduct as a termination, and so bring an action for wrongful dismissal. In other words, the conduct of the employer amounts to a repudiation of the employment contract, which the employee may act on by bringing the contract to an end and suing for damages for wrongful dismissal.

The classic explanation of what constitutes a repudiation of the contract is set out in *Rubel Bronze & Metal Co. v. Vos* (1917), [1918] 1 K.B. 315, as follows:

> Dismissal may be effected by conduct as well as words. A man may dismiss his servant if he refuses by word or conduct to allow the servant to fulfil his contract of employment. The refusal must of course be substantial in the sense that it is not a mere repudiation of some minor rights of the servant or of non-vital provisions of the contract of employment. The question is ever one of degree. If the conduct of the employer amounts to a basic refusal to continue the servant on the agreed terms of the employment, then there is at once a wrongful dismissal and a repudiation of the contract. I see no distinction in such a case as the present between repudiation by the defendants of their contractual obligations and "a wrongful dismissal" in the ordinary sense of that phrase. (at p. 323)

In *Dauphinee v. Major Foods Ltd.* (1983), 56 N.S.R. (2d) 517, 117 A.P.R. 517 (T.D.), affirmed (1984), 62 N.S.R. (2d) 381, 136 A.P.R. 381 (C.A.), Mr. Justice Natherson summarized the law of constructive dismissal as follows:

> Constructive dismissal arises from the failure of the employer to live up to the essential obligations of the contract of employment in existence between the employer and the employee. (at p. 528)

In addition, Natherson J. quoted with approval the following statement:

> An employer's refusal to fulfill the essential terms of the employment contract releases the employee from his obligation to perform under the contract of employment. The employer's breach of that contract must be fundamental if it, coupled with the resignation of the employee, is to be treated as constructive dismissal. In such circumstances, the employer is viewed as having repudiated the contract by his behaviour. Accordingly, the employee's resignation is seen in the eyes of the law as a dismissal forced by the employer and not a voluntary act of resignation. The employee will be treated in all respects as if he was subject to a wrongful dismissal by the employer. . . . (at p. 528)

In *Smith v. Viking Helicopter Ltd.* (1989), 24 C.C.E.L. 113, 68 O.R. (2d) 228, 31 O.A.C. 368 (C.A.), the employee claimed that he had been constructively dismissed, as a result of the amalgamation of two corporate offices. His allegation was based upon two incidents: the movement of the company from Ottawa to St. Clet, Quebec and his meeting with a person in the Quebec office who performed the same tasks which he performed, from which he inferred that his position was redundant. Added to these incidents was a general lack of information from the defendant as to what moving expenses it was going to cover for its Ottawa employees. Mr. Justice Finlayson, as to the general principle of constructive dismissal, stated:

> In my opinion a damage action for constructive dismissal must be founded on conduct by the employer and not simply on the perception of that conduct by the employee. The employer must be responsible for some objective conduct which constitutes a fundamental change in employment or a unilateral change of a significant term of that employment. A decision to change its manner of conducting business or a move to another place of business does not necessarily result in such a fundamental breach of its contract with its employees as to constitute a constructive dismissal. See *Cdn. Bechtel Ltd. v. Mollenkopf* (1978), 1 C.C.E.L. 95 (Ont. C.A.) at p. 98:
>
> > The evidence led in this respect may have been relevant on the issue as to whether the assignment to new responsibilities was made in good faith and not as a disguised means of discharging the plaintiff. However, even if the jury were of the view that Inco's complaints about the plaintiff were unjustified, and the employer erred in its assessment of the plaintiff's capabilities, such a finding would not be decisive. The plaintiff had no vested right in the particular job initially given to him. If the employer, although mistaken, acted in good faith and in the protection of its own business interests, the plaintiff would have had no right to refuse the transfer. (at pp. 116-117)

Therefore, constructive dismissal allegations will be viewed by the Court in an objective manner.

Similarly, in *Islip v. Northmount Food Services Ltd.* (1988), 20 C.C.E.L.

250 (B.C.C.A.), the Court ruled that an employee's subjective impression of his employer's intent did not justify a finding of constructive dismissal. The employee joined the employer in 1981, and was entitled under his contract to a bonus based on profit sharing. For each of two years he received $25,000 in addition to his salary. This sum appears to have been treated as though it were the employee's share of the company profits.

In 1984 the employer experienced some business reversals. The former president died unexpectedly and the new president, who had not been present when the employee's remuneration was set, instituted changes which did not please the plaintiff. Not least of these was the termination of the profit-sharing plan. Instead, a discretionary bonus of $3,000 was awarded for 1984. The plaintiff was also asked to move to a smaller office and to make detailed reports of his sales efforts. The plaintiff alleged that these changes amounted to constructive dismissal.

Mr. Justice Lambert, for the Court, gave the following reasons for upholding the trial judgment and dismissing the plaintiff's action:

> Having eliminated from consideration the change of office location, the change in formalized reporting requirements and the business trip as not being sufficiently significant either in themselves or together to constitute a fundamental breach of the contract of employment, the trial Judge turned then to the question of the character of the two payments of $25,000 that had been made, one in 1982 and one in 1983. If the contract of employment was to the effect that the plaintiff was to receive $25,000 extra to his monthly salary each year of his employment, then the trial Judge considered that the refusal or failure to pay that in 1984 would have been a fundamental breach of the contract of employment entitling the plaintiff to accept the repudiation and to sue for wrongful constructive dismissal. If, on the other hand, the $25,000 was payment to which the plaintiff was not entitled as a term of his employment because it was conditional in some way or because it was discretionary, then the trial Judge concluded, in my opinion correctly, that the failure to pay that amount, if it was not shown to be in breach of a condition, did not constitute a repudiation of the contract by the defendant which the plaintiff could rely on to establish constructive dismissal.
>
> The trial Judge in his reasons discussed some of the evidence, but not every item of the evidence, that dealt with the question of the characteristics of the payments of $25,000 each, and what implication could be drawn from those payments with respect to the terms of the contract of employment. (at p. 254)
>
> . . . .
>
> It is not open to this Court to reassess the whole body of evidence that was before the trial Judge. The only question that we are permitted to ask is whether the trial Judge was clearly wrong in the overall assessment that he made. The conclusion that the trial Judge reached was that the plaintiff had failed to establish that there was a term of his contract of employment that entitled him to be paid the additional $25,000 each year, no matter what the fortunes of the company were. In my opinion, it is not possible for this Court to say that the trial Judge was clearly wrong in that conclusion. For that reason I would not accede to the first ground of appeal.

The second ground of appeal was stated in this way by the appellant's counsel:

> The trial judge erred in failing to consider Mrs. Mueller's intention to terminate the plaintiff's employment, when considering whether the cumulative effect of the alterations made to the terms of the plaintiff's employment amounted to constructive dismissal.

In support of the necessity to consider the intention of the defendant or the guiding mind of the defendant, counsel for the appellant relied on this passage from the reasons of Mr. Justice Wallace in *Longman v. Federal Business Development Bank* (1982), 36 B.C.L.R. 115 at 131, 131 D.L.R. (3d) 533 (B.S. S.C.):

> Further, whether or not the breach of the implied term, as in the case of any other term of the contract, constitutes a repudiation of the contract depends on the nature and degree of seriousness of the breach, the intention of the parties and the prevailing circumstances.

In my opinion, Mr. Justice Wallace has summarized the issue of whether the breach of an implied term constitutes a repudiation in a very succinct and accurate way. The question of intention becomes relevant in two aspects. If the breach is an anticipatory breach, that is, an announcement of an intention to commit a breach in the future, then intention is significant. Indeed, the whole of anticipatory breach depends on a statement of intention, and so intention is relevant in that way.

Intention is also relevant in the case of an actual breach to show whether the actual breach was intentional or accidental. If it was intentional then, of course, if the breach is a fundamental term, then it would be a repudiation. If it was accidental, it might not be a repudiation, so intention is relevant in that way as well.

But the nub of the appellant's argument on this point was that a course of conduct was embarked upon by the company with the intention of causing the termination of the plaintiff's employment. Such an intention is not relevant to the question of whether there has been a fundamental breach. That depends on whether there has been an announced intention of an anticipatory breach or an actual breach. If there has been no such announced intention and no actual breach, then a generalized speculation about an intention to bring about a dismissal does not create a repudiation or give rise to a cause of action. In this case, in my opinion, the evidence in relation to intention is not sufficient in itself to give rise to the conclusion that it constituted a repudiation of the contract and, as I have said, the other actual conduct did not constitute a repudiation. (at pp. 255-256)

As well, Mr. Justice Lambert concluded that even if the termination of the profit-sharing plan constituted a breach of a term of the plaintiff's employment contract, the discretionary payment of $3,000 "was greater than the amount that would have been his share in the profit sharing bonus plan, namely, $2,800" (at p. 257). The termination of the plan could not, therefore, constitute a fundamental breach constructively dismissing the plaintiff.

In determining whether a constructive dismissal has occurred, special considerations apply to the case of an employee who is promoted, does not perform satisfactorily and is then returned to the original position. In the case of *Mifsud v. MacMillan Bathurst Inc.* (1989), 28 C.C.E.L. 228, 70 O.R. (2d) 701, 63 D.L.R. (4th) 714, 35 O.A.C. 356 (C.A.), leave to appeal to S.C.C. refused (1990), 73 O.R. (2d) x (note), 68 D.L.R. (4th) vii (note), 39 O.A.C. 153 (note), 113 N.R. 400 (note) (S.C.C.), Mifsud had been promoted from foreman to plant superintendent. The employer, after production problems occurred during the shifts when Mifsud was on duty, returned Mifsud to the position of foreman. There was no reduction in salary or benefits, only in responsibilities and prestige. The Court of Appeal reasoned that while the change was definitely a demotion, it did not necessarily constitute a constructive dismissal, stating:

> I think it is fair to say that at the time of any promotion within an organization, if no specific agreement is reached to the contrary, the parties will have impliedly agreed that if the employee does not function adequately in the new position the employer will be able, without committing a fundamental breach to the employment contract, to return the employee within a reasonable period of time to a position similar to the one vacated. In other words, a reasonable period of probation would normally be considered a term to which the parties would have agreed had they turned their minds to the question. In this case, however, Mr. Mifsud held the position of superintendent for a period of approximately 9 years – clearly not a probationary period. He was then demoted and required to work at another location within the organization. The initial question is, "Was there an implied term of the employment contract that if at any time the company validly considered Mr. Mifsud's performance to be unsatisfactory it could, without his concurrence, demote him, as it did, to a position of lesser responsibility, but equal pay?" I believe that had the parties considered this question at the time of Mr. Mifsud's promotion to superintendent, they would have so agreed. Such an agreement would have protected the company's future position, and Mr. Mifsud would likely have assumed that his performance would continue to satisfy his employer as it had in the past. (at pp. 235-236)

Mifsud, however, was not awarded damages as he had failed, in not accepting the demoted position, to mitigate his losses. The obligation of the employee to accept a lesser position in mitigation of damages is discussed in Chapter 6.3(c).

In considering an allegation of constructive dismissal there are three questions:

1. What are the terms of the particular contract of employment?
2. Has the employer breached the contract of employment?
3. If there has been a breach of the employment contract, is it such a serious and deliberate breach that it amounts to a repudiation of the contract by the employer?

One would think that a situation of constructive dismissal that, having regard to the aforesaid quotations, involves a failure or refusal of the employer to fulfil the essential terms of the employment contract, would by definition exclude any obligation on the part of the employee to accept a lesser position by way of mitigation of damages. There are, however, certain cases in which the courts have held that an employee has an obligation to accept a lesser position with an employer as a means of mitigating damages, notwithstanding the fact that the demotion constitutes a constructive dismissal. The obligation of the employee to accept a lesser position in mitigation of damages is discussed in Chapter 6.3(c).

Faced with a change that may amount to a constructive dismissal, an employee may be concerned that acceptance of the position in order to mitigate damages will be viewed as an acceptance or waiver of the right to allege constructive dismissal. In *Cayen v. Woodwards Stores Ltd.* (1993), 45 C.C.E.L. 264, 75 B.C.L.R. (2d) 110, [1993] 4 W.W.R. 11, 100 D.L.R. (4th) 294, 22 B.C.A.C. 32, 38 W.A.C. 32 (C.A.), the Court found that the legal and practical considerations that cause an employee to incline to accept a new position as a means of mitigating damages make it unlikely that such conduct will be viewed as a waiver. In this regard, the Court observed:

> I understand the foregoing might sometimes impose a difficult evidence burden upon an employee who accepts a new position in order to mitigate and who then or later alleges constructive dismissal. Such an employee might then be faced with an argument that she has waived her right to claim that she has been constructively dismissed.
>
> In my judgment, a very heavy burden would rest upon the employer to show that there was a real waiver, regardless of whether constructive dismissal was asserted at the time of transfer or not. At the end of the day, however, the question of whether the employer has repudiated the employment will be a question of fact to be decided upon a consideration of all of the circumstances. But the employer cannot have it both ways, that is mitigation and waiver, and it will be rare indeed when an employer will succeed on a plea of waiver after an employee has mitigated his or her damages after accepting a new position. It would be different, of course, if the employee continues in the new employment after the expiration of a reasonable period roughly equivalent to what the law would impose by way of reasonable notice. (at p. 275)

In order to understand the general principle it is helpful to consider the different types of changes that can constitute constructive dismissal. It must be borne in mind, however, that since the results in each case depend upon the terms of the particular contract, one cannot generalize. Thus, there is no legal principle that determines what kinds of changes in job description, or in geographic location are, or are not, permissible. In each case the question is what, if anything, the parties have agreed to with respect to the subject matter of the proposed change. Having stated that qualification, it may be of assistance to consider the reported cases grouped according to the type of proposed change in issue.

5.2 CHANGE IN JOB DESCRIPTION

In many cases a threshold question will arise as to whether the employee was hired to do one particular job or whether the employer enjoys the latitude to assign the employee suitable alternative duties.

At one extreme is *Brown v. Can. Biscuit Co.*, 8 M.P.R. 102, [1934] 3 D.L.R. 216 (N.B. C.A.), reversed [1935] S.C.R. 212, [1935] 2 D.L.R. 81, in which the Supreme Court of Canada upheld a trial decision in which the charge to the jury stated in part:

> If a person undertakes to do certain work for another person for hire, for reward, well then he is entitled to insist that he shall do that work alone; that is when a person is hired under a definite capacity, specified and unequivocal, well then he may not be forced under that contract to do anything else; he can legally and lawfully refuse to do anything else but what he undertook to do under his contract. (quoted at p. 111, N.B.C.A. decision).

The authority of the trial Judge's statement of the law was somewhat qualified by Chief Justice Duff, who stated (at D.L.R. p. 83) that certain aspects of the charge might "convey a false impression" if taken out of context. It is, however, consistent with the general principles set out that if an employee is, in fact, hired to do one particular job, then he is entitled to insist upon that job.

It is suggested, however, that it is unlikely that the Court would find that an employee was hired for one particular job, in the absence of clear and unequivocal evidence. In practical terms such a term prevents the employer from adapting to changed circumstances. Further, to the extent that broad experience in a business is a prerequisite to advancement, such a term would work against the employee.

In most cases, where there is no compelling evidence as to the agreement or intent of the parties, the decisions suggest that an employer does have the right to alter the responsibilities of an employee. In *Buchanan v. Can. Valve Inc.* (1987), 17 C.C.E.L. 273, 59 O.R. (2d) 681, 39 D.L.R. (4th) 268 (H.C.), the Court stated as follows:

> It is not necessary to engage in a review of the cases on constructive dismissal due to demotion. It goes without saying that, unless it amounts to an unwarranted demotion, an employer is entitled to change the responsibilities of its executives: see, for example, *Gillespie v. Ont. Motor League Toronto Club*, Ont. H.C., Eberle J., March 4, 1980, and *MacKenzie v. Ralston Purina Canada Ltd.*, Ont. H.C., O'Leary J., June 3, 1981. A sideways move is not necessarily a demotion: see the decision of the British Columbia Court of Appeal in *Reber v. Lloyds Bank Int. Can.* (1985), 7 C.C.E.L. 98, 61 B.C.L.R. 361, 18 D.L.R. (4th) 122. The general principle has been stated by Rutherford J. in *Tymrick v. Viking Helicopters Ltd.* (1985), 6 C.C.E.L. 225 at 230 (Ont. H.C.), as follows: "I think it is clear law that an employer is to be allowed a certain degree of latitude with respect to upward and lateral promotions; not every change in the terms of employment constitutes constructive dismissal." (at p. 278)

A discussion of several cases will help illustrate the applicable principles. *O'Grady v. Insurance Corp. of B.C.* (1975), 63 D.L.R. (3d) 370 (B.C. S.C.), is a case in which the Court tended to the view that the employee was entitled to do one particular job. The plaintiff, a solicitor, had enjoyed the position of secretary and general counsel and as such reported to the general manager and to the board of directors of the defendant. As a result of a corporate reorganization, the plaintiff was offered the position of senior counsel to a division of the defendant reporting to a vice-president who in turn reported to the general manager. The reorganization, however, did not change the plaintiff's income or fringe benefits, and the plaintiff continued to be the senior lawyer in the employ of the defendant.

The Court found that the new position was subordinate to and markedly different in scope from the prior position, and such that the plaintiff would suffer a "serious loss of status and prestige" by accepting the new employment (at p. 378). As a result the Court found that there had been a constructive dismissal.

The *O'Grady* decision was interpreted, or misinterpreted, as suggesting that:

(*Continued on page 5-7*)

1. employees generally had the right to do their own job and no other;
2. any adverse change in the employment contract would be viewed as a demotion and amount to constructive dismissal;
3. an employee could not be obliged to accept a position that would involve a loss of status or prestige or that would cause embarrassment to the employee.

Longman v. Federal Business Development Bank (1982), 36 B.C.L.R. 115, 131 D.L.R. (3d) 533 (S.C.), however, marked a retreat from these interpretations, or misinterpretations, of *O'Grady*. In this case the employer accommodated requests by the employee for a transfer to British Columbia despite the fact that there was no suitable permanent position available at the time of transfer. The employee was placed in a position which was inferior to his prior position with the bank in that:

1. the job title given the employee had less "official status" and prestige than his previous title;
2. the employee would be required to report to a person who had previously been junior to him in the bank hierarchy;
3. although no salary reduction was imposed, the new position was in a lower salary range.

Mr. Justice Wallace found, however, that there were other aspects of the position that were equivalent to, or even superior to, the former position of the employee. Wallace J. distinguished *O'Grady* on the basis that O'Grady had been engaged as the secretary and general counsel of the company and that was the only position that he had agreed to accept. In contrast,

> [i]t is different where an employee has not been hired for a specific position but has entered the company's employment, usually without any express contract, at a very junior position presumably in the hope that he would prosper and be promoted as time goes by and—from the employer's point of view—that he would become a skilled, experienced employee who would benefit the company. In such instances, one must look at all the circumstances to determine the terms of the employment contract. (at p. 124)

Mr. Justice Wallace began his analysis by noting that, as in virtually all cases in which the parties do not have a written employment contract, there was no express contractual term as to the changes that could, or would not, be implemented by the employer. Wallace J. then quoted a number of leading authorities, including the following passage from *Trollope & Colls Ltd. v. North West Metropolitan Regional Hospital Bd.*, [1973] 2 All E.R. 260, [1973] 1 W.L.R. 601 at 609 (H.L.), in which Lord Pearson stated:

> The court's function is to interpret and apply the contract which the parties have made for themselves. If the express terms are perfectly clear and free from ambiguity, there is no choice to be made between different possible meanings: the clear terms must be applied even if the court thinks some other terms would have

been more suitable. An unexpressed term can be implied if and only if the court finds that the parties must have intended that term to form part of their contract: it is not enough for the court to find that such a term would have been adopted by the parties as reasonable men if it had been suggested to them: it must have been a term that went without saying, a term *necessary* to give business efficacy to the contract, a term which, though tacit, formed part of the contract which the parties made for themselves. (quoted at (B.C.L.R.) p. 127)

Mr. Justice Wallace then stated:

Applying the "bystander" test to the instant case, one who asks, "What will happen if—in arranging a transfer at an employee's request to a regional office, where there is not a comparable opening available, a position is created to accommodate both the employee and the employer—certain aspects of the new position carry less prestige than the employee had previously enjoyed?"

One may speculate on the variety of responses such a question might elicit. The employer might reply, "It will depend on the circumstances—we will do the best we can for our employee—but he will have to cooperate and put up with certain aspects of the transfer that may not be to his liking." On the other hand, the employee might well agree to such conditions when engaged and later, having acquired certain status, might well take exception to status changes being effected without his consent.

I find it difficult to envisage *both* parties, at the time of the engagement, immediately responding, "Oh, on such a transfer, or indeed, at any time there is a change in position, the employee's salary, status, title, responsibilities or duties, including to whom he reports, will not be in any way diminished from that of the position he holds at the time of the transfer". (at pp. 127-128)

. . . .

I am of the opinion it is not necessary for the business efficacy of this contract to imply a term that an employee will not, under any circumstances, be appointed by management to a position in any way inferior to the position held at the time of the appointment. Nor can I conceive that, if someone suggested such a term to the parties, the defendant corporation would have agreed to it. (at p. 129)

Mr. Justice Wallace then concluded that:

On all of the evidence, I cannot find an implied term prohibiting such a partial diminution in the employee's status incidental to effecting a transfer requested by the employee. Accordingly, I do not find that the employer, taking the steps described to effect the plaintiff's transfer to British Columbia, committed a breach of the plaintiff's employment contract.

If I am in error in reaching this conclusion, then it is my opinion that the degree of the breach in the circumstances of this case did not constitute a repudiation of the contract by the defendant. I find the bank did not, at any time, indicate an unqualified refusal to perform their obligations under the contract but rather made every effort to accommodate the plaintiff's wishes. In my view, the plaintiff's action in view of the extent to which the bank had attempted to satisfy his request for a transfer within the structure of the regional office, was indeed precipitous. The plaintiff erred in construing minor aspects of the new position as a repudiation by the bank of its contract. Had he settled down to do a

> job in British Columbia, I have no doubt the parties would have been successful in revising those minor aspects of the new position with which he did not find satisfaction. It was the plaintiff's attitude and action that negated this possibility. (at pp. 132-133)

A majority of the British Columbia Court of Appeal approved of the legal analysis in *Longman*, and applied it in *Reber v. Lloyds Bank International Can.* (1985), 7 C.C.E.L. 98, 61 B.C.L.R. 361, 18 D.L.R. (4th) 122 (C.A.), to dismiss a claim for constructive dismissal. The employer had offices throughout the world and from the time the employee joined the employer in 1974, until 1983, he had been on the "fast track" in terms of promotion. The employer, however, was dissatisfied with his performance as a branch manager in Vancouver, and decided to transfer him to an account executive position as the head of a bank division in New York. While the New York position was at the same job level it was common ground that, with the proposed transfer, Reber would no longer be on the fast track for promotion. The trial Judge had found that the New York position would involve a "humiliating loss of prestige and position." The Court of Appeal however, stated:

> The transfer from Vancouver branch to division 2B was a development which did not bode well for Mr. Reber's future advance in the bank. It does not follow that it was a demotion within the terms of the contract. There is no finding that it was a term of the contract that Mr. Reber would always advance and that the company would never effect a transfer which would reflect adversely on his prospects of future advancement. Nor can I find anything in the evidence which would justify a conclusion that that was a term of the contract. (at p. 105)

With respect to the matter of prestige and position the Court stated:

> Whether any given loss of prestige and position would be "humiliating" is something subjective to the individual suffering the loss. Some are easily humiliated - others have more fortitude in these matters. Nevertheless, it having been found as a fact that the transfer involved a loss of prestige and position, which Mr. Reber's peers would see as a demotion, does it follow that the transfer was a breach of contract going to its root? It seems clear that there was no express term of the contract that there would be no transfer involving a loss of prestige and position. Was there an implied term? (at pp. 106-107)

In allowing the appeal the Court explained that the trial Judge erred because he

> proceeded on the basis, which in my view is not supportable in law, that any transfer which involved a loss of prestige and position is a "demotion" and that nothing more is required to justify the employee in treating the contract as terminated by the act of his employer. In some respects, the proposed transfer could be seen as a demotion. It simply does not follow that it was a breach of the contract going to its root. (at p. 108)

In *Lesiuk v. B.C. Forest Products Ltd.* (1986), 15 C.C.E.L. 91, 8 B.C.L.R. (2d) 297, 33 D.L.R. (4th) 1 (C.A.), a majority of the Court found that the poor economic climate, which necessitated certain changes in job responsibilities, should be considered in determining whether there had been a constructive dismissal. In this case the employee had been employed for approximately 16 years, latterly as the project engineer responsible for new construction at the defendant's mill. In 1982 the mill closed and the plaintiff was laid off. However, the mill reopened in 1983 and the plaintiff was offered the position of plant engineer at the same salary which he had previously enjoyed. The plaintiff had held the position of plant engineer, prior to being appointed as project engineer, and as plant engineer he would be required to report to a lower level of management than previously.

In finding that there had been no constructive dismissal, a majority of the Court reasoned as follows:

> As I view this matter, to accede to the submission of the appellant on the issue of constructive dismissal would be tantamount to saying to the employer, "You must keep this man in employment as a project engineer, even though there are no funds for capital projects and, hence, no requirement for the services of a project engineer. If you do not keep him in employment in that capacity, you must pay him 18 months' salary and benefits in lieu of notice."
>
> I do not think either the law or the evidence in this case supports that conclusion. The evidence shows the employer was compelled by economic circumstances to make the management changes it did. The economic facts cannot be ignored, though they ought not to be given more than an appropriate share of consideration. With respect, I think Mr. Justice Spencer gave too little weight to that aspect and placed too much emphasis on the extent to which the plaintiff's duties were changed. (at p. 99)
>
> . . . .
>
> It was not contended the defendant could not unilaterally alter the management structure. The complaint before the trial Judge was that the plaintiff's position in the hierarchy is lower than it was before. The Judge rejected that complaint and I think he was right to do so. That leaves for consideration the changes in the plaintiff's duties. One of the contentions of the plaintiff was that he had been moved from a staff to a line position and was supervising employees doing maintenance work in a way he had not done before. Another contention was that the engineering aspect of his duties had been reduced. I do not think the plaintiff can complain of the move from a staff to a line position, which I regard as analogous to the lateral transfer which took place in *Reber*. The engineering aspect of his duties was certainly altered but that was due to the cut-back in capital projects and not because of dissatisfaction by the defendant with the plaintiff's performance as project engineer. Of necessity the emphasis shifted from expansion and large-scale renewal of plant to efficient production and maintenance.
>
> Taking all the circumstances into account, my opinion is there was not a breach by the defendant of a fundamental term of the contract of employment. I would therefore allow the cross-appeal and dismiss the action. (at p. 101)

Mr. Justice Lambert, concurring in the result, found that although in his view there had been a constructive dismissal, the plaintiff was nevertheless required to work out his period of reasonable notice in the position offered to him.

In *Merilees v. Sears Can. Inc.* (1986), 15 C.C.E.L. 302, 24 B.C.L.R. (2d) 165, 32 D.L.R. (4th) 539 (S.C.), affirmed (1988), 22 C.C.E.L. 317, 24 B.C.L.R. (2d) 172, 38 B.L.R. 118, 49 D.L.R. (4th) 453 (C.A.), the Court considered whether the imposition of a requirement that the employee work on Sunday constituted a constructive dismissal. In this case Sears had traditionally been open Monday through Saturday, and had opposed Sunday opening. In 1984, however, Sunday opening became legal in British Columbia and Sears determined that it had to open on Sunday to meet the competition. As a result, Sears assigned the employee work on Sunday, and when she declined to work on Sunday her employment was terminated.

The Court found that there had been a constructive dismissal, reasoning as follows:

> I conclude that when the plaintiff took employment on the sales floor with the defendant, the hours and days of store opening as they then were, were part of the contract of employment. The change to include Sunday as a day of work is not a trivial alteration; it is a material alteration. An employer has no right to make such an alteration: see *Hill v. Peter Gorman Ltd.* (1957), 9 D.L.R. (2d) 124 (Ont. C.A.), applied in *C.A.I.M.A.W., Loc. 14 v. Paccar of Can. Ltd.* (1986), 32 D.L.R. (4th) 523 (B.C. C.A.) [leave to appeal to the Supreme Court of Canada granted March 26, 1987 (S.C.C.)]. (at p. 306)

Again, the focus is on the terms of the particular employment contract in question. The result would, therefore, not necessarily be the same if an employee accepted employment, and was assigned to work between Monday-Saturday by an employer that was also open on Sunday. In such a case, it would be far easier to imply a term that the employee could be assigned other workdays within the normal workweek of the employer. This is, however, a matter that can be easily and clearly addressed in a written employment contract.

It bears repeating that each case will turn on factual findings as to the terms of the particular contract. There can be no sweeping legal generalization as to the applicable contractual terms. Having made that point, however, employers will find some comfort in the decision of the Ontario Court of Appeal in *Canadian Bechtel Ltd. v. Mollenkopf* (1978), 1 C.C.E.L. 95 (Ont. C.A.).

In *Bechtel*, the employee was hired as a purchasing agent and assigned duties in relation to a project which the employer had undertaken for its customer, International Nickel Company. The employer received certain complaints from the International Nickel Company regarding the employee's performance and, as a result, decided to terminate the employee's involvement with that customer, and to transfer him to its head office. There was, however, no diminution in job classification or salary. The employee refused to accept the transfer and was discharged.

The trial was held before a Judge and jury. The Court of Appeal allowed the employer's appeal on the grounds that the Judge's charge to the jury was unsatisfactory. Of particular interest, however, is the following statement by the Court of Appeal:

> However, even if the jury were of the view that Inco's complaints about the plaintiff were unjustified, and the employer erred in its assessment of the plaintiff's capabilities, such a finding would not be decisive. The plaintiff had no vested right in the particular job initially given to him. *If the employer, although mistaken, acted in good faith and in the protection of its own business interests, the plaintiff would have had no right to refuse the transfer.* (at p. 98) [emphasis added]

5.3 CHANGE IN REMUNERATION

From an employee point of view, remuneration is usually the most essential term of the employment contract. Thus, as a general rule, any unilateral change imposed which reduces the remuneration of the employee will constitute a constructive dismissal. As the law is quite clear, there have been relatively few reported cases involving a reduction in remuneration.

Oxman v. Dustbane Enterprises Ltd. (1986), 13 C.C.E.L. 209 (Ont. H.C.), reversed on other grounds (1988), 23 C.C.E.L. 157, 21 O.A.C. 154 (H.C.) is, however, typical of the sort of situation that may arise when there is a change in ownership or management. In this case the employee had traditionally enjoyed a salary, and a generous bonus plan. There was, however, a change in ownership and the new owner proposed that the employee receive a salary of $100,000, with no opportunity for bonus. At the time this offer was made the employee indicated that, by his forecast, he might earn $110,000 on the salary plus bonus plan. In any event, the employee reacted poorly to the change in compensation and ultimately resigned his employment. Thereafter, he took the position that he had been constructively dismissed.

The Court found that the proposed change in the means of compensation did not constitute a constructive dismissal, stating:

> The planned change was not designed to reduce his income nor can it reasonably be so interpreted. (Indeed the president was content to equate Oxman's salary with his own, although I do not take that as a conclusive test.) The proposal was a reasonable one intended to provide a fair substitute for the bonus system. In my opinion, on the facts of this case, this is not constructive dismissal. (at p. 231)

Any significant reduction in remuneration will, however, constitute constructive dismissal. Thus, in *Nerada v. Hobart Can. Inc.* (1982), 1 C.C.E.L. 116, 22 B.L.R. 17 (S.C.), the Court found that the act of the employer in depriving the employee of the use of a company vehicle constituted a constructive dismissal. In this regard the Court stated:

> The supplementary or fringe benefit of having the free use of a company vehicle to drive to and from work, or compensation in lieu thereof, was of significant value to the plaintiff. It was of major importance, not merely of minor importance, in considering the over-all terms of the employment contract. Its withdrawal would cause the plaintiff to incur additional annual expense of

between $2,000 and $2,500 per year, plus the cost of the acquisition of a vehicle. It was a material ingredient of the contract, and its withdrawal constituted a repudiation of the contract by the defendant. (at pp. 120-121)

In the same vein, reference may be made to *Cardwell v. Young Manufacturer Inc.* (1988), 20 C.C.E.L. 272 (Ont. Dist. Ct.). The employee was hired by the employer chain of clothing stores as a director of operations for its outlets outside Toronto. He was told that "he would receive a bonus of $1,000 a week for each week that the stores for which the plaintiff was responsible achieved a 5 per cent or higher profit" (at p. 275).

Several months later the president of the defendant, Goldgrub, met with the employee and stated, for the first time, that in order for the employee to receive the bonus, the average profitability of the stores must be at least 5% for an extended period.

Finding in favour of the employee, Judge Mandel stated:

> I have found that what was stated by Mr. Goldgrub to the plaintiff was that the plaintiff would receive a bonus of $1,000 a week for each week that the stores, for which the plaintiff was responsible, achieved 5 per cent or higher profit.
>
> This was understood by the plaintiff to mean that he earned the bonus each week if such stores achieved 5 per cent or higher profit, and not as the defendant contends that the stores must maintain a 5 per cent average for a specific period ending on the last day of February, which is what the defendant had in mind, but did not specifically inform the plaintiff of until November 24, a period in excess of 2 months after the meeting of September 11 when the agreement was struck with the plaintiff.
>
> . . . .
>
> In the case at bar the words and language spoken by Mr. Goldgrub to the defendant on December 11, 1982, concerning the bonus are clear. Such words do not, and could not, bear the interpretation put on them by the defendant. A reasonable man hearing that language would take it that the plaintiff would earn a bonus of $1,000 a week for each week that the stores, for which he was responsible, achieved a 5 per cent or higher profit. (at p. 278)

The Court concluded that:

> the change in the bonus structure, as put forth by Mr. Goldgrub on November 24, 1982, was a material change in the terms of employment, for by such change, any monies already earned by the plaintiff, could potentially be wiped out.
>
> An example of this is shown on Ex. 11, which was prepared by the defendant. For the period from October 23, 1982, to January 1, 1984, according to Ex. 11, there were 3 weeks that the stores achieved a 5 per cent or better profit.
>
> According to the agreement arrived at on September 11, 1982, between the parties, the plaintiff would have earned $3,000 for such period, if he had remained in the defendant's employment. However, during such period, the total profit percentage after deducting losses was 35.5 per cent. The period is 11 weeks so that the stores did not maintain a 5 per cent average during such period, and according to what the defendant advanced at the meeting of November 24, 1982, the plaintiff would not have been entitled to any bonus whatsoever. This is constructive dismissal. (at p. 282)

The question whether a particular change in remuneration constitutes a constructive dismissal must be considered in context. To a person earning $20,000 per year, virtually any adverse change to remuneration would constitute a constructive dismissal. At the other extreme, a person earning $200,000 per year may have to suffer significant changes in remuneration, particularly if his or her income level has been volatile and if there is a history of alterations to the compensation package. Further, the change must be considered having regard to the particular contract of employment to determine if the contract speaks to this issue. For example, a written employment agreement may expressly provide that the employee may have to accept a reduction in compensation, or such a provision may be implicit in the particular contract of employment.

5.4 CHANGE IN GEOGRAPHIC LOCATION

Questions may also arise as to the right of the employer to alter the employee's place of work. In *Smith v. Viking Helicopter Ltd.* (1989), 24 C.C.E.L. 113, 68 O.R. (2d) 228, 31 O.A.C. 368 (C.A.), the employee argued that he was constructively dismissed for a number of reasons, including the requirement that he relocate from Ottawa to St. Clet, Quebec. On the issue of change of location Mr. Justice Finlayson stated that:

> As I understand counsel for the respondent in this Court, he was of the view that the company could not relocate its business to the financial detriment of the respondent without creating a fundamental breach of its contract of employment. Consequently, the move itself was the fundamental breach. Counsel seemed to equate the terms of employment with the personal situation of the respondent, a lifelong resident of Ottawa, who had a family and a home with a mortgage. It has never been my understanding that an employee is entitled to a job for life in a place of his choosing. If he wishes to remain an employee of a given company, he must expect reasonable dislocations in that employment including the place where it is to be performed. There was no evidence in this case that Viking acted unreasonably in notifying the respondent of its intended move or of its desire that he and others should accompany it. The sole complaint was about its lack of timeliness and specificity as to what moving expenses it would be prepared to absorb. (at p. 118)

As the conduct of the company was reasonable, there was no ground for complaint by the employee. Each case will, however, depend on the trial Judge's view of the facts and brief reference to the following cases may be of assistance.

In *Birnbaum v. Lambda Mercantile Corp.*, [1977] 1 A.C.W.S. 394 (Ont. H.C.), the Court found that the employee had an obligation, as part of his duty to take reasonable steps to mitigate damages, to move from Montreal to Portage la Prairie, Manitoba. In *Hunt v. Cimco Ltd.* (1976), 2 A.R. 514 (T.D.), however, the Alberta Supreme Court held that the employee, who was told to relocate from Calgary to Winnipeg, was justified in refusing to do so. The Court in *Hunt v. Cimco* may have been influenced in its decision by the fact that although the parties had an "understanding" that the employee would have a higher salary in Winnipeg, there was no commitment by the employer as to what the salary would be or what financial assistance, if any, would be provided with respect to moving expenses.

In *Kozak v. Hallmark Engineering Ltd.* (1983), 1 C.C.E.L. 113 (B.C. S.C.), the Court found that it was an implied term of the plaintiff's employment that he would have permanent residence in Vancouver. The Court, therefore, found that an offer requiring the plaintiff to move to Calgary constituted a breach of his employment contract. However, the Court went on to find that, notwithstanding the term of his employment contract that he be permitted to remain in Vancouver, the plaintiff was nevertheless required to move to Calgary in an attempt to mitigate his damages. This decision is, however, questionable in that it operates to deprive the employee of the benefit of the implied term of his contract that he be entitled to remain in Vancouver. Further, the decision, in effect, requires the employee in mitigation of damages to take the first position offered to him, in Calgary, notwithstanding that this requires him to uproot his family.

Employer publications and employment practices may assist a court in determining the latitude of the employer to reassign job location. In the absence of a written contract, or any persuasive employer practices or procedures, a court will probably enunciate the principle that an employee is obliged to accept reasonable changes in job location, and then wrestle with the application of that principle in particular cases.

5.5 EMPLOYER CONDUCT INCOMPATIBLE WITH CONTINUED EMPLOYMENT

There are also situations in which the employer, although not acting to change the terms of the employment contract, nevertheless creates a situation in which it is untenable for the employee to continue. Such conduct on the part of the employer can properly be regarded as constructive dismissal.

Wilcox v. Philips Electronics Ltd. (1984), 6 C.C.E.L. 43, 64 N.S.R. (2d) 352, 143 A.P.R. 352 (T.D.), provides an example of such conduct. The employee, age 59, had resided in the Halifax area for approximately 14 years, and held the position of area sales supervisor. He was then offered the position of western Canada sales manager and was assured that he would not "lose by the move." The employee regarded this as a promotion and moved to Edmonton. Unfortunately, however, there was a very major failure to communicate. Bechtel, a superior of the employee, was under the misapprehension that the employee had occupied a somewhat lesser position in Halifax, and viewed the move to Edmonton as a lateral transfer to the same type of lesser position. The supervisor also rationalized the description of the employee as western Canada sales manager on his business cards as a device to impress customers. Further, because he regarded the transfer as lateral, as opposed to a promotion, he took the position that no salary increase was justified.

The Court did not mince words in stating its conclusions as follows:

> It is unnecessary to further recite the evidence of the defendant on this point. I reject the view that these classifications are the same. Similarly, I reject the notion that the business cards are solely to impress the customer. In fact, I consider that a shocking proposition. In my view the plaintiff suffered with Mr. Bechtel as a result of the error in his personnel record. From the documentation it appears that everyone else in the company considered the plaintiff to be an Area Sales Supervisor but not Mr. Bechtel.
>
> I find, as a fact, that the plaintiff considered his move to be a promotion and that it was announced as a promotion. Further, the defendant was aware that the plaintiff considered it a promotion and did nothing to dispel that view until long after the move took place. In fact, no one ever took the time to face the situation and deal with it. One would have expected that a full explanation of the move and the terms of employment would have been provided in writing to the plaintiff shortly after he agreed to move.
>
> In my view the plaintiff's expectations were reasonable and the defendant must have been aware that the plaintiff, then aged 56, would not move his long established place of residence and move to a higher cost economy without some upward adjustment.
>
> All in all, I find that the plaintiff was, indeed, promoted. He was then shoddily treated by his employer, particularly considering his long service. The evidence of the defendant is more a retrospective reconstruction to support a denial of the claim. It does not face the issue, nor does it explain, the failure of the defendant to meet the problems and deal with it before the move and subsequent difficulties occurred.
>
> I find, therefore, that it was a term of the plaintiff's contract that on his transfer to the west he was promoted to Western Canada Sales Manager and that there was to be a salary increase and that while he received the promotional title, the defendant did not provide the salary increase. In my view such a finding is reasonable, necessary and justified by the previous dealings of the parties. As well, it is necessary to implement the parties' presumed intention on the evidence here and to give business efficacy to the employment contract. (at pp.52-53)

Tolman v. Gearmatic Co. (1986), 14 C.C.E.L. 195 (B.C. C.A.), provides an additional, and rather stark, example of employer conduct incompatible with continued employment. The employee, who had been employed for some 24 years, declined to take a computer course as required by the employer. The employer chose to regard this as a resignation and posted a general notice to employees indicating that the employee had resigned his employment and wishing him every success in his endeavours. The Court had little difficulty in finding that this constituted a constructive dismissal, stating:

> The actions of the employer in the posting of the notice with the announcement that the plaintiff would be leaving the company to devote full time to his horse breeding interests and the subsequent offer of a lesser position amounted to constructive dismissal. (at p. 201)

In general terms, any employer conduct which is perceived to be unfair and which renders it untenable for the employee to continue in employment will be found to be a constructive dismissal. In determining what is untenable, the Court is very likely to state that it is judging the issue by an objective standard, namely, how a reasonable employee would react. In practice, however, it is likely that considerable weight will be given to the actual reaction of the employee.

6

DAMAGES

6.1 WHAT CONSTITUTES REASONABLE NOTICE OF TERMINATION

(a) General Principles

In the absence of just cause, an employer is obliged to provide the employee with reasonable advance notice of termination or a payment in lieu thereof. In assessing damages, a court seeks to put the employee in the same position that the employee would have enjoyed had reasonable notice been given.

The classic statement as to what constitutes "reasonable notice" is set out in *Bardal v. Globe & Mail Ltd.*, [1960] O.W.N. 253, 24 D.L.R. (2d) 140 (H.C.), as follows:

> There could be no catalogue laid down as to what was reasonable notice in particular classes of cases. The reasonableness of the notice must be decided with reference to each particular case, having regard to the character of the employment, the length of service of the servant, the age of the servant and the availability of similar employment, having regard to the experience, training and qualifications of the servant. (at p. 255)

Chief Justice McEachern, of the British Columbia Supreme Court, commented at some length on the *Bardal* principles in *Ansari v. B.C. Hydro & Power Authority*, 13 C.C.E.L. 238, 2 B.C.L.R. (2d) 33, [1986] 4 W.W.R. 123 (S.C.). In this case, the defendant had terminated a large number of graduate engineers as being surplus to its requirements. The Court, therefore, heard a number of representative cases, in order to assist in settling many other outstanding cases. In his reasons Chief Justice McEachern discussed the *Bardal* factors at considerable length and left no doubt that, in his opinion, any non-*Bardal* factors are of relatively slight importance. Due to the representative nature of the case, McEachern C.J.B.C. gave an unusually detailed explanation and analysis of the *Bardal* factors, which it is useful to refer to in detail. In this regard McEachern C.J.B.C. explained:

> In *Gillespie v. [Buckley] Valley Forest Industries Ltd.*, [1975] 1 W.W.R. 607, 50 D.L.R. (3d) 316 (B.C. C.A.), it was said that the factors enumerated by McRuer C.J.H.C. should not be regarded as exhaustive but with great respect, they are indeed the most important factors, and other matters which have crept into the assessment of this kind of damages are not of great significance. (at p. 243)
>
> . . . .
>
> Further, it does not appear useful to attempt nice distinctions between the comparative employment functions of these employees. Thus, in my view, it is not necessary minutely to investigate the degree or level of specialization of these plaintiffs. It is enough to observe that they are all highly skilled graduate engineers whom B.C. Hydro was satisfied to employ in responsible positions. Those factors alone are sufficient to entitle these employees to a longer notice period than in many other cases.
>
> Also, I do not consider it useful to make distinctions between these professional employees who did or did not supervise other employees. Such a concept is pervasive in some disciplines, but it is not a particularly relevant consideration when employees are professionally skilled and are employed because of such skill.
>
> The next important factor in fixing the period of reasonable notice is length of service. This is the only important factor that does bear directly upon the employee's prospects for future employment although long service may add materially to the age of the employee which does bear upon employment possibilities.
>
> For reasons which are largely subjective and which I would not presume to disturb, the law requires a longer notice period for a long-term employee even though discharged employees of the same age, skill and responsibility suffering under the same economic factors must be assumed to require an equal period to obtain equivalent employment. The reasons for this anomaly may be that a long-term employee has a moral claim which has matured into a legal entitlement to a longer notice period.
>
> Advancing years are also an important factor to be considered along with years of service because age bears so importantly upon the prospects for other similar employment. The Court cannot be unmindful of the fact that employment opportunities for older engineers are extremely limited. (at p. 245)
>
> . . . .
>
> But the law is also clear that there is a "rough upper limit" for the notice period

which has lately been substantially increased as in *Suttie* [*Suttie v. Metro Transit Operating Co.*, 1 C.C.E.L. 123, 42 B.C.L.R. 234, 3 W.W.R. 71 [supplementary reasons at 45 B.C.L.R. 394, [1983] 5 W.W.R. 247, 148 D.L.R. (3d) 354 (S.C.)], varied 9 C.C.E.L. 19 (C.A.)], supra, where a period of 24 months was approved for a 58 year old employee who had exercised senior management responsibilities and had served his employer for 39 years, and in *Sorel v. Tomenson Saunders Whitehead Ltd.* (1985), 9 C.C.E.L. 226 (B.C. S.C.), where a 60 year old senior executive with 37 years service was awarded 30 months.

In other words, the law seems to place a cap of reasonableness upon the notice period and does not compensate a discharged employee to retirement age, whatever that may be, even if there is no likelihood of alternative equivalent employment. I believe this is because:

(a) such a law would amount to a guarantee of life-time income;

(b) it would fix the employer with all responsibility for the lack of employment opportunities; and

(c) the law presumes that no employer would accept such an onerous responsibility at the time of engagement.

Subject, therefore, to exceptional cases such as *Suttie* and *Sorel*, supra, where the degree of responsibility, age, and years of service were very extensive, it seems to me that 18 to 24 months is the rough upper limit for reasonable notice, and other cases should be scaled downward from there unless there are extenuating circumstances which cannot all be enumerated in this crude attempt to provide guidance for the settlement of the many cases still outstanding. (at pp. 247-248)

. . . .

What all this means, in my view, is that the general statement of factors quoted above from *Bardal* are the governing factors, and it would be better if other individual or subjective factors had not crept into the determination of reasonable notice. In my view such other matters are of little importance in most cases. (at p. 248)

In *Cronk v. Canadian General Insurance Co.* (1994), 6 C.C.E.L. (2d) 15, 94 C.L.L.C. 14,032, 19 O.R. (3d) 515 (Gen. Div.), the Court addressed whether that part of the *Bardal* formula which gives weight to the "character of the employment" was appropriate. Mr. Justice MacPherson put the issue as follows:

Edna Cronk was older than 45 when she was dismissed. She had worked for her company for more than 20 years. But she was not a senior manager; she was essentially a clerical employee with some minor administrative duties.

The pivotal question which this case raises is whether an employee's position in the hierarchy of a company is a major factor in setting the period of compensation to which the employee is entitled when she is dismissed without cause.

This question can be illustrated quite graphically by comparing Edna Cronk's situation to that of the plaintiff in one of the leading Ontario cases in the wrongful dismissal domain. Geoffrey Stevens was a renowned journalist and senior manager for the Globe and Mail newspaper for 24 years. When he was fired he was 46 years of age. He was awarded compensation for 21 months' salary by a judge of this court in 1992 [*Stevens v. Globe & Mail (The)* (1992), 39 C.C.E.L. 1 (Ont. Gen. Div.)].

Edna Cronk had been employed by the defendant insurance company for 29 years when she was fired. She was 55 years of age. However, unlike Geoffrey

> Stevens, she was not a highly visible and renowned employee occupying a senior management position. Viewed from an external perspective, she was in fact an invisible, unknown and junior employee — a small cog in a large corporate enterprise.
>
> The question which this case poses squarely is whether the law of Ontario provides as much protection to Edna Cronk for the loss of her job as it did to Geoffrey Stevens when he lost his job. (at 6 C.C.E.L. (2d), p. 17)

Mr. Justice MacPherson rejected the argument that senior, specialized employees have greater difficulty in finding new employment for the following reasons:

> I have great difficulty accepting this argument, for three reasons. First, the defendant has offered no evidence to support its argument.
>
> . . . .
>
> Second, a close examination of the table above dealing with the six Ontario employees who have been awarded 20 and 21 month notice periods contradicts the defendant's argument at its crucial point. It will be recalled that the defendant asserts that the principal rationale for the long notice periods is the great difficulty these senior employees will have in securing new employment. Yet the average period of post-dismissal unemployment for these six employees was nine and one third months. Ms. Cronk was unemployed for almost eight months when this motion was heard, and her unemployment [sic] prospects were very bleak indeed. It is difficult to see how her employment prospects are better than the senior managers in the decided cases.
>
> Third, the reality is — as we are all told by our parents at a young age — that education and training *are* directly related to employment. The senior manager and the professional person are better, not worse, positioned to obtain employment, both initially and later in a post-dismissal context. Higher education and specialized training correlate directly with *increased* access to employment. [Emphasis in original.] (at 6 C.C.E.L. (2d), p. 25)

Mr. Justice MacPherson concluded that any distinction between managerial and clerical employees, for the purpose of determining reasonable notice, was not well founded. As such, he awarded a 20-month notice period.

There is no reliable formula or rule of thumb as to how to weigh the *Bardal* factors to arrive at a reasonable period of notice. While precedent cases are the lawyers' stock-in-trade, the judicial attitude is exemplified by Mr. Justice Robertson of the British Columbia Court of Appeal who stated in *Gillespie v. Buckley Valley Forest Industries Ltd.*, [1975] 1 W.W.R. 607, 50 D.L.R. (3d) 316, with reference to precedent cases:

> I get next to no help from them, for each depended on its own facts, just as this case does. (at p. 608)

An experienced lawyer should be able to provide a prediction of the period of reasonable notice within a range of approximately three months. The judicial weighing of the factors is, however, very subjective and the Court of Appeal is naturally reluctant to interfere. For that reason a party who is unsympathetic, i.e., the indifferent employee or the arbitrary employer, may well receive an award outside the range.

In general terms the cases below bear out the proposition put by Chief Justice McEachern that the non-*Bardal* factors are to be given relatively little weight. The only notable exception to this proposition is the factor of inducement (see Chapter 6.1(c)), which McEachern C.J.B.C. did not need to consider. Inducement can be a very important, and even dominant, factor in determining the period of reasonable notice in certain cases.

In *Bartlam v. Saskatchewan Crop Insurance Corp.*, 49 C.C.E.L. 141, [1993] 8 W.W.R. 671, 112 Sask. R. 136 (Q.B.), the Court considered a case in which the plaintiff, who had a grade eight education, had been employed for approximately 16 years and had been promoted to a senior management position supervising approximately 650 employees. In considering the period of reasonable notice, the Court noted the different approaches in the *Bardal* and *Lazarowicz* cases. In this regard the Court stated:

> While the principle of reasonable notice is well understood, there is a divergence of opinion as to what theoretical approach or test should be followed in determining a reasonable notice period for a specific employment contract. On the one hand is a series of decisions suggesting that reasonable notice is to be determined by the court as of the date an employment contract was terminated. These decisions do not require the court to consider what the parties would have negotiated at the time they entered into their contract had they directed their minds to such issue or to other matters such as: whether the employee, if he were to leave his or her employment, would be prepared to give the employer the same notice period the court considers reasonable to require the employer to provide the employee. This approach, which for ease of reference I shall refer to as the "Bardal Approach", is based on the decision of McRuer C.J.H.C. in *Bardal v. Globe & Mail (The)* [*Bardal v. Globe & Mail Ltd.*], [1960] O.W.N. 253, 24 D.L.R. (2d) 140 (H.C.) where at p. 255 he stated:
>
> > There could be no catalogue laid down as to what was reasonable notice in particular classes of cases. The reasonableness of the notice must be decided with reference to each particular case, having regard to the character of the employment, the length of service of the servant, the age of the servant and the availability of similar employment, having regard to the experience, training and qualificiations of the servant.
>
> On the other hand is a series of decisions suggesting that a period of reasonable notice should be determined as of the time the parties entered into their employment contract with the length of the notice to be implied by the court being the same whether the employer or the employee is terminating the employment contract. These decisions direct the court to look at all relevant factors existing at the time the employment contract was entered into and then imply a notice provision of the kind the parties would have agreed to had they considered the same. This approach, which for ease of reference I shall refer to as the "Lazarowicz Approach", is based on the decision of Roach J.A. in *Lazarowicz v. Orenda Engines Ltd.* [(1960)], [1961] O.R. 141, 26 D.L.R. (2d) 433 (C.A.), where at pp. 144 and 145 he said:

> Having concluded that his hiring was for an indefinite period, the next question is, to what notice was he entitled on the termination of that employment? The answer may be given that he was entitled to a reasonable notice. To put it in that language is not too informative because another question immediately follows, namely, what is reasonable? Opinions might differ as to what was reasonable, but in reaching an opinion a reasonable test would be to propound the question, namely, if the employer and the employee at the time of the hiring had addressed themselves to the question as to the notice that the employer would give in the event of him terminating the employment, or the notice that the employee would give on quitting, what would their respective answers have been? (at pp. 148-149)
>
> . . . .
>
> In my opinion the Bardal Approach and the Lazarowicz Approach are irreconcilable and when applied to the same facts may lead to substantially different conclusions. The degree of divergence is illustrated in *Tysoe v. Plant Forest Products Corp.* (1990), 34 C.C.E.L. 124 (B.C. S.C.) where Hutchinson J., while considering what constitutes a reasonable notice period, concluded on the facts before him that a notice period of 12 months was appropriate if the Bardal Approach was applied and 6 months if the Lazarowicz Approach was applied. He applied the Bardal Approach. (at pp. 150-151)

While a theoretical distinction may be drawn between the two approaches, in practical terms there is little difference. This may well be because, as pointed out in *Yosyk v. Westfair Foods Ltd.; Vernon v. Westfair Foods Ltd.; Vivian v. Westfair Foods Ltd.*, (*sub nom. Yosyk v. Westfair Foods Ltd.*) [1988] 3 W.W.R. 155, 49 D.L.R. (4th) 260, 51 Man. R. (2d) 191 (C.A.), additional reasons at (1988), 55 Man. R. (2d) 173 (C.A.) by Mr. Justice Twaddle, the employment relationship is not static and is amended from time to time in relation to compensation and responsibilities. As such, even on the *Lazarowicz* approach, the focus may be the intent of the parties at the time the contract was last entered into or amended, which in most cases is not more than one or two years prior to the date of termination.

The question of whether the *Bardal* approach or the *Lazarowicz* approach is appropriate was revisited in *Wiebe v. Central Transport Refrigeration (Man.) Ltd.* (1994), 3 C.C.E.L. (2d) 1 (Man. C.A.) in which the Court concluded that the *Bardal* approach was to be preferred and was, in fact, endorsed by the Supreme Court of Canada in *Machtinger v. HOJ Industries Ltd.*, 40 C.C.E.L. 1, 7 O.R. (3d) 480 (note), [1992] 1 S.C.R. 986, 92 C.L.L.C. 14,022, 91 D.L.R. (4th) 491, *(sub nom. Lefebvre v. HOJ Industries Ltd.; Machtinger v. HOJ Industries Ltd.)* 136 N.R. 40, 53 O.A.C. 200. In that case, Mr. Justice Iacobucci, writing for the majority, stated:

> For the purposes of this appeal, I would characterize the common law principle of termination only on reasonable notice as a presumption, rebuttable if the contract of employment clearly specifies some other period of notice, whether expressly or impliedly.

. . . .

What constitutes reasonable notice will vary with the circumstances of any particular case. The most frequently cited enumeration of factors relevant to the assessment of reasonable notice is from the judgment of McRuer C.J.H.C. in *Bardal, supra*, at p. 145:

> There can be no catalogue laid down as to what is reasonable notice in particular classes of cases. The reasonableness of the notice must be decided with reference to each particular case, having regard to the character of the employment, the length of service of the servant, the age of the servant and the availability of similar employment, having regard to the experience, training and qualifications of the servant. (at pp. 998-999)

(b) Economic Circumstances

(i) *General Economic Circumstances*

In *Bohemier v. Storwal International Inc.* (1982), 40 O.R. (2d) 264, 142 D.L.R. (3d) 8 (H.C.), varied (1983), 3 C.C.E.L. 79, 44 O.R. (2d) 361, 4 D.L.R. (4th) 383 (C.A.), leave to appeal to the Supreme Court of Canada refused (1984), 3 C.C.E.L. 79 (S.C.C.), the Court was concerned with an employee having 35 years of service in what were generally non-management positions, such as spot welder, press operator and inspector. Mr. Justice Saunders indicated that "to a certain extent he was a victim of the current scarcity of employment opportunity." Saunders J. then discussed the general principles, and in particular the impact of the general economic circumstances as follows:

> Experience, training and qualification of an employee must be taken into account in considering availability. A chief executive officer of a large corporation likely has fewer opportunities of similar alternative employment than does a general labourer. Therefore, it is said that the former is entitled to a longer period of notice. Most of the decided cases deal with employees who have held positions superior to that of the plaintiff in this action. It was argued that the character of the plaintiff's employment was only relevant to assist in determining the availability of similar employment. It was argued that age and length of service are

(*Continued on page 6-5*)

> also only relevant for that purpose. The plaintiff had great difficulty in obtaining any employment and from this the court was asked to conclude that employment at even the most modest level was generally unavailable. It was submitted that in the current period of great unemployment a chief executive officer and a general labourer were in the same situation and that there was no social reason why one should be entitled to more notice than the other. In either case, it was submitted an employer had an obligation to give an amount of notice sufficient to enable a discharged employee to obtain new employment. On the other hand, it was submitted on behalf of Storwal that even in periods of general unemployment there are fewer opportunities for those of higher rank and that more notice is always required for more senior employees. The general increase in unemployment in the past few years has been reflected in the trend in court decisions to extend the period of notice. (at p. 268)
>
> . . . .
>
> . . . It seems to me that the character of the employment of the plaintiff with Storwal does not entitle him to a lengthy period of notice on the basis of decided cases and the reasons I have stated. If the issue had been addressed at the time he was first employed, it would not have been reasonable for his employer to have agreed to a notice period sufficient to enable him to find work in difficult economic times. In saying this, I hope that it is not thought that I am unsympathetic to the plight of the plaintiff. His claim, however, is based on contract and it is not reasonable to expect that his employer would or could have agreed to assure that his notice of termination would be sufficient to guarantee that he would obtain alternative employment within the notice period. (at p. 269)

After the trial Judge weighed the various factors he concluded that eight months' notice was reasonable. On appeal, however, the Court of Appeal increased the notice period to 11 months, stating:

> As to the award for inadequate notice, each case must turn on its own facts, there is really no precedent. We agree Saunders J. was right in taking into account the economic factors when considering the case for each of the parties. We think he correctly discerned all of the proper principles, but we think he did not give sufficient weight to length of term of employment, the various work which he performed with company over his working life (35 years and ten months) and feel that the separation was but two years from the pension entitlement. In our opinion, giving proper weight to these facts and the fact that this concerns really a major employer in a small community, we think 11 months' salary in lieu of notice would have been appropriate and the judgment is varied accordingly. (at p. 80)

Thus, in *Bohemier*, the trial Judge makes it clear that in poor economic times the period of notice may well be less than would be a reasonable period within which to expect the employee to find new employment. The trial Judge, however, recognized implicitly that general economic circumstances were a factor to be considered by observing that the general increase in unemployment then being experienced had been reflected in the trend in court decisions to extend the period of notice.

In *Isaacs v. MHG International Ltd.* (1984), 4 C.C.E.L. 197, 45 O.R. (2d)

693, 7 D.L.R. (4th) 570, 3 O.A.C. 301 (C.A.), the Court, in giving oral reasons for judgment, stated:

> It may be that the trial Judge gave too much weight to the economic climate prevailing at the time of the respondent's termination in calculating the appropriate length of the notice. The trial Judge said [at p. 82, 2 C.C.E.L.]:
>
> > I believe, however, that the notice period must be determined in this case primarily on the nature of the plaintiff's employment, which I have dealt with above, and the fact that he was being thrust into a marketplace in which it would be very difficult for him to obtain employment in which he could employ his present skills.
>
> The fact that the termination occurred at a time when the alternate employment was scarce, is not a proper consideration in fixing the length of notice: see *Bohemier v. Storwal Int. Inc., supra.* (at pp. 199-200)

With respect, these reasons are difficult to comprehend. The statement that the trial Judge gave too much weight to the prevailing economic climate certainly suggests that the prevailing economic climate can at least be considered and given some weight. It is then difficult to reconcile that position with the later statement, purporting to rely on *Bohemier*, to the effect that the scarcity of alternative employment (clearly a product of the prevailing economic climate) is not a proper consideration at all.

The significance of the general economic circumstances was also considered in *Hunter v. Northwood Pulp & Timber Ltd.* (1985), 7 C.C.E.L. 260, 62 B.C.L.R. 367 (C.A.). In this case the Court determined to reconcile the opinions in *Bohemier* and *Isaacs* as follows:

> While the language used by the Ontario Court of Appeal in the *Isaacs* case is difficult to follow, it appears to me that when *Bohemier* and *Isaacs* are read together the result is as follows:
>
> (1) The lack of available employment opportunities resulting from a depressed economy is a factor to be taken into account.
> (2) The economic factor must not be given undue emphasis. (at pp. 270-271)

While this reconciliation of the case law is lacking in precision, there is probably little else that could have been said. General economic circumstances must be taken into account, while on the other hand the employer cannot be put in the position of a guarantor in tough economic times.

(ii) *Economic Circumstances of the Employer*

Bohemier v. Storwal International Inc. (1982), 40 O.R. (2d) 264, 142 D.L.R. (3d) 8 (H.C.), varied (1983), 3 C.C.E.L. 79, 44 O.R. (2d) 361, 4 D.L.R. (4th) 383 (C.A.), leave to appeal to Supreme Court of Canada refused (1984), 3 C.C.E.L. 79, also provides authority for the Court to consider the economic circumstances of the employer as a factor to reduce the period of notice that would otherwise be required. In *Bohemier* the employee had been employed for 35 years in a variety of positions. At the time of termination, in 1981, the employee had an inspector's job at a salary of $14,400 per annum. In considering the appropriate period of notice, Mr. Justice Saunders stated:

> The claim is for damages for breach of contract. In determining the amount of notice to be given to an employee, the principal concern has rightly been to consider what is reasonable in the circumstances in which the employee finds himself. In my opinion, there is another factor to be considered. As this is a contract matter, the notice period must also be reasonable for the employer. What may be a reasonable period to allow a discharged employee to find new employment may be more than an employer should be asked to pay. An employer may dismiss for cause without notice but the economic requirements of the business or even the incompetence or negligence of the employee do not constitute cause. If the period of notice is extended too far, the ability to dismiss employees for economic or other reasons may be seriously impaired or rendered illusory.
>
> . . . Payment in lieu of notice involves a cost to the employer for which there is no corresponding production or benefit. In my view, there is a need to preserve the ability of an employer to function in an unfavourable economic climate. He must, if he finds it necessary, be able to reduce his work force at a reasonable cost. If he can not do so, the alternative may be bankruptcy or receivership. It seems to me that when employment is unavailable due to general economic conditions, there has to be some limit on the period of notice to be given to discharged employees even if they are unable to secure similar employment within the notice period. The case at bar is illustrative of the problem. (at pp. 268-269)

It is somewhat difficult to appreciate the scope of the principle being established. The basic *Bardal* factors do not equate a reasonable notice period with the period of time that it is likely to take the employee to find new employment, and to some extent *Bohemier* simply notes this fact. On the other hand, *Bohemier* seems to require a different assessment of the notice period for prosperous employers as opposed to employers who may be facing financial hardships. While the concept that the damages suffered by the innocent party to a contract may be reduced by the economic circumstances of the person in breach of the contract is novel, the trial decision was upheld on appeal.

Although *Bohemier* is the law in Ontario, it is becoming apparent that the principle enunciated is unwieldy in application. If an employer pleads economic circumstances as a mitigating factor, an employee will be interested in evidence particularizing the present economic state of the employer, including historical information as to how the present economic state came about, and information relating to the economic state of parent, subsidiary or affiliated corporations. Thus, an employer may be forced to divulge sensitive financial information, such as information relating to executive remuneration, and dividends paid to shareholders. The result may well be that a relatively simple wrongful dismissal action will require lengthy consideration of economic evidence concerning the economic well-being of groups of related corporations.

Pechenkov v. Borg-Warner (Can.) Ltd. (1983), 2 C.C.E.L. 237 (Ont. Co. Ct.), provides an example of the potential problems. The employer was a wholly owned subsidiary of a United States corporation. The division in which the employee was employed was affected by a general downturn in the economy resulting in the termination of the employee.

Counsel for the employer argued that the notice period should be reduced according to the principle in *Bohemier*. While accepting *Bohemier* as legally correct, County Court Judge Waisberg gave it little weight, stating:

> In the case before me, it was argued that because of the downturn in the economy and the fact that layoffs were economically necessary, that that should also be taken into consideration.
>
> While not ignoring that fact, I must also take into consideration, in deciding upon "reasonableness", the position of the defendant as a branch of a much larger organization. I do not think it would be equitable to allow the parent organization to skim off the profits in good years and leave the branch organization to struggle through the lean years, and then argue that because they are lean years for the branch organization, that the length of reasonable notice should be shortened by that fact.
>
> In that respect, it is interesting to look at Ex. 5, which is an annual report for the year 1982 of the parent corporation, and it gives a figure of 227.3 million dollars as the operating profit of all the segments for the year 1982, of which Canada contributed 10.4 million dollars. (at p. 239)

Thomson v. Bechtel Can. Ltd. (1983), 3 C.C.E.L. 16 (Ont. H.C.), affirmed (1985), 6 C.C.E.L. xxxv (Ont. C.A.), adopted a similar view. The employer was the Canadian arm of what was described as the largest private company in the world. Again, while accepting *Bohemier* in principle, the Court gave it little weight on the facts of the case, finding:

> While the defendant is a separate corporate entity, it would be illogical and unreal to disregard its close connection with its profitable United States international parent. (at p. 20)

It is implicit in the reasons for judgment in *Bechtel* and *Borg-Warner* that the profits of the parent organization were relevant. This would mean that financial records of the parent were relevant and subject to production and cross-examination. Thus, the defendant should give careful consideration prior to invoking the *Bohemier* principle. In many cases the *Bohemier* principle may be of limited assistance in minimizing the claim but may open the door to the employee having broad discovery of the otherwise confidential financial affairs of the defendant and related corporations.

(c) Inducement

In determining the proper notice period, the Court will also consider whether the terminated employee had been induced to leave previous secure employment. *Makhija v. Lakefield Research* (1983), 14 C.C.E.L. 131 (Ont. H.C.), affirmed (1986), 14 C.C.E.L. xxxi (Ont. C.A.), is illustrative of the general principle. The employee was 43 years of age and he had received a Ph.D. in analytical chemistry in 1966. Between 1966 and 1980 the employee held a number of positions, none of them for more than three years. In 1980 the employee joined the federal government. In the spring of 1981 the employee became aware that the employer was interested in hiring a chief chemist, and the employee initiated contact with the employer. The Court described the discussions leading up to the hiring of the employee as follows:

> The plaintiff in his discussions with Mr. Wyslouzil made known to him that his major concern was the permanency, the security of the position he was being offered. He was assured by Mr. Wyslouzil that the position was permanent, barring a complete collapse of the defendant. Mr. Wyslouzil told him the defendant did not "fire" people. Mr. Wyslouzil pointed out to him that he had been with the defendant for 25 years and that other employees had been there 15 to 30 years. Mr. Wyslouzil assured him that if the unlikely happened and the position had to be discontinued he would be given sufficient notice to permit him to find comparable employment elsewhere.
>
> Relying on these assurances of job security the plaintiff resigned from his position with the Department of the Environment and accepted the position of head chemist with the defendant. He began his work with the defendant on June 15, 1981. (at p. 134)

The employment of the plaintiff was then terminated on August 31, 1982, for economic reasons. Despite the fact that the plaintiff had only been employed for 13½ months, the Court found that a 15-month notice period was appropriate. In this regard the Court stated:

> The plaintiff had only been working for the defendant for 13½ months when he was discharged, however the defendant knew when it hired him that he would only give up his government job which carried maximum security if the job he was going to was also secure. Specifically he was told his job would last as long as the defendant continued to operate and that if some circumstance made it necessary to terminate his employment he would be given sufficient notice to permit him to find comparable employment elsewhere. That he was given such assurance before he accepted employment is in my view an important factor for the Court to take into account in determining the length of notice to which the plaintiff was entitled. (at p. 142)

It is also noteworthy that in this case the Court gave an additional reason for concluding that 15 months' notice was reasonable, stating as follows:

> It is further my conclusion that if the plaintiff and the defendant had directed their minds in May 1981 to the exact amount of notice of termination the plaintiff would be entitled to they would have concluded that on termination the plaintiff would not likely find a comparable position elsewhere in less than 15 months and given the plaintiff's great concern about job security and the adequacy of notice that they would have both felt that 15 months' notice would be reasonable notice.
>
> I am not suggesting that in every action for wrongful dismissal the Court must pick that period of notice that the parties would themselves have considered reasonable if at the time the contract was entered into they had available to

> them all the facts that later transpired. Often it would be improper for the Court to fix as the proper period of notice the period of notice the parties themselves would have arrived at.
>
> I am simply saying in this case that the notice which is appropriate in all the circumstances as they now are known happens to be the same notice that the parties must themselves have considered reasonable when the plaintiff was hired. (at pp. 143-144)

Thus, a case that might ordinarily have merited a three-month notice period became converted into a 15-month notice period based upon findings of fact as to conversations at the time of hiring. From the employer point of view the extreme difficulty in refuting alleged representations, i.e., in this case the representation, in effect, that "if we need to fire you we will give you time to find a comparable position," presents another compelling argument in favour of employment contracts.

Brief reference to the following cases will also assist in demonstrating that the factor of inducement may be the single most important factor in determining the period of reasonable notice:

1. *Cathcart v. Longines Wittnauer Watch Co.* (1980), 1 C.C.E.L. 287 (Ont. H.C.): The 54-year-old employee was induced to leave employment of 11 years duration a few months prior to becoming entitled to a vested pension benefit and in the face of a reasonable expectation of a promotion to a vice-presidency. The employee was terminated after one year of service, and the Court found that a one-year period of notice was appropriate.
2. *Brisbois v. Casteel Inc.* (1983), 2 C.C.E.L. 35 (Ont. H.C.): The employee was 33 years of age, and had been induced to leave a secure and successful position after eight years of service, to accept a slightly lower salary in anticipation of greater opportunities with his new employer. In order to accept the new employment the plaintiff had to relocate his family. The employee was dismissed after 10 months of service and the Court found that a reasonable period of notice was 12 months.
3. *Hooker v. Audio Magnetics Corp. of Can.* (1984), 3 C.C.E.L. 288 (Ont. Co. Ct.): The 56-year-old employee was recruited and left a position which the Court indicated was secure and "which would have continued indefinitely into the future." The employee was terminated after approximately 11 months of service, and the Court found that a 14-month period of notice was reasonable.
4. *I.S.S. Information System Services Ltd. v. Smyth* (1985), 7 C.C.E.L. 35 (B.C. Co. Ct.): The employee had 12 years of prior experience as a systems analyst, and was induced to relocate from Northern Ireland to accept new employment. An arrangement was made whereby his expense in relocating was described as a loan repayable over 36 months. However, the monthly payment was forgiven in each month that employment continued. He was dismissed after four months of service and the Court found that a six-month period of notice was reasonable.

In summary, in considering the impact of an alleged inducement a court will consider

1. the position, remuneration and security enjoyed in the previous employment;
2. whether it was the employer or employee who initiated contact with respect to the new employment and/or pursued the negotiations leading to the new employment;
3. representations made by the new employer as to the position, remuneration and prospect for secure employment and advancement at the new employment; and
4. the length of service at the new employment.

There are no clear statements as to the extent to which the period of reasonable notice may be extended as a result of inducement. In considering this, however, it may be helpful to consider the period of reasonable notice to which the employee would have been entitled at his previous employment. Inducement will have its greatest impact in cases of previous long standing and secure employment, followed by strong inducement to leave that employment and a short period of service prior to termination at the new employment. For practical purposes the maximum impact of inducement should be to aggregate the prior length of service with the current service and count the cumulative service in applying the *Bardal* factors. In most cases, however, the Court will recognize that there is an element of assumption of risk when a person leaves one job to take another and will accord the factor of inducement somewhat less than the suggested maximum impact. The suggested maximum impact of inducement, however, could be exceeded in a case such as *Makhija, supra*, in which the employer's inducement included a specific representation that, in the event of termination, the employee would be given sufficient advance notice to find comparable new employment.

In *Kennedy v. Gescan Ltd.* (1991), 41 C.C.E.L. 134 (B.C.S.C.), the Court was concerned with an employee induced to leave secure employment who was terminated after four years of service. The Court found that inducement was not relevant to determining the period of reasonable notice stating:

> I think inducement is a subjective factor applicable only in cases where an employee is terminated relatively early in his new position, having been induced to leave his previously secure position, and is basically a compensating factor for the short period of new employment, but ceases to be a factor as the length of service increases: *Ansari* [*Ansari v. British Columbia Hydro & Power Authority*, 13 C.C.E.L. 238, 2 B.C.L.R. (2d) 33, [1986] 4 W.W.R. 123 (S.C.)], supra, at pp. 41 and 43 [B.C.L.R.]; *Mott v. Hayward Securities* (June 30, 1986), Doc. Vancouver C844853, McEachern C.J.S.C. (B.C. S.C.), at pp. 6-7; *Skene v. Dearborn Motors Ltd.* (1990), 29 C.C.E.L. 107 (B.C. C.A.), at p. 108. It is also applicable only in situations where the inducement and subsequent termination behaviour of the employer results in unconscionable prejudice to the dismissed employee: *Web-*

ster v. British Columbia Hydro & Power Authority (1990), 31 C.C.E.L. 224 (B.C. S.C.). (at pp. 138-139)

While it certainly makes sense that inducement be a less significant factor as time passes, it is submitted that it is incorrect to view it as a factor only when the employee "is terminated relatively early in his new position". Surely it makes sense to treat the two- or four-year employee induced from long-term secure employment differently from a comparable employee who was unemployed at the time of hiring.

(d) Continuity of Service

(i) *Introduction*

There are two distinct circumstances where continuity of service may affect the determination of reasonable notice. In the first circumstance, the Court must consider the weight to attach to an interruption in service with the same employer. In the second, the same determination must be made when service continues but the identity of the corporate employer changes.

(ii) *Interruption in Service with the Same Employer*

Although the case law is not consistent, it is generally fair to state that the longer the interruption in service, in proportion to the overall period of employment, the more likely it is that the Court will disregard the period of employment prior to the interruption in assessing reasonable notice. There is, however, no formula or test to correlate the length of service, as compared to the length of the interruption in service, to determine the effect on the period of reasonable notice. The Court will, in each case, closely examine the facts to attempt to ascertain the significance of the interruption in service. It is, however, helpful to consider a number of cases which illustrate the judicial attitude in this area.

In *Roscoe v. McGavin Foods Ltd.* (1983), 2 C.C.E.L. 287 (B.C.S.C.), the plaintiff worked in the defendant's bakeries in various capacities from 1956 until 1971. At this time, he voluntarily left the employ of the defendant to take a position with a Crown corporation. Eight months later he was offered and accepted a management position with the defendant. He again held a number of management positions with the defendant and in 1980 was promoted to regional manager for the Province of British Columbia. Prior to accepting this position, the plaintiff expressed concerns to the defendant with respect to his abilities to perform effectively in the new position.

In early 1982, the overall performance of the area for which the plaintiff was responsible deteriorated. The defendant made unilateral changes to address the problem. The plaintiff, although not pleased with the changes, agreed to do whatever was necessary to improve the area's performance. Shortly thereafter, the plaintiff was summarily terminated by the defendant. In all the circumstances, the Court found that the defendant did not have just cause for dismissal.

With respect to the appropriate notice period to which the plaintiff was entitled, the Court stated:

> I turn now to a consideration of what notice should properly have been given to the plaintiff in the circumstances. The plaintiff occupied a senior management position with the defendant company. He was urged to take that position notwithstanding his own modest misgivings, and the defendant's knowledge of his potential shortcomings. He did not seek out or pursue the job. He was, in effect, lured from a position in which he had excelled and placed into a job which required him to deal with matters of which he had little or no knowledge. In so doing the defendant company told him there would be no turning back; that is, he could not go back to the job which he had done so well for the company for almost 26 years in the event this new position did not suit him. In just over 12 months a lifetime career with the defendant company ended. He was 45 years of age when that happened. (at p. 294)

With respect to the plaintiff's voluntary, albeit short, interruption of employment, the Court stated:

> I have given anxious consideration to the manner in which I should view the plaintiff's prior employment with the defendant company in light of the voluntary interruption of that employment for approximately eight months in 1971-72. I have come to the conclusion that for the purpose of considering what, in the circumstances, would have been proper notice to the plaintiff I should ignore that interruption. I do so for two reasons. Firstly, while the plaintiff left the defendant company voluntarily he was, in fact, actively pursued by the defendant who obviously wanted him to return. The evidence was that the holiday time was given to him by the company on his return was based upon a seniority level which

(Continued on page 6-13)

ignored the interruption of employment. Secondly, counsel for the defendant conceded, rightly so in my view, that I should consider the plaintiff for these purposes as one who had more than ten years on the job.

In all of the circumstances I am of the view that the proper notice to which the plaintiff was entitled upon termination of his employment would have been 15 months. (at pp. 294-295)

In a somewhat similar case, *Gordon v. St. John Shipbuilding & Dry Dock Co.* (1983), 47 N.B.R. (2d) 150, 124 A.P.R. 150 (Q.B.), the plaintiff had worked with the defendant for approximately 39 years, beginning in 1940, with a one-year interruption in service between 1970 and 1971. Upon the plaintiff's return to the employ of the defendant, he assumed the same position he held prior to his voluntary break in service. He was terminated in 1980.

In this case, the Court also disregarded the break in service in assessing the notice to which the plaintiff was entitled. On this point, the Court stated:

Having said that, I want just briefly to deal with the question of Mr. Gordon's interruption in service in 1970-71. As I said, he was rehired at the same position with an increase in salary. In addition, he appears to have picked up his vacation entitlement which had been earned through his past thirty years service. In the circumstances, I am not convinced that it is a matter of substantial importance in considering the notice to which Mr. Gordon is entitled, that is, should it be based on nine years or thirty-nine years.

Two things are clear; one, that he did, in fact, work for the company for thirty-nine years; secondly, he did have an interrupted service in 1970-71. I will take into account the appropriate factors to be considered and which were set out by Chief Justice McRuer in *Bardal v. Globe & Mail*, [1960] O.W.N. 253, at page 255 . . . .

No matter which period I use, nine or thirty-nine, the appropriate notice would be in excess of the seven months that he was in point of fact unemployed. In this particular case, I do not feel that the interruption of service in 1970-71 affects the considerations which I must give in determining the length of appropriate length of notice.

It is my view, considering the matters referred by Chief Justice McRuer and other matters such as the economic climate at the time, twenty-one months would have been an appropriate notice here. It is purely gratuitous for me to say that if Mr. Gordon's service, in fact, must run from 1971 and no regard to be had for the previous thirty years work with the company, the length of notice should have been somewhere in the range of fifteen to eighteen months. The important considerations which I think attach to this particular case, namely, the skill of the employee, his age, and his dedication to the company indicate such a period would be appropriate notice for Mr. Gordon if he had only nine years service. (at pp. 155-156)

The reasoning in *Roscoe* and *Gordon* was again applied in *Krewenchuk v. Lewis Construction Ltd.* (1985), 8. C.C.E.L. 206 (B.C.S.C.). In *Krewenchuk*, the plaintiff commenced employment with the defendant at age 18 as a carpenter's apprentice. In 1960, after completing a four-year period of apprenticeship, he became a journeyman carpenter with the defendant pursuant to an oral contract. He was so employed until 1972 when the plaintiff and defendant "terminated their relationship graciously and cordially." From time to time in the first period of employment, the plaintiff was laid off when there was insufficient work.

In 1975, the plaintiff approached the defendant for employment and was rehired. He was terminated without notice in April of 1982. Again during the latter period of employment the plaintiff was laid off for certain periods of time due to work shortages.

As to the weight to attach to the periods of interrupted employment, the Court stated:

> Here I view the interruptions in employment as being relatively unimportant and look on the plaintiff as being a long-term employee who was trusted sufficiently by his employer that he was named foreman of many projects. In my view, he should have received 12 months' notice. (at p. 212)

It is of interest that the Court did not specifically address what period it considered to be the plaintiff's length of service in determining the notice period. Having regard to the fact that the plaintiff was 44 when terminated, and was a foreman with managerial responsibilities, an assessment of notice based upon a 23-year period of employment would probably have resulted in a notice period in excess of 12 months. The Court may, therefore, have reduced the notice period somewhat having regard to the interruptions in service.

In other cases, however, the Court has viewed an interruption in service as being quite significant in assessing the period of reasonable notice. For example, in *Balchin v. Die-Cast Marwest Ltd.* (1987), 46 Man. R. (2d) 201 (Q.B.), the plaintiff was employed for a period of seven years in various positions, ranging from supervisor to production manager. The plaintiff was initially employed from December 1976 to September 1983. The plaintiff then left the defendant's employ for a period of ten months and returned for an 11-month period from July 1984 until April 1985, when he was terminated.

With respect to the interruption in service, the Court stated:

> Considering all the circumstances, the interruption in employment ought not to be disregarded for the purpose of establishing a reasonable notice period. Unlike the facts in the *Gordon* case, he did not receive back his position that he terminated. He was not "lured from a position in which he excelled and placed into a job which required him to deal with matters of which he had little or no knowledge" as in the *Roscoe* case. Unlike the instant case, in *Krewenchuk* the interruptions in employment were relatively unimportant.
>
> . . . .
>
> If doubt were to otherwise exist with respect to two separate and distinct periods of employment, the terms of his subsequent engagement must be reviewed. Although he assumed part of his former responsibilities, he was hired as a production manager. Neither did he assume his prior position with the company, nor did he receive the same salary. His duties were specified in Exhibit 6.

> His substantially reduced salary was subject to review, as well as his performance. (at p. 205)

The Court found that three months' notice was reasonable having regard to the factors set out above and the fact that the plaintiff was 55 years of age when dismissed.

Another interesting decision in this area is *Salituro v. Construction & General Workers Union, Local 602* (1988), 22 C.C.E.L. 183 (B.C.S.C.). In this case, the plaintiff was employed by the defendant union as a union organizer for approximately five years. The plaintiff quit on two separate occasions and was rehired on June 6, 1986, the day following his second resignation, on terms which were set out in a letter to him listing five conditions for his re-employment. The plaintiff was then terminated on July 15, 1986.

With respect to the appropriate notice period, the Court stated:

> In settling on the appropriate period of notice, I give little weight to the plaintiff's period of service prior to his rehiring on June 6, 1986. When he quit, unequivocally and without notice, on June 4, 1986, Mr. Salituro intended to terminate that employment and effectively did so. I must consider what term as to notice would be reasonable to imply when the plaintiff thereafter entered into the new contract of June 6 - one under which he was rehired on what I have found was essentially a trial basis. In arriving at that figure, having in mind the circumstances of his departure and rehiring, I believe reasonable people in the position of these parties would not at that time have given much weight to the previous term of employment. His age then was 39 or 40, and save to the extent that he himself damaged them in his dealings with the defendant, Mr. Salituro would have been thought to have good re-employment prospects within the union movement. (at p. 186)

The Court, therefore, found that six weeks was the appropriate notice period in all the circumstances. The Court was clearly influenced by the fact that the plaintiff had terminated his employment and was rehired on substantially different terms, which included a probationary period.

In *Roger Attridge v. Intertan Canada Ltd.* (15 March 1986), Doc. No. 20795/87 (Ont. H.C.), Mr. Justice R.E. Holland found that an interruption in service was of some significance in assessing reasonable notice. The plaintiff commenced employment with Radio Shack in 1976. The Radio Shack stores are franchises, joint venture arrangements, or are company-operated. Over the next 11 years the plaintiff held various positions, including sales clerk, manager of joint venture stores and district manager. He resigned for four months in 1982 and was reinstated. His final position, from July 1985 until his termination in March of 1987, was that of district manager for Toronto, central and northern Ontario.

With respect to the period of reasonable notice, the Court stated:

> I realize that when he was a joint venturer, he was not an employee. But in assessing the period of notice, some consideration should be given to the periods of association with the company in joint venture. The employment was not

> continuous. It was interrupted twice, each time for a short period. Again, some consideration should be given to the prior periods of employment. (at p. 6 of the judgment)

Having regard to the fact that the plaintiff was 48 years old, and had latterly held employment which required him to manage some 27 stores with direct responsibility for approximately 150 to 175 employees, the Court fixed the period of reasonable notice at ten months. Had the Court considered the plaintiff's employment as continuous, a greater period of notice would probably have been awarded.

An important consideration for the Court is the length and frequency of the interruptions as compared to the overall employment period. As well, the Court will look at the terms on which employment was resumed. Reinstatement with seniority, job title, pay, benefits and *de facto* responsibilities equal to or greater than those enjoyed before the interruption, will suggest that prior service has been taken into account by the parties. This implication is particularly strong if the employee has been induced to come back. The converse is true where the employee was rehired subject to demotion or probation.

(iii) *Interruption in Service: Change in Corporate Employer*

The leading case dealing with interruption due to a change in corporate employer is *Addision v. M. Loeb Ltd.* (1986), 11 C.C.E.L. 100, 53 O.R. (2d) 602, 25 D.L.R. (4th) 151, 13 O.A.C. 392 (C.A.), reversing (1984), 3 C.C.E.L. 277, 45 O.R. (2d) 399, 6 D.L.R. (4th) 566 (H.C.). In this case, the plaintiff commenced employment at a food store in May of 1963 in a clerical capacity. He quickly rose to the rank of assistant manager, which position he held until September 1981 when the business went into receivership. Two weeks later the receiver sold the assets of the business to the defendant. The defendant operated the store until April 1983, when the store was sold to a new owner-operator.

Upon the sale of the business to the defendant, each of the employees was requested to sign an employment agreement with the defendant. The plaintiff executed such an agreement and was given an increase in pay. The defendant also agreed to retrain the plaintiff as there was some question about the quality of the plaintiff's work. The plaintiff was later terminated without notice, upon the sale of the business by the defendant to the new manager/operator.

At trial, Mr. Justice Steele found that the plaintiff had only been employed by the defendant directly for approximately eighteen months and as such was entitled to six months' notice as a result of his wrongful dismissal. On appeal to the Court of Appeal, the plaintiff was awarded twelve months' salary in lieu of notice. The salient portion of judgment is as follows:

> If the employee is offered and accepts employment by his new employer, a new contract of employment is entered into. The consequences to an employee in such circumstances are, I think, fairly set forth in an article by M. Norman Grosman in (1984-85), 5 Advocates' Quarterly 500 at p. 502 as follows:

Once the employee accepts employment with the new employer, thereby establishing a new contract, he will probably "mitigate himself right out of his cause of action" against his former employer. If he fails to accept the new job and it is in all respects fundamentally the same as his old one, he is likely precluded by the doctrine of mitigation from recovering any loss sustained on the constructive termination on the basis that such loss could reasonably have been avoided. The unfortunate employee is caught in a bind and will inevitably suffer at least the loss of his perhaps lengthy service with the former employer. If, on the other hand, the new employer declines to employ the individual, the termination becomes express rather than constructive and the former employer will remain liable for any properly recoverable damage sustained by the employee.

I think that s. 13(2) of the Employment Standards Act, R.S.O. 1980, c. 137, (the "Act"), was enacted to avoid, to some extent, such unfairness and to give some recognition to an employee for his past services when his employer sells the business. Section 13(2) reads as follows:

> 13(2) Where an employer sells his business to a purchaser who employs an employee of the employer, the employment of the employee shall not be terminated by the sale, and the period of employment of the employee with the employer shall be deemed to have been employment with the purchaser *for the purposes of Parts VII, VIII, XI and XII.* (at pp. 103-104) [emphasis added]

The Court, however, rejected the submission that the *Employment Standards Act* provisions resulted in continuity of employment, for all purposes, on the sale of a business. The Court stated:

> It was submitted that the words of s. 13(2) which read, "Where an employer sells his business to a purchaser who employs an employee of the employer, the employment of the employee shall not be terminated by the sale", can stand by themselves, and thus on the sale of a business there is a continuity of employment with the new employer for all purposes. With respect, I do not think that s. 13(2) can be given such a broad interpretation. On such an interpretation there would have been no need to add the subsequent words of the Act since without them the employee would have received the benefits of s. 40(1). I think it is clear that what was intended by the statute and what it covers is that for the purposes of Pts. VII, VIII, XI and XII the employment of the employee shall not be terminated by a sale, but only for such purposes. (at p. 104)

In the result, the Court had regard to the various factors affecting the period of reasonable notice and stated:

> Although in a technical sense the appellant may have been a new employee of the respondent, it was clear on the evidence that he was not treated as such. According to the respondent's records, the commencement of the appellant's employment was stated to be May 1963. The appellant was given a wage increase which appears to be commensurate with other employees of long standing. There was a clear inference that both he and the respondent considered him as such.
>
> In these circumstances and in the absence of an express understanding to the contrary, it would, I think, be unfair to assess the appellant's damages for

> wrongful dismissal in the same manner as if he had walked into the store for the first time after the respondent purchased the business and became a new employee of the respondent, even at the rank of assistant manager. An examination of the authorities in cases where an employee has been employed by a purchaser of a business after having been employed for some time by the vendor and has subsequently been wrongfully dismissed discloses no clear principle other than that in the majority of the cases some recognition is given to the period of employment with the predecessor employer. (at p. 106)

In all the circumstances, the Court of Appeal awarded the plaintiff twelve months' salary in lieu of notice.

In the case of *Lyons v. Gainers Inc.* (1987), 17 C.C.E.L. 245 (Ont. Dist. Ct.), however, the *Addison* decision referred to above was distinguished. In *Lyons* the issue was whether, under a company personnel policy, an employee was entitled to be treated as a "separating employee," notwithstanding that the employee became employed by a purchaser of the business. In this case, although the plaintiff was employed by one company from 1956 to 1981, when the business was sold the plaintiff became an employee of the defendant on the closing of the transaction for the sale of the business. In 1983 the defendant sold its assets to another company. The next business day after the sale the plaintiff became an employee of the purchaser with no loss of benefits. In this case, the plaintiff claimed that he was terminated without just cause by the second company, the defendant in this case, even though he was immediately rehired by the purchaser of the business.

In essence, the plaintiff claimed that under the personnel policy manual of the defendant, a "separating" employee would include an employee whose job is terminated due to an asset purchase and thus this employee would be entitled to a severance allowance. The defendant's strongest argument was that the plaintiff was not a separating employee and that a novation of the contract had occurred so that the employment of the plaintiff was never severed (novation being a substitution, with the consent of the employee, of the purchaser in the place of the vendor). The defendant argued that by novation, the plaintiff's employment continued, so that his job was not severed.

A careful review of the company personnel manual resulted in a determination by the Court that "taken together, these paragraphs spell out that the company would pay separation allowance or would continue service to a person rehired, but not both, as is requested in this claim." (at p. 240)

The Court, referring with approval to the case of *Sorel v. Tomenson Saunders Whitehead Ltd.* (1987), 16 C.C.E.L. 223, 15 B.C.L.R. (2d) 38, 39 D.L.R. (4th) 460 (C.A.), stated:

> [I]t was found that the contract of employment between the purchaser of a business and the firm's employees includes an implied term that the workers will receive credit for their previous years service with the vendor for matters such as salaries, bonuses, and notice of dismissal. The situation was described beginning at p. 4 of the decision [p. 40 B.C.L.R.]:

1. When a purchaser acquires a business as a going concern, there is an implied term in the contract of employment between it and those employees continuing in the service of the business, that the employees will be given credit for years past service with the vendor for purposes of such incidents of employment as salaries, bonuses and notice of termination.
2. This implied term may be negated by an express term to the contrary. In other words, the purchasing employer may, at his option, advise the employees that he does not intend to give them credit for past services to the vendor. If this is done, the employees have the option of entering into the new contract of employment on these terms or of declining to work for the purchasing company and suing the vendor for wrongful dismissal and damages in lieu of notice.
3. Where the new employer does not advise the employees that he is unwilling to contract on the basis that the employees have credit for past years of service, the employer is deemed to have contracted with the employees on the basis that the employees will be given such credit.

In the case at Bar, Mr. Lyons would fall under points 1 and 3. Therefore, the contract of employment between Mr. Lyons and Gainers would be subject to an implied term that Mr. Lyons would be given full credit for his years of service with Gainers. It follows that severance pay would not be payable, as employment was not interrupted. (at pp. 252-253)

On the issue of novation, the Court stated:

A recent case on this subject is *Paul v. Etiquette C.W.L. Ltée*, a decision of the Honourable Judge Heather Smith, April 2, 1986, in this Court. This was a wrongful dismissal case, involving a purchase of assets of the defendant company. At p. 3 of the decision, Judge Smith states:

> The plaintiff himself acquiesced in working with and for the defendant by working in exactly the same capacity, on the same unique terms, with the same responsibility, servicing the same clients, and producing the same type of product. He was not required to sign anything or to change anything as he continued doing his job for the defendant after July 1983. The employment was continuous and on exactly the same basis as prior to the change of employer. No new employment relationship had to be created, just the substitution of a new employer, in essence, in novation of the original employment contract on exactly the same terms on the implied consent of both parties.
>
> Was the contract thus renewed or at least confirmed then by the acquiescence of both parties? Ordinarily on the sale of a business, an employee's contract of employment would automatically terminate unless the parties agree to assign it to the new owner. See *Nokes v. Doncaster Amalgamated Collieries Ltd.* (1940) A.C. 1014 (H.L.). In *Nokes*, it was held that there was automatic termination unless the parties agreed to assign the contract to the new owner, in which case it could be said that the new owner was assuming the employee's contract including the obligations as to dismissal. The case seems to go beyond express assignments and includes implied assignments or novations. One must look to the facts in a particular case to see whether there is an implied assignment or novation and look to whether or not an

> employee continues to provide the same services which are accepted by the new owner.
>
> On the facts before me, I am content that novation has occurred. The critical factors appear to be that the plaintiff continued to work in the same manner, on the same unique terms, on the same material and in the same capacity as before the asset purchase. By the defendant's act of paying the plaintiff and taking his finished products on exactly the same terms there was a clear novation of the original employment contract and a substitution of the liability of the old employer by the new. From that pattern of conduct, it can be concluded that a term of the plaintiff's continuing contract of employment was that it commenced as the time of first employment before the asset purchase. (at pp. 253-254)

The Court went on to distinguish the *Addison* decision on the basis that "there was no contract in that case whereby the purchaser of assets agreed to offer the employment on substantially the same terms and conditions, so that novation was not an issue." (at p. 255)

In the result, the Court found:

> (1) The plaintiff did not fit within the definition of a "separating employee"; and
>
> (2) novation occurred, by the implied assent of the plaintiff, so that his contract of employment was never terminated upon the sale by Gainers to Canada Packers.
>
> In effect, I find an employee, continuing his job with a business that is sold to another and he receiving continuing substantially similar benefits, should not obtain also the severance pay entitlements in his former company's personnel manual, the latter being often regarded as protection for employees terminated upon a sale. (at pp. 255-256)

The Court may also have been influenced by the fact that, if successful, the plaintiff would have obtained double recovery as he claimed a separation payment from the first employer despite the fact that he was continuously employed throughout.

(e) Job Performance

It has long been accepted that a court will, at least implicitly, recognize that a skilled and valuable employee is deserving of a somewhat longer notice period than a mediocre employee. This is so notwithstanding that as a matter of law both have been dismissed without just cause.

A few cases, however, went so far as to explicitly recognize that the period of notice should be reduced for poor performance and this was sometimes referred to as the doctrine of "near cause." Similarly, other cases found that superior performance justified a somewhat longer period of reasonable notice. For example, see *Smith v. Dawson Memorial Hospital* (1978), 29 N.S.R. (2d) 277, 45 A.P.R. 277 (T.D.); *Morrell v. Grafton-Fraser Inc.* (1981), 44 N.S.R. (2d) 289, 83 A.P.R. 289 (S.C.), affirmed (1982), 51 N.S.R. (2d) 138, 102 A.P.R. 138 (C.A.); *Taylor v. Dave Buck Ford Sales Ltd.*, [1978] 1 A.C.W.S. 497 (B.C.S.C.).

The notion that the notice period should be increased or decreased having regard to the performance of the employee was firmly rejected by the Ontario Court of Appeal in *Helbig v. Oxford Warehousing Ltd.* (1985), 9 C.C.E.L. 75, 51 O.R. (2d) 421, 6 C.P.R. (3d) 460, 20 D.L.R. (4th) 112, 9 O.A.C. 145 (C.A.), leave to appeal to Supreme Court of Canada refused (1985), 52 O.R. (2d) 754 (headnote only), 64 N.R. 157 (note), 14 O.A.C. 240 (note) (S.C.C.). Writing for the Court, with respect to this issue, Mr. Justice Finlayson stated:

> In arriving at an 18-month period, the learned trial Judge laid particular stress on the very high quality of the employee in question and the contribution that he had made to the company. This ignores the fact that the test in *Bardal* is an objective one. We are not concerned with the personality of the employee but with the characterization of the employment. This is very well put by McEachern C.J.S.C. in *Steinicke v. Manning Press Ltd.*, [1984] 4 W.W.R. 491, 55 B.C.L.R. 320, 4 C.C.E.L. 294 at 297 (B.C. C.A.):
>
>> The employees' remedy for loss of employment is limited to reasonable notice or pay in lieu thereof. All relevant facts must be taken into account in determining what is reasonable notice, but the test is an objective one, and the fact that the plaintiff may have been wiser than the defendant, if such was the case, and I make no findings in that connection, does not increase the plaintiff's damages, except to the extent if any, that those facts bear on the question of notice.
>
> Similarly, the Court cannot extend the period of notice just to compensate the plaintiff for the extra efforts he put into the operation on behalf of his employer. I must assume that he was paid for what he did during the period of his employment.
>
> This Court has already stated in *Harold Johnson v. Gen. Tire Can. Ltd.* (unreported), released April 22, 1985, that conduct of an employee, which is not sufficient to justify discharge, cannot be weighed against him in determining an appropriate severance time. Similarly, as here, the fact that the employee had made a significant contribution to the company is equally irrelevant because he was hired and paid to make a significant contribution. (at pp. 86-87)

As was noted, however, in *Babcock v. C. & R. Weickert Enterprises Ltd.* (1993), 50 C.C.E.L. 1, (*sub nom. Babcock v. Weickert (C. & R.) Enterprises Ltd.*) 126 N.S.R. (2d) 170, 352 A.P.R. 170 (C.A.):

> A moderation in this position may be indicated in a decision of the Ontario Court of Appeal in *Queensbury Enterprises Inc. v. J.R. Corporate Planning Associates Inc.* (1989), 27 C.C.E.L. 56 (Ont. C.A.). At trial, Catzman J. concluded that a submission by the defence that the period of reasonable notice should be reduced by reason of the plaintiff's impaired performance, was "foreclosed in principle to the defendant by the decisions of the Court of Appeal of this province."
>
> The Ontario Court of Appeal, in affirming the finding of just cause, stated [at p. 57]:
>
>> . . . we are not prepared to hold as a matter of law that a defendant may never claim a reduction in the damages for wrongful dismissal for conduct short of that justifying dismissal, but we are satisfied that there can be no reduction in the circumstances of this case. (at p. 11)

The Nova Scotia Court of Appeal in *Babcock* adopted what it referred to as the "moderated damages" principle.

Without discussing the authorities, the Court in *Rock v. Canadian Red Cross Society* (1994), 5 C.C.E.L. (2d) 231, 94 C.L.L.C. 14,048 (Ont. Gen. Div.), additional reasons at (1994), 7 C.C.E.L. (2d) 146 (Ont. Gen. Div.) reduced what it said would have been a 24-month notice period to 20 months, having regard to the fact that the plaintiff had admittedly breached certain employer policies leading to her termination.

The "near cause" or "moderated damages" principle was rejected by the Saskatchewan Court of Appeal in *Page v. Jim Pattison Industries Ltd.*, 4 C.C.E.L. 283, [1984] 4 W.W.R. 481, 10 D.L.R. (4th) 430, 33 Sask. R. 253 (C.A.). In this case, the employee had been dismissed for refusing to accept a transfer which would have involved an advancement in his employment. At trial, the Court found an implied term in the employee's contract of employment that required him to accept a reasonable transfer not involving a demotion. The trial Judge, while finding that termination was justified, held that the employer was not entitled to summarily dismiss the employee. The trial Judge, therefore, awarded the employee a reduced amount of compensation in lieu of notice.

The Court of Appeal, while affirming the trial Judge's view that the term relating to transfers was implicit in the contract, allowed the employer's appeal, holding that the employee's refusal of the transfer entitled the employer to terminate the employee immediately without notice. Mr. Justice Vancise, speaking for the Court of Appeal, suggested that this was an unusual case for the application of the concept of "near cause" in that the concept had usually been applied where an employee had been guilty of some misconduct which was insufficient to justify termination without notice. In any case, the Court denied that "near cause" had any place in a wrongful dismissal action:

> There is no middle ground. The employer either has cause or he does not. The employee is either satisfactorily discharging the employment obligations undertaken by him under the contract of employment, or he is not. An employee who repudiates the contract of employment, is not entitled to "some" notice because he or she has been a "good" employee prior to such repudiation. (at p. 293)

The conclusion that performance (other than performance amounting to just cause for dismissal) is irrelevant to determining the period of notice probably benefits both employers and employees. The number of wrongful dismissal lawsuits would rise dramatically if it were open to the parties to dispute levels of performance. Further, the duration, and hence, cost, of the litigation would soar if it became relevant in every case to consider the quality of the performance of the employment contract.

(f) Reasonableness of Employer Offer

An interesting development which bears on reasonable notice is the concept of "ballpark justice" or "fairness." The concept of ballpark justice, if given widespread judicial acceptance, would extend considerable comfort to employers.

The concept first appeared in the following trilogy of cases in the Supreme Court of Ontario: *Perry v. Gulf Minerals Can. Ltd.* (1985), 30 A.C.W.S. (2d) 524 (Ont. H.C.); *Rivers v. Gulf Can. Ltd.* (1986), 13 C.C.E.L. 131 (Ont. H.C.); and *McKee v. NCR Can. Ltd.* (1986), 10 C.C.E.L. 128 (Ont. H.C.).

The classic statement on ballpark justice was made by Mr. Justice R.E. Holland in *Perry*, as follows:

> It appears to be me that in judging the severance arrangements I should not arbitrarily fix what I consider to be a proper period of notice based on the facts of the case and the authorities, but rather should approach the matter first on the basis of whether or not the employer's severance arrangements were fair. If the period of notice under the severance arrangements was reasonable, then I do not think that I should interfere or tinker with the result. If the period notice was unreasonable, that is a different matter and the Court should interfere. (at p. 6 of the judgment)

This doctrine was subsequently applied in *McKee* by Mr. Justice Reid of the Ontario Supreme Court. In that case, the employee had been offered 12 months' notice upon termination by the employer. In all the facts of the case, Reid J. found that he might have granted 12 to 15 months' notice. Applying the ballpark justice doctrine, however, Mr. Justice Reid found that the employer's offer of 12 months' notice was within the "reasonable range" and awarded the employee 12 months' notice.

(*Continued on page 6-23*)

This concept was considered by Mr. Justice Smith of the Ontario High Court in *De Freitas v. Cdn. Express & Transportation Ltd.* (1986), 16 C.C.E.L. 160 (Ont. H.C.), affirmed (1988), 18 C.C.E.L. xxiii (Ont. C.A.). The employee had been employed continuously from September of 1959 until November of 1984 in various capacities. In 1984, the defendant corporation merged with another corporation and a number of positions, including that of the plaintiff, were eliminated. The employer offered the employee a severance package which included six months' full salary regardless of whether the employee obtained other employment during the six months, and further provided for up to a maximum of nine months' salary should the employee be unemployed for longer than six months. The employee was also provided with a relocation counselling service at a cost of $6,000.

Mr. Justice Smith stated:

> My brothers, in those cases, would cast a threshold onus upon a plaintiff to show the unreasonableness of any offer made by the employer. As I understand their position, it is somewhat like an appellate Court refusing to interfere in an assessment of damages even when the amount is lower or higher than the appellate Court would have been prepared to allow, as long as it is not grossly inadequate.
>
> The Court of Appeal has not passed upon this suggested gloss. On the one hand, I find the approach attractive because in a wrongful dismissal suit, the Court is engaged in the exercise of determining whether an implied term of the contract was breached, namely the term that when the contract is for an indefinite term, it will not be terminated except upon reasonable notice.
>
> The reasoning is then as follows: the Court may well prefer a lengthier or shorter period without being prepared to brand the employer's offer as unreasonable. In such a case, the plaintiff should lose, because he would not have established a breach of the implied term.
>
> On the other hand, this view makes me uneasy, for it can lead to the Court's abdication of its function in favour of the employer, who could then be said to be usurping a judicial function. So long as the difference between the notice offered and the notice judged appropriate by the Court in all of the circumstances and taking account of all of the recognized principles is minimal, I suppose my reticence can be overcome.
>
> In this case, counsel for the defendant conceded that the margin of permissible error, so to speak, should be about three months. My brothers, Galligan and Reid appeared to be approximately of the same view, that a three-month difference or less would not trigger the Court's interference. (at pp. 161-162)

Although Mr. Justice Smith discussed the concept of "a threshold onus upon a plaintiff to show the unreasonableness of any offer made by the employer," in the result he found that the offer by the defendant corporation was unreasonable by any standard and fixed the period of notice at eighteen months. The *De Freitas* case was appealed to the Ontario Court of Appeal. The appeal was dismissed and no comment made by the Court on the concept of ballpark justice.

The concept of ballpark justice was applied in *Mirza v. Polysar Ltd.* (1988), 23 C.C.E.L. 316 (Ont. H.C.), varied (March 18, 1991), Doc. CA 48/89 (Ont. C.A.). The employee, Mirza, was 52 years old and had worked 22 years as an engineer, earning approximately $43,000 per year when dismissed. Polysar offered a settlement package to Mirza which included 12 months' salary plus benefits, tuition payments for his daughters, office space and support staff to aid in the search for new employment and counselling services. Mirza refused this offer and brought an action for wrongful dismissal. Mr. Justice Rutherford examined the principle enunciated in *Perry* and concluded that the offer made by Polysar was reasonable. Mirza's notice and damages were, therefore, limited to the settlement proposed by Polysar.

In *McCrea v. Conference Board of Canada* (1993), 45 C.C.E.L. 29 (Ont. Gen. Div.), the Court specifically rejected the "ballpark justice" or "reasonable range" approach in wrongful dismissal cases. After considering the precedents, Mr. Justice Rutherford stated:

> While the "reasonable range" approach has a certain appeal, not the least of which might be to discourage litigation, I am inclined to prefer the traditional approach. For one thing, as pointed out by O'Driscoll J. in *Grant v. MacMillan Bloedel* [*Grant v. MacMillan Bloedel Industries Ltd.* (1982), 83 C.L.L.C. 12,007 (Ont. H.C.)], curial deference to the assessment of another, unless the assessment is clearly unreasonable, is normally reserved for judicial review of a decision taken in a judicial or quasi-judicial setting where a reasonable result is the duty of the authority making the assessment. There is no such mandate on employers, other than what flows, perhaps, from moral expectation. Nor is there any reason to expect that employers will generally, upon termination, accord employees notice or compensation in lieu thereof other than at the lower or minimal point within the range of what might be considered appropriate. Moreover, I do not see any basis for proceeding in a fashion which has the result of placing the dismissed employee in a position of having an onus to show that the notice given was beyond the bounds of what anyone considers reasonable.
>
> It is all very well to say that it is consonant with the requirement that reasonable notice be given, that the notice or payment in lieu thereof must therefore be assessed to determine if it was reasonable. But should that really lead to anything other than the traditional approach in which what is reasonable is determined in court as a matter of fact, or mixed fact and law? In negligence actions, what amounts to reasonable conduct has not been subjected to some special ballpark or range theory whereby a plaintiff must show that a settlement or offer is beyond the range of what might be considered reasonable, before being able to proceed to trial.
>
> Particularly in circumstances such as those in the present case, in which both the period of employment and the period of reasonable notice are relatively short, a relatively small departure from what was offered makes a relatively large difference in percentage terms. Adding only three months, for example, would double the award or entitlement. Such a small, but relatively significant difference might well be preferred by a court which, at the same time, might be reticent to brand the employer's action as unreasonable. We all know that reasonable people may differ on matters but that, in my view, should not deprive

the plaintiff in a wrongful dismissal action from seeking the uncompromised judgment of the court.

Adopting this traditional approach does not discourage employers from giving reasonable notice or amounts in lieu thereof to terminated employees, nor should it encourage employees to litigate points of principle for their own sake. The cost of litigation and particularly the costs consequences of failure to recognize a reasonable award for what it is constitute a real discipline in this regard.

For the foregoing reasons, I am not prepared nor do I think it appropriate for me, on a motion for summary judgment in this wrongful dismissal action, to assess the compensation given by the employer in lieu of reasonable notice against the range of what might be reasonable in the circumstances with a view to granting judgment to the defendant unless the plaintiff shows the compensation to fall outside of that range. (at pp. 35-36)

In *Garvin v. Rockwell International of Canada Ltd.* (1993), 50 C.C.E.L. 295 (Ont. Gen. Div.), Mr. Justice Ferguson gave extensive reasons rejecting the ballpark justice principle as follows:

Reason 1

I do not think the threshold approach is consistent with the established theory as to what the court's function is in a termination case. As I understand it the court is to determine the length of the period of notice which is an implied term of the contract of employment. (at p. 299)

. . . .

Reason 2

The threshold approach is unfair in allocating the risk of litigation between the employer and the employee. The employee is the disadvantaged party because of the termination and it is not fair to burden the employee with the greater risk of losing the litigation by saying, in effect, that if the employer offers something which is in the range of what the court thinks is appropriate then the employee will lose his case and risk paying the employer's costs.

. . . .

Reason 3

The threshold approach is not consistent with the established approach to making similar determinations in other types of cases.

In tort cases the court performs an analogous function in assessing damages. In a personal injury case the court does not consider as a threshold issue whether the amount of damages offered before trial is reasonable; the court decides what reasonable compensation is and only then finds out what, if anything, has been offered. The same approach is followed in making other assessments such as the amount of support in a family law case.

. . . .

Reason 4

I do not think the threshold approach is consistent with the role of a trial court in our adversary system. For instance, if a defendant has made an offer before trial

> the plaintiff does not lose or even forfeit her right to costs simply because the trial judge decides the offer was in the range of what was reasonable. The judge makes a determination as to a specific amount and the plaintiff receives that amount — not a lower previously offered amount which is in the reasonable range. The plaintiff typically recovers her costs of the proceeding if, as stated in r. 49.10, she obtains a judgment as "favourable as or more favourable than the terms of the offer." The determinative criterion is not a range but a specific figure determined by the court.
>
> *Conclusion*
>
> In considering why the threshold approach was adopted in earlier cases, Justice Smith in *De Freitas* [*supra*] speculated that it was based on the theory that "it is somewhat like an appellate Court refusing to interfere in an assessment of damages even when the amount is lower or higher than the appellate Court would have been prepared to allow, as long as it is not grossly inadequate." (at pp. 161-162)]
>
> I do not think the analogy is apt. An appellate court may refuse to interfere when it concludes that the trial judge's assessment is in a range of what is reasonable. But the reason it refuses to interfere is that a decision has been made by an impartial judge who has made the determination on established legal principles. To suggest that the trial court should not interfere where one of the litigants has proposed something in the reasonable range for indeterminable reasons is entirely different.
>
> In my view it is not appropriate to apply a threshold or ballpark approach. In my view the trial court should not express its view by reference to a range but should make a specific determination as to what it thinks is the reasonable period of notice in the circumstances and then award judgment if the employee received any less. (at pp. 302-304)

The ballpark justice principle has received some consideration in other jurisdictions. In *Locke v. Avco Financial Services Can. Ltd.* (1987), 85 N.B.R. (2d) 93, 217 A.P.R. 93 (Q.B.), the Court approved of the ballpark justice principle. The Court stated that:

> There is logic to this approach. Settlements should be encouraged and as well employers should be encouraged under these circumstances to make reasonable proposals rather than treating the matter in a totally adversary fashion. (at p. 99)

The Court, however, concluded that:

> In the present circumstances the defendant's proposal was for nine months firm and the possibility of a further six months on a month to month basis. In addition there was disagreement between the parties with respect to pension contributions and bonus payments. As I shall detail shortly it is my finding that the plaintiff was entitled to recognition of these compensations. In the appropriate case one might well be inclined to follow the rationale referred to. On the facts in the present case I do not feel that the proposal put forward by the defendant was such as to modify my consideration of a period of 18 months notice as being reasonable. (at pp. 99-100)

Thus, although the Court approved of the logic behind reasonable settlement offers, the Court did not find that the three-month difference, combined with the arguments over the pension and bonus payments, was a sufficiently minor difference to place the settlement offer within the ball park.

Similarly, in the case of *Michalchuk v. B.C. Hydro & Power Authority* (1987), 4 A.C.W.S. (3d) 418 (B.C.S.C.), the ballpark justice doctrine was considered. The Court held:

> While I respectfully prefer not to adopt the approach mentioned by Holland and Galligan, J.J. as an invariable rule, I agree that the selection of a notice period is

(*Continued on page 6-25*)

> not a precise exercise and the Plaintiff has not satisfied me that 15 months is not reasonable compensation in lieu of notice in this case. (at p. 4 of the judgment)

In *Michalchuk*, the employee had worked for 18½ years and was 48 years of age. At the time of dismissal he was earning approximately $48,000. The employee's position was that if he had received 19 months' notice his pension rights would have fully vested. Instead he received a refund of amounts he had paid into the pension fund. The employee's solicitor originally claimed 15 months' pay in lieu of notice. The employer had offered 40 weeks' pay in lieu of notice. The employer responded to the employee's offer of 15 months' pay with an offer of 12 months' pay plus 30 per cent on account of benefits, which the Judge felt was equivalent to 15 months' pay. The employee did not accept this offer and claimed for 19 months' notice at trial. As stated before, the Court awarded the 15 months' notice on the basis that the employer offer was reasonable. It is unclear whether the Court in fact did apply the ballpark justice doctrine at all.

The doctrine was specifically rejected in *Heinz v. Cana Construction Co.* (1987), 55 Alta. L.R. (2d) 382, 82 A.R. 197 (Q.B.). In that case, Mr. Justice Stratten explained his reasons for rejecting the notion of ballpark justice as follows:

> It was submitted by the defendant that its last offer to the plaintiff given with its 2nd June 1986 letter offering 12 months in lieu of notice was reasonable under all the circumstances and, even if I should consider it lower than what I would award, if I nevertheless consider it to be "within the ball park" of reasonableness, then I should not interfere with it. I do not agree with that approach. It seems to confuse the concept of "curial deference" as it may sometimes apply to a review of decisions of a quasi-judicial tribunal with the proper test applicable to wrongful dismissal cases. I agree with the following comments of O'Driscoll J. in *Grant v. MacMillan Bloedel Indust. Ltd.* (1982), 83 C.L.L.C. 12007 at 12012 (Ont. H.C.), in dealing with a similar argument:
>
> > Counsel for the defendant submitted that I should not interfere with the discretion of the defendant management's decision of 12 months' notice unless I should find that 12 months' notice was an error in principal (*sic*). It was argued that I should not order a greater or lesser period of notice simply because I would have awarded a longer or shorter period of notice.
> >
> > In my view, such a submission is appropriate when dealing with the decision of the Master, a judicial officer. I cannot, however, see how such analogy could possibly be applicable to the defendant's management; it is not an impartial nor an independent third party judicial arbitrator. (at pp. 389-390)

It is respectfully submitted that if the ballpark justice principle is to be applied it should be limited to those cases in which the Judge is truly undecided where the period of notice should fall within a certain, and relatively narrow, range. In such cases it would be consistent with the general principles of contract law to look at the conduct of the parties. If either of the contracting parties has made an offer within the range, then this element of conduct, although perhaps deserving of only slight weight, may be enough to tip the judicial scale in favour of finding that the offered notice corresponds with reasonable notice. It is, however, submitted that the ballpark doctrine should not be given any broader scope by reason of the fact that, as stated by Mr. Justice O'Driscoll, the determination of the period of notice by the employer, or the employee, is not entitled to the deference that would be due the decision of a judicial or quasi-judicial body.

(g) Disability Arising During the Period of Reasonable Notice

In *Dunlop v. B.C. Hydro & Power Authority* (1988), 23 C.C.E.L. 96, 32 B.C.L.R. (2d) 334, [1989] 2 W.W.R. 518 (C.A.), the Court considered the case of a 61-year-old employee who was dismissed after 10 years of service. B.C. Hydro terminated the employee and paid him 8 months' salary in lieu of notice; however, a necessary consequence of his termination was that the employee lost the right to participate in the B.C. Hydro disability plan upon termination. Eight months after termination, while doing volunteer work at his church, the employee suffered a disabling injury which continued for 12 months. The trial Judge found that a 20-month period of notice was reasonable but ruled that the employee had failed to prove any loss due to the fact that, had the employee received reasonable advance notice of termination, his entitlement to salary would have ended at the time his disability arose. The Court of Appeal allowed an appeal and compensated the employee for lost salary and fringe benefits to the conclusion of the 20-month period of reasonable notice. Mr. Justice Lambert, for the Court, reasoned as follows:

> In considering that issue it is important to understand the nature of the implied term in the contract of employment. The implied term is a term to the effect that each party must give reasonable notice of termination to the other. The implied term is not a term to the effect that the employer may give pay in lieu of notice. There are a number of reasons why the latter term is not implied from the employment relationship as part of the contract of employment. It would be a more complicated term than can readily be implied by following the business efficacy and officious bystander rules. It would not operate in the same way with respect to the employee as it would with respect to the employer. It would mean that if an employer elected to give pay in lieu of notice, the employer would be complying with the contract and not breaking it. And the contract would require the full payment to be made immediately. The true nature of the implied term, namely, as being a term that each party must give the other reasonable notice of termination, is indicated by the customary application of the principle of mitigation. If the implied term were to be considered to contain a provision for pay in lieu of notice, and if the employer elected to invoke that term and gave no notice of termination, there would be no obligation on the part of the employee to mitigate damages by seeking other employment, even if the employer did not pay the full amount that such a term would have required, because such a term would require immediate payment of the full amount with regard to the measurement of any loss actually suffered by the employee. But the principle of mitigation is consistently applied, even where the employer elects to make a payment in lieu of notice. The reason is that, when an employer gives pay in lieu of notice, he does so

as an attempt to compensate for his breach of the contract of employment, not as an attempt to comply with an implied term of the contract of employment.

For the purposes of this case, the point to be derived from an understanding of the nature of the implied term is that when B.C. Hydro dismissed Mr. Dunlop without notice but with a payment in lieu of notice, it broke the contract of employment.

. . . I disagree with the conclusion that Mr. Dunlop had not proved any loss. In my opinion, the events which might have occurred if the employer had complied with the contract of employment, and so given the employee reasonable notice, but which did not actually occur, cannot determine the amount of damages suffered by the employee when the employer breaks the contract of employment and makes those events inconsequential. At that stage the employer cannot avail itself of any hypothetical alternatives, such as disability, which might have arisen if the contract had not been broken. By dismissing Mr. Dunlop, B.C. Hydro had elected to disqualify him from the disability benefit plans. B.C. Hydro, in those circumstances, cannot later say that it would not have had to pay salary while Mr. Dunlop was disabled, if it hadn't broken its contract, and if he had still been in its employment serving out the notice period. When B.C. Hydro broke the contract of employment it lost its right to rely on the provision in that contract that no salary would be paid with respect to a period of disability. And it must be borne in mind that if Mr. Dunlop had not been dismissed he would not have been working in his church basement on a weekday and would not have been injured.

I add that, in considering the significance of events following the dismissal, the proper principle, in my opinion, is that an event which occurs after a wrongful dismissal and before trial, or before the end of the notice period, whichever comes first, may be considered in assessing the damages actually suffered by the dismissed employee. The legal significance to be attached to the event will depend on the nature of the event and on the other relevant factors in the case. But, to the extent that the damages are derived from a determination of the proper notice period, that notice period is determinable once and for all at the time of the breach of contract and is not, itself, affected by subsequent events.

In this case Mr. Dunlop's disability does not have any effect on the period of reasonable notice, and, because of B.C. Hydro's breach of contract, that disability cannot be relied upon by B.C. Hydro, under the breached contract of employment, to diminish Mr. Dunlop's damages or to deny his claim. (at pp. 100-101)

The exposure of the employer to damages in the event that a disability arises during the period of reasonable notice is discussed in Chapter 6.4(b)(vi).

(h) Other Factors

(i) *Employment in Remote Community — Lifetime Commitment from Employees*

In *Johnston v. Algoma Steel Corp.* (1989), 24 C.C.E.L. 1, 89 C.L.L.C. 14,012 (Ont. H.C.), the Court found that a 48-year-old foreman, who had been terminated after 23 years of "devoted service," had been wrongfully dismissed. In coming to the conclusion that a 24-month notice period was appropriate, Mr. Justice Granger stated:

At the time of termination, Johnston was 48 years of age, having devoted most of his working life to Algoma. As I listened to the evidence of the Algoma employees, it was apparent that their employment at Algoma was a major part of their lives, and early retirement left a large void in their lives.

Algoma, from all the evidence which I heard, was a caring employer who sought a lifetime commitment from its employees. Apparently Algoma was successful in this regard as the management people who gave evidence appeared to be content in their positions and their commitment to Algoma was life-long. Algoma must realize its responsibility to long-term lower management personnel and the difficulties a long-term employee would have in finding alternative employment.

Algoma, as the largest employer in Sault Ste. Marie, has a responsibility to its foremen which cannot be discharged by giving 9-12 months' notice. If an employer in a relatively small northern community lacking similar large industry encourages employees to stay in its employ, the company must accept the responsibility of lengthy notice. Surely Algoma should not be entitled to consume most of the working life of a foreman such as Johnston and then discharge him with 9 months' notice as suggested by Algoma. Such notice does not discharge Algoma's responsibility to Johnston or the community.

In determining the length of time required to obtain alternative employment for a foreman, I must take into account the potential mobility of the employee and the available alternative employment in the area.

In many ways, it would be more difficult for a foreman or supervisor to find alternative employment than an executive who is probably more mobile and can consider alternative employment in a variety of areas. A vice-president who travels across Canada would have numerous contacts nation wide and would be familiar with hiring practices across the land.

If a vice-president or manager has worked in various parts of the country with different corporations, there will be less shock on termination and a greater ability to find alternative employment than that experienced by a foreman or supervisor who has worked for one employer and had never considered leaving the area.

In *Blakeley v. Victaulic Co. of Can. Ltd.*, released 21 February 1979, (Ont. H.C.), Carruthers J. stated:

> I have to think in my own mind that at age 54, having spent 24 years, nearly if not all of his working life, with one company, doing only that kind of work that is available through that company, it would be virtually impossible for a person such as the plaintiff to ever regain that type of employment during the remaining working years that are left to him.

The bleak prospects of Johnston for similar employment must be balanced against the right of the employer to select its employees. In *Warren v. Super Drug Markets Ltd.* (1965), 53 W.W.R. 25, 54 D.L.R. (2d) 183 (Sask. Q.B.), Tucker J. stated, at p. 34 (W.W.R.):

> While no master is obliged to retain in his employ a servant under a contract of indefinite hiring with whom he is not satisfied for any reason whatsoever, such servant may not be dismissed without reasonable notice unless there is just ground for dismissal: *Guildford v. Anglo-French Steamship Co.* (1885), 9 S.C.R. 303, affirming 14 N.S.R. 54; *Bole v. Pelissier's Ltd.* [1930] 3 W.W.R. 510, 25 Sask. L.R. 210; *Havard v. Freeholders Oil Co., supra*; *Tracey v. Swansea Const. Co., supra.*

Balancing the rights and responsibilities of Algoma to its foreman Johnston, reasonable notice would be 24 months. (at pp. 12-13)

(ii) *Notice of Likelihood of Termination*

In *Harper v. Bank of Montreal* (1989), 27 C.C.E.L. 54 (Ont. Div. Ct.), the Court found that in determining the period of reasonable notice, some weight should be given to the fact that for approximately 11 weeks prior to termination the plaintiff "had reasonable grounds to believe he would likely be terminated and in fact was actively seeking other employment." The Court also noted that the actual time taken by an employee to find employment related solely to the issue of mitigation and was not a factor to be considered in determining the period of reasonable notice. This is consistent with the reasoning in *Ostick v. Novacorp International Consulting Inc.* (1989), 27 C.C.E.L. 286 (B.C. S.C.), in which the Court held that the fact that the plaintiff commenced alternative employment immediately after termination was irrelevant to the determination of the appropriate notice period.

In *Porter v. Highmont Operating Corp.* (1990), 29 C.C.E.L. 164 (B.C. S.C.), reversed in part (1991), 36 C.C.E.L. 1 (B.C. C.A.), the plaintiff was employed for 20 years in different capacities in relation to a mine owned by the defendant. A decision was made to close the mine and thereafter the plaintiff accepted a position as a security guard. The plaintiff knew that his position would be terminated when the assets were sold. After approximately four years had elapsed, the defendant had sold most of the mine assets and had no further need for a security guard. As a result, the Court found that the plaintiff could not be treated as a 24-year employee and should instead be treated as a person who accepted employment as a security guard "for a comparatively short term which would expire when all the company assets had been sold". In these peculiar circumstances, the Court found that a three-month notice period was appropriate.

(iii) *Wrongful Accusation of Theft*

In *Trask v. Terra Nova Motors Ltd.* (1991), 35 C.C.E.L. 208, 89 Nfld. & P.E.I.R. 130, 278 A.P.R. 130 (Nfld. T.D.), the Court considered the effect of a wrongful accusation of theft on the determination of the reasonable notice period. In this regard, Mr. Justice Barry stated:

> In the present case, considering Carl Trask's age of 33, his length of service of 7 years, his Grade X education at the time of termination, his limited work experience outside of the automobile industry, and his general work experience within that industry, I hold that, in the normal course of events, Carl Trask would be entitled to 9 months' notice or pay in lieu of notice.
>
> However, events were not normal in these circumstances. Carl Trask testified that, following his dismissal, he searched for employment with other automobile dealers. One, in particular, was Hickman Motors Limited. There the person who interviewed him gave general assurances that there might be employment if his references checked out. Later that day he was told by the interviewer that he didn't get the job. Philip Gibbons testified that he had been contacted by Hickman Motors Limited concerning Carl Trask and that he had told them that Carl had been involved in the taking of oil by another employee.
>
> In *McHugh* [*McHugh v. City Motors (Nfld.) Ltd.* (1989), 26 C.C.E.L. 57, 58 D.L.R. (4th) 753, 74 Nfld. & P.E.I.R. 263, 231 A.P.R. 253], our Court of Appeal,

at [74 Nfld. & P.E.I.R.] 267, applied the rule of *Hadley v. Baxendale* (1854), 156 E.R. 145, 9 Exch. 341, [1843-60] All E.R. Rep. 461, 18 Jur. 358, 2 W.R. 302, 2 C.L.R. 517, where Baron Alderson said, at [E.R.] 151:

> Now we think the proper rule in such a case as the present is this: — Where two parties have made a contract which one of them has broken, the damages which the other party ought to receive in respect of such breach of contract should be such as may fairly and reasonably be considered either arising naturally, i.e., according to the usual course of things from such breach of contract itself, or such as may reasonably be supposed to have been in the contemplation of both parties, at the time they made the contract, as the probable result of the breach of it.

I believe it was foreseeable, at the time of hiring Carl Trask, that if he were wrongfully accused of being involved with theft during the course of his employment, and if that accusation was made known to other potential employers, then he would need more time than normal, following termination, to search for other employment. In other words, the reasonable time to search for other employment, which may reasonably be supposed to have been in the contemplation of the parties at the time of entering into the employment contract and, indeed, at the time of termination, would be longer in those circumstances. Accordingly, I hold that 18 months' notice would be reasonable in the circumstances. I hold that Carl Trask is entitled to 18 months' pay, less income, from any employment during that period. (at pp. 214-215)

(iv) *Years of Part-Time Service*

In *Starcevich v. Woodward's Ltd.* (1991), 37 C.C.E.L. 46, 58 B.C.L.R. (2d) 254 (S.C.), the Court considered that five years of part-time service, which preceded six years of full-time service, should be considered in determining the period of reasonable notice. The Court indicated that the weight to be given to part-time employment would vary according to the extent and duration of the part-time employment.

(v) *Employer Persuading Employee to Reject Offer of Alternative Employment Prior to Termination*

In *McCallion v. Canadian Manoir Industries Ltd.* (1991), 39 C.C.E.L. 269 (Ont. Gen. Div.), the Court regarded the fact that the employer had persuaded the employee to turn down an offer of comparable alternative employment only a month prior to the termination as a factor tending to lengthen the period of notice. The Court, therefore, found that a 37-year-old vice-president and engineer, having 9 years' service, was entitled to 12 months' notice.

(vi) *Termination While Absent on LTD Not a Factor*

In *McGarry v. Bosco Homes Edmonton* (1992), 42 C.C.E.L. 198 (Alta. Q.B.), the Court found that the fact that the employee was constructively dismissed while absent on long-term disability benefits was not a relevant factor in determining the period of reasonable notice. This case should not, however, be regarded as a licence to terminate disabled employees. As a general rule it is not prudent to terminate an employee who is disabled and the human rights implications must be considered carefully (see Chapter 13.9, Discrimination on the Basis of Handicap).

(vii) *Eligibility Date for Early Retirement Benefits Not a Factor*

In *Webster v. British Columbia Hydro & Power Authority* (1992), 42 C.C.E.L. 105, 66 B.C.L.R. (2d) 129, 91 D.L.R. (4th) 272, 13 B.C.A.C. 84, 24 W.A.C. 84 (C.A.), leave to appeal to Supreme Court of Canada granted (1993), 74 B.C.L.R. (2d) xxx (note) (S.C.C), the Court was concerned with the termination of a 20-year employee who, at the time of termination, was 26 months away from being entitled to an early retirement pension. At trial the Judge found that this was a significant factor in finding that the employee was entitled to a 26-month notice period. The Court of Appeal, however, rejected this contention and reduced the notice period to 18 months, reasoning as follows:

> In my respectful opinion, the learned trial judge erred in considering that the wrongful dismissal of the plaintiff was a benefit to the employer and therefore a reason for concluding that the plaintiff was entitled to an extensive period of notice. By taking into account that the plaintiff was 26 months away from being eligible for early retirement as an extenuating or exceptional factor to warrant a notice period of 26 months, the judge construed the contract of employment as if it contained a guarantee of employment until retirement or a guarantee of a retirement pension. No employer would hire an employee on those terms. It cannot be said that it was an express or implied term of the plaintiff's contract of employment that he would be given that guarantee. If the parties had put their respective minds to the matter at the time of the making of the contract, Hydro would not have agreed to guarantee the plaintiff's employment until he reached retirement age or to guarantee a pension on early retirement. Nor would the plaintiff have expected that he would be employed to retirement age or to receive a pension on early retirement. (at p. 112)

(viii) *Prior Service in Same Type of Business Not a Factor*

In *Dahdouh v. Hugin Sweda Inc.* (1993), 45 C.C.E.L. 56 (B.C.S.C.), the Court assumed, without deciding, that "a moral claim to a longer notice period arises where the employee had devoted the majority of his working life to the same type of business as that carried on by his employer, as the result of which his employer derives a direct benefit . . ." (at p. 60) In that case, however, the Court concluded that the employee had not been previously employed in the same type of business. While the employee had an extensive background in the distribution and servicing of the products of the defendant, he similarly had experience in working with the products of direct competitors. The Court stated:

> I do not conclude from the evidence that his work as a technician, notwithstanding he is highly experienced with respect to the defendant's products, was so exclusive to the defendant's business that the defendant became obliged to treat him as an employee of long-standing. (at p. 60)

(ix) *Notice Entitlement With Previous Employer*

In *Wegg v. National Trust Co.* (1993), 47 C.C.E.L. 104, 93 C.L.L.C. 14,036 (Ont. Gen. Div.), the Court considered the case of a Vice-President of Network

Services who had been employed for 19 months. The Court decided the case on the basis that the employee was bound by a written employment contract which limited his entitlement to that provided by employment standards legislation. The Court however, as is customary, proceeded to assess damages at common law in the event that the Court of Appeal concluded that the employment contract was not binding. Mr. Justice Granger concluded that a reasonable notice period would be 15 months having regard to the narrow specialty of the employee and the fact that to the knowledge of National Trust he had a 15-month entitlement in the event of termination by his previous employer. Granger J. reasoned as follows:

> The plaintiff was a senior executive with both Wardair and National Trust. As the number of employers using the Unisys system is extremely limited, National Trust must have known that it would be extremely difficult for Wegg to find alternative employment. Although National Trust did not entice Wegg away from secure employment at Wardair, it was aware that Wegg had an opportunity to continue his employment with Wardair and perhaps be transferred to PWA in Vancouver. It was important for National Trust to hire an executive who was familiar with the Unisys system to head up its computer operation in Stratford. In addition, National Trust was aware that the severance package which Wegg would receive from Wardair if he was terminated was fifteen months. (at p. 114)

(x) *Excessive Level of Compensation*

In *Gareau v. Oracle Corp. Canada* (1992), 47 C.C.E.L. 202 (Ont. Gen. Div.), the Court considered a 42-year-old who had a high school education and was employed as director of marketing services at $125,000 per annum. The Court found that the employer had overpaid the employee which made it even more difficult for her to find reasonably comparable employment and that this factor increased the period of reasonable notice. In this regard, the Court stated:

> Miss Gareau is forty-two. She had six years and one month service in a variety of senior positions, culminating in a senior executive position. At the time of her dismissal she was earning, as I found, compensation of $125,000 per annum, although in previous years she had received as much as $148,000 annually. She has a high school education. It is perhaps not surprising to hear that despite diligent effort, she has been unable to secure employment. She is in the unenviable position of having perhaps been overpaid by Oracle. That is not her fault. It was brought about by Oracle, and Oracle cannot reasonably force her to scale down her expectations, although she probably realizes that that is precisely what she must do.
>
> But for this factor, I would have been inclined to fix ten months as a reasonable period. However, having regard to all the circumstances, I view twelve months as a reasonable period. (at pp. 207-208)

(xi) *Commencing Employment At or After Age 60*

In *Ferguson v. Eddy Group Ltd.* (1993), 47 C.C.E.L. 54, 136 N.B.R. (2d) 161, 347 A.P.R. 161 (Q.B.), the Court considered a situation in which an individual with 28 years' experience in the electrical supply business commenced employment with the defendant at age 60 and was terminated 20 months later. The Court concluded that the appropriate notice period was six months and declined to extend the notice period having regard to the age of the plaintiff stating:

> But in my view an employee who begins working for an employer at age 60 should not expect extra severance pay at age 62 on account of his age. If the courts were to allow that, then I would agree with the observation of Kyle, J. that such older "persons seeking employment will find ever greater difficulty": *Kemp v. Sask. Oil & Gas Corp.* (1992), 42 C.C.E.L. 6 [103 Sask. R. 206 (Q.B.)] at p. 8. (at p. 56)

(xii) *Employer Allegation of Incompetence*

In *Wallace v. United Grain Growers Ltd.*, 49 C.C.E.L. 71, [1993] 7 W.W.R. 525, 87 Man. R. (2d) 161 (Q.B.), the plaintiff was a salesman who had been summarily dismissed after 14 years of service. Several days after the termination the defendant advised that the dismissal was on the basis of incompetence. The defendant defended the action for wrongful dismissal on the basis of incompetence and this pleading was not withdrawn until the opening day of trial. The plaintiff was 59 years old, and had an annual income of approximately $78,000 at the time of termination. Taking into account the usual factors of age, length of service, position and the availability of comparable employment and, "particularly the fact that the peremptory dismissal and the subsequent actions of the defendant made other employment in his field virtually unavailable" (at p. 82), the Court concluded that the period of reasonable notice was 24 months.

(xiii) *Not For Profit Status of Employer Not a Factor*

In *Russell v. Winnifred Stewart Assn. for the Mentally Handicapped* (1993), 49 C.C.E.L. 177, 12 Alta. L.R. (3d) 444, (*sub nom. Russell v. Stewart (Winnifred) Assn. for the Mentally Handicapped*) 144 A.R. 74 (Q.B.), the Court reasoned that:

> [W]hen a "not-for-profit" corporation decides to hire employees, it comes within the provisions of the general law relating to employment. Such an employer becomes obligated to treat its employees fairly according to law. Morally, it may well be the case that "charity begins at home"; an association that aims to do good in the community should aim to do well by its employees. However, whether or not a moral standard applies, it is clear that a legal standard applies. No general relief is given to "not-for-profit" corporations from the application of employment law. If such a company wished to impose on its employees a restriction on the common law right to notice, it could try to do so by contract. (at p. 180)

(xiv) *Statutory Minimums are Reasonable for Certain Junior Employees*

Statutory entitlements to termination and/or severance pay are typically expressed to be "minimum" requirements with the employee being entitled to any greater benefit provided by contract. In the vast majority of cases the statutory minimums are ignored in the determination of the period of reasonable notice. The question then arises whether the statutory entitlements are so minimal that they cannot be considered "reasonable" for employees at any level.

In *McLennan v. Apollo Forest Products Ltd.* (1993), 49 C.C.E.L. 172 (B.C.S.C.), the Court considered a 38-year-old lumber sorter at a sawmill who had been employed for a total of nine months, with only the last five months being full-time employment. The statutory entitlement was to two weeks of termination pay. While the Court determined that three weeks was the reasonable period of notice for the plaintiff, the Court did accept the proposition that the minimum standards will be considered reasonable for certain employees, stating:

> I am of the opinion that the minimum standards set out by the *Employment Standards Act* should be applicable to the situations where, by virtue of the character of the employment, the age of the employee, the length of service and the availability of similar employment, the dismissed employee's chances of regaining his lost employment are maximized. I am satisfied that this is not such a case and that the minimum notice period of the *Employment Standards Act* should not be applicable. Nevertheless, we have a very short term of employment of nine months of which only five months was permanent full time employment, we have entry level employment with little responsibility, an employee that is not disadvantaged by youth or advanced age and similar employment which was readily available although not as readily available as some less remunerative employment. (at pp. 175-176)

(xv) *Failure to Provide Appropriate Letter of Reference*

In *Sharpe v. Computer Innovations Distribution Inc.* (1993), 1 C.C.E.L. (2d) 28 (N.B.Q.B.), affirmed (1994), 2 C.C.E.L. (2d) 157 (N.B.C.A.), the lower Court considered that the failure of the employer to provide anything more than a perfunctory letter of reference was a factor in determining the reasonable period of notice.

In *Boldon v. Computer Innovations Distribution Inc.* (1993), 50 C.C.E.L. 263 (N.B.Q.B.), the employee was 34 years of age and had been employed for nine years, initially as a sales representative and later as an account executive. The Court found that a reasonable period of notice was eight months taking into account "the failure of the defendant to provide her with any more than the most perfunctory letter of reference."

(xvi) *Narrow Field of Specialization*

In *Veach v. Diversey Inc.* (1993), 1 C.C.E.L. (2d) 242 (B.C.S.C.), the Court considered a commission sales representative, age 59, who had been terminated after 21 years of service. The plaintiff was responsible for the sale of chemical products and the position required specialized knowledge and skill in relation to these chemical products. There was a limited market for such chemical products and the knowledge and skill required could not easily be transferred to the sale of other products. The Court concluded that an 18-month notice period was appropriate taking into account that "[t]he position required very specialized knowledge of chemical products being sold in a narrow and limited market" (at p. 246).

(xvii) *Termination Provision in Earlier Employment Contract Not a Factor*

In *Slater v. Sandwell Inc.* (1994), 5 C.C.E.L. (2d) 308, 94 C.L.L.C. 14,031 (Ont. Gen. Div.), an engineer in a senior managerial position was terminated after two years and two months of service. During the first two years of employment, his written employment contract provided that either party could terminate on two weeks' notice. The Court rejected the argument that the notice period should be determined taking into account the original contract termination provision. In the result the Court determined that a four-month notice period was appropriate.

(xviii) *Existence of a Restrictive Covenant*

In *Murrell v. Burns International Security Services Ltd.* (1994), 5 C.C.E.L. (2d) 123 (Ont. Gen. Div.), additional reasons at (June 1, 1994), Doc. Ottawa 53490/91 (Ont. Gen. Div.), at the time of termination the plaintiff had been employed for approximately three years as Ottawa Branch Manager. The plaintiff was subject to a 12-month non-competition covenant and the Court stated:

> The plaintiff claims 12 months' notice on the basis that he was a senior manager and subject to a 12 month non-competing agreement.
>
> There is some doubt as to whether a non-competing agreement could be invoked by an employer who dismisses the employee but the existence of such an agreement is one factor to consider in determining proper notice.
>
> I do not feel 12 months' notice was called for in these circumstances. The defendant claims three to four months is sufficient notice on the basis of one month per year's service. When I consider the managerial position of the plaintiff and the abruptness of his dismissal, as well as the non-competing agreement, I consider that eight months' notice would be proper. (at 5 C.C.E.L. (2d), p. 130)

6.2 TABLE OF SAMPLE NOTICE PERIODS

As discussed in Chapter 6.1(c), the factor of inducement from prior employment, if present, can be an overriding factor in determining the period of notice.

(*Continued on page 6-35*)

For that reason, Part (a) of the Table deals with cases that apply, for the most part, the *Bardal* factors and which do not involve inducement. Part (b) of the Table provides examples of cases in which inducement is considered as a factor in determining the period of reasonable notice.

TABLE OF SAMPLE NOTICE PERIODS

(a) Sample Notice Periods (Inducement not a Factor)

Case	Age of Employee	Length of Service	Position or Salary	Notice Period (months)
Sorel v. Tomenson Saunders Whitehead Ltd. (1987), 16 C.C.E.L. 223 (B.C.C.A.)	60	37 yrs.	Regional vice-president $82,000	24
Suttie v. Metro Transit Operating Co. (1986), 9 C.C.E.L. 19 (B.C.C.A.)	58	39 yrs.	Division manager $61,000	24
Paitich v. Clarke Institute of Psychiatry (1988), 19 C.C.E.L. 105 (Ont. H.C.), affirmed (1990), 30 C.C.E.L. 225 (Ont. C.A.)	53	23 yrs.	Psychologist —	24
Lyonde v. Cdn. Acceptance Corp. (1983), 3 C.C.E.L. 220 (Ont. H.C.)	64	24 yrs.	Vice-president administration $52,700	24
Johnston v. Algoma Steel Corp. (1989), 24 C.C.E.L. 1 (Ont. H.C.)	48	23 yrs.	Foreman $43,000	24
Gaunt v. Consolidated Freightways Corp. of Delaware (1990), 33 C.C.E.L. 255, 68 Man. R. (2d) 149 (Q.B.), varied (1991), 73 Man. R. (2d) 123, 3 W.A.C. 123 (C.A.)	61	21 yrs.	Terminal manager $58,500	24
Fraser v. Kelowna (City) (1993), 1 C.C.E.L. (2d) 127 (B.C.S.C.)	60	22 yrs.	Assistant manager of electrical utilities $54,000	24
McAndrew v. Kelowna (City) (1993), 1 C.C.E.L. (2d) 127 (B.C.S.C.)	59	23 yrs.	Manager of electrical utilities $57,000	24
Trudeau-Linley v. Plummer Memorial Public Hospital (1993), 1 C.C.E.L. (2d) 114 (Ont. Gen. Div.)	46	21 yrs.	Nurse—department head $57,000	22
Brause v. Microtel Ltd./Microtel Ltée (1989), 27 C.C.E.L. 260 (B.C. S.C.)	60	33 yrs.	Quality control engineer —	20

Case	Age of Employee	Length of Service	Position or Salary	Notice Period (months)
Dunlop v. B.C. Hydro & Power Authority (1988), 23 C.C.E.L. 96 (B.C.C.A.)	61	10 yrs.	Engineer $45,000	20
Ansari v. B.C. Hydro & Power Authority (1986), 13 C.C.E.L. 238 (B.C.S.C.), affirmed (1986), 55 B.C.L.R. (2d) xxxiii (note) (C.A.)	50	19 yrs.	Engineer $46,000	20
Yeager v. R. J. Hastings Agencies Ltd. (1984), 5 C.C.E.L. 266 (B.C.S.C.)	55	30 yrs.	Salesman $36,000	18
Tennant v. Greyhound Lines of Can. Ltd. (1988), 22 C.C.E.L. 299 (B.C.S.C.)	56	24 yrs.	Bus driver for 22 years and thereafter safety co-ordinator $38,000	18
Lacouvee v. McGavin Foods Ltd. (1993), 47 C.C.E.L. 131 (B.C.S.C.)	54	30 yrs.	Route operations manager $48,000	18
Rivers v. Gulf Can. Ltd. (1986), 13 C.C.E.L. 131 (Ont. H.C.)	51	28 yrs.	Senior administrator $39,000	16½
Roberts v. Versatile Farm Equipment (1987), 16 C.C.E.L. 9 (Sask. Q.B.)	55	18 yrs.	Regional sales manager $61,000	16
Gillespie v. Union Optics Corp. (Can.) (1987), 18 C.C.E.L. 58 (Ont. H.C.), additional reasons at (1987), 22 C.C.E.L. 81 (Ont. H.C.), affirmed (1989), 26 C.C.E.L. xxiv (Ont. C.A.)	42	7 yrs.	President $36,000	16
Lightburn v. Mid Island Consumer Services Co-Op. (1984), 4 C.C.E.L. 263 (B.C. Co. Ct.)	49	10 yrs.	Manager, hardware dept. $30,000	15
Anderson v. Pirelli Cables Inc. (1984), 5 C.C.E.L. 156 (Ont. H.C.)	54	12 yrs.	Machine operator $50,000	15
Furuheim v. Bechtel Can. Ltd. (1988), 22 C.C.E.L. 257 (Ont. H.C.), varied (1990), 30 C.C.E.L. 146 (Ont. C.A.)	60	24 yrs.	Engineer —	15

Case	Age of Employee	Length of Service	Position or Salary	Notice Period (months)
Makarchuk v. Midtransportation Services Ltd. (1985), 6 C.C.E.L. 169 (Ont. H.C.)	—	5 yrs.	Truck salesman $36,000	14
Kenzie v. Standard Motors (77) Ltd. (1985), 8 C.C.E.L. 173 (Sask. Q.B.)	54	36 yrs.	Sales manager $30,000	14
Leclerc (Syndic de) c. Roneo Vickers Can. Ltd. (1988), 23 C.C.E.L. 42 (C.A. Qué.)	—	15 yrs.	Quebec regional director and marketing director for eastern Canada —	12
Brock v. Matthews Group Ltd. (1988), 20 C.C.E.L. 110 (Ont. H.C.), varied (1991), 34 C.C.E.L. 50 (Ont. C.A.)	40	11 yrs.	Chief operating officer $110,000	12
Shiels v. Sask. Government Insurance (1988), 20 C.C.E.L. 55 (Sask. Q.B.)	—	10 yrs.	Assistant vice-president, traffic and safety $60,000	12
Durand v. Quaker Oats Co. of Can. (1988), 20 C.C.E.L. 223 (B.C.S.C.), reversed (1990), 32 C.C.E.L. 63 (B.C. C.A.)	—	18 yrs.	Sales, planning and development manager for western Canada $40,000	12
Lockhart v. Chrysler Can. Ltd. (1984), 7 C.C.E.L. 43 (B.C.C.A.)	48	18 yrs.	Lease manager $37,000	12
Balogh v. Citicom Inc. (1987), 17 C.C.E.L. 35 (Ont. Dist. Ct.), varied (1988), 26 C.P.C. (2d) 226 (Div. Ct.)	54	19 yrs.	Parking lot manager $25,000	12
Poniecki v. Polysar Ltd. (1987), 18 C.C.E.L. 191 (Ont. H.C.)	62	8 yrs.	Draftsman —	12
Arnot v. General Wire & Cable Co. (1982), 2 C.C.E.L. 208 (Ont. H.C.)	40	4½ yrs.	Production and inventory manager $29,000	12
Wuorinen v. W.C.B. (1983), 1 C.C.E.L. 29 (B.C.S.C.)	53	5 yrs.	Education manager $50,000	12
Springer v. Merril Lynch, Royal Securities Ltd. (1984), 4 C.C.E.L. 81 (Ont. H.C.)	—	14 yrs.	Institutional bond salesman $35,000	12

Case	Age of Employee	Length of Service	Position or Salary	Notice Period (months)
Bardal v. Globe & Mail Ltd., [1960] O.W.N. 253 (H.C.)	—	17 yrs.	Advertising department manager $11,000	12
Thomson v. Bechtel Can. Ltd. (1983), 3 C.C.E.L. 16 (Ont. H.C.)	48	13 yrs.	Project procurement manager $45,000	11
Merilees v. Sears Can. Inc. (1988), 22 C.C.E.L. 317 (B.C.C.A.)	—	9 yrs.	Assistant manager cosmetics and hosiery —	9
Robinson v. Tingley's Ltd. (1988), 20 C.C.E.L. 263 (N.B.Q.B.)	—	10 yrs.	Meat-cutter at grocery store $20,000	9
Jackson v. SNC Inc. (1985), 8 C.C.E.L. 274 (Ont. H.C.)	44	6 yrs.	Civil engineer $41,000	9
Lewarton v. Walters (1985), 8 C.C.E.L. 86 (B.C.S.C.)	38	2 yrs.	Audit supervisor $41,000	9
Carrick v. Cooper Can. Ltd. (1983), 2 C.C.E.L. 87 (Ont. H.C.)	56	1 yr.	Vice-president, operations and planning $50,000	9
Pechenkov v. Borg-Warner (Can.) Ltd. (1983), 2 C.C.E.L. 237 (Ont. Co. Ct.)	29	5½ yrs.	Mechanical engineer $30,000	9
Garvin v. Rockwell International of Canada Ltd. (1993), 50 C.C.E.L. 295 (Ont. Gen. Div.)	45	21 yrs.	Quality control engineer $31,000	8.5
Macdonald v. Richardson Greenshields of Can. Ltd. (1985), 12 C.C.E.L. 22 (B.C.S.C.)	40	5 yrs.	Commission stock and bond holder $48,000	8
Shulman v. Xerox Can. Inc. (1986), 15 C.C.E.L. 200 (N.S.T.D.)	40	6½ yrs.	Sales executive $35,000	8
Surveyer, Nenniger & Chênevert Inc. c. Jackson (1988), 22 C.C.E.L. 242 (C.A. Qué.), leave to appeal to S.C.C. refused (1989), 23 C.C.E.L. xxxvi (note) (S.C.C.)	56	8 yrs.	Vice-president $84,000	7
Dickinson v. Northern Telecom Can. Ltd. (1985), 7 C.C.E.L. 139 (Ont. Co. Ct.)	38	6½ yrs.	Security guard $25,000	7

Case	Age of Employee	Length of Service	Position or Salary	Notice Period (months)
Zelisko v. "99" Truck Parts & Equipment Ltd. (1985), 8 C.C.E.L. 201 (B.C.S.C.)	34	14 yrs.	Mechanic $24,000	7
Cadenhead v. Unicorn Abrasives of Can. Ltd. (1984), 5 C.C.E.L. 241 (Ont. H.C.)	38	6 yrs.	Regional sales manager $36,000	7
McBride v. W.P. London & Associates Ltd. (1984), 5 C.C.E.L. 314 (Ont. H.C.)	51	8 yrs.	Senior draftsman —	7
Deacon v. MacMillan Bloedel Ltd. (1982), 3 C.C.E.L. 166 (Ont. Dist. Ct.)	38	6 yrs.	Shift foreman $20,000	7
White v. B.C. Timber Ltd. (1983), 3 C.C.E.L. 284 (B.C.S.C.)	37	6 yrs.	Engineering technician $32,000	7
Zutter v. Stuart Nassim Developments Ltd. (1988), 23 C.C.E.L. 8 (B.C.S.C.)	40	6 yrs.	Superintendent of apartment complex $27,000	6
Keighan v. Kool-Fire Ltd. (1984), 6 C.C.E.L. 196 (Ont. H.C.)	64	3 yrs.	Vice-president and secretary-treasurer $18,000	6
Clark v. Optyl (Can.) Ltd. (1985), 7 C.C.E.L. 1 (N.B.C.A.)	35	6 yrs.	Foreman $30,000	6
Pearl v. Pacific Enercon Inc. (1985), 7 C.C.E.L. 252 (B.C.C.A.)	37	3 yrs.	Sales manager $73,000	6
Siu (Sui) v. Westcoast Transmission Co. (1984), (*sub nom. Yui-Ming Siu v. Westcoast Transmission Co.*) 7 C.C.E.L. 281 (B.C. S.C.), reversed on other grounds (1986), 14 C.C.E.L. 117 (B.C. C.A.)	35	3 yrs.	Process engineer	6
Ewasiuk v. Estevan Area Home Care Dist. No. 9 (1985), 9 C.C.E.L. 267 (Sask. Q.B.)	—	1½ yrs.	Manager of home care nursing programme $21,400	6
Mann v. Andres Wines Ltd. (1988), 19 C.C.E.L. 1 (Ont. Div. Ct.)	50	8 yrs.	Clerical staff —	6

Case	Age of Employee	Length of Service	Position or Salary	Notice Period (months)
Plummer v. W. Carsen Co. (1985), 10 C.C.E.L. 19 (Ont. Dist. Ct.)	43	9 yrs.	Accounts payable clerk $21,000	6

(*Continued on page 6-39*)

Case	Age of Employee	Length of Service	Position or Salary	Notice Period (months)
Johnson v. Able-Atlantic Taxi Ltd. (1987), 17 C.C.E.L. 239 (Ont. Dist. Ct.)	35	15 yrs.	Dispatcher and supervisor $30,000	6
McIntosh v. Sask. Water Corp. (1988), 23 C.C.E.L. 143 (Sask. Q.B.), varied (1989), 26 C.C.E.L. 196 (Sask. C.A.)	43	2 yrs.	Resource economist $45,000	6
Adams v. Coseka Resources Ltd. (1988), 22 C.C.E.L. 164 (Alta. Q.B.)	—	13 mos.	Corporate counsel to small oil company $70,000	5
Moore v. Zurich Insurance Co. (1984), 4 C.C.E.L.188 (Ont. Co. Ct.)	34	11 yrs.	Dicta typist $14,000	4
Hubler v. Geneva Cosmetics Inc. (1984), 4 C.C.E.L. 318 (Ont. Co. Ct.)	47	4½ mos.	Marketing director $32,000	4
Ahmad v. Procter & Gamble Inc. (1987), 18 C.C.E.L. 124 (Ont. H.C.), affirmed (1991), 1 O.R. (3d) 491 (C.A.)	49	16 yrs.	Sales forecaster (had been laid off 2 months prior to dismissal) $30,000	4
Tremblett v. Aardvark Pest Control Ltd. (1987), 16 C.C.E.L. 306 (Ont. Dist. Ct.)	31	14 mos.	Manager of small office $14,000	4
Aubin v. H.B. Group Insurance Management Ltd. (1987), 18 C.C.E.L. 75 (Ont. Dist. Ct.)	39	18 mos.	Underwriting manager $40,000	4
Kozak v. Aliments Krispy Kernels Inc. (1988), 22 C.C.E.L. 1 (Ont. Dist. Ct.)	40	5 wks.	District sales manager $14,000	4
Warren v. Orlick Industries Ltd. (1993), 47 C.C.E.L. 198 (Ont. Gen. Div.)	46	7 yrs.	Labourer $25,000	3½
Cardwell v. Young Manufacturer Inc. (1988), 20 C.C.E.L. 272 (Ont. Dist. Ct.)	42	11 wks.	Director of operations outside Toronto $60,000	3
George v. Muller Sales & Services Ltd. (1984), 3 C.C.E.L. 106 (Sask. Q.B.)	40	2 yrs.	General manager $25,000	3

Case	Age of Employee	Length of Service	Position or Salary	Notice Period (months)
Wansborough v. N.W.P. Northwood Products Ltd. (1984), 3 C.C.E.L. 177 (Ont. H.C.)	53	2 yrs.	Office administrator $22,000	3
Morby v. Tozer Plymouth Chrysler Ltd. (1986), 14 C.C.E.L. 221 (N.B.Q.B.)	—	9 yrs.	Warranty clerk and service supervisor $13,000	9 wks.
Lavallee v. Prairie Equipment Ltd. (1988), 20 C.C.E.L. 182 (Man. Q.B.)	—	1 yr.	Mechanic $24,000	1

(b) Sample Notice Periods (Inducement a Factor)

Case	Age of Employee	Length of Service	Position or Salary	Notice Period (months)
Makhija v. Lakefield Research (1983), 14 C.C.E.L. 131 (Ont. H.C.), affirmed (1986), 14 C.C.E.L. xxxi (Ont. C.A.)	43	13½ mos.	Analytical chemist —	15
Hooker v. Audio Magnetics Corp. of Can. (1984), 3 C.C.E.L. 288 (Ont. Co. Ct.)	59	1 yr.	Marketing strategist (U.S.) $38,000	14
Cathcart v. Longines Wittnauer Watch Co. (1980), 1 C.C.E.L. 287 (Ont. H.C.)	54	12	President $42,500	12
Brisbois v. Casteel Inc. (1983), 2 C.C.E.L. 35 (Ont. H.C.)	33	10 mos.	Operations manager $29,000	12
Chang v. Simplex Textiles Ltd. (1985), 6 C.C.E.L. 247 (Ont. C.A.)	50	10 wks.	Plant manager (U.S.) $35,000	8
Zylawy v. Edmonton (City) (1985), 8 C.C.E.L. 93 (Alta. Q.B.)	39	2 yrs.	Supervisor of space, planning and co-ordination $37,000	8
Jackson v. Makeup Lab Inc. (1989), 27 C.C.E.L. 317 (Ont. H.C.)	38	Less than 3 mos.	Plant manager $45,000	8
Magnusson v. Laing Property Corp. (1991), 35 C.C.E.L. 248 (B.C. S.C.)	36	3 yrs.	Lawyer acting as Lease Administrator $54,000	8

Case	Age of Employee	Length of Service	Position or Salary	Notice Period (months)
Horvath v. Joytec Ltd. (1989), 27 C.C.E.L. 269 (Sask. Q.B.)	34	0	Personnel co-ordinator	6
I.S.S. Information System Services Ltd. v. Smyth (1985), 7 C.C.E.L. 35 (B.C. Co. Ct.)	—	4 mos.	Systems analyst $30,000	6
Gibson v. Pemberton Houston Willoughby Inc. (1985), 9 C.C.E.L. 295 (B.C.S.C.)	27	18 mos.	Chartered financial analyst $39,000	6
Adamson v. Watts & Henderson (Atlantic) Ltd. (1987), 16 C.C.E.L. 74 (Ont. H.C.), additional reasons at (1987), 21 C.P.C. (2d) 215 (Ont. H.C.)	52	9 mos.	Project manager $50,000	6

6.3 MITIGATION OF DAMAGE

(a) General Principles

McGregor on Damages, 15th ed. (London: Sweet & Maxwell, 1988), at pp. 168-169, describes three related rules which together explain the significance of mitigation of damage in quantifying damages. These three rules are as follows:

> (1) The first step and most important rule is that the plaintiff must take all reasonable steps to mitigate the loss to him consequent upon the defendant's wrong and cannot recover damages for any such loss which he could thus have avoided but has failed, through unreasonable action or inaction, to avoid. Put shortly, the plaintiff cannot recover for avoidable loss.
> (2) The second rule is the corollary of the first and is that, where the plaintiff does take reasonable steps to mitigate the loss to him consequent upon the defendant's wrong, he can recover for loss incurred in so doing; this is so even though the resulting damage is in the event greater than it would have been had the mitigating steps not been taken. Put shortly, the plaintiff can recover for loss incurred in reasonable attempts to avoid loss.
> (3) The third rule is that, where the plaintiff does take steps to mitigate the loss to him consequent upon the defendant's wrong and these steps are successful, the defendant is entitled to the benefit accruing from the plaintiff's action and is liable only for the loss as lessened; this is so even though the plaintiff would not have been debarred under the first rule from recovering the whole loss, which would have accrued in the absence of his successful mitigating steps, by reason of these steps not being ones which were required of him under the first rule. Put shortly, the plaintiff cannot recover for avoided loss.

The first rule cited by *McGregor* is hereinafter discussed in considering the obligation of the employee to mitigate damages by finding new employment, commencing self-employment or accepting a lesser position with the same employer. (See Chapter 6.3(c), (d) and (e).) The second rule is discussed in Chapter 6.4(a)(vii). The third rule, which is not the subject of further discussion, would apply in the rare circumstance in which an employee in fact mitigated damages, although under no legal obligation to do so. This might occur if an employee, in order to mitigate, took a clearly inferior position to that which was previously enjoyed. The employee may have been able to take the position that the position offered was so inferior that it did not have to be accepted as part of a reasonable effort to mitigate damages. The fact is, however, that the employee did accept the position, and the amounts earned in mitigation must be deducted from any damage claim.

It should be remembered, however, that in every case, it is necessary to consider the terms of the particular employment contract. It is open to the parties to agree that the employee will not be under an obligation to mitigate damages in the event that the contract is terminated. Thus, in *Paquin v. Gainers Inc.*, 33 C.C.E.L. 80, 76 Alta. L.R. (2d) 68, [1990] 6 W.W.R. 640, 108 A.R. 304 (Q.B.), affirmed 37 C.C.E.L. 113, 80 Alta. L.R. (2d) 278, [1991] 6 W.W.R. 45, (*sub nom. Paquin v. Gainer's Inc.*) 117 A.R. 61, 2 W.A.C. 61 (C.A.), the plaintiff was employed pursuant to an employment contract for a fixed term of three years which provided that, apart from termination for just cause, the employer would continue payments to the end of the term regardless of whether the agreement was terminated and regardless of whether services were rendered by the plaintiff. The conclusion of the Court, stated succinctly, was as follows:

> In summary, the parties to the contract explicitly agreed on the term during which remuneration would be paid to the plaintiff and identified the sole circumstance in which such payments would cease. That circumstances did not arise; the employer must complete all the payments. (at pp. 84-85)

(b) Application to Fixed Term and Indefinite Term Contracts

The law is clear that, subject to an agreement to the contrary, an employee employed for an indefinite term has an obligation to take such reasonable steps as may be necessary to mitigate the damages suffered after termination of the employment contract.

The weight of authority also favours the view that an employee employed for a fixed term has the same obligation to mitigate damages. In *Neilson v. Vancouver Hockey Club Ltd.*, 20 C.C.E.L. 155, 25 B.C.L.R. (2d) 235, [1988] 4 W.W.R. 410, 51 D.L.R. (4th) 40 (C.A.), leave to appeal to Supreme Court of Canada refused, 22 C.C.E.L. xxxv (note), 29 B.C.L.R. (2d) xxxii (note), [1988] 6 W.W.R. lxix (note), 92 N.R. 240 (note) (S.C.C.), the Court considered the case of a professional hockey coach who had entered into a written employment contract having a four-year term, but which provided that it could be terminated after three years upon the giving of certain notice and payment of a lump sum of $60,000. In fact, Neilson was terminated after approximately $2\frac{1}{2}$ years, which was in breach of his employment contract. During the following $1\frac{1}{2}$ years, Neilson was employed by the Los Angeles Kings and the Chicago Black Hawks and the question was whether the amounts earned from these two teams should be deducted from the amounts that Neilson was otherwise entitled to. The majority of the Court ruled that these amounts should be deducted, stating as follows:

> Kellock J. in *Sinclair v. Canadian Ice Machine Co.*, [1955] S.C.R. 777 at 780-81, [1955] 5 D.L.R. 1 (S.C.C.) dealt with repudiation of an employment contract in which there was a 5-year term without provision for termination during the term:
>
> > It is unquestionable, therefore, in my opinion, that the monthly instalments were to be made in consideration of services to be rendered by the respondent, although it was for the appellant to require the performance of such services from time to time as it saw fit. That being so, as Mr. Starr contends, the contract was an "employment" contact for a fixed term with the usual result that upon repudiation without cause on the part of the employer, the appellant company became liable for the consequent damages with a corresponding obligation on the part of the respondent to mitigate those damages. The law is clearly settled that the remedy of a person in the position of the respondent in such case is to sue for damages. He is not entitled to wait until the termination of the period for which he was engaged and sue for the whole amount of the wages which have fallen due in the interim.
>
> English courts have also applied the principles of mitigation to fixed term contracts. In *Yetton v. Eastwoods Froy Ltd.*, [1967] 1 W.L.R. 104, [1966] 3 All E.R. 353 (Q.B.), the question was whether the plaintiff wrongfully dismissed from a fixed term contract of employment had sufficiently mitigated his damages. Blain J. said (at p. 362):
>
> > The basic principle of damages is restitutio in integrum: the plaintiff should have what he has lost through the defendants' fault; but of course, if a plaintiff in fact, in the case of a contract of service, earns something elsewhere through being at liberty so to do, then he has lost that much less as the consequence of the default.
>
> In my view, whether a contract of employment is for a fixed period or an indefinite time the usual rules of mitigation apply and earnings from other sources after termination are taken into account unless the contract provides otherwise. (at pp. 167-168)

Mr. Justice Carrothers, dissenting in the Court of Appeal, would have upheld the trial judgment finding that there was no obligation to offset amounts earned against the amount claimed in the action. Carrothers J.A. reasoned as follows:

> I consider this case to have the attributes of a special one, as wrongful dismissal cases go, for three reasons. First, this is not a case of an indefinite hiring, as found in most wrongful dismissal cases, but rather a hiring for a fixed term. Second, this is a case of a hiring to a specific position with a high public profile, with the potential of exceptional detrimental consequences to the employee in the event of wrongful dismissal, that is, dismissal without cause.
>
> Third, as the issue of mitigation of damages for wrongful dismissal is raised on this appeal, I note at this juncture, for a better understanding of what follows, that the order appealed is, in effect, not an award of damages for wrongful dismissal but rather a money judgment for the balance of wages contracted for over the fixed term but unpaid to an employee fired without cause and under circumstances which precluded the employee from earning that balance of wages. (at p. 157)

As stated, the weight of authority favours the view that an employee employed for a fixed term has an obligation to mitigate damages and that amounts earned in mitigation are offset against any award of damages. It should be noted, however, that the principle applies only in the absence of an agreement to the contrary. Thus it is open to the parties to specify whether or not there is an obligation to mitigate damages. Having regard to the dissenting reasons in the *Neilson* case, and the possibility that they might be applied elsewhere, it would be prudent to specify, in a fixed term contract, whether the employee is subject to an obligation to mitigate damages.

Further, an agreement whereby an employee is entitled to a stipulated sum on termination (e.g., one month's pay per year of service), in effect, excludes the obligation to mitigate damages. This entitlement arises in a fixed amount at the time of termination and it would be untenable to construe such a contract to limit the entitlement of the employee, yet afford the employer the opportunity to benefit from efforts in mitigation.

(c) Mitigation Through Accepting Lesser Position with Same Employer

Prior to the case of *Mifsud v. MacMillan Bathurst Inc.* (1989), 28 C.C.E.L. 228, 70 O.R. (2d) 701, 63 D.L.R. (4th) 714, 35 O.A.C. 356 (C.A.), leave to appeal to S.C.C. refused (1990), 73 O.R. (2d) x (note), 68 D.L.R. (4th) vii (note), 39 O.A.C. 153 (note), 113 N.R. 400 (note) (S.C.C.), the weight of authority was against requiring an employee to accept a lesser position with the same employer in order to mitigate damages. In the *Mifsud* case, however, the Court found that an employee was obliged to accept a significant demotion as a means of mitigating damages. The demotion was from plant supervisor to foreman, which required the employee to rotate through three, as opposed to two, shifts. The Court of Appeal, however, held that the employee was not entitled to damages due to his failure to take reasonable steps to mitigate his loss. McKinlay J.A. stated:

> The doctrine of mitigation was concisely stated by Chief Justice Laskin in *Michaels v. Red Deer College*, [1976] 2 S.C.R. 324, [1975] 5 W.W.R. 575, 5 N.R. 99, 75 C.L.L.C. 14,280, 57 D.L.R. (3d) 386 at 390:
>
>> The primary rule in breach of contract cases, that a wronged plaintiff is entitled to be put in as good a position as he would have been if there had been proper performance by the defendant, is subject to the qualification that the defendant cannot be called upon to pay for avoidable losses which would result in an increase in the quantum of damages payable to the plaintiff. The reference in the case law to a "duty" to mitigate should be understood in this sense.
>>
>> In short, a wronged plaintiff is entitled to recover damages for the losses he has suffered but the extent of those losses may depend upon *whether he has taken reasonable steps to avoid their unreasonable accumulation*. (Emphasis added.)
>
> There is no doubt that the duty of the plaintiff to take steps to mitigate his damages applies in all wrongful dismissal cases. The question is simply whether or not the steps taken by the plaintiff were reasonable.
>
> When an employer wishes to dismiss an employee (other than for cause) the employer may choose either to give the employee reasonable notice of his termi-

nation date and require that he work out the notice period, or he may require the employee to leave immediately, thus rendering the employer liable for damages equal to the employee's remuneration and benefits for the reasonable notice period. If the employee leaves immediately, he is required to take reasonable steps to mitigate his loss and, barring any agreement to the contrary between the parties, any moneys earned in mitigation must be credited against his damages.

Is the situation substantially different when an employer does not wish to dismiss an employee but, being unsatisfied with his performance, or for some other valid reason, wished to place him in a different position at the same salary? Why should it not be considered reasonable for the employee to mitigate his damages by working at the other position for the period of reasonable notice, or at least until he has found alternative employment which he accepts in mitigation?

The fact that the transfer to a new position may constitute in law a constructive dismissal does not eliminate the obligation of the employee to look at the new position offered and evaluate it as a means of mitigating damages. In all cases, comparison should be made to the contractual entitlement of the employer to give reasonable notice and leave the employee in his current position while a search is made for alternative employment. Where the salary offered is the same, where the working conditions are not substantially different or the work demeaning, and where the personal relationships involved are not acrimonious (as in this case), it is reasonable to expect the employee to accept the position offered in mitigation of damages during a reasonable notice position, or until he finds acceptable employment elsewhere.

It must be kept in mind, of course, that there are many situations where the facts would substantiate a constructive dismissal, but where it would be patently unreasonable to expect an employee to accept continuing employment with the same employer in mitigation of his damages.

In this case, Mr. Mifsud improperly rejected the opportunity to mitigate his damages by maintaining an employed status from which to seek a preferable position elsewhere. (at pp. 237-239)

Ritchie v. King Truck Engineering Ltd. (1983), 1 C.C.E.L. 102 (Ont. H.C.) is illustrative of this proposition, and contains a good review of the authorities. Ritchie was hired as Toronto sales manager at a salary of $28,000 per year plus five per cent of branch gross profits on certain sales which, it was anticipated, would afford a total annual income of approximately $40,000. It turned out that Ritchie lacked the necessary management skills and, for that reason, the employer reassigned him to act as a sales representative in Toronto with an annual salary of $18,000 plus a commission on sales which, it was anticipated, would afford him in excess of $40,000 per year. Ritchie refused to act as a sales representative, and it was conceded by the employer that the reassignment to sales representative constituted a constructive dismissal. Mr. Justice Cromarty then found that by refusing to take up duties as a sales representative Ritchie failed to act reasonably to mitigate his damages and on that basis the action was dismissed. In support of his conclusions, Cromarty J. cited with approval the following statements of law:

In certain cases of personal service it may be unreasonable to expect a plaintiff to consider an offer from the other party who has grossly injured him; but in commercial contracts it is generally reasonable to accept an offer from the party in default. However, it is always a question of fact. About the law there is no difficulty. . . .

A[s] I see the matter, it is a plain question of fact for the court in any particular case, whether any particular refusal to accept alternative employment which would reduce a plaintiff's loss is a reasonable or an unreasonable refusal, and factually, even if not as a strict matter of law, personal factors clearly are more likely to be of weight or are likely to be of greater weight in cases of personal service than in what I call (for want of a better word) soulless cases of sale of goods contracts where money may often be the only important factor. Certainly personal factors do not have to be ignored in the making up of a dismissed servant's mind when he comes to make a decision reasonable or unreasonable. (at pp. 107-108)

In *Campbell v. Merrill Lynch Canada Inc.* (1992), 47 C.C.E.L. 248 (B.C.S.C.), the Court considered a situation in which the employer had laid off more than 75 per cent of its staff in the course of a restructuring. As a consequence the plaintiff, a corporate debt financing specialist, was effectively precluded from being able to pursue her speciality. While the Court concluded that the change in role amounted to a constructive dismissal, it found that the plaintiff had an obligation to continue her employment as a means of mitigating damages. In this regard, Mr. Justice Finch reasoned as follows:

In my view, the risk of diminished bonus income to the plaintiff as a result of the defendant's changed circumstances was not sufficient reason for her to refuse continued employment with the defendant as a way to mitigate her loss of income. The risk of income fluctuation was inherent in the line of work the plaintiff chose to pursue. Acceptance of big bonuses in good years, carried with it the implied risk of lesser bonuses in difficult times. The plaintiff's position sought to place all of the burden of a down-turn upon her employer.

The second aspect of this issue, is whether the risk of potential harm to the plaintiff's reputation, by continuing in a role with almost no hope of success, was sufficient to justify her refusal of continued employment with the defendant. . . . It was suggested that the plaintiff's continued efforts in such a losing cause would be seen in the industry as harassment or irritation of potential clients, with a consequent negative reflection upon her.

. . . .

I find it hard to believe that her continued employment with the defendant in the suggested circumstances, would have had an overall negative effect on her reputation. Rather, in my view the objective observer would have been impressed had she continued her employment with the defendant, both with her employer's continued confidence in her, and with her loyalty and dedication to duty in the most difficult circumstances.

I conclude that there was no adequate reason for the plaintiff's refusal of continued employment with the defendant as offered by the defendant in its letter of February 15, 1991. While there was some risk to her of diminished income, or loss of reputation, or both, had she continued her employment, those risks were relatively small. They were outweighed considerably by the assurance of gainful employment in an industry where she was established, at a time when that industry was in difficulty, and when many employees were being laid off. It was unreasonable

> for the plaintiff to refuse to continue her employment, at least for the period of time equivalent to reasonable notice. (at pp. 256-257)

Herrschaft v. Vancouver Community College (1978), 91 D.L.R. (3d) 328 (B.C. S.C.), provides an example in which an employee was not obliged to accept a lesser position with the same employer in order to mitigate damages. In this case the employee had been the director of curriculum of a college. Due to a reorganization her position became redundant and she was offered an alternative position at the same salary. The new position, however, involved acquiring additional instructional space, which was not within her area of expertise or competence. On the facts the Court stated:

> But what about her duty to mitigate? First of all, should she have stayed on drawing the same salary but doing entirely different work? I do not think so. Her position, in a sense, was no different than the plaintiff's in *O'Grady v. Ins. Corp. of British Columbia* (1975), 63 D.L.R. (3d) 370, where there was a change in the executive structure of the Insurance Corporation of British Columbia which resulted in his position as secretary and general counsel being abolished. Anderson, J., held, at p. 378, that the plaintiff did not have to mitigate by accepting a new appointment with the defendant as he would suffer "a substantial loss of prestige with consequent embarrassment and humiliation". (at p. 337)

The cases in Chapter 5, "Constructive Dismissal," are also instructive on the question of when an employee may be obliged to accept a lesser position with the same employer.

(d) Mitigation By Finding New Employment

It is very difficult for the employer to prove that a terminated employee has failed to use reasonable efforts to mitigate damages by finding new employment.

In *Michaels v. Red Deer College*, [1976] 2 S.C.R. 324, 75 C.L.L.C. 14,280, 57 D.L.R. (3d) 386, 5 N.R. 99, [1975] 5 W.W.R. 575, Chief Justice Laskin, for a majority of the Supreme Court of Canada, adopted the following from *Williston on Contracts* (Vol. 11, 3d ed. (1968) at p. 312):

> It seems to be the generally accepted rule that the burden of proof is upon the defendant to show that the plaintiff either found, or, by the exercise of proper industry in the search, could have procured other employment of an approximately similar kind reasonably adapted to his abilities, and that in absence of such proof the plaintiff is entitled to recover the salary fixed by the contract. (at p. 332)

It is, however, clear that employees are not obligated to accept any offer of employment. In *Forshaw v. Aluminex Extrusions Ltd.* (1989), 27 C.C.E.L. 208, 39 B.C.L.R. (2d) 140 (C.A.), the wrongfully dismissed plaintiff turned down three job offers involving positions materially different from his former job, at which time he started his own business. The issue on appeal was whether the plaintiff acted reasonably in declining offers of alternative employment. The Court held that the duty to take reasonable steps to obtain comparable employment does not amount to an obligation on the part of the dismissed employee to act in the employer's interest. In this regard the Court stated:

That "duty" — to take reasonable steps to obtain equivalent employment elsewhere and to accept such employment if available — is not an obligation owed by the dismissed employee to the former employer to act in the employer's interests. It would indeed be strange that such a duty would arise where an employer has breached his contractual obligation to his employee, having in mind that no duty to seek other employment lies on an employee who receives proper notice.

The duty to "act reasonably", in seeking and accepting alternate employment, cannot be a duty to take such steps as will reduce the claim against the defaulting former employer, but must be a duty to take such steps as a reasonable person in the dismissed employee's position would take in his own interest — to maintain his income and position in his industry, trade or profession. The question whether or not the employee has acted reasonably must be judged in relation to his own position, and not in relation to that of the employer who has wrongfully dismissed him. The former employer cannot have any right to expect that the former employee will accept lower-paying alternate employment with doubtful prospects, and then sue for the difference between what he makes in that work and what he would have made had he received the notice to which he was entitled.

The learned trial Judge was, in my view, entitled to find the plaintiff justified in rejecting the offer of employment in question. He plainly regarded the position in question, while similar in terms of the level of managerial responsibility and the nature of the business involved to that which he held with the defendant, as not similar in terms of the scope of business to be done and the opportunity for achieving the income which he previously enjoyed. (at pp. 212-213)

Difficult questions may arise as to whether an employee is obliged to mitigate by moving to a new locale or whether the employee must take a particular job. It is difficult to be more precise than to say that the employee must act reasonably in light of the circumstances and the contract of employment in question.

In assessing what is reasonable the courts will consider many of the same factors as are considered in determining whether certain changes in the employment contract constitute a constructive dismissal (see Chapter 5.2, "Change in Job Description"; Chapter 5.3, "Change in Remuneration"; and Chapter 5.4, "Change in Geographic Location").

In comparing the constructive dismissal cases, however, one major distinction should be noted. In determining whether a change constitutes a constructive dismissal the Court generally is concerned with a set of facts at a particular time; for example, whether the employee is obliged to accept a transfer from Vancouver to Toronto at the time it is offered. In contrast, the obligation to mitigate extends throughout the period of reasonable notice. It stands to reason that what is reasonable for the employee to do in mitigation may vary over time. Thus, an employee who has been terminated in Vancouver may not, on the facts of the particular case, be obliged to accept a transfer to Edmonton or, alternatively, accept a job offer in Edmonton received immediately after termination. The same employee, however, may be obliged to accept employment in Edmonton after several months of searching for a job demonstrates that positions are not readily available in Vancouver. Similarly, a recently terminated employee may act reasonably in rejecting alternate employment that is in any material respect a lesser position than previously held. This would not, however, be the case for an employee who had been unemployed for a considerable period and so had learned that, for whatever reason, comparable or superior employment was not readily available.

As a practical matter, it is virtually impossible for an employer to prove a failure to mitigate damages in the absence of evidence that the employee rejected a suitable position or made no efforts whatsoever to find other employment. Thus, whether the failure of an employee to find new employment is due to either mental depression that inhibits a proper job search, or inexperience or lack of diligence at a job search, it is generally the employer who will ultimately bear the cost of a deficient job search over the period of reasonable notice. This suggests that an employer do everything possible, consistent with its legal position on just cause, to assist an employee in finding new employment.

(*Continued on page 6-41*)

(e) Mitigation Through Self-Employment

A terminated employee may attempt to mitigate damages by starting a business. In some cases this may occur after a relatively lengthy and unsuccessful search for employment. In such a case it is difficult to take issue with the fact that starting a business constitutes a reasonable step in the process of attempting to mitigate damages.

A much more difficult question arises when the terminated employee simply decides that, for long-term and personal reasons, self-employment is preferable. Quite commonly, and quite naturally, this decision is prompted by the fact of the wrongful dismissal itself.

The typical pattern when starting a business is that there are substantial organization and start-up costs, a period after start-up when expenses exceed income and finally, if all goes well, long-term profitability. Given that the majority of wrongful dismissals give rise to a notice period of less than one year, this pattern usually dictates that no net income is derived from the new business over the period of notice. On the other hand, the employee may well, during the period of notice, have established a business that will generate profits for many years into the future.

In the few reported cases, the courts have tried to balance the legitimate interest of the employee in having the freedom to make the best long-term career decision against the interest of the employer in realizing the benefit accruing from the legal obligation to mitigate damages.

In *Brdlik v. Comtech Group International Ltd.* (1980), 7 A.C.W.S. (2d) 416 (Ont. H.C.), affirmed (1981), 11 A.C.W.S. (2d) 396 (Ont. C.A.), the Court considered a case in which the terminated employee did not attempt to find employment, and instead proceeded to form his own company. Mr. Justice Hughes found that the failure to first look for employment did not mean that the employee had not acted reasonably to mitigate his damages, stating:

> Generally speaking, [the cases which] have dealt with the attempt to make a living through a company are dealing with situations where incorporation has followed an unsuccessful search for salaried employment. But the courts have recognized that company or firm activity is a proper one to be taken into account for mitigation of damages and it seems to me to be largely a matter of diligence and good faith rather than whether or not one should be tried before the other, particularly when the prospects for a successful launching of a company are good.
>
> In this connection Mr. Filion relies on the evidence of the plaintiff who said that because of various mergers the market for his services was better in the first year of his severance from the defendant than in the second year; therefore, he should have reversed the order of his activities and applied for salaried employment first before he devoted his energies to what I think has been described as his status as an entrepreneur. All I can say about that, is that there is no evidence other than the assessment of the situation by Mr. Brdlik to support the view that he failed to mitigate and admittedly on the authority of the Supreme Court of Canada, in *Red Deer College v. Michaels*, the onus is on the defence to establish that the climate was better in 1978 than it was in 1979. Not only the climate but

> the actual existence of suitable positions would be such evidence before me and which the defence has not adduced.
>
> I am, accordingly, impelled to conclude that the plaintiff made a reasonable and sustained attempt to mitigate his damages, an attempt which was not successful, during the year following his separation, and in respect of which I have found he should have received either notice of termination or money in lieu thereof. (at pp. 120-121 of the trial transcript)

It may be significant that in *Brdlik* the Court made a specific finding that the plaintiff had an "entirely reasonable apprehension of success" when he started his business. It would also appear from the reasons that the new business was bidding on potentially lucrative projects so that, if successful, profit would be realized during the period of notice. In other words, the employee was acting with the intent of achieving profits, thereby mitigating damages, during the period of notice. In a brief endorsement the Court of Appeal dismissed an appeal, stating that it was not persuaded that the trial Judge misconstrued or misapplied any relevant principle in relation to mitigation.

In *Battell v. Canem Systems Ltd.* (1981), 31 B.C.L.R. 345 (S.C.), the dismissed employee, instead of looking for employment or immediately starting his own business, spent four months studying for a real estate licence. The Court recognized that the real estate licence had value, and would result in future income. As a result the Court deducted $3,500 from the damage award, not on the basis that the employee had earned income, but on the basis that he had devoted his time to acquiring a valuable asset, namely, the real estate licence.

It is submitted that the *Battell* case makes good sense and should be applied in those cases in which a terminated employee embarks upon self-employment, recognizing that the nature of the new venture is such that no profit can be expected during all, or a substantial part, of the applicable notice period. It makes no sense to deduct from a damage award those financial benefits in the form of income from employment and ignore other financial benefits, more capital in nature, such as acquiring a licence or laying the foundation for a business. This is not, however, to say that the courts will have an easy time valuing non-income financial benefits and, pursuant to the general principle in the area, it is the employer who will bear the onus of establishing the extent of the non-income financial benefit to the employee.

A further issue arises when the effort to start a business results in a net loss during the notice period. In *Rajakaruna v. Peel (Regional Municipality)* (1981), 10 A.C.W.S (2d) 522 (Ont. Co. Ct.), the Court awarded as special damages $1,358, being the business loss suffered by the employee in attempting to establish a business as a financial consultant. Similarly, in *Rooney v. Reed Ltd.* (1978), 20 O.R. (2d) 665, 88 D.L.R. (3d) 414 (H.C.), the Court awarded the plaintiff $320, being the amount of the loss he suffered in operating a consulting firm, pursuant to his obligation to attempt to mitigate damages. Awarding damages with respect to these losses is consistent with the second rule respecting mitigation of damages, as stated in *McGregor on Damages*, 15th ed., and as cited in Chapter 6.3(a). To be recoverable, the loss must arise during the notice period and must be reasonably foreseeable.

(f) Mitigation Due to Receipt of Collateral Benefits

(i) *General Principles*

By virtue of a termination of employment, the employee may become entitled to receive money from a source which would not have been available had employment continued. An obvious example is an employee who, upon termination, is entitled to apply for and receive pension benefits.

The difficult questions surrounding the treatment of collateral benefits have most often been considered in the context of a tort claim for personal injury. An issue typically arises as to whether the innocent party, who has suffered a personal injury, is entitled to recover for the full measure of lost wages notwithstanding that the innocent party has already received payments from an insurer, employer or pension fund which would not have been received, but for the fact of the injury.

In *Boarelli v. Flannigan*, [1973] 3 O.R. 69, 36 D.L.R. (3d) 4 (C.A.), the Ontario Court of Appeal made a broad pronouncement indicating that welfare payments, unemployment insurance, private insurance, wage replacement payments under collective agreements or contracts of employments and *ex gratis* payments should not be deducted in computing damages in a tort action for negligence.

The economic and policy considerations pertaining to collateral benefits were considered at length in *Ratych v. Bloomer*, 30 C.C.E.L. 161, 73 O.R. (2d) 448 (note), [1990] 1 S.C.R. 940, 3 C.C.L.T. (2d) 1, 69 D.L.R. (4th) 25, 107 N.R. 335, 39 O.A.C. 103, [1990] R.R.A. 651 (headnote only) (S.C.C.). The Court, by a five to four majority, found that wage benefits paid to a police officer pursuant to a collective agreement should be deducted from the damages awarded to the police officer in a civil action for negligence relating to an automobile accident, which caused the police officer to be off work for three months. The reasoning of Madam Justice McLachlin, for the majority, may be summarized as follows:

> The general principles underlying our system of damages suggest that a plaintiff should receive full and fair compensation, calculated to place him or her in the same position as he or she would have been in had the tort not been committed, insofar as this can be achieved by a monetary award. This principle suggests that in calculating damages under the pecuniary heads, the measure of the damages should be the plaintiff's actual loss. It is implicit in this that the plaintiff should not recover unless he can demonstrate a loss and, then, only to the extent of that loss. Double recovery violates this principle. It follows that where a plaintiff sustains no wage loss as a result of a tort because his employer has continued to pay his salary while he was unable to work, he should not be entitled to recover damages on that account. (at p. 184)

. . . .

> As a general rule, wage benefits paid while a plaintiff is unable to work must be brought into account and deducted from the claim for lost earnings. An exception to this rule may lie where the Court is satisfied that the employer or fund which paid the wage benefits is entitled to be reimbursed for them on the principle of subrogation. This is the case where statutes, such as the *Workers' Compensation Act*, R.S.O. 1980, c. 539, expressly provide for payment to the benefactor of any wage benefits recovered. It will also be the case where the person who paid the benefits establishes a valid claim to have them repaid out of any damages awarded. Absent legislation or a third-party claim, the only device available to the Court to effect transference to the third party would be trust. Given that the third party has effective ways apart from trust of enforcing the claim, I would not extend the trust doctrine applied in *Teno* [*Arnold v. Teno*, [1978] 2 S.C.R. 287] and *Thornton* [*Thornton v. Prince George Board of School Trustees*, [1978] 2 S.C.R. 267] to collateral benefits in the usual case. At the same time, I would not rule out that a judge might use this device to transfer payment to a third party where the judge is satisfied that this is both necessary and apppropriate in the interests of justice. Generally speaking, however, some sort of obligation, moral if not legal, to repay the third party would need to be established to permit application of the trust device. (at p. 185)

While the *Ratych* case deals with a tort action, the fact that it is a decision of the Supreme Court of Canada, which considers the broad policy and economic issues, suggests that it should be considered in attempting to discern how collateral benefits will be treated in the context of a wrongful dismissal action.

(ii) *Pension Benefits*

Since we are considering whether the receipt of pension benefits is relevant to the calculation of damages in a wrongful dismissal action, in most cases the employee will have been terminated prior to the normal retirement date. In that event, any pension benefits which the employee is entitled to elect to receive, will probably be one of the following types:

1. Actuarially Reduced Benefits:

   This pension benefit will be reduced, typically by fixed percentage, multiplied by the number of years that the employee falls short of normal retirement age.

2. Unreduced Benefits:

   This type of pension benefit is typically calculated in the same manner as it would be calculated at normal retirement age, and is typically a function of the number of years of service and/or the wage rate of the employee calculated on the basis of the highest three or five years of earnings. In this situation, the employee does receive a marginally lower pension benefit than if he or she had been permitted to work out the period of reasonable notice. If the employee had been able to do that, then he or she would have had marginally longer service, and the three or five year average earnings would also be somewhat higher.

Most pensions are funded, in whole or substantial part, by the employer. Further, it is self-evident that it is impossible, in the ordinary course of events, for an individual to receive wages and pension benefits with reference to the same period of time and the same employer. An employee who has age and service sufficient to elect to receive pension benefits immediately can elect to retire and receive pension benefits or, in the alternative, can continue to work and receive wages and accrue additional service for pension purposes. As stated, however, the employee cannot receive pension benefits, and wages, for the same period.

Thus, to the extent that such benefits are paid prematurely on an actuarially reduced basis, it would not be sensible to deduct such payments from an award of damages. In such a case, the employee has earned a particular pension benefit and if the employee elects to receive certain pension benefits earlier than otherwise anticipated, the consequence is that there is a corresponding reduction in the payments. As such, to deduct the pension benefits received during the period of notice would give the employee something less than full compensation for the period of notice and the full pension benefit. However, this would not be the case if pension benefits are paid on an unreduced basis. In such a case, if unreduced pension benefits are not deducted from wrongful dismissal damages, the employee receives a double recovery. The Supreme Court of Canada in *Ratych* permitted a tortfeasor, a stranger and wrongdoer, to deduct collateral benefits to avoid double recovery by the innocent party. It is submitted that the economic and policy reasons against double recovery apply with even greater force when a person is attempting to recover damages, not from a stranger and wrongdoer, but from his or her own employer. It is, therefore, submitted that pension benefits received on an unreduced basis should be deducted from damages awarded in a wrongful dismissal action. To ensure that the plaintiff does receive full recovery, he or she should be awarded, as one of the positive components of the damage calculation, an amount to compensate for the fact that the person would have received a marginally higher pension had they worked out the period of reasonable notice (see chapter 6.4(b)(v)).

This issue has not been discussed in great detail in the cases reported to date. In *Rivers v. Gulf Canada Ltd.* (1986), 13 C.C.E.L. 131 (Ont. H.C.) and *Laakso v. R.* (1986), 15 C.C.E.L. 139, 5 F.T.R. 87 (Fed. T.D.), it was held that pension payments received during the period of reasonable notice should be deducted from damages awarded in a wrongful dismissal action.

In *Tedford v. Woodward Stores Ltd.* (1990), 31 C.C.E.L. 1 (B.C. C.A.), the Court appeared to recognize that pension benefits should be offset against wrongful dismissal damages. The case is of limited utility as a precedent, however, because the trial judge gave very brief reasons which failed to identify the value of the enhanced pension benefits.

In *Tedford*, the plaintiff was approximately nine months short of his fifty-fifth birthday and, therefore, not entitled to elect early retirement. The employer, however, treated the employee as if he was age 55. The actuarial lump sum value of the pension at age 55 was approximately $34,000 as compared to approximately $14,000 at age 60. While the issue was not discussed, there was no dispute that had the employee been provided with reasonable advance notice of termination, he would have worked until after age 55. Thus, the plaintiff may well have been entitled to have his damages assessed on the basis that he was entitled to elect pension benefits at age 55. In any event, based upon an admittedly inadequate record, the Court of Appeal adopted the rough and ready approach of deducting 50 per cent of the actuarial value of the pension enhancement from the damage award. The Court of Appeal adopted the approach of the trial Judge and expressed this as a reduction in the number of months of the notice period. It is, however, respectfully submitted that it would be more logical and precise to determine the period of reasonable notice in accordance with the generally accepted principles, calculate damages over that period and then simply regard the pension benefit as an amount deducted from the total damages.

The *Tedford* decision was followed in *Regan v. Commercial Union Assurance Co. of Canada* (1993), 48 C.C.E.L. 208 (B.C.S.C.), in which the employer, anticipating the need to have to terminate a number of employees, amended its pension plan to provide increased early retirement benefits to qualifying members terminated during a five month window of opportunity. The plaintiff was terminated during this time and he elected to accept the early retirement benefits. The Court was provided with evidence that the enhanced pension benefit was worth $54,000, on a present value basis, and 75 per cent of this amount was deducted from the damages awarded to the plaintiff. Again, the case is not particularly helpful as a precedent, in terms of the appropriate percentage to deduct, because there was incomplete evidence concerning matters such as the tax advantages of receipt of periodic pension payments as opposed to damages.

(iii) *Unemployment Insurance Benefits*

As discussed at Chapter 8.2, the employee has an obligation to repay unemployment insurance benefits upon receipt of a damage award referable to the same period of time as benefits have been received. As such, unemployment insurance benefits would clearly not apply as collateral benefits reducing the damage award.

(iv) *Disability Benefits*

In *McGarry v. Bosco Homes Edmonton* (1992), 42 C.C.E.L. 198 (Alta. Q.B.), the Court was concerned with an unusual situation in which an employee, absent from work and receiving long-term disability benefits, was constructively dismissed. The employee brought a civil action. The Court considered conflicting decisions as to whether long-term disability benefits should be deducted from wrongful dismissal damages stating:

> The other cases are employment cases. In *Jack Cewe* [*Jorgenson v. Jack Cewe Ltd.*, [1980] 1 S.C.R. 812, [1980] 4 W.W.R. 494, 10 B.L.R. 287, 22 B.C.L.R. 297, 111 D.L.R. (3d) 577, [1980] C.T.C. 314, C.E.B. & P.G.R. 8102, 80 D.T.C. 6233, 32 N.R. 1], the Supreme Court of Canada held against deductibility of unemployment insurance payments received by the plaintiff from an award in his favour for wrongful dismissal. *McKay v. Camco* [(1986), 11 C.C.E.L. 256, 11 O.A.C. 356, 53 O.R. (2d) 257, 24 D.L.R. (4th) 90 (C.A.)], supra, in the Ontario Court of Appeal, was a case

> 257, 24 D.L.R. (4th) 90 (C.A.)], supra, in the Ontario Court of Appeal, was a case where the plaintiff, having been dismissed by the defendant, became ill, and was paid the equivalent of five and one-half months' salary by the defendant as "disability benefits". The court held that disability benefits and damages for wrongful dismissal serve different purposes, the majority holding that the purposes of damages in that context were to allow the employee to search for new employment, something that he could not do while disabled, and that accordingly the damages should be paid without reduction. The court noted that the application of the so-called "collateral benefits rule" had not been considered in a wrongful dismissal context in that province. The court says (pp. 100-101 [D.L.R.] that it
>
>> . . . involves the relationship between two separate and independent rights of an employee under a contract of employment. The first right arises from the express items of the contract providing for the payment of disability benefits. The second right arises from the implied term, recognized by the courts, that an employee be given reasonable notice in the event of dismissal without cause.
>>
>> The rights conferred on the appellant by the express and implied terms of his contract of employment are, in my respectful opinion, qualitatively different. The disability plan provided for the maintenance of the appellant's income during the period of disability. It was a benefit which formed part of the bargain between the appellant and the respondent. I agree with my brother Finlayson that nothing turns on the fact that the payments to the appellant during disability were provided directly by the respondent employer rather than through a third party insurer.
>
> The court goes on to hold by a majority of three to two that the "collateral benefits" rule should not apply to wrongful dismissal cases. The court holds that the tort cases are not relevant to the case before the court where no third party tortfeasor is involved and appellant employee seeks merely to enforce his contractual rights against the respondent employer. In reaching this conclusion, the Ontario Court of Appeal disagreed with the decision of the New Brunswick Court of Appeal in *Bursey v. Acadia Motors Ltd.* [(1981), 35 N.B.R. (2d) 587, 88 A.P.R. 587 (C.A.)], supra, which held that sick benefits paid to a dismissed employee under a sickness and accident policy paid for by the employer could be deducted from damages for wrongful dismissal. It also disagreed with the Alberta Court of Appeal in *Salmi v. Greyfriar Developments Ltd.* [7 C.C.E.L. 80, [1985] 4 W.W.R. 463, 36 Alta. L.R. (2d) 182, 58 A.R. 364, 17 D.L.R. (4th) 186 (C.A.)], which also proceeds on the theory that disability payments "provided" by an employer (in that case, provincial workers' compensation payments) are deductible from damages for wrongful dismissal.

In the result, the Court deferred to the reasoning of the Alberta Court of Appeal in the *Salmi* case. The Court did, however, sympathize with the reasoning of the Ontario Court of Appeal in *McKay v. Camco*. The decision in *McKay v. Camco* was followed in *Datardino v. Royal Trust Corp. of Canada* (1993), 49 C.C.E.L. 255, 85 B.C.L.R. (2d) 214, [1994] 2 W.W.R. 176 (S.C.). While *McKay v. Camco* represents the law in Ontario, this issue can only be finally resolved by the Supreme Court of Canada.

(g) Discount or Deduction if Judgment Rendered During the Period of Reasonable Notice

With the advent of amendments to the Court rules in a number of provinces, to provide a broader right to claim summary judgment, came the possibility that judgment might be rendered during the period of reasonable notice. In *Cousins v. Woodward Stores Ltd.* (1990), 32 C.C.E.L. 210 (B.C. Co. Ct.), the application for summary judgment was made four months after the date of termination. The Court found that the appropriate period of reasonable notice was 18 months. The Court, however, calculated damages based upon a 16-month notice period. The reduction of two months was, in effect, a contingency to take into account the possibility that the plaintiff might obtain employment prior to the end of the period of reasonable notice.

6.4 QUANTIFYING DAMAGES

(a) General Principles

The first step in quantifying damages is to determine the period of reasonable notice for the employee having regard to the factors discussed in Chapter 6.1. In general terms, damages are then calculated by assessing the dollar difference between the position that the employee would have been in had the employee continued to work for the employer during the period of notice and the position realized by the employee over that period having regard to amounts received by the employee, and certain amounts expended by the employee during the period of reasonable notice.

In the real world, virtually all terminations are made effective immediately and the employee is not permitted to work out a period of reasonable notice. With respect to the non-salary elements of the damage calculation there is a threshold question as to whether the parties have agreed that certain benefits will be payable after the date that active employment ceases. For example, in *Brock v. Matthews Group Ltd.* (1991), 34 C.C.E.L. 50, 43 O.A.C. 369 (C.A.), the Court found that the terms of a share-option plan were such that it was agreed that the employee would not have any rights after active employment ceased, and notwithstanding that the employee may not have received reasonable advance notice of termination. As such, no damages with respect to the share-option plan, referable to the period of notice, were awarded.

The positive elements of the damage calculation are hereinafter set out. From the sum of the positive elements it is necessary to deduct all amounts received, and the value of all benefits received, by the employee during the period of reasonable notice pursuant to the obligation of the employee to mitigate damages (see Chapter 6.3, "Mitigation of Damages").

(b) Elements of the Damage Calculation

(i) *Salary and Salary Increments*

The most significant loss suffered by an employee is usually the loss of salary during the period of reasonable notice. In quantifying damages the positive element to be included is the salary that the employee would probably have received during the period of reasonable notice. In virtually all cases this will be the salary enjoyed at the time of termination.

A question often arises as to whether the employee should be entitled to the benefit of any salary increments that may have been implemented during the period of reasonable notice. The answer will depend upon the proper interpretation of the particular contract of employment.

In *Turner v. Cdn. Admiral Corp.* (1983), 1 C.C.E.L. 130 (Ont. H.C.), Mr. Justice Robins gave the following reasons for granting the employee the benefit of salary increments:

> In my view, the plaintiff is entitled to both. If the bonus or salary increase were purely ex gratia payments, I would agree with the defendant's contention. But those payments were not made by the company on that basis. On the uncontradicted evidence (and I pause to say that the defendant did not call any evidence in this case) persons at the plaintiff's level received an annual increase and bonus as a matter of course. Historically, increases and bonuses were forthcoming every year. The immediate past president of the company testified that these sums were regarded as part of the total compensation package of senior management. As I view the pattern, they formed an integral part of the applicable salary structure, and as far as the plaintiff and others in comparable positions were concerned, they were "money in the bank", so to speak. The defendant is not entitled to deny the plaintiff the salary increase and bonus that would have accrued to him during the notice period. While technically there may be a discretion, as the defendant argues, as to whether these payments should be made to a particular employee, that discretion has never been exercised against an employee and it would be unfair here, in my opinion, to deprive the plaintiff of these salary payments. (at p. 133)

On the other hand, in *Rooney v. Reed Ltd.* (1978), 20 O.R. (2d) 665, 88 D.L.R. (3d) 414 (H.C.), Mr. Justice Southey refused to award damages on account of salary increments stating:

> The plaintiff has claimed the benefit of normal salary increases which other employees received during the 12-month period in respect of which he might have been entitled to notice. In my judgment, he is not entitled to receive the benefit of those increases. If his employer had given him 12 months' notice in June of 1977, his employer was under no obligation to increase his salary during that 12-month period in the same way as the salaries of other employees were increased. (at p. 669)

Since each case depends upon the interpretation of a particular contract, it serves little purpose to cite example after example. It is, however, submitted that with respect to salary increments that are routinely granted in a certain base amount, for example, at the rate of inflation, a good argument can be made that even an employee working out a notice period should receive this type of increment. Such an increment is not so much a reward or an improvement, as a salary adjustment to maintain the status quo in terms of real income. On the other hand, it is submitted that all other types of salary increments should not be included in the damage calculation. The employer is generally entitled to terminate upon giving the employee reasonable advance notice of termination, and it is difficult to conceive that one can imply a term that the employer is obliged to grant an employee, who is subject to notice and so leaving the employer, a salary increment which is based on merit or in anticipation of future service.

(ii) *Commissions*

In certain types of employment, commission income is, in whole or part, substituted for salary income. In calculating damages, the principle is the same as for salary income, namely, that the employee is entitled to receive the commission that the employee would probably have earned during the period of reasonable notice.

Employers sometimes have policies, or enter agreements, whereby commissions are only payable up to the date of termination. A simple provision of this sort may be ineffective in that the employee can argue that such a policy or provision cannot be construed to limit the liability of the employer when the employer has been guilty of a breach of contract such that the date of termination is immediate, as opposed to falling at the conclusion of a period of reasonable notice. In effect, the employee can argue that under the provision or policy the date of termination should be regarded as the date termination would have occurred had both parties fulfilled the contract. On this argument, therefore, the employee is entitled to compensation for commissions that would have been payable throughout the period of reasonable notice. This argument was accepted in *Rooney v. Reed Ltd.* (1978), 20 O.R. (2d) 665, 88 D.L.R. (3d) 414 (H.C.), in assessing damages related to a company stock plan. (See Chapter 6.4(b)(vi).)

It is, however, open to an employer and employee to clearly and specifically agree that commission entitlement ceases on the date that the employee ceases active employment and regardless of whether the employee is entitled to reasonable notice or a payment in lieu thereof. This is, of course, subject to compliance with any statutory minimum entitlements such as are provided for in the *Employment Standards Act*.

(iii) *Bonuses*

There is no legal principle that describes when bonuses are to be included in the damage calculation. The entitlement in each case depends upon the evidence of the agreement between the parties. For the purpose of analysis, however, it may be helpful to categorize types of bonus compensation as follows:

(a) formula bonus
(b) quasi-formula bonus
(c) non-formula bonus.

A formula bonus is a bonus determined according to an arithmetical formula, such as a percentage of sales or profits. The entitlement to compensation for such a bonus, over the period of reasonable notice, is comparable to the entitlement to commissions discussed in Chapter 6.4(b)(ii). Such bonus compensation is generally recoverable on the principle that the employee is entitled to receive the amounts that would ordinarily have been received if the employee had in fact worked throughout the period of reasonable notice. Further, and as in the case of commissions, employment policies or contracts intending to limit the entitlement to formula bonus compensation over the period of reasonable notice must be carefully drafted to accomplish their purpose.

A quasi-formula bonus is one in which amounts are allocated according to specified factors, some or all of which are subjective in nature. For example, an amount for accomplishing certain tasks or for managerial skills. The entitlement to compensation for such a bonus, over the period of reasonable notice, is comparable to the entitlement to a formula bonus. The only difference is that there will be considerable uncertainty in attempting to prove what would be a fair appraisal of the employee's performance in relation to the specified subjective factors.

A non-formula bonus is one in which the performance of the employee is assessed without obligation on the part of the employer to take into account specified factors, or to weigh factors in a specified manner. The entitlement to such a bonus, over the period of reasonable notice, is comparable to the entitlement to the benefit of a salary increment during the period of reasonable notice discussed in Chapter 6.4(b)(i). Thus, to the extent that such bonuses are routinely awarded in a certain amount, or in a certain range, a good argument can be made that such bonuses should be included in the damage calculation. It is, however, submitted that other bonuses should not be included in the damage calculation. Surely an employer is not subject to an implied contractual obligation to grant a bonus, based on meritorious performance, to an employee who is at the same time under notice of termination. If that is correct, it follows that to put the employee in the same position as if the employee had been permitted to work out the period of notice it is not necessary to compensate for such a bonus.

In *Ivanore v. Bastion Development Corp.* (1993), 47 C.C.E.L. 74 (B.C.S.C.), the Court considered an executive who had a contractual entitlement to a bonus. The method of calculation was not stipulated. In fact, the practice was to assess bonus entitlement based upon three components being the personal job performance, including interpersonal relationships with other employees, performance on projects and overall profitability of the corporation. The Court concluded that while there was an element of discretion in the awarding of bonus, it was necessary that the discretion "be exercised reasonably and on the basis of objective criteria" (at p. 80). The Court found that a complete denial of bonus was unwarranted and constituted a breach of contract.

With respect to all types of bonuses, it is also relevant to consider the period with respect to which bonus eligibility is determined, i.e. calendar year, fiscal year, quarterly. In *Nugent v. Midland Doherty Ltd.* (1989), 31 C.C.E.L. 235, 41 B.C.L.R. (2d) 249, 90 C.L.L.C. 14,027, 65 D.L.R. (4th) 694 (C.A.), the Court considered a discretionary bonus which was payable at fiscal year end. The plaintiff claimed to be entitled to two-thirds of the bonus because he worked for two-thirds of the period to which the bonus related. While the Court might simply have dismissed the claim on the basis that the bonus was discretionary, the Court did discuss the significance of the fact that the employee had not worked to the end of the period of bonus eligibility. In this regard, the Court stated:

> But, if he stayed until after March 31, 1987, he had a reasonable expectation of earning as much, more, or less than he had before, depending upon the profitability of the company on a national scale and upon the company's assessment of the performance of the various people who might be entitled to share in the bonus pool. There was no basis upon which he could reasonably conclude that he would be paid a proportionate share of the bonus he might have earned had he stayed. On the contrary, there were many sound commercial and policy reasons why a bonus would not be paid to an employee who resigned before the end of the fiscal year. A bonus rewards loyalty and encourages employees to stay in the employ of the company. No one else who had left had been paid a bonus. Loyal employees may have resented payment to Nugent. A bonus is paid not only to recognize past performance but to encourage good future performance. A bonus is based, in part, on profits and performance. But, the period of the year in which those factors occur may influence the amount of the bonus. Accrual of a bonus on a periodic basis is inconsistent with those factors and could not have been in the reasonable contemplation of the parties.
>
> In my opinion, there is no basis in the evidence for deeming the bonus to be part of the employee's wages, accruing as the services were performed, and to be paid on a proportionate basis whether the employee stayed with the company or not.
>
> Finally, I agree with the trial Judge that in the circumstances, the case must be determined in accordance with the rule of law relating to entire contracts.
>
> The rule is stated by the respondent in its factum in this way:
>
>> Where, under a contract of employment, remuneration is payable at the end of a certain period, the contract is an 'entire contract' and the employee is bound to complete that period before he becomes entitled to receive the remuneration. (at p. 243)

A different approach was taken in *Daniels v. Canadian Tire Corp.* (1991), 39 C.C.E.L. 107, 5 O.R. (3d) 773 (Gen. Div.), in which a bonus plan was non-discretionary in that entitlement was based upon corporate profit and not individual performance. The employee in question was a long-service employee who resigned in November and the issue was whether profit-sharing entitlement based upon the December 31 results should be paid on a *pro rata* basis. Associate Chief Justice McMurtry found that the employee was entitled stating:

> I am of the opinion, however, that where a bonus scheme has become an integral part of an employee's compensation and is non-discretionary in the sense that it is related to profits generally and not the employee's performance, that if the employer wishes to include a condition of continuing employment, that the employer must make the condition known to the employee as a specific term of his employment. (at pp. 111-112)

It bears repeating, however, that in every case the Court is concerned first with ascertaining the intention of the parties. Thus, the starting point is always to attempt to determine if there is any evidence of that intent.

(iv) *Fringe Benefits*

In *Davidson v. Allelix Inc.* (1991), 39 C.C.E.L. 184, 7 O.R. (3d) 581, 86 D.L.R. (4th) 542 (C.A.), the Court considered whether damages for loss of fringe benefits should be restricted to losses or expenses actually incurred. In rejecting this proposition, the Court found that in Ontario:

> [T]he law is settled that a wrongfully dismissed employee may claim, in addition to lost salary, the pecuniary value of lost benefits flowing from such dismissal. This principle was referred to with approval by this court in *Peck v. Levesque Plywood Ltd.* (1979), 27 O.R. (2d) 108, 7 B.L.R. 250, 80 C.L.L.C. 14,005, 105 D.L.R. (3d) 520, where Dubin J.A. said, at pp. 259 and 260 (B.L.R.), pp. 113-114 (O.R.), pp. 525-526 (D.L.R.) and p. 18 (C.L.L.C.):
>
>> In a successful action for wrongful dismissal, an employee is entitled to damages for the breach of his contract of employment.
>>
>> In Batt on the Law of Master and Servant (5th ed., 1967), at pp. 262-3 the following proposition is enunciated:
>>
>> "The law is that an employee's claim for damages is not limited to the wages or salary he would have received had he been given proper notice. The dismissal, if wrongful, is a breach of contract, and all damages flowing therefrom are recoverable."
>>
>> In the case of *Lawson v. Dom. Securities Corpn. v. Harris & Partners Ltd.*, March 30, 1977 (unreported) this Court held:
>>
>> "The recovery of lost income is not limited to salary. In this case the appellant conceded that pension plan benefits should also be included . . . . other income items should be admitted including contractual profit-sharing, a share purchase option, and many fringe benefits such as a company car, club membership, pension, disability and medical plans . . . .: *McGregor on Damages* (13th ed.), para. 885 at 595." (at pp. 192-193)

(*Continued on page 6-47*)

In the case of *Bull v. Realty Capital Corp.* (1980), 8 C.C.E.L. 229 at 230 (Ont. H.C.), varied (1981), 8 C.C.E.L. 229 (Ont. C.A.), the employee, Bull, had suffered back injuries while moving a machine at work. The injury occurred well before notice of dismissal. After the injury Bull had returned to work, but the condition became aggravated and she had to be hospitalized for treatment. While in hospital she was dismissed, although the communication did not reach her immediately. The dismissal was without cause. Bull tried to claim short-term disability benefits, but they were refused by the insurer on the advice of the defendant. At trial Bull claimed for the loss of short and long-term disability payments. The trial Judge found that Bull was disabled and as such had been wrongfully denied short-term disability benefits. The trial Judge also awarded damages on account of long-term disability benefits on the basis that the denial of short-term benefits had destroyed the right of Bull to claim long-term disability benefits.

The Court of Appeal overturned the trial Judge's ruling on the long-term disability benefits. The Court of Appeal held that:

> The learned trial Judge held that the appellants had destroyed the respondent's status to claim and recover long-term disability benefits from her insurer (who was not a party to the action), and therefore were responsible for the payment of those benefits. When the record is examined, we can find no evidence to support this conclusion. The respondent was free and entitled to sue her insurer at any time during the period she was suing her employers. Indeed, she submitted a claim for long-term disability with her insurer on the 30th of March 1978, the writ being issued against the appellants on February 13, 1978. Her right of action was clearly against the insurer and the evidence indicates that the insurer had left the final decision on her claim open. There was no suggestion in the correspondence or in the evidence given at the trial by the insurer's representative that the insurer was taking the position that the appellants' assertion throughout the proceedings that the respondent was not totally disabled, destroyed the respondent's status to claim. (at p. 241)

The duty of the employer to process disability claims was examined in *Tarailo v. Allied Chemical Can. Inc.*, 26 C.C.E.L. 209, 68 O.R. (2d) 288, 39 C.C.L.I. 85, 89 C.L.L.C. 14,040, [1989] I.L.R. 1-2427 (H.C.) (under appeal and cross-appeal). Tarailo alleged wrongful dismissal and claimed damages including damages on account of lost long-term disability benefits. In an interesting judgment the Court awarded damages relating to the benefits even though the employer had just cause for dismissal.

Tarailo had suffered from schizophrenic paranoia before his employment at Allied. During his employment with Allied he visited a doctor for treatment. His performance at Allied was less than desirable and in February 1978, Tarailo wrote a letter to the personnel department of Allied requesting a leave of absence for three months and after that date to be considered laid-off. This letter was treated by Allied as a letter of resignation. At the end of his leave of absence, Tarailo wrote to Allied requesting permission to return. Permission was granted with conditions.

Tarailo again proved to be an unsatisfactory employee. A letter was delivered to him detailing his unsatisfactory performance. Tarailo sent the letter back unopened. It was then presented personally by his superior. This time Tarailo crumpled the letter and threw it at his superior. The following day Tarailo was to be presented with a letter of termination; however, he resigned. Tarailo's illness after this date grew worse.

In November of the year following his resignation, Tarailo wrote to Allied explaining his illness and asking to be reinstated. However, Allied refused. After this Tarailo worked briefly for Home Foundries.

In November 1981, two years after his previous letter, Tarailo again wrote to Allied requesting a position. Allied again refused. On March 30, 1982 Tarailo made a claim for disability benefits. This claim was dismissed by the insurer upon the advice of Allied. Tarailo died in 1986 and thereafter his action was maintained by his wife.

The Court found that Allied had just cause for dismissing Tarailo but did, however, award damages on account of the disability benefits.

The Court held, with respect to the entitlement to short-term disability payments, that:

> The defence raised appears to be that Mr. Tarailo was not disabled and that Allied's obligations to Mr. Tarailo ceased on the termination of employment.
>
> I am satisfied that Mr. Tarailo was prevented by illness from working and earning his regular income in the 6-month period following September 6, 1978. There is little evidence to the contrary. He did attempt to engage in some stock market activity without much success. He suffered from the delusion that he had solved the secret of the stock market. He was seriously mentally ill.
>
> The brochure provides that in order to participate in the benefit program "you must be a permanent, full time employee of Allied."
>
> Mr. Tarailo was a permanent, full-time employee of Allied when he became ill. He became entitled to benefits when his illness prevented him from working. Allied could not cut off Mr. Tarailo's benefits by discharging him or by telling him he was to be discharged and then accepting his resignation. (at p. 218)

The Court also found that Tarailo had a valid claim for damages on account of long-term disability payments against both his employer and the insurance carrier. The long-term disability brochure provided by the insurer stated that:

> Claims
>
> All claims should be referred to the Employee Relations Department who will assist in completing the required forms. First notice of a possible claim should be filed not later than the fourth month of disability. (at p. 222)

This statement in the long-term disability brochure led the Court to conclude that:

> Allied was in possession of claims forms supplied by Mutual. The letters of November 5, and 16, 1979, advising of Mr. Tarailo's physical and mental illness

should have alerted Allied to the fact that their ex-employee might have a claim for disability payments, in spite of the fact that the notice was late. (at p. 222)

Because the Employee Relations Department was to assist in completing the required forms, the Court held that the employer owed a duty of care to the employee to assist in the claim process. On this issue the Court stated that:

> It should have been in the contemplation of the officers or employees of Allied, upon receiving the letters of November 1979, that carelessness on their part may be likely to cause damage to their ex-employee. It was not up to them to decide whether or not there was a valid claim but rather to ''assist in completing the required forms.'' Mr. Tarailo may well have been so mentally ill that he did not appreciate that he might have a claim. I conclude that a duty was owed to him. There do not appear to be any considerations which ought to negative, or to reduce or limit the scope of the duty or the damages to which a breach of it may give rise. Allied did nothing to assist Mr. Tarailo. (at p. 223)

This conclusion that Allied owed a duty of care to the employee allowed the Court to find that Allied had breached this duty and that Tarailo's inability to receive the payments was a loss resulting from the breach. The Court also concluded that the insurer was liable on the basis that Allied was acting as their agent in this matter.

In the case of *Dunlop v. B.C. Hydro & Power Authority* (1988), 23 C.C.E.L. 96, 32 B.C.L.R. (2d) 334, [1989] 2 W.W.R. 518 (C.A.), the employee was 61 years old and had been employed by Hydro for 10 years, with a final salary of approximately $46,000. He was offered a separation package of eight months' salary plus 25 per cent of that amount on account of fringe benefits. By virtue of his age the employee also started to receive his pension. Seven months after his dismissal he suffered a disabling injury while moving furniture at his church.

The trial Judge concluded that a 20-month period of notice was reasonable. The receipt of a retirement pension did not affect the notice period. The trial Judge did, however, conclude that the disability that the employee suffered affected the award of damages as the employee would not have been able to work during his period of disability and so would not have been paid for that period by the employer. Because he would not have been paid by the employer, the trial Judge did not award damages for the 12 months that the employee was disabled.

The Court of Appeal disagreed with the trial Judge, stating that:

> The trial Judge said that Mr. Dunlop had not proved any loss because he was paid for 8-months, plus 25 per cent for fringe benefits, giving the equivalent of 10 months at straight salary, and thereafter, because of his injury, he would not have been paid if he had been working out his notice period, in accordance with the contract of employment, at the time of his injury. I disagree with the conclusion that Mr. Dunlop had not proved any loss. In my opinion, the events which might have occurred if the employer had complied with the contract of employment, and so given the employee reasonable notice, but which did not actually occur, cannot determine the amount of damages suffered by the employee when the employer breaks the contract of employment and makes those events inconsequential. At that stage the employer cannot avail itself of any hypothetical alternatives, such as

> disability, which might have arisen if the contract had not been broken. By dismissing Mr. Dunlop, B.C. Hydro had elected to disqualify him from the disability benefit plans. B.C. Hydro, in those circumstances, cannot later say that it would not have had to pay salary while Mr. Dunlop was disabled, if it hadn't broken its contract, and if he had still been in its employment serving out the notice period. When B.C. Hydro broke the contract of employment it lost its right to rely on the provision in that contract that no salary would be paid with respect to a period of disability. And it must be borne in mind that if Mr. Dunlop had not been dismissed he would not have been working in his church basement on a weekday and would not have been injured.
>
> I add that, in considering the significance of events following the dismissal, the proper principle, in my opinion, is that an event which occurs after a wrongful dismissal and before trial, or before the end of the notice period, whichever comes first, may be considered in assessing the damages actually suffered by the dismissed employee. The legal significance to be attached to the event will depend on the nature of the event and on the other relevant factors in the case. But, to the extent that the damages are derived from a determination of the proper notice period, that notice period is determinable once and for all at the time of the breach of contract and is not, itself, affected by subsequent events. (at pp. 100-101)

In *Koor v. Metropolitan Trust Co. of Canada* (1993), 48 C.C.E.L. 216 (Ont. Gen. Div.), additional reasons at (November 29, 1993), Doc. 45186/90 (Ont. Gen. Div.), the Court concluded that the plaintiff was entitled to not only salary over the period of notice but also to vacation pay. In this regard, the Court stated:

> The authorities tend to agree that vacation pay should be given during the notice period. (See, for example, *Oxman v. Dustbane Enterprises Ltd.* (1988), 23 C.C.E.L. 157, 32 O.A.C. 154 (Ont. C.A.) at p. 160 (C.C.E.L.).) Taking into account the duty to mitigate and the fact that services during the notice period are purely notional, this appears to me to be a sensible approach. (at p. 235)

The *Oxman* case, however, contains no discussion as to the principle on which an employee should recover vacation pay in addition to salary over the period of reasonable notice. Certainly if the employer had provided the employee with reasonable advance notice of termination one would expect that the employer would have insisted that the employee take any vacation time during the period of notice. As such this does appear to be double recovery and has the effect of putting the employee in a better position than if the employee had been provided with reasonable advance notice of termination.

If the employee proves that she/he did not take any vacation during the notice period, and constantly sought to mitigate damages, then it is submitted that the recovery of additional vacation pay is defensible. In many cases, however, the evidence is that terminated employees do take vacation during the period of reasonable notice and courts typically recognize that this is not inconsistent with the duty to take all reasonable steps to mitigate damages. It is submitted that vacation pay should only be recoverable over the period of reasonable notice in the event, and to the extent that the employee proves that she/he did not take vacations and could not reasonably take vacations having regard to her/his efforts to mitigate.

In contrast, in *Scott v. Lillooet School District No. 29* (1991), 60 B.C.L.R. (2d) 273, (*sub nom. Scott v. Board of Education, Lillooet School District No. 29*) 5 B.C.A.C. 254, 11 W.A.C. 254 (C.A.), the Court adopted dissenting reasons given by Mr. Justice Esson in an earlier case (*Stauder v. B.C. Hydro & Power Authority* (1988), 25 B.C.L.R. (2d) 40 (C.A.)) as follows:

> It may be useful to consider what the position would have been had B.C. Hydro, instead of electing to make payment in lieu of notice, elected to give Mr. Stauder 18 months' prior notice of termination. Let us assume a four week entitlement and that, at the beginning of that period, he had received all vacation time to which he was then entitled. He would then have been entitled to the stipulated period of vacation during that period of notice, i.e., a total of six weeks in 18 months. If, at the end of the 18 month period, he had received only four weeks' vacation, he would have been entitled to be paid for the two weeks he had worked beyond his contractual obligation.
>
> . . . .
>
> But, except for the first month during which Mr. Stauder was required to provide services, B.C. Hydro elected to pay in lieu of notice. The result is that, in respect of a 17 month period, he had been paid a lump sum equivalent to his full salary for that period. In that period, he was free of any obligations to go to work or effort on behalf of B.C. Hydro. The time was his to do with as he wished. The substance of the matter is that, during the 18 month notice period, Mr. Stauder had 17 months' vacation.
>
> The appellant submits, however, that Mr. Stauder's time was not his to do with as he wished because he had a duty to B.C. Hydro to mitigate his loss and a duty to himself and his dependents to use his time to obtain other employment. Therefore, it is argued, he could not take a vacation (in the sense of "going on holidays") lest it later be held against him that he had not carried out his duty to mitigate; and also because his situation was such that he could not enjoy a holiday. I cannot accept those considerations as creating an obligation on the employer to pay "vacation pay" during the 17 month period. The duty to mitigate requires only that reasonable steps be taken. I cannot visualize as a realistic possibility that a discharged employee who rested from his mitigation efforts for a period equivalent to the vacation period provided in his contract would be held to have failed for that reason to have acted reasonably. The same, in my view, is true of the submission based on enjoyment. The fact remains that he was effectively free to use the time as he wished. (at p. 278)

The Court, therefore, summarized the law as follows:

> Vacation pay arises as a result of the contract of employment providing for a period of time during the employment year when the employee is not required to "work" but yet is entitled to pay.
>
> During the 15-month notice period awarded to the respondent, he was free from any obligations to the appellant, either to go to work or to expend any effort on its behalf.
>
> In the case at bar, the respondent led no evidence of loss or expense associated with lost vacation benefits nor did he lead any evidence that he had suffered in any way as a result of his not being able to take a meaningful holiday.
>
> To award the respondent damages for vacation pay, on top of an award of full salary for the period of notice to which he was entitled, (which necessarily includes

> payment of his salary for any vacation he may have taken had he worked during that notice period), is to provide double indemnity, or put another way, to provide compensation for loss that he has not suffered. (at p. 280)

Thus, the British Columbia Court of Appeal has generally accepted that vacation pay should not be recoverable, in addition to lost salary, in the absence of evidence that the employee has suffered from not being able to take vacation during the notice period. It is submitted that this approach is most consistent with the fundamental principle that an award of damages should put the employee in the position she/he would have enjoyed had she/he been provided with reasonable advance notice of termination.

(v) *Loss of Pension Benefits*

Each pension plan will have its own criteria as to when vesting occurs. The *Pension Benefits Act*, R.S.O. 1990, c. P.8, however, provides that vesting must occur:

1. with respect to the period prior to January 1, 1987, not later than the time at which the individual is 45 years of age and has 10 years of service;
2. with respect to service after January 1, 1987, after not more than 24 months of service.

It should be noted that certain pension plans, such as those applicable to provincial and municipal government employees, teachers, and those pension plans registered federally are not governed by the *Pension Benefits Act*. The vast majority of private sector employees in Ontario are, however, subject to the *Pension Benefits Act*.

In terms of pension benefits as a factor in computing damages in a wrongful dismissal action there are essentially four fact situations, as follows:

1. **The terminated employee did not at the time of termination have a vested pension benefit and would not have had a vested pension benefit had employment continued to the conclusion of a period of reasonable notice**:

(*Continued on page 6-51*)

In such a case the employee does not suffer any pension loss by virtue of the wrongful dismissal since the employee is left in the same position the employee would have enjoyed had reasonable advance notice of termination been given. The employee is entitled to a refund of the employee pension contribution, if any, plus interest, but derives no additional benefit as a result of the employer pension contribution. (See *Hokanson v. Sheet Metal Workers International Assn., Local 280* (1985), 12 C.C.E.L. 231 (B.C. S.C.).)

2. **The terminated employee did not at the time of termination have a vested pension benefit but would have had a vested pension benefit had the employment continued to the conclusion of a period of reasonable notice:** In this case an employee should be entitled to recover as damages the amount found by:
   (a) taking the amount calculated to be the present value of what would have been the vested pension on the last day of the applicable notice period;

   minus

   (b) the total of employee contributions refunded, if any (and interest on that amount, calculated to the last day of the applicable notice period), and the amount of employee contributions, if any, that would have been made over the period of reasonable notice. (See *Sturrock v. Xerox of Canada Ltd.* (1976), [1977] 1 A.C.W.S. 202 (B.C. S.C.).)
3. **The terminated employee had a vested pension benefit at the time of termination, which vested benefit would have had a higher value at the conclusion of a period of reasonable notice:**
   In this case an employee should be entitled to recover as damages the amount found by taking:
   (a) the amount calculated to be the present value of the vested pension benefit on the last day of the applicable notice period;

   minus

   (b) the total of the amount calculated to be the present value of the vested pension benefit on the date of termination, and the amount of employee contributions, if any, that would have been made over the period of reasonable notice. (See *Ansari v. B.C. Hydro & Power Authority*, 13 C.C.E.L. 238, 2 B.C.L.R. (2d) 33, [1986] 4 W.W.R. 123 (S.C.), affirmed (1986), 55 B.C.L.R. (2d) xxxiii (note) (C.A.); *Rivers v. Gulf Can. Ltd.* (1986), 13 C.C.E.L. 131 (Ont. H.C.); *Zeggil v. Foundation Co. of Can.* (1980), 2 C.C.E.L. 164 (Ont. H.C.).)
4. **The terminated employee had a vested pension benefit at the time of termination but would have been entitled to additional benefits, i.e., an enhanced early retirement option, had the employment continued to the conclusion of a period of reasonable notice:**
   In this case an employee would be entitled to the amount found by taking:

(a) the amount calculated to be the present value of the vested pension benefit, which will include the value of the additional benefits, on the last day of the applicable notice period;

minus

(b) the total of the amount calculated to be the present value of the vested pension benefit on the date of termination, and the amount of employee contributions, if any, that would have been made over the period of reasonable notice. (The cases cited under the third fact situation also support this calculation.)

(vi) *Other Losses Consequent on Termination*

It is often the case that the right of the employee to receive a certain type of benefit will either depend upon the employee continuing employment or being employed on a particular date. Examples would include the right of an employee to exercise a share option at less than market value on a future date, or the right to qualify for a reimbursement of moving expenses after a specified period of employment. It would be open to the parties to enter into an express agreement that such benefits are lost if the employee ceases to be employed and regardless of whether the dismissal is wrongful. Such express agreements are rare. In the absence of such an express agreement, and consistent with the general principles applicable to damage calculations, the Court attempts to put the employee in the same position that the employee would have been in had the employee received reasonable advance notice of termination.

This issue was addressed in *Rooney v. Reed Ltd.* (1978), 20 O.R. (2d) 665, 88 D.L.R. (2d) 414 (H.C.), in the context of considering whether an employee should be obliged to resell company stock to the company at the date of termination as opposed to enjoying the benefit of the appreciation of the stock that occurred over the period of reasonable notice. In this regard, Mr. Justice Southey stated:

> In my judgment, the proper interpretation of the agreement between the defendant and its employees is that the employee is obliged to sell the stock back on the date on which his employment could have been lawfully terminated by the company; that is, that it is implicit in the agreement that the company will not break its contract in discharging its employees. An employee hired for an indefinite term cannot require his employer to employ him for the rest of his life, but he is entitled to receive reasonable notice of discharge. If the plaintiff had been given 12 months' notice, which in my view was reasonable notice, he would have been entitled to hold the stock for a year, because he would have remained in the employ of the company for a year. As it turned out, however, he received a very satisfactory offer of employment with another company as of April 28, 1978, and I think that the proper way to assess damages in respect of his interest in the shares is on the footing that he would have left the employment of the defendant on April 28, 1978, to join his new employer had he been given 12 months' notice, and that the damages in respect of the shares should be calculated on the basis of

> the price at April 28, 1978. Had he sold his shares on that date to the company, he would have made a gain of $1,060. (at pp. 668-669)

In *Johnston v. Algoma Steel Corp.* (1989), 24 C.C.E.L. 1, 89 C.L.L.C. 14,012 (Ont. H.C.), the Court found that it was a term of a foreman's contract that, in the event of dismissal for other than just cause, he would be entitled to be reinstated in the bargaining unit. The company did not offer the foreman a bargaining unit position on termination. The Court found that the foreman had been wrongfully dismissed and as a result awarded additional damages in this regard. Damages in the approximate amount of $300,000 were calculated on the basis of the present value of the future earnings of the employee in the bargaining unit for the balance of his working career. The damages were then discounted to provide for the contingency that the employee, who had an alcohol problem, would have been terminated from the bargaining unit for just cause prior to his ordinary retirement date.

In *Prince v. T. Eaton Co.* (1990), 32 C.C.E.L. 174, 47 B.C.L.R. (2d) 310 (S.C.), additional reasons (1990), 34 C.C.E.L. 228 (B.C. S.C.), varied (1992), 41 C.C.E.L. 72, 67 B.C.L.R. (2d) 226, 91 D.L.R. (4th) 509 (C.A.), the employer terminated the plaintiff and paid a total of 42 weeks' pay in lieu of notice or on account of severance pay. The Court of Queen's Bench found that the plaintiff had suffered a long-term disability commencing within the 42-week period. As a result, the Court concluded that the plaintiff would be entitled to damages based upon the value of the long-term disability coverage. In the circumstances of the case, however, the insurer was a corporation owned by the defendant and the Court, therefore, simply found that the plaintiff was entitled to benefits under the applicable long-term disability plan.

Mr. Justice Lysyk reasoned as follows:

> Eaton's position comes to this. Provided an employee is given severance pay equivalent to salary for a period of reasonable notice, Eaton's is under no obligation to provide fringe benefits for that period or any part of it. It can avoid financial responsibility for any, or presumably all, fringe benefits by a simple expedient. It can tie the benefit to employment status and then terminate such status without notice or upon such notice as Eaton's is pleased to provide.
>
> . . . .
>
> The point has been made that recovery for loss during the period of reasonable notice is not limited to salary. The basic principle is that damages for breach of the contract of employment are to put the plaintiff in the same position, so far as possible, as if the contract had been performed: see, e.g., *Harris v. Robert Simpson Co.* (1984), 7 C.C.E.L. 202, [1985] 1 W.W.R. 319, 34 Alta. L.R. 64 at pp. 70 and 78, 56 A.R. 201 (Q.B.).
>
> . . . .
>
> A defence raised by an employer in similar circumstances was considered and rejected by Mr. Justice Griffiths in his reasons for judgment in *McDonald v. Lac Minerals Ltd.* (25 September 1987), Doc. No. 7021/85 (Ont. H.C.). There the plaintiff had been summarily dismissed, and the issue related to his right to

> damages for the loss of stock options. Under the stock option plan, an employee had 30 days after termination to exercise his option. Griffiths J. (now J.A.) stated (at p. 13):
>
> > Although the regulation calls for the termination of the option after the employee ceases to be an employee, I would interpret that as meaning when he lawfully ceases to be an employee. Here, where the plaintiff was wrongfully dismissed, it is my view his termination in law, for the purposes of this regulation, should take effect at the end of the reasonable notice period.
>
> Accordingly, the plaintiff was compensated for the stock option on the basis that he had not ceased to be an employee for purposes of the regulation until his termination in law, that is, upon expiry of the reasonable notice period.
>
> I would adopt and apply the reasoning of Mr. Justice Griffiths to the circumstances of the present case. (at pp. 187-189)

In dismissing an appeal, the Court of Appeal in *Prince* was in substantial agreement with the trial Judge although the Court of Appeal found that the damages should be assessed on a present-value basis that took into account contingencies, including the possibility of re-employment, instead of declaring that the plaintiff was entitled to an annuity to age 65.

It was fundamental to the decision in *Prince* that the employer, by failing to give reasonable advance notice of termination, was inevitably in breach of contract. In this regard, the trial Judge in *Prince* cited *Dunlop v. B.C. Hydro & Power Authority* (1988), 23 C.C.E.L. 96, 32 B.C.L.R. (2d) 334, [1989] 2 W.W.R. 518 (C.A.), in which the Court had stated:

> In considering that issue it is important to understand the nature of the implied term in the contract of employment. The implied term is a term to the effect that each party must give reasonable notice of termination to the other. The implied term is not a term to the effect that the employer may give pay in lieu of notice. (at p. 100)

However, it is submitted that conclusion of the British Columbia Court of Appeal in *Dunlop*, that the implied term in an employment contract is that the employer must give notice of termination, and that to provide pay in lieu of notice is in breach of contract, is:

(a) contrary to clear Ontario authority to the contrary; and
(b) inconsistent with the basic contract law principles governing implied terms.

Ontario cases that indicate clearly that an employer may, without breaching the employment contract, terminate the employment contract and provide compensation in lieu of notice include the following:

1. In *Posluns v. Toronto Stock Exchange*, [1964] 2 O.R. 547, 46 D.L.R. (2d) 210, was affirmed without dealing with this point [1966] 1 O.R. 285, 53 D.L.R. (2d) 193, which was affirmed [1968] S.C.R. 330, 67 D.L.R. (2d) 165, Mr. Justice Gale (as he was then) stated:

> Is it also correct to conclude that a breach of the contract of employment rather than its lawful termination was the result of the action by the Exchange? Admittedly, the contract of employment could have been brought to an end by a contemporaneous arrangement between the parties to that effect, or by reasonable notice or compensation in lieu thereof, or for cause, or if there were any express or implied term in the original engagement giving either party that right. (at p. 600)
>
> . . . .
>
> In somewhat the same vein, counsel for the Exchange contended that the Daly company could have lawfully terminated its relationship with the plaintiff by providing him with compensation in lieu of notice. *Konski v. Peet*, [1915] 1 Ch. 530 was cited on the point. There, Neville, J., held that as between the contracting parties, the payment by the employer of a week's salary in lieu of giving the week's notice provided in the contract, was not a breach of such contract by the employer since it was not an agreement to provide employment while paying wages. Surely, however, the principle that an employer does not breach his contract by paying compensation to an employee, in lieu of giving him reasonable notice (where no period of notice is specified in the contract), does not enable a third party who is alleged to have procured a breach of contract, to contend without any supporting evidence, that he contemplated that the employer, in discharging the employee immediately, would pay adequate compensation in lieu of notice. (at p. 605)

2. In *Brown v. Waterloo (Region) Commissioners of Police* (1983), 2 C.C.E.L. 7, 43 O.R. (2d) 113, 23 B.L.R. 41, 4 Admin. L.R. 113, 150 D.L.R. (3d) 729 (C.A.), Mr. Justice Weatherston, for the Court of Appeal, stated:

> It is trite law that an employer is entitled to terminate his employee's contract of employment either on reasonable notice or by giving compensation in lieu of notice. (at p. 17)

3. In *Brock v. Matthews Group Ltd.* (1991), 34 C.C.E.L. 50, 43 O.A.C. 369 (C.A.), in a per curiam judgment, the Court of Appeal stated:

> Brock was discharged from his employment on November 8, 1984. He had, in law, a right to reasonable notice or compensation in lieu of such notice. (at p. 58)

Further, in *Posluns*, Mr. Justice Gale, who was concerned with a contract of employment, referred to the circumstances under which a contractual term would be implied stating:

> As to the instances when the Court will imply a term in a contract, see *The "Moorcock"* (1889), 14 P.D. 64, and the language of Bowen, L.J., at p. 68, where he indicates that a term will be implied to give effect to the presumed intention of the parties, in order to give such business efficacy to the transaction as must have been intended. MacKinnon, L.J., stated the test in *Shirlaw v. Southern Foundries (1926), Ltd.*, [1939] 2 K.B. 206 at p. 227:
>
> > Prima facie that which in any contract is left to be implied and need not be expressed is something so obvious that it goes without saying; so that, if, while the parties were making their bargain, an officious bystander were to

> suggest some express provision for it in their agreement, they would testily suppress him with a common "Oh, of course!" (at p. 601)

It is respectfully submitted that a requirement that employers must give reasonable advance notice of termination or be in breach of contract, is inconsistent with the previous statement of the law concerning implied terms, having regard to the following:

1. It appears quite clear from the many reported cases, that it is common practice for employers to almost always terminate with immediate effect. This is particularly the case with management employees.
2. It is reasonable to conclude that the employer and employee would "of course" agree that the employer could terminate the employment contract by providing compensation in lieu of notice rather than actual notice of termination.
3. It would not contribute to "business efficacy" to require an employee to always provide advance notice of termination such that the employee was required or permitted to actually work out the period of reasonable notice. This is particularly the case with management employees. It is self-evident that an employee who is being terminated may be indifferent, or even antagonistic, to the best interests of the employer. To retain such a person, for reasonable notice periods of up to 24 months, would be unthinkable and contrary to ordinary business practice.

If the value of lost long-term disability benefits is recoverable as part of damages in a wrongful dismissal action, this would place an employer in the position of becoming an insurer throughout the period of reasonable notice. If the provision of long-term disability benefits, or other benefits, puts an employer in the position of a de facto insurer during the period of reasonable notice, it will serve as a strong disincentive to the introduction of such benefit plans.

If one accepts that a termination with compensation in lieu thereof is in compliance with, and not in breach of the contract of employment, then it is submitted that the appropriate level of compensation must be ascertainable at the time of termination. It would not be reasonable to imply that the parties intended that the level of compensation to be paid by one contracting party would be determined by a highly unlikely and random event occurring after the decision of the employer to terminate.

It is, therefore, respectfully submitted that the parties would "of course" have agreed that compensation in lieu of notice would be salary and the cost actually incurred in replacing the fringe benefit coverage which can be replaced. The parties would not reasonably have contemplated that, with respect to long term disability benefits that cannot be continued, the employer would become the insurer.

Further, even if it can be said that a termination without reasonable advance notice constitutes a breach of contract, it is questionable whether the damages suggested in *Prince* should be awarded.

In *Coopérants Société Mutuelle d'assurance-vie c. Colard (Succession de)*, 38 C.C.E.L. 107, [1991] R.R.A. 937 (C.S. Qué.), an employment contract provided that certain fringe benefits, including life insurance coverage, would continue until the later of the date of termination, or the last day of the period of reasonable notice. The group life insurance policy, however, provided that benefits continued only for 31 days after termination. The employee died after the group life insurance policy coverage ceased, but during the period of reasonable notice. In the circumstances, the Court found the employer liable to pay the estate the amount of the applicable life insurance.

In *Brock v. Matthews Group Ltd.* (1991), 34 C.C.E.L. 50, 43 O.A.C. 369 (C.A.), the plaintiff was the president and chief operating officer of the defendant company when he was terminated without advance notice. The defendant alleged termination for just cause, and as such did not provide the plaintiff with compensation in lieu of notice. This was, therefore, quite clearly a breach of contract since the Court ultimately found that there was no just cause.

The plaintiff Brock had purchased shares in the defendant company pursuant to an agreement which provided that, "in the event of the employee ceasing to be an employee" the shares would be sold to the defendant at an agreed price. In this case, the plaintiff was advised that his employment was being terminated on November 8, 1984, and his active employment ceased on that date. At trial, the Court reasoned, as in *Prince*, that the plaintiff should be put in the same position as if he had been provided with reasonable notice of termination. The Court determined that a one-year period of reasonable notice was appropriate and, therefore, awarded damages on the basis of the plaintiff being able to exercise share options which he would have been entitled to exercise up to the end of the notice period on November 8, 1985. The Court of Appeal, however, reversed the trial Judge on this issue stating as follows:

> The trial Judge's numbers were based upon his view that the "notice of dismissal", "dismissal", and "ceasing to be an employee" did not contemplate the wrongful dismissal that occurred in the present case. Accordingly, he held that Brock could have exercised his option up to November 8, 1985, the expiration of the period of reasonable notice, and he made his calculations of the numbers on that basis.
>
> With respect, we are of the view that he was in error. Brock was discharged from his employment on November 8, 1984. He had, in law, a right to reasonable notice or compensation in lieu of such notice. But the proper focus of the question relating to the interpretation of the share option agreements is not the determination of the period of reasonable notice or the quantification of compensation in lieu of thereof. The proper focus of that question is the meaning, within the contemplation of the option agreements, of the words "notice of dismissal", "dismissal", and "ceasing to be an employee". In our view, that meaning is the same for all of the events described, and the date on which all three events occurred is the same: November 8, 1984. It was on November 8, 1984, that

> Brock was given notice that he was dismissed; it was on that day that he was, in fact, dismissed; and it was on that day that he, in fact, ceased to be an employee. Accordingly, in our view, the number of shares to which Brock was entitled to exercise his option under the option agreements must be tested by reference to that date. (at pp. 58-59)

Brock, therefore, provides strong support for the argument that since long-term disability insurance benefit coverage (which almost invariably is available only to persons actively employed) ceases upon termination, no damages should be awarded as a consequence of a disability during the subsequent period of reasonable notice.

(vii) *Expenses Incurred in Mitigating Damages*

The corollary to the obligation of the employee to make a reasonable effort to mitigate damages is the right of the employee to be compensated for expenses incurred in this regard. This principle is explained in *McGregor on Damages*, 15th ed. (London: Sweet & Maxwell, 1988) at p. 168:

> [W]here the plaintiff does take reasonable steps to mitigate the loss to him consequent upon the defendant's wrong, he can recover for loss incurred in so doing; this is so even though the resulting damage is in the event greater than it would have been had the mitigating steps not been taken. Put shortly, the plaintiff can recover for loss incurred in reasonable attempts to avoid loss.

In considering whether a particular expense was incurred in order to mitigate damages it is necessary to bear in mind that damages are only recoverable over a period of notice. Thus, expenses incurred after the conclusion of the period of notice are not recoverable. Similarly, expenses which at the time incurred exceed the damages that would otherwise result through to the conclusion of the period of notice should not be fully recoverable. By way of example, an employee resident in Toronto and entitled to a nine-month period of notice may be offered a new job in Vancouver to start at the end of the eighth month of the notice period. If the damages for the ninth month are $3,000, it would not be reasonable for the employee to incur a moving expense of $10,000, and recover that full amount as damages. In such a case it would seem consistent with the general principle to allow the employee recovery of $3,000, which might be characterized as either salary for the ninth month on the basis that no net amount was earned in mitigation through new employment, or alternatively on the basis that the recovery of expenses incurred in mitigation is subject to a ceiling, being the balance that the employee would otherwise have been entitled to receive through to the conclusion of the period of notice.

Subject to the foregoing comments, recoverable expenses of mitigation include basic job search expenses such as for printing resumes, arranging and attending interviews, relocation counselling to the extent the services rendered were reasonably necessary for an effective job search and costs incurred in moving to take up new employment.

The recoverability of legal fees and real estate commissions incurred, and capital losses suffered, as the result of a sale of real property consequent on a termination, were considered in *Earl v. Northern Purification Services Ltd.* (1981), 1 C.C.E.L. 267 (Ont. H.C.), affirmed without written reasons (1981), 1 C.C.E.L. 267 (note) (Ont. C.A.), leave to appeal to Supreme Court of Canada denied (1982), 1 C.C.E.L. 267 (note) (S.C.C.). The facts of this case were unusual in that the employer had relocated its business from Toronto to Barrie and required the employee to move to Barrie rather than commute. With the active participation of the employer, the employee agreed to buy a house in Barrie, after which the employee intended to sell his house in Toronto. The employee closed the purchase in Barrie after being advised by the employer to do so, notwithstanding certain financial difficulties the employee faced, only to be told two weeks later that unless conditions improved his employment would terminate in two weeks' time. In the circumstances the employee took his Toronto house off the market and listed and sold his Barrie house at a loss of $9,000. Mr. Justice R.E. Holland awarded the employee damages on account of legal fees, real estate commissions and for his capital loss, reasoning as follows:

> Moving expenses and legal fees incurred by an employee as a result of wrongful dismissal are recoverable. See *Johnston v. Northwood Pulp Ltd.*, [1968] 2 O.R. 521, 70 D.L.R. (2d) 15 (H.C.) and *Vos v. Security Trust Co.* (1969), 68 W.W.R. 310 (Alta.). I see no reason why the principle should not extend to real estate commission, carrying costs and interest which were all foreseeable damages caused by the breach. I have some concern in connection with the $9,000, being the loss on the sale. Was this loss reasonably foreseeable? I think it is certainly foreseeable that real estate will fluctuate in value — up or down. If the plaintiff had made a profit of $9,000 on this sale I am quite sure that the defendant would have required him to deduct this profit from the expenses that he is claiming and I have come to the conclusion that it was foreseeable that the property would sell at a loss. The plaintiff should therefore recover the full amount of $28,129.65 less the tax saving of $2,825 for a net recovery of $25,304.65, together with costs. (at p. 272)

It is respectfully submitted that legal fees and real estate commissions are recoverable as expenses of mitigation in accordance with the general principles, and subject to the limitations previously stated. Thus, it would not make sense to make such expenses recoverable to the extent they exceed the damages that would otherwise have been suffered. Further, it might not be reasonable to incur substantial moving expenses without making every effort to find employment in the same locale.

The question of the capital loss, however, is quite different. Real estate values fluctuate up and down and the fact of the termination is irrelevant to the value of property at a particular time. The fact that the termination may result in a sale of real property does not give rise to any real economic loss or gain. There is no logical or causal connection between the fact of the termination and the capital gain or loss that is realized on the sale and, therefore, it is impossible to find that the gain or loss was a foreseeable consequence of the termination. Thus, as a general principle, the capital gain or loss that may

(*Continued on page 6-55*)

result from the sale of a house should not be recoverable. This is not, however, to say that the decision in *Earl*, on highly unusual facts, was necessarily wrong. In that case the employer, in effect, caused the employee to buy the house and actively participated in and approved of the purchase. This conduct on the part of the employer, coupled with the fact that the abrupt termination of employment would cause a reasonable employee to have to sell under severe time and financial constraints, made it reasonably foreseeable that a loss would result. See *Hennessey v. La France Textiles Can. Ltd.* (1981), 12 A.C.W.S. (2d) 233 (Ont. H.C.), for an example of a case in which the Court found the capital loss on the sale of a home to be unforeseeable and too remote to be recoverable.

6.5 DAMAGES FOR MENTAL DISTRESS

(a) General Principles

The leading case on mental distress damages is the Supreme Court of Canada decision in *Vorvis v. Insurance Corp. of B.C.*, 25 C.C.E.L. 81, [1989] 1 S.C.R. 1085, 36 B.C.L.R. (2d) 273, [1989] 4 W.W.R. 218, 58 D.L.R. (4th) 193, 94 N.R. 321, affirming (1984), 4 C.C.E.L. 237, 53 B.C.L.R. 63, 9 D.L.R. (4th) 40 (C.A.), reversing in part (1982), 17 B.L.R. 150, 134 D.L.R. (3d) 727 (S.C.). Mr. Justice McIntyre (Beetz and Lamer JJ. concurring) delivered the judgment of the Court. Madam Justice Wilson (Madam Justice L'Heureux-Dubé concurring) dissented. The facts in issue were summarized by Wilson J. as follows:

> The appellant is a solicitor who was employed by the respondent, Insurance Corporation of British Columbia (I.C.B.C.), in its legal department from 1974 to 1981. He had graduated from law school in 1972 after a successful career as an engineer with DuPont of Canada Ltd. He left DuPont to enter law school rather than accept a transfer to eastern Canada. He was Western District Sales Manager for DuPont at the time. He took up his employment with the respondent as a junior solicitor on September 24, 1973 when the respondent was starting up its business. His work initially was of a routine nature and included the preparation of leases and real estate purchases with a view to the establishment of claim centres and other facilities for the corporation throughout the province. He was promoted from the position of solicitor I to solicitor II on July 1, 1976 and given merit increases in salary in 1978, 1979 and 1980. In January 1981 his employment was abruptly terminated and he was required to vacate his office by February 13, 1981. He was 49 years old at the time.
>
> On October 1, 1979 the respondent had hired as general counsel a Mr. Reid who was given a mandate to improve the quality of the corporation's legal work with specific attention to productivity. He became the appellant's immediate superior. Difficulties arose between Mr. Reid and the appellant, Mr. Reid being of the view that the appellant took too long to get his work done. For example, Mr. Reid complained that the appellant wrote in long-hand as opposed to using a dictating machine. There was no complaint about the quality of the appellant's work or that he failed to meet deadlines required for his assignments nor was it alleged that he did not carry his fair share of the workload. He was simply

> conscientious to a fault, according to the learned trial Judge, and, in the words of Mr. Reid, was prone "to produce a Cadillac when a Ford would do".
>
> Mr. Reid became increasingly dissatisfied with the pace of the appellant's work. By November 1980 he had set up "productivity meetings" each Monday morning in which he reviewed the appellant's work in relation to the number of hours he spent on each project. The trial Judge found that these meetings "became an inquisition" and "as the pressure increased the plaintiff became tense, agitated and distressed, finally resorting to medical attention and a tranquillizer."
>
> The appellant was dismissed on January 21, 1981 without any particular precipitating event but simply because, according to the trial Judge, he did not fit into Mr. Reid's plans for the department. The trial Judge found that the appellant was "an honest, loyal, trustworthy and diligent employee" and was dismissed without cause and without reasonable notice. The respondent offered to pay his salary and certain benefits for an 8-month period if he agreed by January 23, 1981 to release the corporation from any claims arising out of his employment and its peremptory termination. Since the appellant was not prepared to admit that he was incompetent and that his employer had just cause for his dismissal on account of his incompetence, he refused the offer. He left the respndent's employ on January 23, 1981 and was paid up to February 15, 1981. He obtained other employment in September of 1981 but not as a solicitor. (at pp. 105-106)

The Supreme Court of Canada was concerned with whether aggravated damages or punitive damages could be awarded in the circumstances.

In his majority judgment Mr. Justice McIntyre differentiated between aggravated damages and punitive damages, stating:

> Before dealing with the question of punitive damages, it will be well to make clear the distinction between punitive and aggravated damages, for in the argument before us and in some of the materials filed there appeared some confusion as to the distinction. Punitive damages, as the name would indicate, are designed to punish. In this, they constitute an exception to the general common law rule that damages are designed to compensate the injured, not to punish the wrongdoer. Aggravated damages will frequently cover conduct which could also be the subject of punitive damages, but the role of aggravated damages remains compensatory. The distinction is clearly set out in S. M. Waddams, *The Law of Damages* 2d ed. (Toronto: Canada Law Book, 1983), at p. 562, para. 979, in these words:
>
>> An exception exists to the general rule that damages are compensatory. This is the case of an award made for the purpose, not of compensating the plaintiff but of punishing the defendant. Such awards have been called exemplary, vindictive, penal, punitive, aggravated and retributory, but the expressions in common modern use to describe damages going beyond compensatory are exemplary and punitive damages. "Exemplary" was preferred by the House of Lords in *Cassell & Co. Ltd. v. Broome*, but "punitive" has also been used in many Canadian courts including the Supreme Court of Canada in *H.L. Weiss Forwarding Ltd. v. Omnus*. The expression "aggravated damages", though it has sometimes been used interchangeably with punitive or exemplary damages, has more frequently in recent times been

> contrasted with exemplary damages. In this contrasting sense, aggravated damages describes an award that aims at compensation, but takes full account of the intangible injuries, such as distress and humiliation, that may have been caused by the defendant's insulting behaviour. The expressions vindictive, penal and retributory have dropped out of common use.
>
> Aggravated damages are awarded to compensate for aggravated damage. As explained by Waddams, they take account of intangible injuries and by definition will generally augment damages assessed under the general rules relating to the assessment of damages. Aggravated damages are compensatory in nature and may only be awarded for that purpose. Punitive damages, on the other hand, are punitive in nature and may only be employed in circumstances where the conduct giving the cause for complaint is of such nature that it merits punishment. (at pp. 95-96)

Mr. Justice McIntyre then examined the authorities, beginning with the cases of *Addis v. Gramophone Co.*, [1909] A.C. 488, 78 L.K.J.B. 1122 (H.L.), and *Peso Silver Mines Ltd. v. Cropper*, [1966] S.C.R. 673, 58 D.L.R. (2d) 1, 56 W.W.R. 641, which establish the rule that in cases of breach of contract damages are generally limited to the financial loss suffered by the innocent party and cannot include damages for the manner of breach, for injured feelings, or for loss sustained from the fact of the breach, such as the increased difficulty an employee might encounter in obtaining new employment after a wrongful dismissal. McIntyre J. then concluded that aggravated damages should not be awarded to Vorvis based upon the findings of fact and the manner in which Vorvis had framed his claim. McIntyre J. stated:

> From the foregoing authorities, I would conclude that while aggravated damages may be awarded in actions for breach of contract in appropriate cases, this is not a case where they should be given. The rule long established in the *Addis* and *Peso Silver Mines* cases has generally been applied to deny such damages, and the employer/employee relationship (in the absence of collective agreements which involve consideration of the modern labour law régime) has always been one where either party could terminate the contract of employment by due notice, and therefore the only damage which could arise would result from a failure to give such notice.
>
> I would not wish to be taken as saying that aggravated damages could never be awarded in a case of wrongful dismissal, particularly where the acts complained of were also independently actionable, a factor not present here. As noted by Hinkson J.A. in the Court of Appeal, at p. 46:
>
> > It was not suggested by the plaintiff that Reid's actions in the months prior to his termination constituted a breach of contract. Upon the basis of the reasoning in the *Brown* case, Reid's conduct was not a separate head of damages in the claim for breach of contract.
>
> His reference to the *Brown* case was to the words of Weatherston J.A. in *Brown v. Waterloo Regional Board of Commissioners of Police*, supra, p. 736, where speaking for the Court, he said:
>
> > If a course of conduct by one party causes loss or injury to another, but is not actionable, that course of conduct may not be a separate head of damages in

> a claim in respect of an actionable wrong. Damages, to be recoverable, must flow from an actionable wrong. It is not sufficient that a course of conduct not in itself actionable, be somehow related to an actionable course of conduct. (at p. 99)

Mr. Justice McIntyre concluded that:

> Turning to the case at Bar, it is clear from the judgments below that the appellant's superior, Reid, treated him in a most offensive manner. As has been noted, the trial Judge would have awarded punitive damages had he been of the view that it was open to him to do so. The question before us now is whether the trial Judge was right in concluding that it was not open to him to award the punitive damages. In my view, while it may be very unusual to do so, punitive damages may be awarded in cases of breach of contract. It would seem to me, however, that it will be rare to find a contractual breach which would be appropriate for such an award. In tort cases, claims where a plaintiff asserts injury and damage caused by the defendant, the situation is different. The defendant in such a case is under a legal duty to use care not to injure his neighbour, and the neighbour has in law a right not to be so injured and an additional right to compensation where injury occurs. The injured party is entitled to be made whole. The compensation he is entitled to receive depends upon the nature and extent of his injuries and not upon any private arrangement made with the tortfeasor. In an action based on a breach of contract, the only link between the parties for the purpose of defining their rights and obligations is the contract. Where the defendant has breached the contract, the remedies open to the plaintiff must arise from that contractual relationship, that "private law", which the parties agreed to accept. The injured plaintiff then is not entitled to be made whole; he is entitled to have that which the contract provided for him or compensation for its loss. This distinction will not completely eliminate the award of punitive damages but it will make it very rare in contract cases.
>
> Moreover, punitive damages may only be awarded in respect of conduct which is of such nature as to be deserving of punishment because of its harsh, vindictive, reprehensible and malicious nature. I do not suggest that I have exhausted the adjectives which could describe the conduct capable of characterizing a punitive award, but in any case where such an award is made the conduct must be extreme in its nature and such that by any reasonable standard it is deserving of full condemnation and punishment. (at p. 102)

The conduct of the supervisor, Reid, was found not to be sufficiently offensive, standing alone, to constitute an actionable wrong and, therefore, no punitive damages were awarded by the majority of the Supreme Court of Canada.

Madam Justice Wilson, in her dissenting opinion, formulated a different test than Mr. Justice McIntyre for aggravated damages. Wilson J., instead of following *Addis, supra*, and *Peso Silver Mines, supra*, placed emphasis upon the decisions of Lord Denning in *Jarvis v. Swans Tours Ltd.*, [1973] 1 All E.R. 71, [1973] Q.B. 233 (C.A.), and Mr. Justice Weatherston in *Brown v. Waterloo Regional Commissioners of Police* (1983), 2 C.C.E.L. 7, 43 O.R. (2d) 113, 4 Admin. L.R. 113, 23 B.L.R. 41, 150 D.L.R. (3d) 729 (C.A.). She also referred to

Professor G.H.L. Fridman's treatise, *The Law of Contract in Canada*, 2d ed. (Toronto: Carswell, 1986) at 675, and quoted from it as follows:

> By intangible loss is meant such consequences as loss of reputation, insult, annoyance, aggravation, nervous shock, inconvenience, mental distress, or other emotional or sentimental suffering. In recent years in England and Canada, there has been a growing realization that such results of a breach of contract should also be the subject of compensation, as long as the doctrine of *Hadley v. Baxendale* is applicable. There has been a greater acceptance of the idea that such damages can, and should be awarded in appropriate cases. (at (C.C.E.L.) p. 109)

Madam Justice Wilson also notes Professor Fridman's suggestion that employment contracts are subject to these awards for intangibles because of the nature of the relationship, one of trust and confidence, between employer and employee. To this suggestion Wilson J. adds that these awards also may arise in employment situations because of the vulnerability of the employee to the superior authority of the employer. The test, therefore, for aggravated damages that Wilson J. supports is one of reasonable foreseeability following the principle of *Hadley v. Baxendale* (1854), 9 Ex. 347 (note), 18 Jur. 358, 156 E.R. 148. She states this test as follows:

> It is my view that the established principles of contract law set out in *Hadley v. Baxendale* provide the proper test for the recovery of damages for mental suffering. The principles are well-settled and their broad application would appear preferable to decision-making based on a priori and inflexible categories of damages. The issue in assessing damages is not whether the plaintiff got what he bargained for, i.e., pleasure or peace of mind (although this is obviously relevant to whether or not there has been a breach) but whether he should be compensated for damage the defendant should reasonably have anticipated that he would suffer as a consequence of the breach. (at p. 114)

Madam Justice Wilson did, however, conclude that it was not reasonably foreseeable, in these circumstances, that Vorvis would suffer mental distress. As such she concurred in the result that aggravated damages for mental distress should not be awarded.

Madam Justice Wilson also disagreed with the test formulated by Mr. Justice McIntyre respecting punitive damages. She supported the position espoused by Linden J. in *Brown v. Waterloo Regional Commissioners of Police* (1983), 2 C.C.E.L. 7, 43 O.R. (2d) 113, 4 Admin. L.R. 113, 23 B.L.R. 41, 150 D.L.R. (3d) 729 (C.A.). Wilson J. stated:

> I do not share my colleague's view that punitive damages can only be awarded when the misconduct is in itself an "actionable wrong". In my view, the correct approach is to assess the conduct in the context of all the circumstances and determine whether it is deserving of punishment because of its shockingly harsh, vindictive, reprehensible or malicious nature. Undoubtedly some conduct found to be deserving of punishment will constitute an actionable wrong but other conduct might not. I respectfully adopt the following statement made by Clement J.A. in *Paragon Properties Ltd. v. Magna Investments Ltd.*, at p. 167 [24 D.L.R. (3d)]:

> It is the reprehensible conduct of the wrongdoer which attracts the principle, not the legal category of the wrong out of which compensatory damages arise and in relation to which the conduct occurred. To place arbitrary limitations upon its application is to evade the underlying principle and replace it with an uncertain and debatable jurisdiction.
>
> Nor would I draw the wide divergence that my colleague does between the duties owed to a neighbour under the law of tort and the duties that are breached in contract by the type of flagrant and deliberate misconduct that would merit an award of punitive damages. I agree with the appellant that it would be odd if the law required more from a stranger than from the parties to a contract. The very closeness engendered by some contractual relationships, particularly employer/employee relationships in which there is frequently a marked disparity of power between the parties, seems to me to give added point to the duty of civilized behaviour. (at p. 121)

Madam Justice Wilson would, therefore, have upheld the award by the British Columbia Court of Appeal of $5,000 in punitive damages.

As was mentioned by the Supreme Court of Canada, the leading case in Ontario, prior to *Vorvis*, was *Brown v. Waterloo Regional Commissioners of Police* (1982), 37 O.R. (2d) 277, 17 B.L.R. 299, 136 D.L.R. (3d) 49 (H.C.), varied (1983), 2 C.C.E.L. 7, 43 O.R. (2d) 113, 4 Admin. L.R. 113, 23 B.L.R. 41, 150 D.L.R. (3d) 729 (C.A.). Brown had been employed as chief of police of the defendant and a finding had been made that he had been wrongfully dismissed. Mr. Justice Linden, in assessing damages, found the following relevant to the claim for damages for mental distress:

1. the fact of the illegal termination;
2. the failure of the Board of Commissioners of Police to advise Brown concerning its true opinion of his performance;
3. public statements made by board officials concerning the termination which resulted in public embarrassment and humiliation to Brown;
4. the failure to pay Brown his salary and the continuing failure of the board to restore Brown to his position as chief of police.

On the issue of mental suffering Mr. Justice Linden stated:

> On the issue of foreseeability, it must be recognized that, normally, one does not anticipate physical or mental suffering as a result of a breach of a contract. Business people can handle contractual disappointments in stride usually. Certain types of contracts are different, however. For example, contracts to arrange holidays, because their very purpose is to supply happiness and enjoyment, can be expected to cause distress if they are breached. Similarly, if a contracting party is *aware* of the vulnerability of the other party, as in the *Newell* [*Newell v. C.P. Airlines* (1977), 14 O.R. (2d) 752, 74 D.L.R. (3d) 574 (Co. Ct.)] case, *supra*, liability may flow for a breach that causes mental anguish to that vulnerable party, because this should have been foreseen. Contracts of employment, because they are so personal and so important to the employee, especially more mature employees, are of this special type as well. (at pp. 287-288)

In the result, Mr. Justice Linden awarded Brown $10,000 to compensate him for his "mental distress, anxiety, vexation, frustration, worry and disappointment, both past and future."

The Court of Appeal, while affirming the principle that general damages can be awarded for mental distress, allowed an appeal by the board against the $10,000 award for mental distress. Mr. Justice Weatherston summarized the law as follows:

> Any breach of contract that results in pecuniary loss to the injured party will inevitably cause some mental distress – rage and frustration at least. But in the ordinary commercial transaction, the reasonable expectations of the parties are that the disappointed party will bear himself with a measure of fortitude, and be satisfied if he can recoup his financial loss. (at p. 15)
>
> . . . .
>
> But it would be surely wrong in principle to hold that a discharged employee could receive compensation for all the mental distress he suffered by reason of the termination of his employment if his notice was insufficient, and none at all if it was sufficient. It is trite law that an employer is entitled to terminate his employee's contract of employment either on reasonable notice or by giving compensation in lieu of notice. If he fails to give reasonable notice, the wrong he does is not the termination of the contract, but the failure to give reasonable notice so, for damages to flow from this wrong, it must have been in the contemplation of both parties, at the time of hiring, that mental distress would be the probable result of a failure to give proper notice, and the mental distress suffered by the discharged employee must flow from the want of reasonable notice, and not from the fact of dismissal.
>
> Finally, on this subject, I refer to *Br. Guiana Credit Corp. v. Da Silva*, [1965] 1 W.L.R. 248 (P.C.), where it was held that the humiliation, embarrassment and loss of reputation of a dismissed employee were not reasonably foreseeable as liable to result from the breach of contract.
>
> The cases that I have referred to show that there may be circumstances where a breach of contract will give rise to a claim for damages for mental distress. In my opinion, the correct rule is stated in Corbin, *supra*, Vol. 5, p. 429, citing the Restatement of the Law of Contracts, para. 341, as follows:
>
> > There is sufficient authority to justify the statement that damages will be awarded for mental suffering caused by the wanton or reckless breach of a contract to render a performance of such a character that the promisor had reason to know when the contract was made that a breach would cause such suffering, for reasons other than pecuniary loss. (at p. 17)

The Court, however, ruled that the mental distress suffered by Brown was not compensable. The principal reason for the conclusion was that the Board of Commissioners of Police, in dismissing Brown, acted in good faith pursuant to its mandate under the *Police Act*. The Court, therefore, relied on the principle that the decision of a public body made in good faith, and within its statutory authority, cannot give rise to an award of damages.

The grounds for awarding mental distress damages were also examined in *Bohemier v. Storwal International Inc.* (1982), 40 O.R. (2d) 264, 142 D.L.R.

(3d) 8 (H.C.), varied (1983), 3 C.C.E.L. 79, 44 O.R. (2d) 361, 4 D.L.R. (4th) 383 (C.A.), leave to appeal to the Supreme Court of Canada refused (1984), 3 C.C.E.L. 79 (S.C.C.). The plaintiff was 59 years of age, and had been employed by the defendant for over 35 years. The plaintiff was informed of his discharge by a letter delivered to his home on a Friday evening. The letter was described as follows by Mr. Justice Saunders:

> In my opinion, the letter was cold and perfunctory. It expressed no gratitude for 35 years of devoted service. It offered no concrete proposal to assist the plaintiff in finding other employment. It did not specify the basis for payment in lieu of notice. It provided no comfort at all to the plaintiff. (at p. 273)

The following week the defendant tendered a cheque for eight weeks' pay in lieu of notice, which was clearly an inadequate period of notice having regard to the length of service of the plaintiff.

Mr. Justice Saunders analyzed the law and found two grounds for awarding damages for mental distress.

> There are said to be two grounds for awarding damages for mental distress which, to an extent, overlap. First, such damages may be awarded on the basis that the injury was in the contemplation of the parties. In *Hadley et al. v. Baxendale et al.* (1854), 9 Exch. 341, 156 E.R. 145, Alderson B. said at pp. 354-55 Exch., p. 151 E.R.:
>
> > Now we think the proper rule in such a case as the present is this: – Where two parties have made a contract which one of them has broken, the damages which the other party ought to receive in respect of such breach of contract should be such as may fairly and reasonably be considered either arising naturally, i.e., according to the usual course of things, from such breach of contract itself, or such as may reasonably be supposed to have been in the contemplation of both parties, at the time they made the contract, as the probable result of the breach of it. Now, if the special circumstances under which the contract was actually made were communicated by the plaintiffs to the defendants, and thus known to both parties, the damages resulting from the breach of such a contract, which they would reasonably contemplate, would be the amount of injury which would ordinarily follow from a breach of contract under these special circumstances so known and communicated.
>
> There is a difficulty in assessing damages under this head. In contracts of indefinite term, an employer has a right to terminate on reasonable notice and such a possibility is within the contemplation of the parties at the time of making and throughout the term of the contract. Nevertheless, if an employer chooses to exercise his right to dismiss, it is reasonably foreseeable that such action will cause mental distress, anxiety, vexation, frustration, worry and disappointment to the employee. However, if reasonable notice or payment in lieu of reasonable notice is given, there is no breach of contract and, therefore, there can be no claim for damages. In most wrongful dismissal cases, the claim is not based on the act of dismissal but rather the failure to give reasonable notice. In *Pilon*, there was a finding that the employer had led the employee to believe that he was secure in his job for his working life; in *Grant* [*Grant v. MacMillan Bloedel Industries Ltd.*

(1982), 83 C.L.L.C. 14,002 (Ont. H.C.)], there was a finding that a statement in a company booklet and management's treatment of the employee had given him "a false sense of security"; and in *Brown* [*Brown v. Waterloo Regional Commissioners of Police, supra*], the decision was based on the finding in another court that the employer had no right to dismiss the employee. In the case at bar, the plaintiff recognized that he could be dismissed but did not expect it to happen. Where the employer has the right to dismiss, the damages must, in my view, flow from the failure to give adequate notice and not from the act of dismissal.

The second basis for awarding damages for mental suffering in wrongful dismissal cases is by way of aggravated damages. In *Brown*, Mr. Justice Linden said commencing at pp. 288-89 O.R.:

> The aim of aggravated damages is to "soothe a plaintiff whose feelings have been wounded by the quality of the defendant's misbehaviour". They are a "balm for mental distress" which is brought about by the wrongful "character of the defendant's wrongdoing". There must be evidence of damage of this type to the plaintiff. Aggravated damages are not meant to punish the defendant. (See Cooper-Stephenson and Saunders, *Personal Injury Damages in Canada* (1981), at p. 55; *Robitaille et al. v. Vancouver Hockey Club Ltd.* (1979), 19 B.C.L.R. 158 at 183 *per* Esson J.; varied 124 D.L.R. (3d) 228, 16 C.C.L.T. 225, 30 B.C.L.R. 286 (C.A.).) In sum, though based on the quality of the defendant's conduct, aggravated damages are compensatory in purpose.
>
> . . . .
>
> Canadian law seems to have recognized the need for something like aggravated damages in contract law by awarding damages, not only for financial losses, but also for any mental suffering incurred by the plaintiff in appropriate cases. (See *Pilon v. Peugeot Canada Ltd.* (1980), 29 O.R. (2d) 711, 114 D.L.R. (3d) 378, 12 B.L.R. 227, for example.) The purpose behind allowing such damages is to compensate for hurt feelings, anxiety and stress caused by certain types of contractual breach, where they are in the contemplation of the parties. Where the conduct of a defendant which violates a contract is particularly callous, the likelihood of mental suffering would be more foreseeable to him.

Linden J. concluded that, if the mental suffering of the plaintiff had not been compensable under *Hadley v. Baxendale, supra*, he would have been inclined to base such an award on aggravated damages. However, he found it unnecessary to do so in view of the recent developments in Canadian law of contract damages for mental suffering. (at pp. 271-273)

Bohemier suffered significant mental distress, as a result of which he visited a psychiatrist on several occasions. On the facts of the case the Court concluded that part of the mental distress was caused by the failure to give adequate notice and the manner in which the termination was effected. The Court awarded $1,500 in damage for mental distress.

The Court of Appeal dismissed an appeal, stating, "as to the award for mental distress, Saunders J. correctly stated the principles applicable and on the findings of fact that he made the judgment is unassailable" (at p. 362).

Having stated the general principles that are applicable it may be helpful, in illustrating the principles, to consider the types of cases in which damages for mental distress have been awarded, and the factors found to give rise to such damages.

(b) Factors Which May Give Rise to Damages for Mental Distress

(i) *Special Relationships - Employment for Life*

In *Pilon v. Peugeot Can. Ltd.* (1980), 29 O.R. (2d) 711, 12 B.L.R. 227, 114 D.L.R. (3d) 378 (H.C.), the Court found that Peugeot represented that its employees were part of a "family" and that in return for accepting less than competitive salary rates they would have "lifetime security." Mr. Justice Galligan stated:

> In my opinion, it cannot fail to have been in the contemplation of the defendant that if it suddenly, without warning, unlawfully discharged a man whom it had led to believe was secure in his job for his working life, there would be the gravest likelihood that such a man would suffer vexation, frustration, distress and anxiety. (at p. 715)
>
> . . . .
>
> . . . I think that the conduct of the defendant and the method used by it in callously, suddenly, and arbitrarily firing a long-devoted, loyal servant, aggravated the mental distress which the defendant's breach of contract caused the plaintiff. Its method of firing increased the distress and in that sense and only in that sense, do I consider the callous conduct of the defendant when I assess the plaintiff's damages for mental distress. (at p. 716)

Similarly, in *Grant v. MacMillan Bloedel Industries Ltd.* (1982), 83 C.L.L.C. 14,002 (Ont. H.C.), the employee, Grant, had served the company for 30 years. He had been led to believe that his work was satisfactory and that he would be able to remain until his retirement in ten more years. The Court held that:

> [t]he red booklet (Exhibit #3) entitled "You and MacMillan Bloedel", given to all managerial staff by the defendant on the purchase of the plant in December 1979, states in Part 1:
>
> > Family security coupled with competitive salaries are essential to a productive and stimulating career, and MB provides both.
>
> In his examination in chief, the plaintiff said: "On November 9, 1980, I felt that I would be at the plant until I retired in 10 years; no one had ever said otherwise; my health was good and I had given the company 100% plus". Just 10 days before November 10, 1980, Mr. Stokes-Rees had taken the plaintiff to Toronto to view equipment at some plants that the defendant had purchased from Continental Canada; the two men looked at the equipment and made recommendations to management.
>
> In my view, the cumulative effect [of the exhibits] and the defendant management's treatment of the plaintiff, especially in the final days of his employment before the "axe fell", gave the plaintiff a false sense of security. The plaintiff's term of employment was for an indefinite term subject to termination upon reasonable notice. However, the defendant terminated the plaintiff's employment at 7:10 a.m. in circumstances which beget a mental picture of an

intelligence unit's covert operation. In my view, the cloak and dagger method used by the defendant aggravated the mental distress of the plaintiff. (at pp. 12,012-12,013)

(ii) *Employer Conduct Inconsistent with Assurances or Representations*

Mental distress damages may result if an employer promises one thing and does another. In the case of *Lightburn v. Mid Island Consumer Services Co-op.* (1984), 4 C.C.E.L. 263 (B.C. Co. Ct.), the employee was ill and in hospital when his wife was assured by Mid Island that he was not to worry about his job, that a position would be available when he was fit. In considering the mental distress damages the Court held that:

> [h]owever, such an award can be made where the employee is assured prior to his dismissal that certain things will be done. Here the assurance was that he would have a job with the defendant when he was able to return to work. He received that assurance on two occasions and I find that that assurance together with the lack of honesty on the part of the defendant's general manager, did cause him mental distress and that mental distress ought to have been reasonably foreseeable by Mr. Glydon, purporting to act on behalf of the defendant. (at p. 270)

Therefore, assurances by the employer to the employee are a factor to be considered in situations of mental distress.

In the case of *Colasurdo v. CTG Inc.* (1988) 18 C.C.E.L. 264 (Ont. H.C.), additional reasons (March 8, 1988), Doc. No. 2651/85 (Ont. H.C.), the employee, Colasurdo, was sought out by CTG and offered inducements to join CTG. One inducement was the ability to become a shareholder in CTG based upon performance. Colasurdo performed well but received no shares. Colasurdo was constructively dismissed through a series of events which undermined his authority at CTG. The Court held that:

> [t]he plaintiff it will be remembered came to CTG only as the result of the persistent efforts of Miville and Lavin and on the basis of the promises made to him that he would have a strong equity position in the company and most probably rise quickly through the ranks to end up in head office in Toronto in a senior executive position. It was on the basis of these promises and only on these promises that Colasurdo left A.E.S., his previous employer where he was very happy. He was lured away by the efforts of Miville who must have known when the contract was struck with the plaintiff that a breach of that contract would cause the plaintiff precisely the type of mental distress he in fact suffered as a result of the events herein described. Any reasonable man would be aware that such emotional distress would be the necessary result of Colasurdo being treated in the fashion he was and effectively demoted without even the courtesy of being so advised. (at p. 291)

In terms of Mr. Justice McIntyre's analysis in *Vorvis, supra,* situations involving a breach of an assurance or representation by the employer can result in mental distress damages as being actionable in that the breach can itself be viewed as actionable.

(iii) *Denial of Opportunity to be Heard*

The *Vorvis* decision *supra*, makes it unclear whether failures by the employer to exercise procedural fairness will result in damages for mental distress. In certain cases the Court will be able to imply a contractual term that the employee will be afforded an opportunity to be heard, by reference to employer publications or representations. In this regard, policy and procedure manuals often allude to the fact that certain procedures will be followed prior to imposing discipline.

In the case of *Young v. Huntsville District Memorial Hospital* (1984), 5 C.C.E.L. 113 (Ont. H.C.), the employee Young had suffered a heart attack due to the pressures resulting from his increased workload. He had asked the hospital for some help doing the work before he had his heart attack. After he returned to the hospital he was suffering from depression, which was known by his superiors. Regardless of this, he was presented with a performance review which alleged that he was unable to perform the tasks required by the position. The performance review also alleged that he had asked to step down from his position. This caused Young to suffer from increased depression. Young's demotion and salary reduction were held by the Court to be a constructive dismissal. After his dismissal Young suffered even greater depression and had to undergo treatment.

In addressing the claim for mental distress damages, the Court stated:

> I have concluded that the mental distress damages, experienced by Mr. Young was caused by the defendant's breach of contract, that is, by the way in which he was terminated (without reasonable notice), rather than by the termination itself. Not only was Mr. Young terminated without reasonable notice, he was effectively not given any notice nor was he given an opportunity to be heard. . . . (at p. 127)

A denial of an opportunity to be heard, therefore, may also be considered by the Court in a claim for mental distress, especially when the accusation in question causes some distress in and of itself.

In the case of *Pilato v. Hamilton Place Convention Centre Inc.* (1984), 3 C.C.E.L. 241, 45 O.R. (2d) 652, 84 C.L.L.C. 14,039, 7 D.L.R. (4th) 342 (H.C.), the purported ground for dismissal was that Pilato had told the Convention Centre Board of Directors that no members of the board had been present when he showed a pornographic videotape in his office. The board at first accepted Pilato's answers but, upon urging by Hamilton City Council, changed its opinion and dismissed Pilato by means of an announcement to the press. On the issue of opportunity to be heard the Court stated:

> Mr. Pilato was not informed by the defendant of the various reasons for his dismissal, nor was he afforded an opportunity to be heard. This was so despite the board's statement issued on January 22, 1982:
>
>> The members of this Board have, at considerable personal inconvenience, accepted the responsibility of acting on the Board and in particular, pursuing the commitment given to City Council on January 14, 1982. All of

us are devoting a significant percentage of our business, professional, recreational and family hours to the task. This Board, more than anyone, would like to conclude the matters in issue, clear the air, and return to the business of running the Convention Centre. We well recognize the urgency of concluding our review.

We are moving as quickly as we can to satisfy ourselves with the aid of our legal counsel and auditors as to the reliability of the information and other evidence being examined.

It would, however, be irresponsible and reckless to specifically and publicly comment on any matter before it is fully investigated.

In short, there is a fundamental conflict between the need to complete with dispatch our investigation and report fully and responsibly to City Council and the public and the equally critical responsibility of being careful to avoid premature statements or conclusions that may damage reputations.

The Board must also satisfy the requirement of due process. Anyone against whom allegations of serious misconduct are made is entitled to have the opportunity to respond to such allegations with the assistance of legal counsel, if he so chooses. This is a basic right in a free democratic society and this Board cannot sacrifice the principles of natural justice and due process on the altar of expediency.

Our legal counsel has outlined earlier the procedures that he will follow in completing the investigation and the Board fully supports his recommendations.

In the light of my earlier remarks and on the instructions of legal counsel, the Board and its Chairman will make no further public comment on the matters under review until our legal counsel has completed his preliminary investigation and reports back to the Board. This will ensure that the investigation is orderly and complete without the distraction of premature public comment by the Board or its Chairman." [The underlining is mine.]

Keith J. in *Reilly v. Steelcase Can. Ltd.* (1979), 26 O.R. 725, 103 D.L.R. (3d) 704 (H.C.), stated that a decision to dismiss an employee for alleged misconduct ought not be made without giving him an opportunity to be heard. This proposition was reiterated by Glube J. in *Pulsifer v. GTE Sylvania Can. Ltd.* (1982), 51 N.S.R. (2d) 298, 102 A.P.R. 298 (T.D.) [since reversed (1983), 56 N.S.R. (2d) 424, 1 C.C.E.L. 62, 117 A.P.R. 424 (C.A.)], who also emphasized that the employee must be informed of the reason for his dismissal. She states at pp. 301-302 [N.S.R.] of the judgment:

> To deny an individual the opportunity to explain, let alone denying him the opportunity to know the reason why he was being dismissed, goes beyond the bounds of reasonableness . . .

It seems clear from the evidence that Pilato was not given an opportunity to be heard. The board made its decision to dismiss him while he was on vacation. The board not only violated its internal policy that "anyone against whom allegations of serious misconduct are made is entitled to have the opportunity to respond to such allegations and the assistance of legal counsel" but it also did not adhere to the principles enunciated in *Reilly*, supra and *Pulsifer*, supra. (at pp. 253-255)

As a matter of contract law, the party in breach has no general right to a hearing prior to the innocent party exercising whatever rights may arise from the breach (see Chapter 4.2(c)). As the foregoing cases demonstrate, however, the failure to afford an opportunity to be heard may give rise to mental distress damages.

(iv) *Failure to Warn of Unsatisfactory Performance*

As with denial of opportunity to be heard, failure to warn of unsatisfactory performance would be an adequate ground for damages for mental distress damages if the Court can find a contractual obligation to warn on the part of the employer. In this regard, it is not unusual for employer publications to refer to the process by which employees are evaluated, and to offer assurances that the employee's performance will be monitored and shortcomings pointed out to the employee. Publications of this sort may give rise to a contractual obligation to warn. The following pre-*Vorvis* cases considered failure to warn as a factor giving rise to mental distress damages.

In *Speck v. Greater Niagara General Hospital* (1983), 2 C.C.E.L. 21, 43 O.R. (2d) 611, 2 D.L.R. (4th) 84 (H.C.), affirmed (1985), 7 C.C.E.L. xxxvii, 51 O.R. (2d) 192, 19 D.L.R. (4th) 576 (C.A.), the uncontradicted evidence was that the employee had received no complaint about her work during the one-year period prior to termination. Mr. Justice Southey referred to the fact that the employee had not received "timely warning that her work was unsatisfactory" as a factor in finding that the employee was entitled to damages for mental distress.

In a similar vein, in *Pilon v. Peugeot Can. Ltd.* (1980), 29 O.R. (2d) 711, 12 B.L.R. 227, 114 D.L.R. (3d) 378 (H.C.), the company encouraged employees to view themselves as part of a "family." Pilon, a long service employee, was terminated and Mr. Justice Galligan commented on the evidence as follows:

> In cross-examination he agreed that if he was not doing his job he could not expect to be kept on for his full working life. He said that he thought (and I think that he was reasonable when he did so) that in a family if there was some complaint about his work he would be given some warning and opportunity to improve. In my opinion, it cannot fail to have been in the contemplation of the defendant that if it suddenly, without warning, unlawfully discharged a man whom it had led to believe was secure in his job for his working life, there would be the gravest likelihood that such a man would suffer vexation, frustration, distress and anxiety. (at p. 715)

(v) *Failure to Make Adequate Provision for the Employee*

The decision in *Vorvis, supra*, makes it doubtful that a simple failure to give reasonable notice can give rise to mental distress damages. Mr. Justice McIntyre, in his majority opinion, indicated that failure to give adequate notice was fully compensable by an award of damages in lieu thereof. It is still possible, however, that a court might find that the terms of a particular contract of employment were such that the parties did not regard damages relating to financial loss during the notice period as the only damages recoverable in the event of a failure to provide reasonable advance notice of termination or a payment in lieu thereof.

In *Bohemier v. Storwal International Inc.* (1982), 40 O.R. (2d) 264, 142 D.L.R. (3d) 8 (H.C.), varied (1983), 3 C.C.E.L. 79, 44 O.R. (2d) 361, 4 D.L.R. (4th) 383 (C.A.), leave to appeal to the Supreme Court of Canada refused (1984), 3 C.C.E.L. 79 (S.C.C.), an employee of 35 years' service was terminated and given a cheque representing eight weeks' salary. Mr. Justice Saunders found that part of the employee's mental distress was "attributable to the failure to give reasonable notice."

Similarly, in *Pilato v. Hamilton Place Convention Centre Inc.* (1984), 3 C.C.E.L. 241, 45 O.R. (2d) 652, 84 C.L.L.C. 14,039, 7 D.L.R. (4th) 342 (H.C.), the Court found that mental distress was caused, in part, by the failure to give any notice of termination.

On the other hand, in *Russello v. Jannock Ltd.* (1987), 15 C.C.E.L. 209, 59 O.R. (2d) 190, 37 D.L.R. (4th) 372, 22 O.A.C. 398 (Div. Ct.), the Court found that it was not within the reasonable contemplation of the parties that the failure to give adequate notice would cause mental distress. In this regard the Court stated:

> In the case at Bar, Russello was engaged on an indefinite hiring and could have been dismissed at any time with proper notice or payment in lieu of notice. It would be reasonable to contemplate that any such dismissal would cause distress and it did so in this case. The learned trial Judge did not specifically consider in his reasons what was in the contemplation of the parties at the time of hiring with respect to termination. We were asked by the respondent to consider all the facts, and in particular, the statement in the letter to the effect that his future with the employer would be as good as he wished to make it. We were then asked to draw an inference that it was in the contemplation of the parties that if Russello were terminated in the manner that he was, that a termination in such a manner would constitute a breach of contract. If such an inference were to be drawn, the breach would either be on the basis of insufficient notice or of wanton or reckless termination.
>
> I am unable to draw the inference on either basis. In the first place, it was in the reasonable contemplation of the parties that termination was a possibility. The statement in the letter had nothing to do with the period of notice that would be given in the event of termination. The learned trial Judge found that the mental anguish was caused by inadequate notice but that is not itself sufficient for an award of damages. There must also be a finding that the parties contemplated that inadequate notice would cause distress. In my opinion, there was no evidence from which such an inference might reasonably be drawn. There was considerably more evidence on which to base such an inference in *Misovic,* supra, and the Court of Appeal found that it was insufficient. I would add, with respect, that it would appear from the evidence that the distress resulted from the fact of dismissal rather than from the period of notice. (at p. 213)

In the case of *Misovic v. Acres Davy McKee Ltd.* (1985), 7 C.C.E.L. 163, 9 O.A.C. 143 (C.A.), *supra*, the damages for mental distress awarded by the trial

Court were set aside by the Court of Appeal. Misovic had been laid off prior to being terminated. The Court of Appeal held that:

> The evidence does not support an inference that it was in the contemplation of the parties at the time of the hiring that mental distress would be a probable result of a failure to give proper notice. Nor does the evidence support an inference that such distress was suffered in any one of these cases from the absence of reasonable notice, rather than from the temporary lay-off of each of the respondents, or their dismissal. (at p. 165)

(vi) *Manner of Communicating Termination*

The employer, by communicating the employee's termination in a reckless or wanton fashion, may cause the employee mental distress. Such communications may also constitute the tort of intentional infliction of mental suffering. (See Chapter 7.6.)

In the case of *Bohemier v. Storwal International Inc.* (1982), 40 O.R. (2d) 264, 142 D.L.R. (3d) 8 (H.C.), varied (1983), 3 C.C.E.L. 79, 44 O.R. (2d) 361, 4 D.L.R. (4th) 383 (C.A.), leave to appeal to Supreme Court of Canada refused (1984), 3 C.C.E.L. 79 (S.C.C.), the plaintiff had worked for the employer for 35 years. He was informed of his discharge by a "cold and perfunctory" letter which was delivered by taxi on a Friday evening. The letter expressed no gratitude for service, offered no proposal to aid in obtaining new employment, and did not specify the basis for payment in lieu of notice.

At trial, Mr. Justice Saunders held that:

> The evidence discloses that the usual practice of Storwal on dismissals was to call the employee into the office of a superior at the end of the last day of work. There is no explanation of why this was not done in the case of the plaintiff. Hughes believes that it was due to inadvertence and that the plaintiff had left the plant before his superior had an opportunity to speak with him. The reason for departing from the usual practice does not matter. Someone in authority at Storwal must have arranged that the notice be delivered by taxi cab. In my opinion, it was reasonably foreseeable that such an action would aggravate the mental suffering of the plaintiff that would inevitably be caused by the act of dismissal and the inadequate period of notice. (at p. 274)

The Court of Appeal upheld the award of damages for mental distress.

In *Pilato v. Hamilton Place Convention Centre Inc.* (1984), 3 C.C.E.L. 241, 45 O.R. (2d) 652, 84 C.L.L.C. 14,039, 7 D.L.R. (4th) 342 (H.C.), the Court awarded both mental distress and punitive damages in a wrongful dismissal situation. A factor which was considered was the manner of communicating the dismissal. In this case, the employee was given no direct notice of his dismissal. Instead, while the employee was on holiday, the employer made a statement to the press publicizing the termination. This method of termination was considered to be "severe and unfair."

As in *Bohemier, Pilato* considered the manner of communicating dismissal to be a factor to be considered in an award of damages for mental distress. In both cases, it was readily foreseeable that mental suffering would occur. It can, therefore, be argued that the conduct in question probably constituted the tort of intentional infliction of mental suffering, and would have resulted in an award of mental distress damages under principles enunciated by the majority of the Supreme Court of Canada in *Vorvis.*

(vii) *Unsubstantiated Allegations of Just Cause*

Whether unsubstantiated allegations of just cause will give rise to mental distress damages depends upon the facts of the particular case.

In *Speck v. Greater Niagara General Hospital* (1983), 2 C.C.E.L. 21, 43 O.R. (2d) 611, 2 D.L.R. (4th) 84 (H.C.), affirmed 7 C.C.E.L. xxxvii, 51 O.R. (2d) 192, 19 D.L.R. (4th) 576 (C.A.), a 56-year-old nurse, who had been employed for approximately 13 years in a supervisory position, was dismissed. The termination was allegedly for just cause and no termination payment was made. Commenting on the grounds for dismissal, Mr. Justice Southey stated:

> The fact that the hospital purported to dismiss for cause when sufficient cause did not exist is nevertheless of great significance to the plaintiff's claim for damages for mental suffering, even though it does not change the basic nature of the breach of contract. I have no hesitation in finding that this conduct on the part of the hospital brings the plaintiff's case squarely within the circumstances defined by Weatherston J.A. in the *Brown* case in which a breach of contract will give rise to a claim for damages for mental distress. While it would not be in accordance with modern usage of the word to describe the conduct of the defendants, Beam, Bent, Weier, and Mawhinney as "wanton", I am satisfied that one or more of them acted recklessly; that is, careless of the consequences of their actions, in purporting to dismiss the plaintiff for cause when sufficient cause did not exist. (at p. 28)

It is unclear whether the circumstances in *Speck* would be sufficiently reckless to provide for an "actionable wrong" as referred to in *Vorvis.*

In *Rahemtulla v. Vanfed Credit Union*, 4 C.C.E.L. 170, 51 B.C.L.R. 200, 29 C.C.L.T. 78, [1984] 3 W.W.R. 296 (S.C.), the employee was a teller for the employer. One day another teller's balance was short by $2,000. On this same day the other teller had transferred large bills to the employee. The employee was called in on her day off regarding the missing money. The supervisor who interviewed the employee told her that she should admit she "borrowed" the money for one day or she would be fired. He also stated that he would spend $10,000 if necessary to get to the bottom of things. The employee denied the supervisor's allegations and was dismissed. The Court awarded Rahemtulla damages for the tort of intentional infliction of mental suffering instead of mental distress damages arising from breach of contract. The fact situation is of the type, however, which might result in an award of damages for mental distress occasioned by a breach of contract.

With respect to the elements of the tort of intentional infliction of mental suffering, Madam Justice McLachlin stated:

The law has long recognized as tortious the uttering of false words or threats with the knowledge that they are likely to cause, and which actually cause, nervous shock and physical injury. One of the earliest cases to set out this duty was *Wilkinson v. Downton*, [1897] 2 Q.B. 57. In that case the defendant falsely represented to the plaintiff that her husband had been injured in an accident, inducing a state of nervous shock, vomiting and prolonged mental and physical suffering. Lord Wright stated at pp. 58-59:

> The defendant has, as I assume for the moment, wilfully done an act calculated to cause physical harm to the plaintiff – that is to say, to infringe her legal right to personal safety, and has in fact thereby caused physical harm to her. That proposition without more appears to me to state a good cause of action, there being no justification alleged for the act. This wilful injuria is in law malicious, although no malicious purpose to cause the harm which was caused nor any motive of spite is imputed to the defendant.

This statement of the law was adopted in *Janvier v. Sweeney et. al.*, [1919] 2 K.B. 316 (C.A.). In that case two private detectives, in an attempt to persuade the plaintiff to show them certain letters, represented themselves as associated with the military and falsely accused her of having corresponded with a German spy. The plaintiff suffered nervous shock and fell ill. It was held that she could recover damages for the injuries she had sustained.

These authorities have been accepted and applied in Canada: *Purdy v. Woznesensky*, [1937] 2 W.W.R. 116 (Sask. C.A.); *Abramzik v. Brenner* (1967), 62 W.W.R. 332, 65 D.L.R. (2d) 651 (Sask. C.A.). In the latter case, Culliton J.A. stated at p. 654:

> There can be no doubt but that an action will lie for the wilful infliction of shock, or a reckless disregard as to whether or not shock will ensue from the act committed.

In the case at Bar, the defendant's agent, Mr. Flack, accused the plaintiff of having stolen $2,000. Accepting that his motive may not have been to inflict shock upon her, but rather to extort a confession and solve the mystery of the missing funds, the fact remains that at very least he acted with a reckless disregard as to whether or not shock would ensue from his accusation. In this respect, the facts are analogous to those in *Janvier v. Sweeney*, where the defendants were found liable notwithstanding the absence of malicious purpose to cause the harm which was caused nor any motive of spite imputed to them.

Counsel for the defendant submitted that for the defendant to be held liable for wilful infliction of nervous shock its conduct must be found to be outrageous. He contended that Mr. Flack was acting bona fide in the interests of the credit union, and that his conduct to this end could not be characterized as flagrant or extreme.

This submission appears to be founded upon the distinction drawn in American cases between mere insult, which is not actionable, and "extreme and outrageous conduct" which is: Linden: Canadian Tort Law (3rd ed.), 48. While this distinction appears not to have been expressly adopted in the Canadian and Commonwealth cases, the conduct considered in the leading authorities such as *Wilkinson v. Downton*, supra, and *Janvier v. Sweeney*, supra, was in fact flagrant and extreme. Moreover, it is difficult to accept that the Courts should protect persons from every practical joke or unkind comment.

> Assuming, therefore that only flagrant and extreme conduct inflicting mental suffering is actionable, the question is whether the defendant's conduct can be so described. In my view, it can. Mr. Flack's conduct went beyond mere insult. His accusation was made in threatening circumstances of the utmost gravity. His conduct was, in my view, equally reprehensible as that of a person posing as a military policeman and accusing another of corresponding with a German spy (*Janvier v. Sweeney*, supra), or of a finance company bombarding one of its debtors who is ill (to its knowledge) with offensive and threatening letters (*Clark v. Associated Retail Credit* (1939), 105 Fed. 2d. 62; see also *Robbins v. C.B.C.* (Que.), [1958] Que. S.C. 152, 12 D.L.R. (2d) 35) – cases where liability has been imposed.)
>
> Allegations of theft should not be made recklessly, without proper care for whether they are true or not. This applies even in a financial institution where great care must be taken in the management of money of others. While the financial institution has the right to dismiss a suspect employee without investigation, the proper conduct of its affairs does not require that it be given the right to make reckless and very possibly untruthful accusations as to the employee's honesty which will foreseeably inflict shock and mental suffering. Considering all these circumstances, I am satisfied that Mr. Flack's conduct can fairly be described as flagrant and outrageous.
>
> A further requirement of the tort of wilful infliction of mental distress is that the defendant's conduct be "plainly calculated to produce some effect of the kind which was produced": *Wilkinson v. Downton*, supra, at p. 59. In the case at Bar this element is established. It was clearly foreseeable that the accusations of theft which the defendant made against the plaintiff would cause her profound distress. That distress could only be exacerbated by the defendant's failure to conduct a proper investigation or allow the plaintiff to defend herself. It was equally foreseeable that the accusations would continue to cause distress into the future, when, in seeking employment, she would be queried by prospective employers as to the reasons for her dismissal from the defendant's employ.
>
> Finally, it must be established that the conduct produced actual harm, a "visible and provable illness": *Radovskis v. Tomn* (1957), 21 W.W.R. 658 at 664, 65 Man. R. 61, 9 D.L.R. (2d) 751 (Q.B.). I have earlier described the distress which the plaintiff suffered as a consequence of the defendant's accusations. Notwithstanding the absence of expert medical evidence, I am satisfied that the plaintiff suffered depression accompanied by symptoms of physical illness as a result of Mr. Flack's accusations. (at pp. 184-186)

In the case of *Ribeiro v. Canadian Imperial Bank of Commerce* (1989), 24 C.C.E.L. 225, 67 O.R. (2d) 385, 89 C.L.L.C. 14,033 (H.C.), varied (1992), 44 C.C.E.L. 165, 13 O.R. (3d) 278 (C.A.), leave to appeal to S.C.C. refused (June 10, 1993), Doc. 23378 (S.C.C.), the employee had been dismissed because of unsubstantiated allegations of fraud. Criminal charges were also laid against the employee. Mr. Justice Carruthers stated, with respect to mental distress damages:

> In the present case, the defendant bank has made much of the fact that the plaintiff's employment with it expressly contemplated that he be honest and act with integrity throughout. The defendant bank wrongfully, and I can also say

> wantonly and recklessly accused the plaintiff of being otherwise and purported to terminate his employment for cause on this basis. I have concluded that this conduct on the part of the defendent bank constituted a breach of its employment agreement with the plaintiff. Having regard to the nature of the agreement, and specifically the requirements for honesty and integrity on the part of the plaintiff, I find that it is reasonable to draw the inference that it was in the contemplation of the parties that if the plaintiff was terminated in this manner he would suffer mental distress. I have already concluded that it did in fact do so. Thus the requirements for the application of the second rule in *Hadley v. Baxendale* have been met, and the plaintiff is entitled therefore to recover damages for his "mental and emotional suffering". (at pp. 281-282)

An appeal by Ribeiro was allowed and the award of damages for mental distress was increased to $20,000.

It would appear that unsubstantiated allegations of just cause, which may also constitute the torts of intimidation or the intentional infliction of mental suffering, will probably result in an award of mental distress damages under the test enunciated by Mr. Justice McIntyre in *Vorvis.*

(viii) *Awareness of Illness or Vulnerability of Employee*

In *Speck v. Greater Niagara General Hospital* (1983), 2 C.C.E.L. 21, 43 O.R. (2d) 611, 2 D.L.R. (4th) 84 (H.C.), affirmed (1985), 7 C.C.E.L xxxvii, 51 O.R. (2d) 192, 19 D.L.R. (4th) 576 (C.A.), the employee had, prior to termination, suffered a reactive depression following a reprimand. Mr. Justice Southey commented on the significance of this knowledge, as follows:

> They [hospital administration] knew that the plaintiff had been under the care of a psychiatrist and had been taking medication for her depression. They also knew that her depression had been of such severity that she had been unable to work for about three months in 1980. They knew, or ought to have known, in June 1981, that the termination of the plaintiff's employment would almost certainly cause a recurrence of her depression, unless it was carried out with the utmost consideration for her feelings. Instead of acting with such consideration, the defendants treated the plaintiff as an employee who had given cause for dismissal; that is, an employee whose performance was so unsatisfactory that it discharged the hospital from further obligations under the employment contract. Instead of giving her liberal notice of termination, giving her help to obtain other employment where her managerial shortcomings would be unimportant, and doing their best to help her preserve her self-respect, they dismissed her with no notice, and had her shown off the premises as though her continued presence constituted a risk to the hospital. All of the individual defendants gave evidence and impressed me as sincere, honest persons. I am satisfied that none of them intended to cause mental suffering to the plaintiff. They all acted in good faith, in what they thought was the best interests of the hospital, but they obviously acted without any thought to what the consequences of the termination would be to the plaintiff. The termination was a breach of contract on the part of the hospital and I find that it was a reckless breach in the circumstances described above. (at pp. 29-30)

Similarly, in *Bohemier v. Storwal International Inc.* (1982), 40 O.R. (2d) 264, 142 D.L.R. (3d) 8 (H.C.), varied (1983), 3 C.C.E.L. 74, 44 O.R. (2d) 361, 4 D.L.R. (4th) 383 (C.A.), leave to appeal to Supreme Court of Canada refused (1984), 3 C.C.E.L. 79 (S.C.C.), the general manager of the company was aware, prior to termination, that the employee had suffered from mental illness, and this appears to have been a factor in awarding damages for mental distress.

An employer who does not have regard to a known weakness in the employee when dismissing that employee may be in breach of a contractual term or committing the tort of intentionally inflicting mental suffering. If so, the Court could award distress damages, even applying the majority test in *Vorvis.*

(ix) *Other Factors*

In *Linkson v. UTDC Inc.* (1991), 40 C.C.E.L. 305, 92 C.L.L.C. 14,037 (Ont. Gen. Div.), the Court awarded damages in the amount of $5,000 having regard to the failure of the employer to comply with the minimum requirements of the *Employment Standards Act*, R.S.O. 1980, c. 137. The Judge stated:

> I find it quite high-handed and cavalier that such a payment would not be made even as the trial proceeds.
>
> The *Employment Standards Act* is not to be used as a bargaining tool to force an employee to accept a less lucrative settlement.
>
> . . . .
>
> [T]o be relieved of your employment and not to get what you are entitled to, and to be forced to sue to collect what you are entitled to as a right, I find most unacceptable. And I reiterate that it is unheard of, and will not be condoned by this court. I therefore fix under the head of damages, aggravated damages, or whatever you wish to call it, mental distress or punitive and aggravated damage, the sum of $5,000. (at pp. 308-309)

In practice it is not unheard of to find employers attempting to withhold statutory entitlements to exert pressure to settle. This is a welcome decision and should do much to deter this type of conduct.

(c) Quantum of Damages for Mental Distress

Case	Award	Facts
Pilato v. Hamilton Place Convention Centre Inc. (1984), 3 C.C.E.L. 241, 45 O.R. (2d) 652, 84 C.L.L.C. 14,039, 7 D.L.R. (4th) 342 (H.C.)	$25,000	The employee was 36 years old and had been employed for two years as the general manager/chief executive officer. The employee was not given an opportunity to respond to serious allegations against him and his dismissal was communicated to the press while he was on holiday. Psychiatric evidence was considered. The employee also received $25,000 in punitive damages.
Ribeiro v. Canadian Imperial Bank of Commerce (1992), 44 C.C.E.L. (2d) 165, 13 O.R. (3d) 278 (C.A.), leave to appeal to S.C.C. refused (June 10, 1993), Doc. 23378 (S.C.C.)	$20,000	The employee was thirty years of age and had been employed by the bank for six years, most recently as a consumer loans officer. After little or no investigation, the bank concluded that the employee had acted dishonestly in connection with the granting of a $1,000 loan that had defaulted, and not only terminated his employment, but also caused criminal charges to be laid against him. The Court concluded that the bank had acted wrongfully, wantonly and recklessly in terminating the employment and as a result had caused the employee to suffer severe depression. The court also awarded $50,000 in punitive damages.
Young v. Huntsville District Memorial Hospital (1984), 5 C.C.E.L. 113 (Ont. H.C.)	$20,000	The employee was 55 years old and had beem employed for 18 years as business manager. He suffered a heart attack and after his return to work his superior demonstrated a lack of understanding and sensitivity in dealing with the employee. The employer incorrectly adopted the position that the employee agreed to accept a lesser position which the employee refused. The Court emphasized the size of the community, the recklessness of the dismissal, the known condition of the

Case	Award	Facts
		employee and the testimony of a psychiatrist.
Speck v. Greater Niagara General Hospital (1983), 2 C.C.E.L. 21, 43 O.R. (2d) 611, 2 D.LR. (4th) 84 (H.C.), affirmed (1985), 7 C.C.E.L. xxxvii, 51 O.R. (2d) 192, 19 D.L.R. (4th) 576 (C.A.)	$15,000	The employee was 56 years old and had been employed for 13 years as a nurse, her final position being head nurse, obstetrics. The employer knew the employee was prone to mental distress from a previous incident but still acted in a wanton and reckless fashion in effecting her termination. Evidence was presented by a psychiatrist.
Carrick v. Cooper Can. Ltd. (1983), 2 C.C.E.L. 87 (Ont. H.C.)	$5,000	The employee was 53 years old and had been employed for approximately 16 months as vice-president of operations and affairs/vice-president finance. The Court examined the arbitrariness of the dismissal and the duty owed by an employer to "a high-ranking dedicated employee to treat him with concern and common decency." Evidence was presented by a psychiatrist.
Antonaros v. SNC Inc. (1984), 6 C.C.E.L. 264 (Ont. H.C.)	$3,500	The employee was 48 years old and had worked for seven months. Factors for consideration were the employer's inducements and promises of security of position. Evidence was presented by his physician. In this case the award of $7,000 was reduced by 50 per cent on the basis that the mental distress of the employee was partly attributable to anxiety over his wife's illness.
Wuorinen v. W.C.B. (1983), 1 C.C.E.L. 29 (B.C. S.C.)	$2,000	The employee was 53 years old and had been employed for eight years, five of which as education manager. Factors for consideration were the humiliating manner of dismissal and promises of security of position.
Lightburn v. Mid Island Consumer Services Co-op.	$1,000	The employee was 49 years old and had been employed for 10 years, eventually attaining the position of hardware man-

Case	Award	Facts
(1984), 4 C.C.E.L. 263 (B.C. Co. Ct.)		ager. The employee became seriously ill and during his absence the employer assured him that his job was secure. Despite this assurance the

(*Continued on page 6-77*)

Case	Award	Facts
		employer later terminated the employee by reason of physical incapacity and refused his offer to take any job available.

6.6 PUNITIVE DAMAGES

(a) General Principle

In the Supreme Court of Canada decision of *Vorvis v. Insurance Corp. of B. C.*, 25 C.C.E.L. 81, [1989] 1 S.C.R. 1085, 36 B.C.L.R. (2d) 273, [1989] 4 W.W.R. 218, 58 D.L.R. (4th) 193, 94 N.R. 321, affirming (1984), 4 C.C.E.L. 237, 53 B.C.L.R. 63, 9 D.L.R. (4th) 40 (C.A.), reversing in part (1982), 17 B.L.R. 150, 134 D.L.R. (3d) 727 (S.C.), both Mr. Justice McIntyre for the majority (Beetz and Lamer JJ. concurring) and Madam Justice Wilson in dissent (L'Heureux-Dubé J. concurring) addressed the issue of punitive damages. In this case, the claim for punitive damages arose from a wrongful dismissal and were based upon the conduct of the employer's supervisor both before and in relation to the termination. The facts in issue were summarized by Madam Justice Wilson as follows:

> The appellant is a solicitor who was employed by the respondent, Insurance Corporation of British Columbia (I.C.B.C.), in its legal department from 1974 to 1981. He had graduated from law school in 1972 after a successful career as an engineer with DuPont of Canada Ltd. He left DuPont to enter law school rather than accept a transfer to eastern Canada. He was Western District Sales Manager for DuPont at the time. He took up his employment with the respondent as a junior solicitor on September 24, 1973 when the respondent was starting up its business. His work initially was of a routine nature and included the preparation of leases and real estate purchases with a view to the establishment of claim centres and other facilities for the corporation throughout the province. He was promoted from the position of solicitor I to solicitor II on July 1, 1976 and given merit increases in salary in 1978, 1979 and 1980. In January 1981 his employment was abruptly terminated and he was required to vacate his office by February 13, 1981. He was 49 years old at the time.
>
> On October 1, 1979 the respondent had hired as general counsel a Mr. Reid who was given a mandate to improve the quality of the corporation's legal work with specific attention to productivity. He became the appellant's immediate superior. Difficulties arose between Mr. Reid and the appellant, Mr. Reid being of the view that the appellant took too long to get his work done. For example, Mr. Reid complained that the appellant wrote in long-hand as opposed to using a dictating machine. There was no complaint about the quality of the appellant's work or that he failed to meet deadlines required for his assignments nor was it alleged that he did not carry his fair share of the workload. He was simply

conscientious to a fault, according to the learned trial judge, and, in the words of Mr. Reid, was prone "to produce a Cadillac when a Ford would do".

Mr. Reid became increasingly dissatisfied with the pace of the appellant's work. By November 1980 he had set up "productivity meetings" each Monday morning in which he reviewed the appellant's work in relation to the number of hours he spent on each project. The trial Judge found that these meetings "became an inquisition" and "as the pressure increased the plaintiff became tense, agitated and distressed, finally resorting to medical attention and a tranquillizer."

The appellant was dismissed on January 21, 1981 without any particular precipitating event but simply because, according to the trial Judge, he did not fit into Mr. Reid's plans for the department. The trial Judge found that the appellant was "an honest, loyal, trustworthy and diligent employee" and was dismissed without cause and without reasonable notice. The respondent offered to pay his salary and certain benefits for an 8-month period if he agreed by January 23, 1981 to release the corporation from any claim arising out of his employment and its peremptory termination. Since the appellant was not prepared to admit that he was incompetent and that his employer had just cause for his dismissal on account of his incompetence, he refused the offer. He left the respondent's employ on January 23, 1981 and was paid up to February 15, 1981. He obtained other employment in September of 1981 but not as a solicitor. (at pp. 105-106)

Mr. Justice McIntyre held that punitive damages could not be awarded in the circumstances. In coming to this decision McIntyre J. clarified the distinction between punitive and aggravated damages, stating that:

Punitive damages, as the name would indicate, are designed to punish. In this, they constitute an exception to the general common law rule that damages are designed to compensate the injured, not to punish the wrongdoer. Aggravated damages will frequently cover conduct which could also be the subject of punitive damages, but the role of aggravated damages remains compensatory. . . . Aggravated damages are compensatory in nature and may only be awarded for that purpose. Punitive damages, on the other hand, are punitive in nature and may only be employed in circumstances where the conduct giving the cause for complaint is of such nature that it merits punishment. (at pp. 95-96)

Mr. Justice McIntyre continued to address the question of when punitive damages can be awarded, stating:

When then can punitive damages be awarded? It must never be forgotten that when awarded by a Judge or a jury, a punishment is imposed upon a person by a Court by the operation of the judicial process. What is it that is punished? It surely cannot be merely conduct of which the Court disapproves, however strongly the Judge may feel. Punishment may not be imposed in a civilized community without a justification in law. The only basis for the imposition of such punishment must be a finding of the commission of an actionable wrong which caused the injury complained of by the plaintiff. This would be consistent with the approach of Weatherston J.A. in *Brown*, supra, and it has found approval in the Restatement on the Law of Contracts, 2d ed. (St. Paul, Minn.: American Law Institute Publishers, 1986), as noted with approval by Craig J.A., at p. 49, where he referred in the Court of Appeal to s. 355, which provides:

> Punitive damages are not recoverable for breach of contract unless the conduct constituting the breach is also a tort for which punitive damages are recoverable. (at p. 101)

MacIntyre J. concluded that:

> Turning to the case at Bar, it is clear from the judgments below that the appellant's superior, Reid, treated him in a most offensive manner. As has been noted, the trial Judge would have awarded punitive damages had he been of the view that it was open to him to do so. The question before us now is whether the trial Judge was right in concluding that it was not open to him to award the punitive damages. In my view, while it may be very unusual to do so, punitive damages may be awarded in cases of breach of contract. It would seem to me, however, that it will be rare to find a contractual breach which would be appropriate for such an award. In tort cases, claims where a plaintiff asserts injury and damage caused by the defendant the situation is different. The defendant in such a case is under a legal duty to use care not to injure his neighbour, and the neighbour has in law a right not to be so injured and an additional right to compensation where injury occurs. The injured party is entitled to be made whole. The compensation he is entitled to receive depends upon the nature and extent of his injuries and not upon any private arrangement made with the tortfeasor. In an action based on a breach of contract, the only link between the parties for the purpose of defining their rights and obligations is the contract. Where the defendant has breached the contract, the remedies open to the plaintiff must arise from that contractual relationship that "private law", which the parties agreed to accept. The injured plaintiff then is not entitled to be made whole; he is entitled to have that which the contract provided for him or compensation for its loss. This distinction will not completely eliminate the award of punitive damages but it will make it very rare in contract cases.
>
> Moreover, punitive damages may only be awarded in respect of conduct which is of such nature as to be deserving of punishment because of its harsh, vindictive, reprehensible and malicious nature. I do not suggest that I have exhausted the adjectives which could describe the conduct capable of characterizing a punitive award, but in any case where such an award is made the conduct must be extreme in its nature and such that by any reasonable standard it is deserving of full condemnation and punishment . . .
>
> In the case at Bar, the plaintiff was entitled to have the salary and benefits agreed upon under the contract of employment while he continued in such employment. Each party had the right to terminate the contract without the consent of the other, and where the employment contract was terminated by the employer, the appellant was entitled to reasonable notice of such termination or payment of salary and benefits for the period of reasonable notice. The termination of the contract on this basis by the employer is not a wrong in law and, where the reasonable notice is given or payment in lieu thereof is made, the plaintiff – subject to a consideration of aggravated damages which have been allowed in some cases but which were denied in this case – is entitled to no further remedy: see *Addis* [*Addis v. Gramophone Co.*], supra, and *Peso Silver Mines* [*Peso Silver Mines Ltd. v. Cropper*] case.
>
> It is argued that the conduct of the defendant, that is, the supervisor Reid, prior to the dismissal was such that it caused mental distress and frustration to

> the appellant. This conduct, however, was not considered sufficiently offensive, standing alone, to constitute actionable wrong (see Hinkson J.A., supra) and in my view was not of such nature as to justify the imposition of an award of punitive damages. (at pp. 102-104)

Madam Justice Wilson, in her dissenting opinion, commented on Mr. Justice McIntyre's analysis with respect to punitive damages, stating that:

> I do not share my colleague's view that punitive damages can only be awarded when the misconduct is in itself an "actionable wrong". In my view, the correct approach is to assess the conduct in the context of all the circumstances and determine whether it is deserving of punishment because of its shockingly harsh, vindictive, reprehensible or malicious nature. Undoubtedly some conduct found to be deserving of punishment will constitute an actionable wrong but other conduct might not. I respectfully adopt the following statement made by Clement J.A. in *Paragon Properties Ltd. v. Magna Investments Ltd.* at p. 167 [24 D.L.R. (3d)]:
>
>> It is the reprehensible conduct of the wrongdoer which attracts the principle, not the legal category of the wrong out of which compensatory damages arise and in relation to which the conduct occurred. To place arbitrary limitations upon its application is to evade the underlying principle and replace it with an uncertain and debatable jurisdiction.
>
> Nor would I draw the wide divergence that my colleague does between the duties owed to a neighbour under the law of tort and the duties that are breached in contract by the type of flagrant and deliberate misconduct that would merit an award of punitive damages. I agree with the appellant that it would be odd if the law required more from a stranger than from the parties to a contract. The very closeness engendered by some contractual relationships, particularly employer/employee relationships in which there is frequently a marked disparity of power between the parties, seems to me to give added point to the duty of civilized behaviour.
>
> In my view, the facts of this case disclose reprehensible conduct on the part of the respondent towards a sensitive, dedicated and conscientious employee. The appellant was harassed and humiliated and, so the learned trial Judge found, ultimately dismissed for no cause after a sustained period of such treatment. Anderson J.A. in dissent described the respondent's conduct as follows at pp. 58-59:
>
>> In the case on appeal, the defendant engaged in a continuous course of reprehensible conduct for several months prior to the date of termination and persisted in its groundless allegations of incompetence against the appellant up to and throughout the trial. The conduct of the defendant, as found by the trial judge, may be summarized as follows:
>>
>> (1) Inquisitorial practices over a substantial period of time;
>>
>> (2) Duress – termination with reasonable notice only if the appellant admitted that he was incompetent;
>>
>> (3) Colourable attempt to find the appellant other employment with the company in a thinly disguised effort to damage the reputation of the appellant;
>>
>> (4) Persistence in groundless allegations of incompetence up to and including the trial.

> Anderson J.A. would have allowed the appeal on the punitive damages issue and awarded the appellant punitive damages in the sum of $5,000. The quantum that Anderson J.A. would have awarded is, I believe, a reasonable one and in keeping with the Canadian experience in the award of relatively modest punitive damages. When the purpose of the award is to reflect the Court's awareness and condemnation of flagrant wrongdoing and indifference to the legal rights of other people, the award does not need to be excessive. I would allow the appeal on the punitive damages issue in this Court in order to give effect to Anderson J.A.'s judgment. I would also award the appellant his costs both here and in the Courts below. (at pp. 121-122)

Thus, *Vorvis* does acknowledge that punitive damages can be awarded for breach of contract, albeit in rare circumstances. Whether a case presents such rare circumstances will to a large extent depend upon the findings of fact, and their characterization and interpretation by the trial Judge. This factual analysis will not lightly be interfered with by Courts of Appeal. It is, therefore, quite possible that the trial courts, while deferring to the legal authority of *Vorvis*, may continue to award punitive damages in the same types of circumstances as punitive damages have been awarded to date. Certainly the award of punitive damages has traditionally occurred in rare cases and the quantum of punitive damages awards has been generally modest. The following cases illustrate the type of situations in which the courts have been prepared to award punitive damages.

In *Brown v. Waterloo Regional Commissioners of Police* (1982), 37 O.R. (2d) 277, 17 B.L.R. 299, 136 D.L.R. (3d) 49 (H.C.), reversed in part (1983), 2 C.C.E.L. 7, 43 O.R. (2d) 113, 4 Admin. L.R. 113, 23 B.L.R. 41, 150 D.L.R. (3d) 729 (C.A.), Mr. Justice Linden advocated the position that punitive damages should be available in breach of contract actions. While, on the facts of the case, he did not see fit to award punitive damages, Linden J. provided a comprehensive statement of the development of the law in this area, which it is useful to quote at length. Linden J. analyzed the state of the law as follows:

> As for punitive or exemplary damages for breach of contract, the Canadian law is in a state of uncertainty. There has been no reluctance evinced by Canadian courts in awarding punitive damages in tort cases. (See Fridman, "Punitive Damages in Tort" (1970), 48 Can. Bar Rev. 373.) So far, however, exemplary or punitive damages have rarely been granted for breach of contract. It has been widely assumed that the *obiter* statement of Mr. Justice Judson in *Dobson v. Winton & Robbins Ltd.*, [1959] S.C.R. 775, 20 D.L.R. (2d) 164 at 169, to the effect that such a claim was "obviously untenable" accurately reflected the law. Madam Justice Boland has declared that "it is quite clear that punitive damages will not be awarded in a breach of contract action in Canada". (See *Cardinal Construction Ltd. v. The Queen in right of Ontario et al.* (1981), 32 O.R. (2d) 575 at 576, 122 D.L.R. (3d) 703; affirmed 128 D.L.R. (3d) 662, without specific reference to this issue; see also *Harvey Foods Ltd. v. Reid* (1971), 18 D.L.R. (3d) 90 at 93, 3 N.B.R. (2d) 444 (C.A.).) These views were based on *Addis v. Gramophone Co., Ltd.*, [1909] A.C. 488 at 495.
>
> There has been evidence of a willingness to reconsider this position in some

recent decisions; however, Mr. Justice Osler in *Cornell v. Pfizer C. & G. Inc.* (1981), 23 C.P.C. 286, refused to strike out a claim for punitive damages for breach of contract in a wrongful dismissal case. Noting that the authority of *Addis v. Gramophone* "has undoubtedly been departed from in recent decisions of this and other Courts", he concluded [at p. 292]

> . . . it is going too far to state that a trial Judge might not properly award punitive damages in such a case as the one at Bar, should he reach certain conclusions of fact . . .

Punitive damages for breach of a collective agreement have been awarded in *New Brunswick Electric Power Commission v. Int'l Brotherhood of Electrical Workers, Local 1733* (1978), 22 N.B.R. (2d) 364, 39 A.PR. 364. Enormous losses were caused as a result of a wildcat strike by the defendant, in violation of its collective agreement. Mr. Justice Dickson explained that there was a claim for punitive damages against the defendant for "wilfully and maliciously harming another by acts or by breach" [at p. 365]. He allowed $50,000 for exemplary damages, in addition to other damages, because the defendants acted "with an utter lack of responsibility to the employer with whom they had contracted and as well with a calloused lack of regard for the citizens of the province" by striking in the "dead of winter" and coming "within an inch of bringing the whole economy of the province to a halt." This case demonstrates the type of shocking circumstances that are required before a court will invoke such a strong sanction, but it shows that, where such conditions are present, the courts will do so.

. . . .

The strongest authority in favour of punitive damages for breach of contract is *Nantel v. Parisien et al.* (1981), 18 C.C.L.T. 79, 22 R.P.R. 1, where Mr. Justice Galligan awarded $35,000 for punitive damages in a breach of contract of lease case. Mr. Justice Galligan found as facts that the defendants, in demolishing their building "exhibited the most arrogant of behaviour toward the plaintiff and her rights", they "exhibited callousness" toward her, they were "prepared to act as they did regardless of whether the plaintiff's rights would be violated by their conduct", and they acted "in a high-handed and shockingly contemptuous manner". They tried to "steam-roll her into acquiescence and when that failed they decided to push her aside like a pest". Mr. Justice Galligan expressed the underlying rationale of the punitive damage award in this unique case, as follows [at p. 89 C.C.L.T.]:

> In this country we live by the rule of law; that woman, in my opinion, had the right to occupy those premises . . . Not only must the law not sanction the deliberate and callous disregard by the powerful of the weaker person's rights, the law must do what it can to ensure, by whatever means are at its disposal . . . that the legal rights of a citizen are protected from the tyranny of another. Many cases have said that exemplary damages must not merely amount to a licence fee or to a reasonable cost or expense of doing business.
>
> It is my opinion that in proper cases damages should act as a deterrent to deter the powerful from subjugating the weaker to their business interests.

This philosophy recognizes that there may be special cases, the particularly shocking ones, where punitive or exemplary damages may be awarded for breach of contract. (at pp. 290-292)

Mr. Justice Linden then advanced the following arguments in favour of allowing the Court to award punitive damages in breach of contract actions:

> Although the *general* principle that punitive damages are not awarded for breach of contract survives, there is no requirement that the general principle be followed invariably. Certainly in the vast majority of situations of contract breach, there would be no possible issue of punitive damages arising. However, just as our courts have recognized the utility of awards for damages for mental suffering caused by breach of contract in appropriate circumstances, so too should punitive damages be allowed where the facts demand that they be awarded. It is clear that such damages would rarely be awarded, but this does not mean that it should *never* be done. To tie the hands of the courts by denying them the power to penalize defendants, who flout contract law in a high-handed and outrageous fashion, is unwise and unnecessary. Punitive damage awards should be part of the judicial arsenal in contract cases in the same way as they are in tort cases. I can see no sound reason to differentiate between them. Canadian courts, unlike English courts, have retained their broad power to award punitive damages in tort cases. Thus, if a high-handed breach of contract also happens to amount to tortious conduct, punitive damages would be awardable pursuant to tort theory. It is said that if this conduct is purely a breach of contract and not tortious, then no punitive damages can be awarded, despite the callousness of the conduct. That makes no sense. It is wrong to treat one contract breach different from another merely because one violates tort principles while the other does not. In recent years, the principles of damages in tort and contract are becoming more consistent. That is good and should be encouraged. By allowing punitive damages for contract breach, that laudable trend will be advanced. Moreover, hopefully those who plan to breach contracts in a callous fashion will think twice.
>
> Consequently, I conclude that is not beyond the power of this Court to award punitive damages in those rare situations where a contract has been breached in a high-handed, shocking and arrogant fashion so as to demand condemnation by the Court as a deterrent. (at pp. 292-293)

Due to the fact that there are very few cases that award punitive damages, it is not possible to attempt to catalogue the factors that may give rise to punitive damages by reference to the decided cases. In each case it is up to the individual judge to determine whether the contract-breaker has, to quote Mr. Justice Linden, acted in such a "high-handed and outrageous fashion" as to warrant punitive damages. The cases hereinafter set out are, however, the leading cases providing guidance as to when punitive damages will be awarded.

In *Ribeiro v. Canadian Imperial Bank of Commerce* (1992), 44 C.C.E.L. (2d) 165, 13 O.R. (3d) 278 (C.A.), leave to appeal to S.C.C. refused (June 10, 1993), Doc. 23378 (S.C.C.), Ribeiro was thirty years of age and had been employed by the bank for six years, most recently as a consumer loans officer. After little or no investigation, the bank concluded that he had acted dishonestly in connection with the granting of a $1,000 loan that had defaulted, and not only terminated his employment, but also caused criminal charges to be laid against him. The Court concluded that the bank had acted wrongfully, wantonly and recklessly in terminating the employment and as a result had caused the employee to suffer severe depression.

At trial, the Court awarded $10,000 in punitive damages. The Court of Appeal, however, increased this award, reasoning as follows:

> The trial judge found that this was a case in which an award of punitive damages was justified. The harsh, vindictive, reprehensible and malicious conduct of the respondents towards the appellant amply justified the trial judge's conclusion. However, in our opinion, his assessment of those damages at $10,000 failed to give effect adequately to the purposes for which punitive damages are awarded, namely, punishment and deterrence. In the circumstances of this case, having found that an award of punitive damages was justified, we think that the trial judge ought to have made an award of a substantially higher amount than he did. We think an amount of $50,000 should be assessed under that head of damages. (at p. 166)

In *Pilato v. Hamilton Place Convention Centre Inc.* (1984), 3 C.C.E.L. 241, 45 O.R. (2d) 652, 84 C.L.L.C. 14,039, 7 D.L.R. (4th) 342 (H.C.), the Court adopted and applied the principles of law enunciated in the *Brown* case. In *Pilato*, the general manager of a convention centre had shown a pornographic videotape in his office. The chairman and vice-chairman of the board of the convention centre were present. The showing of the film came to the attention of the media and at a board meeting Pilato acknowledged showing the film and, in order to avoid embarrassment to the board members present, denied that they had been present. Commenting on this meeting, Mr. Justice Fitzpatrick stated:

> The board expressed no outrage at the December 17th meeting when it learned that Pilato had shown this tape in his office. In fact, some of the board members indicated that if they had known about the tape they also would have attended. (at p. 247)

After learning of the showing of the film the board publicly expressed confidence in the performance of Pilato and granted him a salary increase. Matters took a turn for the worse, however, when City of Hamilton politicians decided to scrutinize matters more closely. At one meeting a city alderman told Pilato to resign, in which case he would receive a favourable recommendation, and that if he didn't "we'll burn you." City Council then directed the board of the convention centre to reconsider its decision. The board viewed this as a directive from City Council to fire Pilato, which the board acted upon. To compound matters Pilato was given no opportunity to be heard and the board announced the termination to the press while Pilato was on vacation. Further, the convention centre defended the action on the basis of just cause consisting of administrative incompetence, dishonesty with respect to expense claims and due to the lies concerning the persons who had viewed the pornographic tape. The Court found that the first two grounds relied upon for just cause were totally unfounded. As to the third ground, relating to the lies, the Court stated:

> I find that Pilato lied only to save the board and its Chairman and Vice-Chairman embarrassment, that he saw no way in which the Centre would be injured by this, and also no way in which he would be benefited, as two men he had lied to to save from embarrassment were no longer board members and in a position to assist him. I find that the lie or lies which Pilato has admitted telling are not of a kind or degree which would justify his dismissal for cause. (at p. 253)

The Court relied upon the law in *Brown v. Waterloo* and awarded Pilato $25,000 in punitive damages, and $25,000 in damages for mental distress, stating:

> When Pilato was dismissed, he was a young man trained in, and very successful in, a narrow and highly specialized field. I accept the evidence of Mr. Phillips that it is improbable that he will be able to get appropriate employment in this field in Canada because of what happened to him in Hamilton. He was dealt with savagely and has been severely, if not irreparably, injured. I find that he has suffered more grievously than he can be compensated for in this action. (at p. 256)

In *Makarchuk v. Midtransportation Services Ltd.* (1985), 6 C.C.E.L. 169 (Ont. H.C.), the terminated employee had been a truck salesman. A fraud was perpetrated on the employer whereby a truck was delivered, and disposed of, without payment. The Court found that the employee was terminated due to a suspicion that he had been party to the fraud. The case was reported to the police and to a bonding company, neither of whom could find any evidence of dishonesty on the part of the employee. Regardless of the fact that there was no evidence against the employee, the employer pleaded and maintained allegations of fraud and dishonesty for the six years it took to bring the case to trial. The allegations were, however, withdrawn at the opening of the trial.

Mr. Justice Rosenberg made the following comments with respect to the conduct of the employer:

> Another important aspect of the evidence, in my view, is the admission by Mr. Brittain that he wanted to give a letter of recommendation to the plaintiff, but that Mr. Patterson instructed him not to do so. This evidence is not consistent with a belief by Mr. Brittain that the plaintiff was dishonest.
>
> In the result, the plaintiff was not only dismissed without reasonable cause, but was seriously hampered in his ability to find similar employment. The community of large truck sales outlets in the Toronto area is a small one. The plaintiff swore that he told every prospective employer his version of the incidents I have described. Without a letter of reference, he would, in any event, have been forced to make such disclosure.
>
> While the belief by Mr. Patterson may have been bona fide with regard to the alleged fraud, it was unfounded. He took no steps, on finding his error, either to try to undo some of the injustice that he had done, nor to withdraw the allegation of fraud.
>
> Accordingly, it is my view that the plaintiff must succeed in this action for wrongful dismissal and that the defendant has not established just cause.

> A further element that should be considered with regard to the plaintiff's claim is that Mr. Patterson admitted that he did not discuss the matter with the plaintiff personally. It would have been appropriate, in view of the serious allegations being made against the plaintiff and the serious consequences to the plaintiff of having this allegation of fraud hanging over him for such a long period, to at least have discussed the matter with him and obtained his view before taking such drastic action. Mr. Patterson did not do this, and Sherway must bear the consequences of his failure in this regard. (at p. 175)

In the result, the Court awarded the global amount of $32,000 on account of a number of heads of damage including punitive, aggravated and exemplary damages.

Edwards v. Lawson Paper Converters Ltd. (1984), 5 C.C.E.L. 99 (Ont. H.C.), presents an unusual fact situation in which the Court dismissed a claim for wrongful dismissal and allowed a counterclaim by the employer claiming damages based upon a competitive business which the employee had founded, and operated for a period of time, prior to the termination of his employment. The Court awarded an additional $1,000 in punitive damages as redress for the fact that the employee had been in flagrant breach of his contract of employment and had also removed company documents, at the time of termination, which he refused to return except under the compulsion of a court order.

Thom Estate v. Goodhost Foods Ltd. (1987), 17 C.C.E.L. 89 (Ont. H.C.), additional reasons at (July 9, 1987), Doc. No. 56543/80 (Ont. H.C.), presents a fact situation so shocking that there can be little wonder at the fact that punitive damages were awarded. The employee had been hired in 1977 as the president and chief operating officer of the defendant. The defendant enjoyed great success and its net worth more than doubled between 1977 and 1979. In 1980 Thom approached the chief executive officer of the defendant and advised him during a brief conversation that he had been working 110 hours per week, that his blood pressure was "off the scale" and that on the advice of his doctor he needed to take a medical leave of absence for approximately three weeks until the commencement of a scheduled three-week holiday period. Thom received no further communication from the defendant until, approximately one week later, he received the following letter:

> I was shocked by the abruptness with which you left the company last Tuesday, the 10th. For the past week I have been trying to gather together as much information as possible about the company and its ongoing operation so as to compensate for the lack of advance notice and planning that we should have expected in a matter of this type for a company for which you had the responsibility as president.
>
> You indicated to me that you were taking a medical leave of absence on information from your doctor which indicated that you were under "a great deal of pressure". As I expressed to you, the pressure which you felt was intolerable is a normal operating climate in our company and I would expect that a chief operating officer would be able to work within the conditions that the job entails.

> Please consider this letter as our acceptance of your resignation. In the circumstances of your leaving the company and in view of the nature of your problem, we have no alternative but to accept and recognize the fact that there is no likelihood of your being able to return to the position that you have left. We must advise that we will begin to search for a replacement as soon as possible. We share with you the recognition that your departure is in the best interests of your health.
>
> As soon as you are in a position to do so, please be in touch with me so that we can make arrangements for the delivery of your personal possessions. (at p. 96)

The defendant then proceeded to defend the wrongful dismissal action on the basis that Thom had resigned his employment or, in the alternative, that he had been terminated for just cause. The particulars of just cause included very serious allegations of misconduct including sexual harassment and the unauthorized drawing of funds.

The Court found that Thom had not resigned, that the chief executive officer knew he had not resigned and that, as such, the reference in the defendant's letter to Thom's resignation was "a work of pure creation." The Court further stated that the letter was otherwise written "without any regard whatever for the truth . . .".

Approximately one year after the termination of his employment, Thom committed suicide. The Court commented on the evidence concerning Thom's mental state as follows:

> Mrs. Thom said that about the second or third week in July, her husband started coming to Toronto to see management people. Up to that point he was resting, he was on medication to keep him quiet and he was getting a lot of extra sleep. She said he tried to get himself back up but he was not successful; he was like a pricked balloon, he had loved his job and now he felt totally useless. (at pp. 111-112)
>
> . . . .
>
> In July 1980 Thom complained of depression, anxiety and frustration and was obsessive about his firing. Dr. Solursh's evidence dealt in detail with his assessment and treatment of Thom through 1980 and into 1981. When asked about the relationship of the firing and the suicide he said: "I have to assume that if it had not been for the firing, he would not have suicided, at least not at that point in time." He went on to say that it is very likely that without the firing, there would have been no suicide. (at p. 113)

The Court declined to award damages for mental distress on the basis that such damages had not been claimed in the Statement of Claim. Mr. Justice Austin then turned to the question of punitive damages and stated:

> The last item is punitive damages. Where the compensatory damages by themselves are sufficient to "punish" the defendant for conduct which is callous high-handed, ruthless, arrogant or arbitrary, then there is no need for punitive

> damages. With the disallowance of the claim of damages for mental distress, this is not such a case.
>
> Here the defendant, knowing that Thom was away ill and suffering from high blood pressure, telephoned him and told him that he was fired. This was followed up with a letter received the following day purporting to accept his resignation. The defendant knew full well Thom had not resigned. Slater said he offered to discuss severance, indicating that he knew he did not have just cause. A few days later, a letter from Thom's lawyers asked that his salary, medical and hospital coverage and all insurance including disability coverage be continued. They were not. The solicitor suggested a meeting as soon as Thom was fit. The evidence does not indicate what happened following that letter of June 24 but the writ in this action was issued on August 6, 1980.
>
> In its statement of defence dated October 6, 1980, the defendant pleaded that Thom mistreated his wife in front of employees of the defendant. This pleading was subsequently abandoned. This statement of defence also alleged that Thom's physical and psychological condition rendered him unfit for and incapable of management of the defendant's business. It also alleged that he sexually harrassed female employees of the defendant. In its amended statement of defence delivered December 16, 1985, these allegations were repeated and in addition it was alleged that Thom fired employees of the defendant improperly and without cause. All of these allegations were abandoned at the outset of the trial.
>
> In my view, in the light of the circumstances listed above, this is an appropriate case for punitive damages and I would fix them at $20,000. (at pp. 119-120)

While the award of punitive damages was clearly appropriate, it is somewhat difficult to understand what is meant by the comment, "[w]here the compensatory damages by themselves are sufficient to 'punish' the defendant . . . then there is no need for punitive damages." In principle, compensatory damages do not "punish" since, by definition, they require the wrongdoer to do nothing more than pay for the damages caused. Punishment is only imposed when the wrongdoer is required to pay an additional non-compensatory amount as a deterrent. It is, therefore, submitted that the award of mental distress damages should not exclude an award of punitive damages if punitive damages would otherwise be appropriate on the evidence.

In *Linkson v. UTDC Inc.* (1991), 40 C.C.E.L. 305, 92 C.L.L.C. 14,037 (Ont. Gen. Div.), the Court awarded damages in the amount of $5000 having regard to the failure of the employer to comply with the minimum requirements of the *Employment Standards Act*, R.S.O. 1980, c. 137. The Judge stated:

> I find it quite high-handed and cavalier that such a payment would not be made even as the trial proceeds.
>
> The *Employment Standards Act* is not to be used as a bargaining tool to force an employee to accept a less lucrative settlement.
>
> . . . .
>
> [T]o be relieved of your employment and not to get what you are entitled to, and to be forced to sue to collect what you are entitled to as a right, I find most unacceptable. And I reiterate that it is unheard of, and will not be condoned by

> this court. I therefore fix under the head of damages, aggravated damages, or whatever you wish to call it, mental distress or punitive and aggravated damage, the sum of $5,000. (at pp. 308-309)

In practice it is not unheard of to find employers attempting to withhold statutory entitlements to exert pressure to settle. This is a welcome decision and should do much to deter this type of conduct.

(b) Quantum of Punitive Damages

Case	Award	Facts
Pilato v. Hamilton Place Convention Centre Inc. (1984), 3 C.C.E.L. 241, 45 O.R. (2d) 652, 84 C.L.L.C. 14,039, 7 D.L.R. (4th) 342 (H.C.)	$25,000	The employee was 36 years old and had been employed for two years as the general manager/chief executive officer. The employee was not given an opportunity to respond to serious allegations against him and his dismissal was communicated to the press while he was on holiday. Psychiatric evidence was considered. He also received $25,000 in mental distress damages.
Ribeiro v. Canadian Imperial Bank of Commerce (1992), 44 C.C.E.L. (2d) 165, 13 O.R. (3d) 278 (C.A.), leave to appeal to S.C.C. refused (1993), 157 N.R. 400 (note), 65 O.A.C. 79 (note) (S.C.C.)	$50,000	The employee was thirty years of age and had been employed by the bank for six years, most recently as a consumer loans officer. After little or no investigation, the bank concluded that the employee had acted dishonestly in connection with the granting of a $1,000 loan that had defaulted, and not only terminated his employment, but also caused criminal charges to be laid against him. The Court concluded that the bank had acted wrongfully, wantonly and recklessly in terminating the employment and as a result had caused the employee to suffer severe depression. The employee also received $20,000 in mental distress damages.

Case	Award	Facts
Thom Estate v. Goodhost Foods Ltd. (1987), 17 C.C.E.L. 89 (Ont. H.C.), additional reasons at (July 9, 1987), Doc. 56543/80 (Ont. H.C.)	$20,000	The president and chief executive officer, who had been working 110 hours per week, developed high blood pressure and was advised by his doctor to rest for three weeks. The employer, by letter, took the position that this constituted a resignation by the employee. The employer then defended the action based upon serious allegations of just cause which were unfounded. The termination was a causative factor in the subsequent suicide of the employee.
Edwards v. Lawson Paper Converters Ltd. (1984), 5 C.C.E.L. 99 (Ont. H.C.)	$1,000	An employer brought an action against a former employee. The employee had carried on a competitive business while still employed and had removed company documents at the time of termination which he refused to return except under compulsion of a court order.

6.7 DAMAGES FOR LOSS OF RETIREMENT BENEFITS

It has become increasingly common for employers to agree to provide continuing group insurance and other benefits to retired employees. Such an ''agreement'' may take several forms, including an express contractual provision in an individual employment contract, a description of benefits set out in an employee booklet or other employee communication, or an oral commitment given at the time of hiring or during the course of employment.

Employers who have agreed to provide such benefits to retired workers should be aware of the Supreme Court of Canada decision in *Dayco (Canada) Ltd. v. C.A.W.*, 13 O.R. (3d) 164 (note), (*sub nom. Dayco (Canada) Ltd. v. CAW — Canada*) [1993] 2 S.C.R. 230, 14 Admin. L.R. (2d) 1, (*sub nom. Dayco v. C.A.W.*) 93 C.L.L.C. 14,032, (*sub nom. Dayco v. N.A.W.*) C.E.B. & P.G.R. 8141, (*sub nom. Dayco (Canada) Ltd. v. C.A.W. — Canada*) 102 D.L.R. (4th) 609, 152 N.R. 1, 63 O.A.C. 1.

Prior to closing its operations in Hamilton in 1985, Dayco entered into a shut-down agreement with the Union on behalf of its active employees. Under that agreement, the existing group benefits program for those employees was to be continued for a period of six months following the plant closure. The most recent collective agreement, which had expired in April 1985, provided for the continuation of certain group benefits to retirees, including group life and accidental death and dismemberment insurance, payment of OHIP premiums and the provision of semi-private hospital coverage. Although the shut-down agreement was silent with respect to retirees, Dayco subsequently informed them that their benefits would also be discontinued concurrent with the termination of coverage for the active employees. A grievance was filed by the Union on behalf of the retirees, demanding the reinstatement of the retirees' benefits. While *Dayco* dealt with a unionized setting, the principles of contract law and interpretation relied upon by the Supreme Court apply to non-unionized employers and employees.

The contractual issue was concerned with the legal entitlement to retiree benefits. In analyzing the issue, the Court first turned to an examination of jurisprudence in the United States. The Court cited the leading U.S. decision in *U.A.W. v. Yard-Man, Inc.*, 716 F.2d 1476 (1983), cert. denied 465 U.S. 1007 (1984), in which a plant closing prompted the termination of a collective agreement and the company advised retirees that life and health insurance benefits would be discontinued. Referring to the *Yard-Man* decision, Mr. Justice La Forest stated:

> [T]he court established the following approach for determining whether retirement benefits have vested. It suggested that courts should look first to the disputed language in the collective agreement, interpreting each provision as part of an integrated whole. If ambiguities exist, courts should then look to other provisions of the agreement, and to the context in which the agreement was negotiated. Finally, the interpretation of the agreement should be consonant with federal labour policy.
>
> Applying this approach, the court concluded that the clause before them respecting retirement benefits was ambiguous as to vesting. The clause read as follows: "The Company will provide insurance benefits equal to the active group benefits . . . for the former employee and his spouse." The agreement did not explicitly contemplate the eventuality of the termination of the collective agreement, and as such was unclear on whether retirees' rights would survive that event. Accordingly, the court reviewed other provisions of the agreement, finding several instances in which the text was indicative of an intent to vest retirement benefits. Finally, it considered the context in which the benefits were negotiated, reasoning as follows, at p. 1482:
>
>> Finally, examination of the context in which these benefits arose demonstrates the likelihood that continuing insurance benefits for retirees were intended. Benefits for retirees are only permissive not mandatory subjects of collective bargaining. . . . As such, it is unlikely that such benefits, which are typically understood as a form of delayed compensation or reward for past services, would be left to the contingencies of future negotiations. . . . The employees are presumably aware that the union owes no obligation to bargain for continued benefits for retirees. If they forego wages now in expectation of retiree benefits, they would want assurance that once they retire they will continue to receive such benefits regardless of the bargain reached in subsequent agreements. Contrary to Yard-Man's assertions, the finding of an intent to create interminable rights to retiree insurance benefits in the absence of explicit language is not, in any discernible way, inconsistent with federal labour law.

> Further, retiree benefits are in a sense "status" benefits which, as such, carry with them an inference that they continue so long as the prerequisite status is maintained. Thus, when the parties contract for benefits which accrue upon achievement of retiree status, there is an inference that the parties likely intended those benefits to continue as long as the beneficiary remains a retiree. This is not to say that retiree insurance benefits are necessarily interminable by their nature. Nor does any federal labour policy identified to this Court presumptively favour the finding of interminable rights to retiree insurance benefits when the collective bargaining agreement is silent. Rather, as part of the context from which the collective bargaining agreement arose, the nature of such benefits simply provides another inference of intent. Standing alone, this factor would be insufficient to find an intent to create interminable benefits. In the present case, however, this contextual factor buttresses the already sufficient evidence of such intent in the language of this agreement itself. (at pp. 290-291)

Some U.S. cases differed with *Yard-Man* as to whether it was proper to infer an intent to continue retiree benefits. Mr. Justice La Forest agreed that intent should be gathered from the evidence and inferences drawn on a case by case basis, and endorsed the American jurisprudence stating:

> Taken as a whole, I find the American jurisprudence to be highly persuasive of the approach this Court should adopt. The American courts have properly focused on the time of retirement as the moment at which certain rights granted under a collective agreement vest. While distinctions can be drawn with respect to the enforceability of the right in Canada, such distinctions, in my view, have no bearing on the present appeal. (at p. 293)

Mr. Justice La Forest also referred with approval to *Pulp & Paper Industrial Relations Bureau v. C.P.U.* (1977), [1978] 1 Can. L.R.B.R. 60, 77 C.L.L.C. 16,109, a little-reported decision of the British Columbia Labour Relations Board in which the Board stated:

> True, the normal legal expectation is that pension benefits are vested as of a certain point in time; and that upon retirement a pensioner has a legal entitlement to his pension which cannot be touched by collective bargaining between a union and an employer. But that would appear to be the product of the typical legal arrangements for pension plans: which require the payment of the employer (and any employee) contribution into a pension trust, which in turn guarantees pension of a certain amount to retirees as beneficiaries under the trust. But the legal situation is not so clear for other kinds of contract benefits. For example, suppose a collective agreement has extended a prescription drug plan to retirees. If a government program has made that benefit redundant, and the parties want to eliminate it and put the money elsewhere, presumably they would be entitled to do so, even in respect of retirees. Undoubtedly, they would be authorized to do so . . . if they built that condition into the contract benefit right from the outset. The reason is that these benefits rest on the private collective agreement and, in the final analysis, the parties who negotiated the contract which created the benefit can also reserve to themselves the authority either to modify or to terminate the benefit. Thus if the parties to a pension plan agreement anticipate this problem, and write into their trust document their mutual authority to alter the level of benefits, one way or the other, then the legal result is that these benefits are no longer absolutely vested in the retiree. (at p. 296)

Mr. Justice La Forest, therefore, concluded:

> To summarize, I am of the view that retirement rights can, if contemplated by the terms of a collective agreement, survive the expiration of that agreement. Moreover, although it is not strictly necessary to decide the point in this appeal, I would also find that these surviving rights vest at the time of retirement, and would survive subsequent collective bargaining that purported to divest such rights. (at p. 305)

A similar analysis may be applied to the case of individual contracts of employment. If a promise to continue group benefits after retirement is made in such a contract, the "vesting upon retirement" principle will apply. Consequently, employers may be precluded from discontinuing or even altering such benefits, unless the terms by which such rights are granted reserve to the employer the ability to amend or revoke those rights in the future. This is an issue which can, and should, be addressed in employment contracts.

In *Dayco*, the Supreme Court of Canada was considering an "all or nothing" situation in which the employer took the position that it had the unilateral right to remove all retiree benefits. This does leave the lower courts with some latitude to find that an employer can, within reasonable bounds, adjust fringe benefits from time to time. In practical business terms, this would make sense because if the retiree fringe benefits are "etched in stone" at the moment of each retirement it would be virtually impossible to have group benefit coverage on standardized terms for all retirees. Further, the argument that the employer does have a reasonable latitude to adjust fringe benefits would be greatly strengthened if retirees have generally shared in changes to the fringe benefit coverage enjoyed by active employees. In other words, if the history is that benefits were generally enhanced, and if retirees generally shared in such enhancements, a court may accept that this reflects an agreement on the part of the parties that retirees will be considered in a manner comparable to active employees.

In conclusion the legal principles in *Dayco* should be considered and, if the parties elect, altered by the terms of an employment contract.

7

TORT LIABILITY

7.1 GENERAL PRINCIPLES

(a) Introduction

Tort law, in broad terms, describes the situations in which a person may be held liable to pay damages in cases not involving breach of contract. As discussed, contract law is concerned with the rights and obligations that flow from an agreement created by the parties. Tort law is concerned with the rights and obligations imposed by the law regardless of whether or not a contract is in existence.

In the context of employment, allegations of tort liability will most often be made as follows:

1. by an employee to render liable a fellow employee. Most employment contracts are between a corporate employer and the employee. Thus, tort law may be invoked by an employee to render other employees, usually more senior managers, personally liable for torts such as intimidation or defamation. This may be of particular significance in the event that the corporate employer is insolvent;
2. by an individual to render liable a former employer. For example, an employee might sue a former employer for defamation;
3. by a corporation to hold liable another corporation and its employees for their acts. For example, a corporation might sue a former employee and his new employer for inducing breach of contract;
4. to claim damages of a different type, or that may be awarded on a more generous scale in tort law, as opposed to contract law.

There are two types of torts: (1) intentional torts, and (2) negligent torts.

An intentional tort involves the intentional infliction of harm. One class of intentional torts is concerned with physical interference with the person, such as assault, battery and false imprisonment. Other intentional torts are concerned with non-physical types of interference and may arise in the employment context. In this regard the torts most often alleged are defamation, inducing breach of contract, intimidation, conspiracy and infliction of mental suffering, all of which are discussed below in greater detail.

The other principal type of tort is the tort of negligence. The law of negligence is chiefly concerned with negligence that causes physical harm. There is, however, a tort of negligent misrepresentation causing economic loss. This tort is of particular relevance in the employment law field in that representations are commonly made to, and acted upon by, employees, often by resigning their employment to accept a new position. Should the inducing representations be negligently made, and if certain other conditions hereinafter described are met, the person who made the representation may be personally liable for the damages suffered.

As the cases discussed below demonstrate, tort claims related to employment are significant and such claims are increasing in number.

To the extent possible the tort claims discussed below arise in an employment context. The vast majority of tort claims, however, arise in a context other than employment. The law concerning torts such as conspiracy and defamation is quite complex and the cases cited below are certainly not intended to provide a comprehensive survey of the areas of tort law listed. Rather, the intention is to provide a description of the legal principles sufficient to describe the tort and demonstrate its potential application in an employment context.

(b) Damages in Tort Law

Under the contract of employment virtually all damages are calculated by reference to the period of reasonable notice for the particular employee. Thus, for example, a junior employee may be terminated by reason of alleged incompetence and, despite his or her best efforts, may remain unemployed for

(*Continued on page 7-3*)

six months. If the Court determines that "just cause" did not exist, then the employer is in breach of contract. Assuming that the age, length of service and position of the employee are such that three months would constitute a reasonable period of notice, the employee will be compensated for three months' remuneration, despite the fact that the employee remained unemployed for six months.

In contrast, however, damages in tort are not related to the period of reasonable notice. Damages in tort are recoverable if a duty exists between the parties, the duty was breached by the party charged with the breach, and the loss flows from the breach. Damages in tort are not limited to those arising during the period of notice or flowing from the lack of proper notice: it is the entire foreseeable loss which may be compensated. Thus, if the same junior employee as just discussed was defamed at the time of termination, or if the termination was brought about by intimidation or an intentional interference with contractual relations, then the employee could claim all damages flowing from the tort, which damages could include compensation for the six-month period of unemployment.

7.2 DEFAMATION

(a) Introduction

The law of defamation is complex, and in certain respects highly technical. The purpose of this section is to describe the law of defamation only to the extent necessary to describe the general principles and alert readers to the circumstances that may give rise to a claim for defamation in the employment context.

(b) What Constitutes Actionable Defamation

A defamatory statement is an untrue statement which harms the reputation of another and lowers his or her esteem in the community or exposes him or her to hatred, contempt or ridicule. In order for a defamatory statement to be actionable, it must be published. A statement is published when it is communicated to a third person other than the defamed individual.

There are two modes of publication: libel and slander. Libel is generally comprised of either written words or pictures. It is actionable without proof of damage because it is presumed that damages will result from a libel having regard to the fact that writing or pictures have a certain permanence and are subject to being reproduced and circulated. Slander, on the other hand, is published through the spoken word which tends to be transitory in terms of its likely impact. In order to maintain an action for slander, it is generally necessary to prove that the slander has caused material or pecuniary loss.

There are, however, some exceptions to the necessity of proving special damages in slander suits. One of these exceptions is slander of a person in connection with that person's business, trade, profession, office or other employment activity. This type of slander is actionable without proof of damage because it is clearly calculated to cause pecuniary damage to the employee. This exception has been codified in Ontario in the *Libel and Slander Act*, R.S.O. 1990, c. L.12, s. 16, which states:

> **16.** In an action for slander for words calculated to disparage the plaintiff in any office, profession, calling, trade or business held or carried on by the plaintiff at the time of the publication thereof, it is not necessary to allege or prove special damage, whether or not the words are spoken of the plaintiff in the way of the plaintiff's office, profession, calling, trade or business, and the plaintiff may recover damages without averment or proof of special damage.

(c) Defences

(i) *Justification*

Justification as a defence, simply put, means that the statement was not defamatory becasuse it was true. This defence requires proof that the words sued upon, construed according to their ordinary and natural meanings, were true in substance and fact. The onus is upon the defendant to prove on a balance of probabilities the substantial truth of the statement sued. This must be done to the extent of justifying every defamatory imputation the words may bear. The *Libel and Slander Act*, in section 22, states that the defence of justification will not fail even if the action consists of two or more charges upon the statement as long as one charge can be justified and the other does not materially injure the plaintiff's reputation, having regard to the truth of the remaining charges.

(ii) *Absolute Privilege*

The proceedings of a legislative body are absolutely privileged and words spoken in the course of a proceeding in Parliament cannot form the basis of a civil action. The principle of absolute privilege of Parliamentary proceedings has been extended to apply to proceedings which are an extension of the proceedings in Parliament. Absolute privilege has been held to apply to:

1. statements made in the course of judicial proceedings;
2. statements made in the course of quasi-judicial proceedings;
3. statements contained in the documents produced in judicial or quasi-judicial proceedings; and,
4. fair and accurate newspaper reports of public proceedings in Court.

(iii) *Qualified Privilege*

Qualified privilege attaches to statements made on a privileged occasion. For qualified privilege to exist, the statement must be made without malice pursuant to a moral, social or legal duty to communicate the information contained in the statement. Concomitant with the duty to speak there must also be an interest or duty in the hearer to receive the communication. Examples of situations in which qualified privilege has been held to exist are:

1. an answer to a *bona fide* request for information from a superior or agent;
2. a statement made in connection with an employee evaluation;
3. a letter of reference to a potential employer;
4. a statement of reasons for dismissal given to a person representing the employee.

(iv) *Fair Comment*

The defence of fair comment relates to the public policy that it is desirable that all persons should be able to freely comment on a matter of public concern. Unlike justification, the opinion itself does not need to be correct; only the facts upon which the statement is based need to be true. This defence will also succeed, according to section 24 of the *Libel and Slander Act*, even if the truth of every allegation of fact is not proved, if the expression of opinion is fair comment having regard to the facts that are proved. This defence would seldom apply in an employment context unless the persons involved were engaged in matters involving public policy or with respect to issues that were of public concern.

(v) *Apology*

Apology is not a true defence. Instead it is a way of mitigating the damage caused by a defamatory statement. The *Libel and Slander Act* states in section 20 that:

> **20.** In an action for libel or slander where the defendant has pleaded a denial of the alleged libel or slander only, or has suffered judgment by default, or judgment has been given against the defendant on motion for judgment on the pleadings, the defendant may give in evidence, in mitigation of damages, that the defendant made or offered a written apology to the plaintiff for such libel or slander before the commencement of the action, or, if the action was commenced before there was an opportunity of making or offering such apology, that the defendant did so as soon afterwards as the defendant had an opportunity.

(d) Examples of Defamation in the Employment Context

In the case of *Spong v. Westpres Publications Ltd.* (1982), 2 C.C.E.L. 228 (B.C. S.C.), the employee was an advertising manager who had been wrongfully dismissed. One of his claims against the employer was for slander. In that case the employee was accused by his superior of making passes at some of the female employees and of having an affair with the wife of one of the employer's clients. His superior also communicated this accusation to the client, who phoned the employee after hearing the accusation. The employee voiced his objections to his superior's accusations. This resulted in the employee being fired.

At trial the employer did not claim that the statements were true. Instead the employer challenged whether the employee could prove special damages as a result of the slander. The Court held that:

> The law is that slander is not actionable without proof of special damage. No special damage has been established. There is, however, an exception. If the slander defamed the plaintiff in his occupation, that is, if it carried the implication that he was unfit to be advertising manager of the Leader, no special damage need be proved. I think that the allegations made by Mr. Hughes cast a shadow over Mr. Spong's observance of the proprieties at the Leader offices and his relations with customers. Pursuing the girls in the production room is not admirable in an advertising manager. Neither is having an affair with a customer's wife. It may be that neither would, by itself, render him unfit to continue in his position, but their tendency would certainly be to show that he was not willing to behave himself at the office and was likely to alienate customers. The result is that the plaintiff does not have to prove special damage. As regards the more serious of these statements - that concerning Mr. Allen's wife - it may seem absurd that Mr. Spong could not sue Mr. Hughes for making this false allegation unless he could show that it would tend to lead Mr. Allen to think less of him as an advertising manager, even though Mr. Allen was no doubt principally concerned that the plaintiff, as a man and as a good friend, should have been having an affair with his wife. That, however, is the law. (at p. 232)

Further, the Court held that there was no qualified privilege on the basis that the communication was made with malice, which destroys the defence of qualified privilege.

In the case of *Stopforth v. Goyer* (1978), 20 O.R. (2d) 262, 4 C.C.L.T. 265, 87 D.L.R. (3d) 373 (H.C.), reversed on other grounds (1979), 8 C.C.L.T. 172 (C.A.), the plaintiff was employed by the Department of Supply and Services as the deputy manager of a project to purchase aircraft for the Department of National Defence. An action was brought against the Minister of Supply and Services as a result of a statement he made to the press after the project collapsed due to lack of proper funding. The statement accused the employee of "misrepresentation or gross negligence." The statement was widely published by the press.

The trial Judge dismissed the defences of fair comment, absolute privilege, qualified privilege, and justification, and held that the Minister was liable for defaming the employee, while the Court of Appeal reversed the trial decision on the basis that the defence of qualified privilege did apply. The trial decision is instructive as to the assessment of damages. In this regard, the Court held that:

> Many problems arise in an assessment of damages for libel.
>
> The Court must address itself to the loss of or damage to the esteem or reputation of the plaintiff for which he must be compensated. In *Littleton v. Hamilton et al.* (1974), 4 O.R. (2d) 283, 47 D.L.R. (3d) 663, Dubin, J.A., in speaking of the assessment of damages for libel said [at p. 287 O.R., p. 667 D.L.R.]: "They are difficult of assessment, and there are no guidelines which can be *clearly set forth.*" (Emphasis mine.)
>
> I have also considered the following cases: (a) *Associated Leisure Ltd. v. Associated Newspapers Ltd.*, [1970] 2 All E.R. 754 (C.A.), and (b) *Fraser v. Sykes*,

[1971] 1 W.W.R. 246 (Alta. S.C. T.D.); affirmed 19 D.L.R. (3d) 75, [1971] 3 W.W.R. 161 (App. Div.); affirmed [1974] S.C.R. 526, 39 D.L.R. (3d) 321, [1973] 5 W.W.R. 484 (S.C.C.).

(*Continued on page 7-7*)

The extent of the injury caused by the libel in this case is very difficult to assess. The defendant had already made substantially the same statement in the House of Commons as he did in the lobby on the occasion complained of apart from some words that he added in addition thereto outside the House. In my view the statement made in the House of Commons on this particular occasion of absolute privilege was bound to get widespread media and press coverage whether anything at all was said afterwards in the lobby. How much more extensive the coverage became after the defendant repeated the statement in the lobby is a very speculative problem.

Once the demotion of the plaintiff had been announced in the House of Commons and that fact became published much damage had already been done to the plaintiff. What damage the plaintiff suffered as a result of the statement made in the lobby of the House as distinguished from the chamber of the House of Commons is a very problematical matter. In my opinion the repetition of the statement already made by the defendant in the House of Commons a short while earlier on an occasion of absolute privilege did not, *per se*, inflict much additional damage to the plaintiff. It is doubtful whether the subsequent or second statement in the lobby had any very serious defamatory or great additional effect on the plaintiff's reputation.

Two types of damage are not applicable to the present action, namely: (1) nominal damages, and (2) contemptuous or ignominious damages.

It is alleged by the plaintiff that the damages were aggravated because:

(1) the defendant added the additional words described in the evidence of Ms. Janigan, including the phrase "I have no confidence in him";

(2) by persisting to the end of the trial in an unreasonable plea of justification; and

(3) by lack of a retraction or apology.

I find that the "additional statement" described by Ms. Janigan was not defamatory *per se*. If the phrase "I have no confidence in him" is an aggravation then it is indeed a slight one. Surely the plaintiff would not have been demoted if his superior officers had continued to have confidence in him. Consequently, I am considering the aggravating feature of this phrase and its effect on the plaintiff's reputation as minor. (at pp. 278-280)

. . . .

I find that the aggravation caused by the persistence in the plea of justification and the defendant's failure to retract or apologize must be considered.

The absence of an apology or retraction is also a factor which must be taken into account in the assessment: see *Morgan v. Odhams Press Ltd.*, [1971] 2 All E.R. 1156 (H.L.). In the English Court of Appeal it was held that the absence of a correction or apology was a relevant factor in assessing the damages and it is generally held to be a relevant factor where there is an opportunity to make an apology and none was made: see *Hubert et al. v. DeCamillis et al.* (1963), 41 D.L.R. (2d) 495 at p. 514, 44 W.W.R. 1 (B.C. S.C.).

Because the defendant received a letter from the plaintiff's solicitor and did not thereafter retract or apologize he aggravated the damages to some extent. It has been held that exemplary damages or punitive damages may be awarded when a defendant has acted in a high-handed fashion "and persists in ignoring the rights of others": see *University of New Brunswick v. Strax* (1968), 1 N.B.R.

> (2d) 112, *per* Barry, J., at p. 124. A Minister of the Crown must take more care to ensure the accuracy of his statement because of the wide circulation any statement by him will receive in the press and in the other media.
>
> I have also considered the following matters:
>
> (a) the conduct, demeanour and attitude of the parties and their counsel throughout;
>
> (b) the position of the parties in society and their standing in the community;
>
> (c) the nature of the libel and whether it was vicious or exaggerated;
>
> (d) the extent of the injury to the plaintiff's reputation;
>
> (e) the extent of the injury to his feelings including mental suffering, anxiety and natural grief and distress.
>
> Having considered all the circumstances of the case and those which rightly touch on the subject, as well as the various constituent components of an award and the various types of awards, and applying the best judgment of which I am capable, I award the plaintiff damages in the sum of $10,000. There will be judgment for the plaintiff for $10,000 and costs. (at pp. 280-281)

In the case of *Hanly v. Pisces Productions Inc.* (1980), [1981] 1 W.W.R. 369 (B.C.S.C.), the plaintiff was a motion picture script supervisor who had been interviewed for a position but was not hired. In response to a request by the plaintiff's union, the defendant wrote a letter stating its reasons for not hiring the plaintiff. This letter included statements that the plaintiff gave the defendant's employee who had conducted the interviews, the "distinct impression that she has little or no confidence in her own work" and also expressed his opinion that "her work record has several suspect areas." The Court held that the letter was defamatory to the plaintiff. The Court did not, however, find the defendant liable because the letter was protected by the defence of qualified privilege. In coming to this decision the Court quoted from the judgment of Lord Atkinson in *Greenlands, Ltd. v. London Assn. for Protection of Trade*, [1916] 2 A.C. 15, [1916-17] All E.R. 452, 85 L.J.K.B. 698 (H.L.), as follows:

> It was decided as long ago, I think, as *Bromage v. Prosser* (1825), 4 B.S.C. 247, 107 E.R. 1051, and many times since, that if one person makes an inquiry of another touching the position or character of a third, and the person inquired of makes a reply which he bona fide believes to be true, and also bona fide believes that the inquirer desires the information, not merely to gratify idle curiosity, but for some purpose in which he, the inquirer, has a legitimate interest of his own, the occasion upon which the answer is communicated to him is a privileged occasion. This will be so, I think, whether either of the beliefs so formed by the person inquired of be reasonable or not - *Clark v. Molyneux* (1877), 3 Q.B.D. 237 (C.A.) — and also whether the inquirer, in fact, desired the information for the purpose mentioned. It will be sufficient if the other person honestly believed he does so require it: *Waller v. Loch* (1881), 7 Q.B.D. 619. (at p. 373)

In summary, if the information which is defamatory was requested for *bona fide* reasons and the reply was honestly made the defence of qualified privilege will prevail.

7.3 INDUCING BREACH OF CONTRACT

The tort of wrongfully inducing breach of contract was described by the then Mr. Justice Gale in *Posluns v. Toronto Stock Exchange*, [1964] 2 O.R. 547, 46 D.L.R. (2d) 210 (H.C.), affirmed [1966] 1 O.R. 285, 53 D.L.R. (2d) 193 (C.A.), affirmed [1968] S.C.R. 330, 67 D.L.R. (2d) 165, as follows:

> While a contract cannot impose the burden of an obligation on one who is not a party to it, a duty is undoubtedly cast upon any person, although extraneous to the obligation, to refrain from interfering with its due performance unless he has a duty or a right in law to so act. Thus, if a person without lawful justification knowingly and intentionally procures the breach by a party to a contract which is valid and enforceable and thereby causes damage to another party to the contract, the person who has induced the breach commits an actionable wrong. That wrong does not rest upon the fact that the intervenor has acted in order to harm his victim, for a bad motive does not *per se* convert an otherwise lawful act into an unlawful one, but rather because there has been an unlawful invasion of legal relations existing between others. (at p. 598)

In employment situations, examples of wrongful inducement of breach of contract would include the following:

1. inducing an employee to quit this or her employment without reasonable notice to the employer;
2. inducing an employer to terminate an employee without reasonable notice;
3. inducing an employee to breach the fiduciary obligation the employee owes the employer, such as obtaining confidential information of the employer for a competitor.

In the case of *Vale v. I.L.W.U., Local 508*, 12 B.C.L.R. 249, 9 C.C.L.T. 262, [1979] 5 W.W.R. 231 (C.A.), the plaintiff was employed as a loading master with two companies. His duties took him to the port of Chemainus which was within the "jurisdiction" of the defendant (the International Longshoremen's and Warehousemen's Union). The defendant's members were on lawful strike in March 1975. During that month the plaintiff, on the orders of his employer, assisted a strike-bound vessel in removing itself from port so it could proceed on its voyage. The strike ended and work resumed. When the vessel returned from its voyage the defendant went on an unlawful strike to force the plaintiff's employer to effect the plaintiff's removal from their jurisdiction. The employer acceded to the union demand and offered to relocate the plaintiff to another jurisdiction. The plaintiff refused to relocate and was dismissed by his employer without notice. The Court of Appeal upheld the trial Judge's finding that the defendant had induced a breach of contract, and stated that:

> . . . As the trial judge expressed it, I think correctly, the end result of the union's conduct was "to get Vale off the waterfront and fired from his job".

"So the end of that job, as far as Vale was concerned, the job of loading master on Vancouver Island, was brought about by the union's act, so therefore, I think the plaintiff has established that the end of Vale's job was a result of union action." (at p. 252)

The Court of Appeal, however, varied the trial Judge's decision that there were no additional damages flowing from the tort since the plaintiff had already received damages for the breach of contract. The Court of Appeal held that the tort loss was a different loss from the breach of contract and awarded the plaintiff $1,500 in damages.

In the case of *Kepic v. Tecumseh Road Builders* (1987), 18 C.C.E.L. 218, 23 O.A.C. 72 (C.A.), the plaintiff was hired by the defendant with a view to obtaining a particular demolition contract. The tender for the contract was successful, in part because of the plaintiff's reputation in the industry. It was agreed between the parties that the plaintiff would receive 50 per cent of the profit on the demolition contract. When it became clear how lucrative the project was, the individuals who controlled the defendant set about to end the plaintiff's involvement in order to increase the defendant's profits. The defendant eventually dismissed the plaintiff, without cause, on 24 hours' notice. The trial court and the Court of Appeal held that the plaintiff had been wrongfully dismissed and awarded him his profit share. On the claim for inducing a breach of contract the Court of Appeal held that:

> It is well established that the directors of a corporation will not be liable for inducing that corporation to breach its contract when they are performing bona fide their functions as corporate officers. See *Said v. Butt*, [1920] 3 K.B. 497 (K.B.); *Thomson & Co. v. Deakins*, [1952] 2 All E.R. 361, [1952] 1 Ch. 6461 (C.A.). This is not the case where a director acts in a fraudulent manner. Fraudulent efforts by a director of a corporation to increase the revenue of that body cannot be said to be bona fide in its best interest. See generally *Einhorn v. Westmount Investments Ltd.* (1969), 69 W.W.R. 31, 6 D.L.R. (3d) 71 (Sask. Q.B.), affirmed (1970), 73 W.W.R. D.L.R. [*sic*] (3d) 509 (Sask. C.A.); *McFadden v. 481782 Ontario Ltd.* (1984), 47 O.R. (3d) 134, 5 C.C.E.L. 83, 27 B.L.R. 173, (Ont. H.C.). After surveying the law on this question, the trial Judge concluded that the Marentettes were personally liable for inducing M.B.L. to breach its agreement with Kepic. The measure for damages for such a tort is the same as that recoverable for the breach induced. See generally *Asamera Oil Corp. Ltd. v. Sea Oil General Corp.*, [1979] 1 S.C.R. 633 at 644, 5 B.L.R. 225, [1978] 6 W.W.R. 301, 12 A.R. 271, 89 D.L.R. (3d) 1, 23 N.R. 181 (S.C.C.).
>
> In the circumstances, the trial Judge was right in holding the Marentettes personally liable for the tort of inducing a breach of the contract by their corporation. (at pp. 222-223)

In the case of *Ribeiro v. Cdn. Imperial Bank of Commerce* (1989), 24 C.C.E.L. 225, 67 O.R. (2d) 385, 89 C.L.L.C. 14,033 (H.C.), varied (1992), 44 C.C.E.L. 165, 13 O.R. (3d) 278 (C.A.), leave to appeal to S.C.C. refused (June 10, 1993), Doc. 23378 (S.C.C.), the plaintiff brought an action against the bank and one of its security division inspectors. This inspector accused the plaintiff of fraud and caused criminal charges to be laid against the plaintiff even though there was no evidence to support the allegations. Mr. Justice Carruthers held that:

(*Continued on page 7-11*)

Another claim by the plaintiff is against Matheson and it is for damages for his having wrongfully induced the breach of the plaintiff's employment agreement. This claim sounds in tort and the elements thereof are outlined in *Posluns v. Toronto Stock Exchange*, [1964] 2 O.R. 547, 46 D.L.R. (2d) 210 (H.C.), aff'd [1966] 1 O.R. 285, 53 D.L.R. (2d) 193 (C.A.), aff'd [1968] S.C.R. 330, 67 D.L.R. (2d) 165. There is no question that all of the elements there listed are found in the present case, except perhaps for that which requires that the breach be [effected] by "wrongful interference" on the part of Matheson.

In order to succeed the plaintiff must establish on a balance of probabilities that Matheson intended to bring about a breach of the agreement here in order to strike at the plaintiff. See Fleming, *The Law of Torts*, 6th ed., (Sydney: The Law Book Co., 1983), at p. 654. As well, it must be demonstrated to the same extent that in doing what he did Matheson was not acting within the scope of his employment with the defendant bank.

At p. 657, Fleming also says:

> A servant or agent, acting within the scope of his employment or authority, is not liable for inducing or procuring a breach of the contract by his employer, at any rate if he acts in good faith for the protection of his employer's interests. Thus, where a company acting by its directors breaks a contract, the party aggrieved is confined to suing the company for breach of contract and has no remedy against the directors in tort. The immunity has been justified on the technical ground that, since the master is responsible for the acts committed by his servant in the course of employment, the "extraordinary result" would otherwise ensue that the master could be held liable not only for breaking his own contract, but also for inducing himself to break it. It may be doubted whether this argument provides a convincing reason for letting off his servant, and it would be more realistic to admit that, on grounds of policy, a privilege is warranted wherever a servant or agent acts, not in capricious pursuit of self advantage, but for the bona fide protection of his employer.

I cannot in good conscience having regard to the manner in which Matheson went about his investigation of the plaintiff and the events giving rise to the plaintiff's wrongful dismissal, consider that Matheson was acting bona fide and in good faith. I can conclude that Matheson was malicious and spiteful towards the plaintiff. In addition, as I have already stated, Matheson went so far on several occasions to fabricate information in order to support his unfounded allegations of criminal activity on the part of the plaintiff. In my opinion he is therefore liable to the plaintiff by reason of having wrongfully induced the breach of the plaintiff's employment contract with the defendant bank. (at pp. 288-289)

7.4 INTIMIDATION

The tort of intimidation occurs when someone coerces a person "by unlawful threats into doing or abstaining from doing something that he would otherwise have every right to do, like firing a particular employee or ceasing to do business with an old customer" (John G. Fleming, *The Law of Torts*, 7th ed. (London: Sweet & Maxwell, 1987) at p. 661). There are two elements necessary in order for the tort of intimidation to occur. There must be an intent to injure and there must be unlawful interference.

In *Roehl v. Houlahan*, (April 13, 1988), Doc. No. Ottawa/Carleton 18513/83, 18514/83 (Ont. H.C.), additional reasons (October 3, 1988), the plaintiff was encouraged by the defendant company to accept new employment when he was 60 years old, as the executive vice-president and general manager of the defendant. There had been internal problems in the company and it was experiencing a reorganization after control had been taken by Swiss interests. The plaintiff was the only one who was hired from outside the company and he had been hired by the Swiss interests. The defendant Houlahan was vice-president of finance and administration. Houlahan, however, resented the fact that the plaintiff had been hired from outside the company and given the position of executive vice-president and general manager.

The Court described the conduct of Houlahan as follows:

> Notwithstanding his evidence and protestations to the contrary, Houlahan resented the plaintiff from the day he first heard of him and before he ever met him. Houlahan looked upon the plaintiff as a "plant" of the Swiss; Houlahan was afraid that Nortec would become a branch plant of Condair. Houlahan resented the plaintiff screening his work and felt that the Swiss had "changed the rules of the game."
>
> My finding is that Houlahan was not alone in these views. Perhaps Guay, unwittingly, expressed it best on cross-examination when he said: "Maybe the staff ganged up on him."
>
> Houlahan was upset that he did not get the general manager's job. He not only did not get the job, he was not considered for the job; indeed, he knew nothing of the fact that at the request of the Swiss, Currie, Coopers and Lybrand Ltd. had advertised and searched for a new general manager. On cross-examination, Houlahan admitted that at some point post-October 6, 1982, he told the plaintiff that he, Houlahan, had been disappointed that he did not get the general manager's job in October 1982. No doubt, Houlahan, a chartered accountant, did not have his disappointment assuaged upon learning that the plaintiff held no degrees of higher learning. (at pp. 49-50, unreported reasons for judgment (13 April 1988))
>
> . . . .
>
> Notwithstanding his denials at trial, I find that Houlahan deliberately "set up" the plaintiff regarding the organizational charts; he saw the charts, he knew they were wrong and he let them go out that way knowing that the plaintiff would reap the wrath of Gary Berlin and Guay as a result thereof.
>
> Houlahan, during his evidence, classified some of the plaintiff's memoranda as a "joke" or as a "complete joke"; "Max did not know what he was talking about."
>
> Why did Houlahan do all of this? Because he was determined that he was going to get the plaintiff fired; Houlahan coveted the general manager's job. And, wonder upon wonder, what happened? In January 1983, after Houlahan had fomented the rebellion and, so to speak, had been its "chef d'orchestre," he told his sad tale of woe to the Board of Directors; he and the others threatened to quit

unless the plaintiff was removed as general manager. Houlahan, of course, had a sympathetic ear on the Board of Directors in the person of the president, Jean Louis Guay, who, from day one, said that he would never have hired the plaintiff. As a result of what Houlahan and the others in this coup told the Board of Directors in January 1983, the plaintiff was "removed from the line" and told to take a low profile, do the Sarco Project until the Howard-Leicester litigation blew over. The plaintiff was frozen out. (at pp. 51-52)

The Court described the conduct of the Board of Directors as follows:

> The Board of Directors, because of the actions of Houlahan and others, saw that Max Roehl was isolated, he was out on the end of a limb. Instead of rescuing Max Roehl, the board chose to cut off the limb. (at p. 55)

Finally, the Court described the conduct of the plaintiff as follows:

> My assessment of the plaintiff is that he is an honest, decent, hardworking gentleman who, unfortunately, walked into a hornet's nest. When the showdown came, his Swiss heroes left him in the lurch and ultimately threw him overboard. Why, because of the actions of Houlahan and his group, the Swiss decided to sacrifice Max Roehl to thwart a threatened mass exodus of middle managers at Nortec. The plaintiff was a victim of time, place, circumstance and people. (at p. 57)

The Court provided the following explanation of the tort of intimidation, and analysis of the law as applied to the case:

> The tort of intimidation (the three-party type) was discussed and summarized by the Supreme Court of Canada in *Central Can. Potash Co. Ltd. v. Minister of Mineral Resources (Sask.)*, [1979] 1 S.C.R. 42, [1978] 6 W.W.R. 400, 6 C.C.L.T. 265, 88 D.L.R. (3d) 609, 23 N.R. 481, at (S.C.R.) 81, per Martland J.:
>
> > The tort of intimidation is defined in *Clerk & Lindsell on Torts*, 14th ed., para 802, p. 414, as follows:
> >
> > "A commits a tort if he delivers a threat to B that he will commit an act or use means unlawful as against B, as a result of which B does or refrains from doing some act which he is entitled to do, thereby causing damage either to himself or to C. The tort is one of intention and the plaintiff, whether it be B or C, must be a person whom A intended to injure."
>
> The very existence of the tort of intimidation was questioned in argument before the House of Lords by Gerald Gardiner, Q.C., (as he then was) in the leading case of *Rookes v. Barnard*, [1964] A.C. 1129, [1964] 1 All E.R. 367, [1964] 1 Lloyd's Rep. 28 (H.L.). The House of Lords confirmed the existence of the tort as had the Court of Appeal in the same case, [1963] 1 Q.B. 623. The difference of opinion between the two Courts was that the Court of Appeal held that intimidation was restricted to acts of violence or threats of a tortious or criminal nature and could not be extended to cover a threat to break a contract, while the House of Lords took the view that a threat to break a contract could be a foundation for the tort.
>
> The facts of that case were these. The plaintiff, an employee of B.O.A.C., resigned from his trade union which had an oral understanding, which was not

> legally binding, with B.O.A.C. that when a section or unit of B.O.A.C.'s employees were all union members it would not thereafter recruit non-union staff for that section. Of the three defendants, B and F were lay officials of the union employed by B.O.A.C. and S was a full-time official employed by the union. These three, in accordance with the terms of a resolution passed at a meeting of union members, threatened B.O.A.C. that a strike of all the employees would take place within three days if the plaintiff non-unionist were not removed. In consequence, B.O.A.C. suspended and later (lawfully and with due notice) dismissed the plaintiff. Under a collective agreement between the union [and] B.O.A.C. the union agreed that employees would not strike. The strike would have been a breach of contract by employees as against B.O.A.C.
>
> It will be noted that the threats which were made were not made to the plaintiff. They were made to his employer, B.O.A.C., which lawfully dismissed the plaintiff. The threatened strike would have been a clear breach of the collective agreement between the union and B.O.A.C. His only recourse, if it existed, and the House of Lords found that it did, was against those persons whose threat to B.O.A.C. resulted in its dismissal of the plaintiff from its employment.
>
> Again, in view of my findings and conclusions set out earlier in these reasons, I hold that the plaintiff has proven intimidation by Houlahan as that term is defined by Martland J., supra. (at pp. 67-68)

In a 2 to 1 decision, however, the Court of Appeal reversed the trial Judge. The case turned on the issue of whether, as a matter of fact, the defendant not only threatened to resign but also threatened "to take the middle management of the company with him". A majority of the Court of Appeal found that there was no evidence to support such a finding while Mr. Brooke, in dissent, found that there was sufficient evidence to support this conclusion. The fact that the appeal was allowed does not, therefore, detract from the general principles of law discussed in the trial decision and the fact that the tort of intimidation may be established against an employee in comparable circumstances.

A defence to the tort of intimidation was successfully argued in *J.C. Kerkhoff & Sons Contracting Ltd. v. XL Ironworks Co.* (1983), 26 C.C.L.T. 1 (B.C.S.C.), reversed on other grounds (1984), 11 C.L.R. 230 (B.C. C.A.). The plaintiff was a general contractor and the defendant was a subcontractor who supplied and erected structural steel components. The union was also a defendant. The subcontractor and the plaintiff were negotiating a contract. The union told the subcontractor that the project which was the subject of the contract was unfair and, in accordance with the union's collective agreement with the subcontractor, no members of the local union would work on the site. Nevertheless, the plaintiff and the subcontractor entered into the contract. The subcontractor then refused to proceed with the contract because of the union's position. The plaintiff successfully sued the subcontractor for breach of contract. The plaintiff also sued the union on the basis of intimidation.

The Court held that when the subcontractor acquiesced to the union's threat, all the elements of the tort of intimidation against the plaintiff were *prima facie* satisfied, there being plainly an intention on the part of the union to injure the plaintiff. However, a defence arose because the union was found to have an honest belief that its collective agreement with the subcontractor permitted it to withhold workers from the job. This honest belief was held to constitute a defence. In finding that an honest belief existed the Court noted that the subcontractor did not question the union interpretation of the collective agreement or challenge the actions of the union before the Labour Board.

7.5 CONSPIRACY

In the case of *Nicholls v. Richmond*, 52 B.C.L.R. 302, [1984] 3 W.W.R. 719 (S.C.), additional reasons at 60 B.C.L.R. 320, 50 C.P.C. 171, [1975] 3

(*Continued on page 7-15*)

W.W.R. 543 (S.C.), the plaintiff had been employed as a solicitor by the defendant municipality. He was dismissed without notice. Part of his claim was against other employees of the municipality for conspiracy to secure his dismissal. Madam Justice McLachlin summarized the applicable legal principles:

> There are two categories of civil conspiracy: (1) where the predominant purpose of the defendants' conduct is to injure the plaintiff; and (2) where the defendants effect their agreed end by unlawful means knowing that the plaintiff may be injured. While only the first category is available in the United Kingdom since the decision in the House of Lords in *Lonrho Ltd. v. Shell Petroleum Ltd.*, [1982] A.C. 173, [1981] 3 W.L.R. 33, [1981] 2 All E.R. 456, both categories are recognized in Canada: *Can. Cement Lafarge Ltd. v. B.C. Lightweight Aggregate Ltd.*, [1983] 6 W.W.R. 385, 21 B.L.R. 254, 24 C.C.L.T. 111, 72 C.P.R. (2d) 1, 145 D.L.R. (3d) 385, 47 N.R. 191 (S.C.C.).
>
> The requirements of conspiracy to injure the plaintiff are an agreement between two or more persons whose predominant purpose is to injure the plaintiff and which when acted upon results in damage to the plaintiff. It is not a requirement that the conduct of the defendants in effecting their agreement be unlawful.
>
> The requirements of the second type of conspiracy, conspiracy by unlawful means, are an agreement between two or more persons which is effected by unlawful conduct where the defendants should know in the circumstances that damage to the plaintiff is likely to ensue and such damage does in fact ensue. Unlike the first category of conspiracy, it is not a requirement of conspiracy by unlawful means that the predominant purpose of the defendants be to cause injury to the plaintiff. Rather, a constructive intent is derived from the fact that the defendants should have known that damage to the plaintiff would result from their conduct. (at pp. 311-312)

Madam Justice McLachlin continued:

> The plaintiff submits that the evidence in the case at bar supports a finding of conspiracy under both categories.
>
> *The agreement*
>
> On either category of conspiracy, the plaintiff must show more than that the defendants independently intended to injure the plaintiff or to commit an unlawful act; an agreement must be established: *Mulcahy v. R.* (1868), L.R. 3 (H.L.) 306 at 317; *Crofter Hand Woven Harris Tweed Co. v. Veitch*, [1942] A.C. 435 at 469, [1942] 1 All E.R. 142 (H.L.).
>
> "Agreement" is not used in the formal sense of a binding contract but rather in the sense of a joint plan or common design: *Humphrey v. Wilson*, 25 B.C.R. 110, [1917] 3 W.W.R. 529 (S.C.); *Gee v. Freeman* (1958), 26 W.W.R. 546, 16 D.L.R. (2d) 65 (B.C.S.C.).
>
> Such an agreement can be proved by direct evidence. But it may also be inferred if the facts justify its inference on the basis of the following test set out by the Lord Chancellor in *Sweeney v. Coote*, [1907] A.C. 221 at 222 (H.L.):
>
> > In such a proceeding [i.e., where civil conspiracy is alleged] it is necessary for the plaintiff to prove a design, common to the defendant and to others, to damage the plaintiff, without just cause or excuse. That, at all events, it is

> necessary to prove. Now, a conclusion of that kind is not to be arrived at by a light conjecture; it must be plainly established. It may, like other conclusions, be established as a matter of inference from proved facts, but the point it is not whether you can draw that particular inference, but *whether the facts are such that they cannot fairly admit of any other inference being drawn from them.* (The italics are mine.)
>
> . . . .
>
> This evidence establishes that a number of the defendants, in some cases at the same time, wanted to terminate the plaintiff's employment. But, as noted above, independent intention to injure or to commit an unlawful act is insufficient: *Mulcahy v. R.; Crofter v. Veitch*, both supra. The question is whether it is plainly established, in the sense that "the facts cannot fairly admit of any other conclusion" (*Sweeney v. Coote*, supra), that there was a joint plan or common design to injure the plaintiff or commit an unlawful act.
>
> In my view, the evidence falls far short of such an inference. The alleged conspirators, whether elected officers or employees, were responsible for the efficient and proper running of the municipal corporation. That responsibility included securing the dismissal of employees whom they concluded should be replaced for the good of the municipality. The most natural inference to be drawn from the evidence, in my view, is that a number of them, largely as a consequence of different incidents, concluded independently that Mr. Nicholls should be replaced. To accept the inference for which the plaintiff contends would be to indulge in the "light conjecture" against which the Lord Chancellor in *Sweeney v. Coote* warned.
>
> I therefore conclude that an agreement, whether to injure the plaintiff or to commit an unlawful act, has not been established.
>
> *Intent to injure*
>
> Having concluded that no agreement is established, it is not necessary to deal with this issue. However, against the possibility I may be found to have erred in that conclusion, I state my conclusion on the issue of fact involved. In my opinion, the evidence does not establish that the predominant purpose of any of the defendants in question was to injure the plaintiff. It establishes, rather, that their concern was with the efficient running of the municipal corporation.
>
> *Conspiracy by unlawful means*
>
> If the means used by the defendants are actionable in tort independent of the conspiracy, or if they offend the criminal law, they are unlawful. Although there would appear to be no case deciding the point, it has been suggested that "a breach of contract should also provide the unlawful means necessary to support an action for conspiracy": Burns, "Civil Conspiracy: An Unwieldy Vessel Rides a Judicial Tempest" (1982), 16 Univ. of British Columbia L. Rev. 229 at p. 246.
>
> In view of my conclusion that no agreement to commit an unlawful act has been established, I need not consider this matter further than to note that in my view none of the defendants ever intended to commit a tort or breach of contract. The evidence shows that at all times they fully intended to fulfil the legal obligations imposed by the municipal corporation's contract with the plaintiff. This is illustrated by the fact that the council's resolution to terminate the plaintiff was coupled with an instruction to negotiate a satisfactory settlement with him. (at pp. 312-315)

7.6 INTENTIONAL INFLICTION OF MENTAL SUFFERING

An employer and fellow employees may be liable for the mental anguish they cause to an employee. This is especially true in wrongful dismissal situations where allegations are made regarding the employee's trustworthiness.

In *Rahemtulla v. Vanfed Credit Union*, 4 C.C.E.L. 170, 51 B.C.L.R. 200, 29 C.C.L.T. 78, [1984] 3 W.W.R. 296 (S.C.), the employee was a teller for the employer. One day another teller's balance was short by $2,000. On this same day the other teller had transferred large bills to the employee. The employee was called in on her day off regarding the missing money. The supervisor who interviewed the employee told her she should admit she had "borrowed" the money for one day or she would be fired. He also stated that he would spend $10,000 if necessary to get to the bottom of things. The employee denied the supervisor's allegations and was dismissed. The Court awarded Rahemtulla $5,000 in damages for the tort of intentional infliction of mental suffering instead of mental distress damages arising from breach of contract. The fact situation is of the type, however, which could easily result in an award of damages for mental distress occasioned by a breach of contract following the decision in *Vorvis*.

Referring to the tort of intentional infliction of mental suffering Madam Justice McLachlin stated:

> The law has long recognized as tortious the uttering of false words or threats with the knowledge that they are likely to cause, and which actually cause, nervous shock and physical injury. One of the earliest cases to set out this duty was *Wilkinson v. Downton*, [1897] 2 Q.B. 57. In that case the defendant falsely represented to the plaintiff that her husband had been injured in an accident, inducing a state of nervous shock, vomiting and prolonged mental and physical suffering. Lord Wright stated at pp. 58-59:
>
>> The defendant has, as I assume for the moment, wilfully done an act calculated to cause physical harm to the plaintiff - that is to say, to infringe her legal right to personal safety, and has in fact thereby caused physical harm to her. That proposition without more appears to me to state a good cause of action, there being no justification alleged for the act. This wilful injuria is in law malicious, although no malicious purpose to cause the harm which was caused nor any motive of spite is imputed to the defendant.
>
> This statement of law was adopted in *Janvier v. Sweeney et al.*, [1919] 2 K.B. 316 (C.A.). In that case two private detectives, in an attempt to persuade the plaintiff to show them certain letters, represented themselves as associated with the military and falsely accused her of having corresponded with a German spy. The plaintiff suffered nervous shock and fell ill. It was held that she could recover damages for the injuries she had sustained.
>
> These authorities have been accepted and applied in Canada: *Purdy v. Woznesensky*, [1937] 2 W.W.R. 116 (Sask. C.A.); *Abramzik v. Brenner* (1967), 62 W.W.R. 332, 65 D.L.R. (2d) 651 (Sask. C.A.). In the latter case, Culliton J.A. stated at p. 654:

> There can be no doubt but that an action will lie for the wilful infliction of shock, or a reckless disregard as to whether or not shock will ensue from the act committed.

In the case at Bar, the defendant's agent, Mr. Flack, accused the plaintiff of having stolen $2,000. Accepting that his motive may not have been to inflict shock upon her, but rather to extort a confession and solve the mystery of the missing funds, the fact remains that at very least he acted with a reckless disregard as to whether or not shock would ensue from his accusation. In this respect, the facts are analogous to those in *Janvier v. Sweeney*, where the defendants were found liable notwithstanding the absence of malicious purpose to cause the harm which was caused nor any motive of spite imputed to them.

Counsel for the defendant submitted that for the defendant to be held liable for wilful infliction of nervous shock its conduct must be found to be outrageous. He contended that Mr. Flack was acting bona fide in the interests of the credit union, and that his conduct to this end could not be characterized as flagrant or extreme.

This submission appears to be founded upon the distinction drawn in American cases between mere insult, which is not actionable, and "extreme and outrageous conduct" which is: Linden: Canadian Tort Law (3rd ed.), 48. While this distinction appears not to have been expressly adopted in the Canadian and Commonwealth cases, the conduct considered in the leading authorities such as *Wilkinson v. Downton*, supra, and *Janvier v. Sweeney*, supra, was in fact flagrant and extreme. Moreover, it is difficult to accept that the Courts should protect persons from every practical joke or unkind comment.

Assuming, therefore, that only flagrant and extreme conduct inflicting mental suffering is actionable, the question is whether the defendant's conduct can be so described. In my view, it can. Mr. Flack's conduct went beyond mere insult. His accusation was made in threatening circumstances of the utmost gravity. His conduct was, in my view, equally reprehensible as that of a person posing as a military policeman and accusing another of corresponding with a German spy (*Janvier v. Sweeney*, supra), or of a finance company bombarding one of its debtors who is ill (to its knowledge) with offensive and threatening letters (*Clark v. Associated Retail Credit* (1939), 105 Fed. 2d 62; see also *Robbins v. C.B.C. (Que.)*, [1958] Que S.C. 152, 12 D.L.R. (2d) 35) — cases where liability has been imposed.

Allegations of theft should not be made recklessly, without proper care for whether they are true or not. This applies even in a financial institution where great care must be taken in the management of money of others. While the financial institution has the right to dismiss a suspect employee without investigation, the proper conduct of its affairs does not require that it be given the right to make reckless and very possibly untruthful accusations as to the employee's honesty which will foreseeably inflict shock and mental suffering. Considering all these circumstances, I am satisfied that Mr. Flack's conduct can fairly be described as flagrant and outrageous.

A further requirement of the tort of wilful infliction of mental distress is that the defendant's conduct be "plainly calculated to produce some effect of the kind which was produced": *Wilkinson v. Downton*, supra, at p. 59. In the case at Bar this element is established. It was clearly foreseeable that the accusations of theft which the defendant made against the plaintiff would cause her profound dis-

> tress. That distress could only be exacerbated by the defendant's failure to conduct a proper investigation or allow the plaintiff to defend herself. It was equally foreseeable that the accusations would continue to cause distress into the future, when, in seeking employment, she would be queried by prospective employers as to the reasons for her dismissal from the defendant's employ.
>
> Finally, it must be established that the conduct produced actual harm, a "visible and provable illness": *Radovskis v. Tomn* (1957), 21 W.W.R. 658 at 664, 65 Man. R. 61, 9 D.L.R. (2d) 751 (Q.B.). I have earlier described the distress which the plaintiff suffered as a consequence of the defendant's accusations. Notwithstanding the absence of expert medical evidence, I am satisfied that the plaintiff suffered depression accompanied by symptoms of physical illness as a result of Mr. Flack's accusations. (at pp. 184-186)

In *Clark v. Canada*, 3 C.C.E.L. (2d) 172, 20 C.C.L.T. (2d) 241, (*sub nom. Clark v. R.*) 94 C.L.L.C. 14,028, [1994] 3 F.C. 323, 76 F.T.R. 241 (T.D.), the Court considered the vicarious liability of the employer, in this case the Government of Canada, for conduct on the part of officers in the R.C.M.P. who condoned the harassment of a female constable. The harassment included advising the female constable that "she wasn't a real woman until she had a child," "that she should go home and start a family" and that she was a "butch" and a "metermaid". On one occasion a pair of plastic breasts were taped to her work station with her regimental number and "RCMP GIRL" written on them.

The Court concluded that the tort of intentional infliction of nervous shock had been established stating:

> I am satisfied that the evidence reviewed above establishes that the conduct directed toward the plaintiff was extreme, and calculated "to produce some effect of the kind which was produced." I have also concluded that the plaintiff's mental and physical deterioration until her reassignment in February 1987 meets the third criterion outlined in *Rahemtulla* [*v. Vanfed Credit Union*, 4 C.C.E.L. 170, 29 C.C.L.T. 78, [1984] 3 W.W.R. 296, 51 B.C.L.R. 200 (S.C.)], i.e., actual harm in the form of illness. [Footnote omitted.] (at 3 C.C.E.L. (2d), p. 195)

The Court also found that the conduct of the defendant was negligent and that the employer was liable for damages caused by such negligence. In the result, the Court awarded the plaintiff $88,000 for lost earnings over a period of approximately three years and $5,000 to provide the plaintiff "a reasonable measure of consolation" for the intentional infliction of nervous shock.

7.7 NEGLIGENT MISREPRESENTATION

In the case of *Queen v. Cognos Inc.*, 45 C.C.E.L. 1, [1993] 1 S.C.R. 87, 14 C.C.L.T. (2d) 113, 147 N.R. 169, 60 O.A.C. 1, 99 D.L.R. (4th) 629, 93 C.L.L.C. 14,019, reversing (1990), 30 C.C.E.L. 1, 74 O.R. (2d) 176, 90 C.L.L.C. 14,024, 69 D.L.R. (4th) 288, 38 O.A.C. 180 (C.A.), reversing (1987), 18 C.C.E.L. 146, 63 O.R. (2d) 389 (H.C.), the employee was a chartered accountant. He left previous employment to join the defendant, which was developing a new "Multiview" computer program to be used by accountants. At his interview the employee was assured by Sean Johnston, the Multiview product development manager, that sales of the program were high, that other versions would be created and that the defendant was committed to the Multiview project. Relying on these assurances the employee joined the defendant pursuant to an employment contract which provided that in the event of termination he would be entitled to receive one month's notice in addition to any notice required by statute. Soon after he commenced employment, senior management of the defendant turned down a proposal by Johnston to fund the development of the Multiview program. The employee was eventually terminated and given three months' notice of termination.

The findings of fact made by the trial Judge were quoted in the reasons of the Supreme Court of Canada as follows:

> I find that misrepresentations were made to the [appellant] by Sean Johnston in the hiring interview. The effect of these misrepresentations was that the [appellant] would have a position in the research and development of the product "Multiview"; that that position would be a significant one and would involve his expertise as an accountant; that he would perform the responsible role of seeing to proper accounting standards being implemented into the product; that beyond the three modules immediately in contemplation were a minimum of four other modules; and that the project of "Multiview", in connection with which [the appallent] would be hired would last a minimum of two years. I find further that Mr. Johnston implicitly represented that management had made a firm budgetary commitment to the develoment of four other modules in addition to those presently under development.
>
> I find further, in all the circumstances, that Sean Johnston made those misrepresentations negligently. Based upon his expertise in the field of computer development, he was aware, according to his evidence, that until there is a feasibility study in which cost estimates have been submitted to and have been considered and approved by senior management, one could not say that the [respondent] had made a firm commitment to the project as Mr. Johnston envisaged it and as he described it to [the appellant] in the interview. (at p. 12,087, quoting (1987), 63 O.R. (2d) 389, at pp. 415-416)

The reasons of the Supreme Court of Canada respecting the findings at trial continued:

> Other circumstances which the trial judge took into consideration in concluding that the misrepresentations were negligently made include the following: (1) Mr. Johnston knew, or ought to have known, that the truth of his representations depended on the approval by the corporate management team of the cost estimates he had prepared for the research and development of the Multiview project; (2) it is reasonable to infer that Mr. Johnston, at the time of the interview, contemplated that the budgetary needs for the Multiview project would be substantial and that approval was at best speculative; (3) Mr. Johnston must have been aware of the continued poor sales performance of the Multiview product line; (4) Mr. Johnston did not disclose to the appellant that senior management had not yet given the financial commitment required to make the plans for the Multiview project a probable reality; (5) Mr. Johnston's expertise in the computer development field should have made him aware that, notwithstanding his conversations with senior management and the meeting of December 21, 1982, there was still a considerable risk that senior man-

> agement would not give budgetary approval to his plans; (6) Mr. Johnston knew that the appellant was relying on the information he was providing during the interview; (7) Mr. Johnston knew that the appellant had a secure, responsible, and well-paying employment as a chartered accountant in Calgary and that coming to Ottawa would involve moving himself and his family across the country; and (8) Mr. Johnston was aware that the appellant was relying on the position with Cognos to enhance his career significantly as an accountant. (at p. 12,087, per Iacobucci J.)
>
> . . . .
>
> White J. further found that the appellant had relied upon the negligent misrepresentions, to his detriment, and that he had sustained substantial damages (at p. 419):
>
>> The misrepresentations induced [the appellant] to quit his job as controller of the Calgary Division of Genstar Development Corporation and to accept employment with the [respondent]. Those representations induced him to sign the contract of employment. But for those representations he would have remained working for the Genstar Development Corporation for some further period of time and would not have become an employee of the [respondent]. (at p. 12,088)

The Court of Appeal had concluded that there was no liability for negligent misrepresentation on the basis that:

1. Johnston believed that representations he had made were true;

(*Continued on page 7-21*)

2. the employment contract signed by Queen contained a termination provision that operated to exclude or limit liability for any misrepresentation.

The Supreme Court of Canada disagreed and allowed a further appeal, summarizing the legal principles, derived from the decision of the House of Lords in *Hedley Byrne & Co. v. Heller & Partners, Ltd.*, [1964] A.C. 465, [1963] W.L.R. 101, [1963] 2 All E.R. 575 at 589, [1963] 1 Lloyd's Rep. 485, as follows:

> The required elements for a successful *Hedley Byrne*, supra, claim have been stated in many authorities, sometimes in varying forms. The decisions of this Court cited above suggest five general requirements: (1) there must be a duty of care based on a "special relationship" between the representor and the representee; (2) the representation in question must be untrue, inaccurate, or misleading; (3) the representor must have acted negligently in making said misrepresentation; (4) the representee must have relied, in a reasonable manner, on said negligent misrepresentation; and (5) the reliance must have been detrimental to the representee in the sense that damages resulted. In the case at bar, the trial judge found that all elements were present and allowed the appellant's claim. (at p. 12,090)
>
> . . . .
>
> While the doctrine of *Hedley Byrne*, supra, is well established in Canada, the exact breadth of its applicability is, like any common law principle, subject to debate and to continuous development. At the time this appeal was heard, there have only been a handful of cases where the tort of negligent misrepresentation was used in a pre-employment context such as the one involved here: see *Steer v. Aerovox Inc.* (1984), 65 N.S.R. (2d) 91 (S.C.T.D.); *H.B. Nickerson & Sons Ltd. v. Woolridge* (1980), 115 D.L.R. (3d) 97 (N.S.S.C.A.D.); *Williams v. School District No. 63 (Saanich)* (1986), 11 C.C.E.L. 233 (B.C.S.C.), aff'd on other grounds (1987), 17 C.C.E.L. 257 (B.C.C.A.); *Grenier v. Timmins Board of Education*, Ont. H.C., No. 1250/82, May 31, 1984, 26 A.C.W.S. (2d) 285; *Pettit v. Prince George & District Credit Union* (1991), 35 C.C.E.L. 140 (B.C.S.C.); and *Roy v. B.N.P.P. Regional Police Commission* (1986), 15 C.C.E.L. 167 (N.B.Q.B.). Without question, the present factual situation is a novel one for this court. (at p. 12,090)

The Supreme Court of Canada then considered the impact of the later employment contract, which stipulated a fixed entitlement in the event of termination stating:

> When considering the effect of the subsequent contract on the representee's tort action, everything revolves around the nature of the contractual obligations assumed by the parties and the nature of the alleged negligent misrepresentation. The first and foremost question should be whether there is a specific contractual duty created by an express term of the contract which is co-extensive with the common law duty of care which the representee alleges the representor has breached. Put another way, did the pre-contractual representation relied on by the plaintiff become an express term of the subsequent contract? If so, absent any overriding considerations arising from the context in which the transaction occurred, the plaintiff cannot bring a concurrent action in tort for negligent

> misrepresentation and is confined to whatever remedies are available under the law of contract. The authorities supporting this proposition, including the decision of this Court in *Central Trust Co. v. Rafuse*, [1986] 2 S.C.R. 147, are fully canvassed in my reasons in *BG Checo* [*BG Checo International Ltd. v. British Columbia Hydro & Power Authority*, [1993] 2 W.W.R. 321 (S.C.C.)]. As alluded to in *BG Checo*, this principle is an exception to the general rule of concurrency espoused by this Court in *Central Trust v. Rafuse*, supra. (at p. 12,091)

The Supreme Court of Canada had no difficulty in concluding that the contractual term relating to termination was not co-extensive or in relation to the same subject-matter as the alleged negligent misrepresentation. This was aptly explained in concurring reasons by Madam Justice McLachlin who noted:

> I agree that the pre-contractual representation was different in scope and effect from the contractual obligation. The matter is not merely one of semantics. It turns on the plaintiff's assessment of the risk involved in leaving his employment and joining Cognos. When a person is deciding to enter a contract with terms governing termination, he or she makes an assessment as to the risk of such termination occurring. A stringent term as to termination may not deter the person from entering into the contract if he or she is satisfied that the risk of termination materializing is low. The representation at issue in this case concerned the risk of termination coming about. The representation was not that Cognos would have the discretion to terminate or transfer the plaintiff on one month's notice. Rather, by implying that the Multiview project was a reality, that it had the financial support of Cognos, and that it had passed through the feasibility and costing stage, Johnston on behalf of Cognos caused the plaintiff to be misled as to the level of the risk to the plaintiff that Cognos might at some point choose to exercise its termination power under the employment contract. The plaintiff, believing Johnston, concluded that the risk of being transferred or terminated was low. (at p. 12,103)

The Court then concluded that Johnston, on behalf of Cognos, had breached the duty of care owned to Queen by representing the positive aspects of the employment opportunity without disclosing the "precarious nature of the respondent's financial commitment to Multiview." In the result Queen was awarded damages of approximately $67,000, including $50,000 for loss of income and $5,000 in general damages for mental distress.

7.8 INJURIOUS FALSEHOOD

Procor Ltd. v. U.S.W.A. (1989), 71 O.R. (2d) 410, 65 D.L.R. (4th) 287 (H.C.), additional reasons at (1990), 71 O.R. (2d) 410 at 434, 65 D.L.R. (4th) 287 at 310 (H.C.), provides a useful summary of the law and a particularly interesting example of how the tort of injurious falsehood can arise in an employment context. The plaintiff was a manufacturer and importer of metal screws and other fasteners. The defendants included the union representing the plaintiff's employees and local, regional and national executives of the union.

The plaintiff had traditionally imported from Japan small quantities of fasteners of a type not ordinarily manufactured in Canada. In late 1983, however, the plaintiff anticipated a lengthy strike at its Montreal manufacturing facility and in order to provide for that contingency ordered a large quantity of fasteners from Japan of the type ordinarily manufactured in Montreal. The plaintiff's ordinary packaging specified ''made in Canada'' and the plaintiff adopted a means of obliterating this marking, with respect to the origin of the product, when packaging the Japanese-made product.

Labour-management relations were poor. In March of 1984 the plaintiff posted a lay-off notice at its Milton, Ontario facility and shortly thereafter the union notified Canada and U.S. customs that the plaintiff was involved in a longstanding and elaborate ''Customs fraud'' in relation to Japanese-manufactured product.

Mr. Justice Rosenberg listed the following false information provided by union officials to the Customs authorities:

> (a) that the individual members of the local bargaining unit had personal knowledge of the detailed facts supporting the allegation;
> (b) that there was a deliberate attempt to obscure and hide the difference between Japanese and Canadian product, for example, by removing the mark in the head of the screws that could be found on Canadian product caused by the dye used in manufacturing the Canadian product;
> (c) that there were and had been two truck-loads of Japanese product per week going to the United States on a regular basis;
> (d) that the Japanese product represented 90% of the production of the plaintiff and that the plaintiff was only manufacturing 10% of the product and then only for special orders with special specifications;
> (e) that the amount of Japanese product being shipped to the United States was more than the company could produce in Canada if it operated for 24 hours per day on all of its equipment and they were not operating at full capacity;
> (f) that the labelling practices and their constant changing was to obscure rather than identify the country of origin;
> (g) that the Japanese product was inferior and being passed on to unsuspecting customers;
> (h) that the customers constantly rejected Japanese product and that there were a number of customers who would not accept Japanese product;
> (i) that the screws imported from Japan could be and in the recent past had been manufacturered in Milton. (at p. 422)

In the result His Lordship concluded that:

> [t]he defendants acted in concert and presented a well-organized and documented case of Customs fraud. The case was founded on falsehoods, half-truths and innuendos. (at p. 429)

The plaintiff suffered substantial damages as a result of the union's allegations. The plaintiff's trucks were frequently stopped or delayed at the border and one truck was turned back. The plaintiff's operation was disrupted by a search and seizure of documentation by Customs officials and the plaintiff incurred substantial legal expenses in that regard. Further, substantial executive and staff time was devoted to dealing with the disruption and refuting the false allegations.

Turning to the law Mr. Justice Rosenberg stated:

> The tort of injurious falsehood requires the making of a false statement with "malice" to some person other than the plaintiff as a result of which the plaintiff suffers damage. W. V. H. Rogers, *Winfield and Jolowicz on Tort*, 12th ed., at p. 288. . . . (at p. 419)
>
> . . . .
>
> The plaintiff having proved publication of falsehoods concerning the plaintiff to third persons which has caused the plaintiff actual damage to succeed must also prove malice. Malice has been described as the absence of *bona fides* proven or reasonably inferred from the facts. Malice in the law of injurious falsehoods is sometimes equated with dishonest or improper motive. Honest belief in an unfounded claim is not malice but the nature of the unfounded claim may be evidence that there was not an honest belief in it. It may be so unfounded that the particular fact that is put forward may be evidence that it is not honestly believed: see *London Ferro-Concrete Co. v. Justicz* (1951), 68 R.P.C. 261 (C.A.). (at p. 420)

Having regard to the facts, the Court had little difficulty in finding that the defendants had acted with malice. The Court awarded the plaintiff $100,000 in general damages, $100,000 in punitive damages and costs on a solicitor-and-client scale. Such costs, after 21 days of trial, were estimated to be approximately $350,000.

While the facts in *Procor* were unusual it is certainly not unheard of for union and non-union employees to engage in similar types of guerrilla warfare. Given the encouragement of the decision in *Procor* it is probable that more actions will be brought in the future claiming damages for the tort of injurious falsehood.

7.9 NEGLIGENCE

In *Clark v. Canada*, 3 C.C.E.L. (2d) 172, 20 C.C.L.T. (2d) 241, (*sub nom. Clark v. R.*) 94 C.L.L.C. 14,028, [1994] 3 F.C. 323, 76 F.T.R. 241 (T.D.), the Court considered the vicarious liability of the employer, in this case the Government of Canada, for conduct on the part of officers in the R.C.M.P. who condoned the harassment of a female constable. The harassment included advising the female constable that "she wasn't a real woman until she had a child", "that she should go home and start a family" and that she was a "butch" and a "metermaid". On one occasion a pair of plastic breasts were taped to her work station with her regimental number and "RCMP GIRL" written on them.

The Court concluded that the tort of negligence had been established stating:

> In order to engage the Crown's vicarious liability under this heading, a plaintiff must show:
>
> . . . (i) that he was owed a duty of care by the [Crown servant]; (ii) that the [Crown servant] should have observed a particular standard of care in order to

perform or fulfil that duty; (iii) that he broke his duty of care by failing to fulfil or observe the relevant standard of care; (iv) that such breach of duty caused damage or loss to the plaintiff; (v) that such damage was not too remote a consequence of the breach so as to render the [Crown servant] not liable for its occurrence.

Canadian courts have used a two-step approach to the test of duty adapted from the classic cases of *M'Alister (or Donoghue) v. Stevenson* [[1932] A.C. 562 (H.L.)] and *Anns v. Merton London Borough Council* [[1977] 2 W.L.R. 1024 (H.L.)]:

> (1) is there a sufficiently close relationship between the parties . . . so that, in the reasonable contemplation of the [defendant], carelessness on its part might cause damage to that person? If so,
>
> (2) are there any considerations which ought to negative or limit (a) the scope of the duty and (b) the class of persons to whom it is owed or (c) the damages to which a breach of it may give rise?

The question whether a duty exists in a given situation is one of law. As to the standard of care required, it is that of the reasonable ordinary man or woman. It is an objective standard. Fridman [*Fridman on Torts*, 8th ed. (Sydney: The Law Book Co., 1992)] summarizes relevant considerations as follows:

> Negligence in law . . . means some failure to do some act which a reasonable man in the circumstances would do, or doing some act which a reasonable man in the circumstances would not do. The test of whether this act or failure is negligent is whether it would be adjudged so by the "man in the street".

I am satisfied that the evidence also establishes negligence that engages the Crown's vicarious liability. In my view there is no doubt that as the plaintiff's immediate supervisor, Cpl. Mazur owed the plaintiff a duty of care and breached that duty consistently. I find that over a lengthy period, he deliberately refused to exercise his authority to put an end to the conduct of harassment of which he was well aware and which he in fact participated in on occasion, thus condoning that behaviour. He further neglected utterly to respond to the plaintiff's distress signals as his position of responsibility required him to do. And, as mentioned earlier, superior R.C.M.P. officers failed to come to the plaintiff's assistance.

In my view, the circumstances of this case present no issue of remoteness or foreseeability. Corporal Mazur was not an unconcerned bystander without authority to exert control over the behaviour of his subordinates; his negligence played a direct causative role in the damage suffered by the plaintiff, and he was clearly acting in the course of his employment. [Footnotes omitted.] (at 3 C.C.E.L. (2d), pp. 197-198)

The Court also found that the conduct of the defendant constituted the tort of intentional infliction of nervous shock. In the result, the Court awarded the plaintiff $88,000 for lost earnings over a period of approximately three years and $5,000 to provide the plaintiff "a reasonable measure of consolation" for the intentional infliction of nervous shock.

7.10 EMPLOYER LIABILITY FOR EMPLOYEE TORTS

In certain circumstances an employer will be found vicariously liable for an employee's torts. An employer's liability in these circumstances does not stem from an action by the employer, but from the employee's torts committed in the course of his employment. In addition to acts committed in the normal course of employment, the employer is also liable for either

1. a wrongful act authorized by the employer, or
2. a wrongful and unauthorized mode of doing some act authorized by the employer.

The second branch of the test means that an employer is responsible not only for what he authorizes his employee to do, but also for the way in which the employee does the task, provided that the acts are still connected with those which the employee was authorized to do. If the unauthorized and wrongful act is not so connected with the authorized act as to be a mode of doing it, but is an independent act, the employer is not responsible. In such a case the employee is not acting within the course of employment.

In *Boothman v. R.*, 49 C.C.E.L. 109, [1993] 3 F.C. 381 (*sub nom. Boothman v. Canada*) 63 F.T.R. 48 (T.D.), the Court considered a case in which the plaintiff had been subjected to intimidation and abuse by her supervisor. The Court concluded that the Crown was liable for the acts of its employee stating, in reference to the supervisor:

> Mr. Stalinski was without supervision. He had ultimate authority to hire, and exercised that authority in a wrongful manner. He was the sole authority in a two person office and, after having been placed in that position by his employer, he used that authority to inflict upon plaintiff mental pain and suffering, to harass her, intimidate her, interfere with her, and on occasion assault her. He was placed in this position notwithstanding the fact that Mr. Sherwin and other senior officials of COGLA knew him to be a difficult individual, abrasive in his behaviour, evasive vis-à-vis his responsibilities, and prone to losses of temper.
>
> The evidence indicates the occurrence of a prior event where, again, a female employee working alone under Mr. Stalinski's orders left her job after suffering a mental breakdown. If senior officials in Ottawa failed to make the connection between the two occurrences, Mr. Stalinski did not as is evidenced by his memorandum of September 1984 to Don Sherwin wherein, in an attempt to get plaintiff terminated, he stated:
>
>> My concern was that Ms. Boothman was exhibiting certain mannerisms also exhibited by a former employee who had some rather serious personality disorders that made it impossible for them to function in a normal work environment.
>
> In my view, when an employer places an employee in a special position of trust, he or she bears the responsibility of ensuring that the employee is capable of trust. That is the rationale which stands behind the vicarious liability of an employer.
>
> Mr. Stalinski used the position of trust in which he was placed by his employer to cause harm to the plaintiff. In so doing, he was acting in the course of his employment and the defendant's liability was thereby engaged. (at pp. 135-136)

In *Clark v. Canada*, 3 C.C.E.L. (2d) 172, 20 C.C.L.T. (2d) 241, (*sub nom. Clark v. R.*) 94 C.L.L.C. 14,028, [1994] 3 F.C. 323, 76 F.T.R. 241 (T.D.), the

Court considered an action by a female former member of the R.C.M.P. alleging that she had been sexually harassed by male officers and that R.C.M.P. supervisors failed to intervene on her behalf. The harassment as described by the Court included the following:

1. telling her "that she wasn't a real woman until she had a child . . .";
2. telling her "that she should go home and start a family . . .";
3. other members referred to her as a "butch" and a "metermaid" . . .";
4. Corporal T.C. Steves began viewing a pornographic movie in the same work area occupied by the plaintiff. She complained, and was told to "hit the road" if she didn't like it;
5. she arrived at her work station to find a pair of plastic breasts taped to her work station with her regimental number and "RCMP GIRL" written on them;
6. on another occasion, members of the Force were displaying the centrefold of a Playboy magazine. When she objected to Cpl. Mazur, he told her they would appreciate it for her;
7. a suit of soft body-armour she had ordered was placed in her basket in an open area of the detachment with "Your playtex cross your heart soft-armour bra" written on the packaging.

The Court found that the Crown was liable, having regard to the principle stated in *Boothman* [*v. R.*, 49 C.C.E.L. 109, [1993] 3 F.C. 381, (*sub nom. Boothman v. Canada*) 63 F.T.R. 48], for the intentional infliction of nervous shock by the fellow R.C.M.P. officers. In this regard, the Court was satisfied that the conduct was in the course of employment.

The Court also found that the Crown, as employer, was vicariously liable for the negligence of the supervisory R.C.M.P. officers stating:

> I am satisfied that the evidence also establishes negligence that engages the Crown's vicarious liability. In my view there is not doubt that as the plaintiff's immediate supervisor, Cpl. Mazur owed the plaintiff a duty of care and breached that duty consistently. I find that over a lengthy period, he deliberately refused to exercise his authority to put an end to the conduct or harassment of which he was well aware and which he in fact participated in on occasion, thus condoning that behaviour. He further neglected utterly to respond to the plaintiff's distress signals as his position of responsibility required him to do. And, as mentioned earlier, superior R.C.M.P. officers failed to come to the plaintiff's assistance. (at 3 C.C.E.L. (2d), p. 198)

In *Plains Engineering Ltd. v. Barnes Security Services Ltd.* (1987), 19 C.C.E.L. 205, 56 Alta. L.R. (2d) 331, 43 C.C.L.T. 129, 83 A.R. 170 (Q.B.), the defendant employer employed a guard who, while on duty, set a building on fire. The owners of the building sued the defendant's employer for the employee's act. The Court stated that,

> if one of two innocent parties must suffer a loss by reason of the wrongful act of an employee of one of the parties, it is more reasonable that the party who employs and

> puts a trust in the employee should be the loser. This statement is tempered where the unauthorized or wrongful act complained of is not connected with the authorized act for which the employer has been engaged so as to be considered to be a mode or method of doing the authorized act, but is an independent act of the employee. In the determination of this issue it is necessary to discover what acts the employer has been authorized to perform and for whom and how such acts are connected to the party suffering the loss. Following this it is necessary to discover whether the employee's wrongful act is so connected with the authorized act as to be regarded as a means or mode of carrying out or performing the authorized act. If the employee's wrongful act is wilful or deliberate, the employer will only be liable if the *tortious* act by the employee is of the same general kind as the employee was authorized to carry out on behalf of the employer, and where the resultant loss can be connected to the employer. (at p. 225)

The Court found that the act of setting fire to the building was not sufficiently connected with the authorized act of providing security services. As a result, the defendant was found not to be vicariously liable for its employee's tort.

On the other hand an employer can be found vicariously liable for its employee's torts in connection with carrying out an authorized activity, even where the employer expressly prohibits the employee from performing certain acts. For example, in *Rose v. Plenty* (1975), [1976] 1 W.L.R. 141, [1976] 1 All E.R. 97, [1976] 1 Lloyd's Rep. 263 (C.A.), an employer was found liable when a milkman employed by the employer allowed a 13-year-old boy on his truck to help him deliver milk, even though he was expressly prohibited from allowing anyone on his truck. The milkman was negligent while driving the truck and the 13-year-old boy was injured. The Court stated that one had to look at the purpose for which the act was done, in order to determine if the act was within the scope of the employee's employment. In this case the act was done for the benefit of the employer's business and, therefore, it was done in the course of employment. The course of the milkman's employment was to distribute the milk, collect the money and to bring back the bottles to the van. He allowed the 13-year-old boy to help him, which was in furtherance of the employer's business. Although the conduct was prohibited it was within the course of the milkman's employment and, therefore, the employer was held responsible.

An issue that one also must consider when determining whether an employer is responsible for his employee's tortious acts is whether the employee is actually an employee or an independent contractor. Generally, an employer is not liable for the acts of an independent contractor. (See Chapter 3.5 regarding the distinction between employees and independent contractors.)

8

STATUTORY OBLIGATIONS RESPECTING TERMINATION PAYMENTS

8.1 INCOME TAX ACT

(a) Retiring Allowance

The definition of "retiring allowance" is found in section 248(1) of the *Income Tax Act*, S.C. 1970-71-72, c. 63, as amended:

> "retiring allowance" means an amount (other than a superannuation or pension benefit, an amount received as a consequence of the death of an employee or a benefit described in subparagraph 6(1)(a)(iv)) received
>
> (*a*) upon or after retirement of a taxpayer from an office or employment in recognition of his long service, or
>
> (*b*) in respect of a loss of an office or employment of a taxpayer, whether or not received as, on account or in lieu of payment of, damages or pursuant to an order or judgment of a competent tribunal
>
> by the taxpayer or, after his death, by a dependant or a relation of the taxpayer or by the legal representative of the taxpayer;

Having regard to the broad definition of "retiring allowance," virtually any type of termination or severance payment made to an employee is to be included in the employee's income. This income inclusion is required whether or not the severance payment is made under a negotiated settlement or a court order. Further, the Department of National Revenue has taken a broad approach to the interpretation of the terms "retirement" and "loss" of employment. Paragraphs 3 and 4 of Interpretation Bulletin IT-337R2, dated May 22, 1984, provide:

3. To be a retiring allowance, the payment must be received upon or after retirement or be paid in respect of a loss of an office or employment. Subject to 4 below, the Department accepts the cessation of employment for any reason as being retirement or loss of employment.

4. Retirement or loss of employment does not include:

(a) transfer from one office or position to another with the same employer, but the mere continuation as a director at nominal compensation is an exception,
(b) termination of employment (other than mandatory retirement) with an employer followed shortly by employment with an affiliate of the former employer, or
(c) termination of employment as a result of death. . . .

Not all amounts paid to an employee at the time of severance will constitute a retiring allowance. For example, where an employee has been paid an artificially low amount over the term of a contract and receives a large lump sum amount upon termination (i.e., a golden parachute), Revenue Canada may take the position that the amount is paid not as compensation for loss of employment or in recognition of long service, but rather as deferred compensation.

Up until now, most employers have assumed that the money paid to employees upon termination of their employment qualified as a retiring allowance for income tax purposes. Recently, however, the proper tax treatment of ''pay in lieu of notice'' under the federal *Income Tax Act* has come into question. It appears that certain amounts that have traditionally been considered to qualify as a ''retiring allowance'' may now be considered by Revenue Canada as ''salary or wages.''

This apparent change is relevant to both employers and employees. For employers, the characterization of pay in lieu of notice for tax purposes has an impact on the determination of the correct amount to be withheld from the sum paid (*e.g.*, in income tax, unemployment insurance, etc.) and the correct tax reporting of the sum paid. For employees, the characterization determines whether an amount qualifies for transfer to a registered retirement savings plan (''RRSP''), as described in Chapter 8.1(f).

Revenue Canada, in several responses to questions raised, has indicated that in its view, pay in lieu of notice is different from a retiring allowance. Notice pay, it has indicated, should be treated as regular salary.

In the positions that it is taking, Revenue Canada is making a distinction between amounts paid in lieu of notice and amounts paid in recognition of long service or in respect of a loss of employment. From a common law perspective, it is generally thought that an amount paid in respect of a loss of employment is, in other words, pay in lieu of notice. Pay in lieu of notice arises in two scenarios. In the first, amounts are paid under the relevant employment standards legislation. In the second, amounts are paid under the terms of a negotiated employment contract. Revenue Canada is taking the more definitive position with respect to amounts paid under the relevant employment standards legislation.

For example, it is Revenue Canada's position that statutory termination pay under section 57 of the *E.S.A.* does not form part of a retiring allowance. Rather, it constitutes regular salary and wages, subject to normal withholdings, and is not qualified to be treated as a retiring allowance. Revenue Canada has further confirmed that statutory severance pay under section 58 of the *E.S.A.* will be a retiring allowance. In light of these comments, when paying an amount considered to be termination pay in accordance with the applicable employment standards legislation, income tax, Canada Pension Plan and Unemployment Insurance should be calculated and deducted as they would be if the amount was salary or wages. The amount paid as statutory severance pay would generally (subject to the discussion below) be treated as a retiring allowance.

With respect to amounts generally paid under an employment contract (other than the minimum statutory requirements), Revenue Canada has stated that

> a payment in lieu of earnings for the period of reasonable notice which is made by virtue of the terms of an employment contract (whether implied or explicit) will be treated as employment income and not as a retiring allowance. Requirements of employment standards legislation are terms of the employment contract and, therefore, the payment relating to the legislation's minimum notice requirement is a term of the employment contract. If the parties agree during the negotiations that after termination the employee is entitled to a notice period greater that that provided by employment standards legislation, then a payment in lieu of such additional notice is also employment income since the employee's right to it was an implicit term of the employment contract. . . . Such amounts should be separately identified by the parties as payments in lieu of notice.

In the same letter, and in response to a question as to whether the full amount of a court award or settlement amount on a wrongful dismissal would qualify as a retiring allowance, Revenue Canada responded:

> If the full amount paid pursuant to the court order or settled between the parties is "in respect of [the] loss of employment," then it is considered to be a retiring allowance in accordance with paragraph (b) of the definition of "retiring allowance" in subsection 248(1) of the Act. If part or all of the amount consists of a payment in lieu of notice, then it is not an amount in respect of the loss of employment, but rather an amount due under the employment contract. It will be considered employment income.

If this stated position is correct, one must question when a payment would ever constitute a retiring allowance. At the Canadian Tax Foundation Conference in December 1993, Revenue Canada was asked to deal with this issue. Its final answer leads to the conclusion that it has reconsidered the position on this point. It now states that if the amount paid by virtue of the terms of the employment contract is for loss of employment, or in recognition of long service, it will be a "retiring allowance." That makes the wording of the employment contract or the negotiated settlement documents increasingly important.

There is still need for clarification on this point from Revenue Canada. Depending on the amounts involved and the circumstances, the most prudent action for employers and employees may be to obtain an advance tax ruling from Revenue Canada confirming how the amounts paid should be treated.

(The discussion of the position of Revenue Canada respecting retiring allowances is excerpted from an article by Susan M. Manwaring which was published in the Hiring and Firing Newsletter by Carswell.)

It is also interesting to note that in *R. v. Albino* (1993), 1 C.C.E.L. (2d) 209 (Fed. T.D.), the Court gave a rather broad interpretation to the definition of ''retiring allowance''. In that case, the Court considered whether a payment under an incentive plan, payable on termination, constituted a retiring allowance. Payments under the incentive plan were based on dividends issued by the company and the market price of the company stock. Amounts were awarded under the incentive plan on an annual basis, but thereafter vested over a nine-year period. As such, the plan encouraged both superior performance and long service.

The Court concluded that the incentive plan payment constituted a retiring allowance, stating:

> [T]he purpose of the Plan was twofold — to provide an employee with a payment for long service and for contributing to the success of the company. Does the fact that the Plan has two objectives, only one of which was to encourage long service, render a payment under the Plan ''remuneration'' under para. 6(3)(*b*) and not a ''retiring allowance'' as defined in subs. 248(1)?
>
> . . . .
>
> In my view, it is implicit in an employee remaining with an employer for a period long enough to be recognized for his or her long service that his or her efforts for the employer must have been at least satisfactory if not better. It would be unrealistic to assume that an amount paid in respect of long service could never also be intended to recognize the contribution of the employee to the employer's business success. In my view, the fact that a plan expressly encourages long service and also expressly encourages an employee to make contributions to the success of the employer's business, does not prevent the amount paid under the plan after retirement from being a ''retiring allowance.''
>
> An amount does not have to be gratuitously paid to qualify as a ''retiring allowance.'' Nothing precludes a ''retiring allowance'' from being provided for in an agreement for considerations and indeed, plaintiff's counsel did not advance such an argument. Section 7 of IT-337R2 states in part:
>
> > . . . Payment of an amount pursuant to a contractual obligation is not disqualified for treatment as a retiring allowance.
>
> The payment in this case is not disqualified from being a ''retiring allowance'' simply because it was provided for in an agreement for consideration. (at pp. 214-215)

Another issue to be considered is whether in fact the employment relationship has been severed. It is not uncommon when negotiating a severance package for the parties to agree that the employer maintain certain benefits for the employee. Careful consideration must be given to the terms of such benefit plans, which often state that only ''employees'' are entitled to receive benefits under the plan. If this is a requirement and a terminated employee is maintained on the plan, notwithstanding the fact the terminated employee is not required to report to work,

Revenue Canada may conclude that the employer/employee relationship has not in fact been terminated and consider any amounts received to be income from employment and not a retiring allowance. For example, in *Serafini v. M.N.R.*, 89 D.T.C. 653, [1989] 2 C.T.C. 2437 (T.C.C.) (under appeal to the Federal Court — Trial Division), the taxpayer appealed an assessment under which the Minister disallowed the deduction of a retiring allowance that the taxpayer had contributed to an RRSP. The Court, in dismissing the taxpayer's appeal, found that the terms of the severance package entered into between Serafini and his employer clearly stated that Serafini was to retire a year after the agreement was entered into. Notwithstanding that Serafini did not attend work between October 30, 1985 and November 1, 1986, he remained a member of the company benefit plan and the pension plan. Taken together, these facts led the Court to conclude that the amounts paid to Serafini between October 30, 1985 and November 1, 1986 were in fact employment income.

(b) Deductibility of Payment

An employer must ensure that the amount paid to an employee as a retiring allowance is reasonable in the circumstances having regard to factors

(*Continued on page 8-3*)

such as length of service, relationship to the amount of remuneration received throughout the years of service, value of pension and other retirement benefits to which the employee is entitled.

Section 67 of the Act provides:

> **67.** In computing income, no deduction shall be made in respect of any outlay or expense in respect of which any amount is otherwise deductible under this Act, except to the extent that the outlay or expense was reasonable in the circumstances.

The Department of National Revenue has indicated in the past that as a rule of thumb a reasonable retiring allowance would be an amount that is not greater than 2½ times the average of the employee's salary earned in the past five years (Taxation of Executive Compensation and Retirement, (1991) Vol. 3, No 4 (published by Federated Press), p. 525).

(c) Employer Obligation to Withhold

Section 153(1)(*c*) of the *Income Tax Act* provides that any person paying a retiring allowance within a taxation year shall withhold an amount set out in the regulations to the *Income Tax Act* and shall remit the amount to the Receiver General at the appropriate time intervals. Any person paying a retiring allowance is also required to report the amount paid on Form T4A supplementary.

Part I of the *Income Tax Regulations*, sections 100 to 109, sets out the rules for determining the amounts which an employer must withhold on account of income tax.

Section 102 of the *Income Tax Regulations* provides the basic withholding rules for employees to whom remuneration is paid on a periodic basis. These rules apply to a retiring allowance which is paid periodically. (A full discussion of the mechanics of section 102 of the *Income Tax Regulations* is beyond the scope of this book. The payroll department of most businesses will be able to carry out the necessary calculations based on regular source deduction tables and formulas.)

The withholding requirements for lump-sum retiring allowance payments are set out in section 103(4) of the Income Tax Regulations. The 1990 Employee Source Deduction Handbook published by Revenue Canada Taxation summarizes the percentage to be withheld from the lump-sum payment to an employee as follows:

> If you make a lump-sum payment to an employee
> — on retirement
> — as compensation for loss of office,
> — in recognition of long service and not out of or under a superannuation fund or plan, or
> — as a retiring allowance,
>
> you must withhold tax from this income at the following federal and provincial composite rates (except for Quebec):

- 10% (5% for Quebec)—if the payment does not exceed $5,000
- 20% (10% for Quebec)—if the payment exceeds $5,000 but does not exceed $15,000
- 30% (15% for Quebec)—if the payment exceeds $15,000.

Note that, from the employee's perspective, these withholding percentages are only estimates and an additional income tax liability for the employee could arise at year end depending on such factors as the level of other income and deductions that may be available for that year.

Special withholding rules apply if the payment is made to a non-resident of Canada. Under section 212(1)(*j*.1) of the *Income Tax Act* a retiring allowance will generally be subject to a 25 per cent withholding tax if payment is made to a non-resident. This 25 per cent withholding tax may be reduced by an applicable tax treaty or convention.

While the definition of retiring allowance is broad, certain components of payments made to an employee upon severance may or may not form part of a retiring allowance and thus may or may not be subject to withholding. Paragraph 6(1)(*a*) of the Act specifically excludes from income from employment any benefit received by a taxpayer derived from counselling services in respect of the re-employment or retirement of the taxpayer. Therefore, to the extent that the employer pays for counselling services in respect of retirement or re-employment, no tax is required to be withheld at source, nor is the value of those services required to be included in the income of the taxpayer. Such an expense is, however, a deductible expense for the employer.

The definition of retiring allowance would certainly include amounts paid on account of lost salary and fringe benefits over the applicable notice period. Uncertainty has arisen, however, in connection with whether amounts paid on account of mental distress and punitive damages, prejudgment and postjudgment interest and costs are properly considered within the definition of retiring allowance.

Revenue Canada was asked to provide clarification with respect to such amounts. By letter dated June 12, 1989, Revenue Canada Taxation has supplied some guidance, with the caution that it will remain "a question of fact as to whether or not any particular amount will form part of a retiring allowance as defined in subsection 248(1) of the Act." Revenue Canada also made the following general observations regarding the withholding requirements for wrongful dismissal payments:

> The phrase "in respect of" which is used in the definition of retiring allowance was given the widest possible scope by the Supreme Court of Canada in *The Queen v. Savage* (83 DTC 5409) and *Nowegijick v. The Queen* (83 DTC 5041). To the extent that an amount can be considered to be in respect of a loss of office or employment and thus a retiring allowance, it is included in the recipient's income and the payor is required to withhold tax.
>
> Where the amount does not form part of a retiring allowance, the nature of the payment must be determined in order to ascertain the extent to which the payor is required to withhold tax.

(i) *Prejudgment Interest*

A technical interpretation issued by Revenue Canada on October 18, 1989 indicated that prejudgment interest is not included in income and as such there is no obligation to withhold tax on account of prejudgment interest (unless paid to a non-resident).

(ii) *Postjudgment Interest*

Revenue Canada made the following comments on postjudgment interest:

> In our view, post-judgment interest is included in income as interest income under paragraph 12(1)(c) of the Act. We confirm that there is no withholding requirement on such an amount.

(iii) *Mental Distress and Punitive Damages*

Revenue Canada made the following comments on mental distress and punitive damages:

> It is a question of fact as to whether or not a particular award for damages, whether punitive, on account of mental distress, or any other kind, is in respect of a loss of office or employment. . . . [I]t is our view that amounts paid for mental distress or as exemplary damages relating to the loss of employment also form part of the retiring allowance.

Accordingly, any amount paid to a taxpayer for mental distress or as punitive damages relating to the loss of employment must be included in an employee's income and an employer is required to withhold tax on that amount.

(d) Legal Expenses

A technical interpretation issued by Revenue Canada on October 18, 1989 indicated that there is no obligation to withhold tax on account of amounts paid with respect to legal expenses incurred by an employee.

Since the enactment of Bill C-28 (S.C. 1990, c. 39), legal expenses incurred are made deductible and legal expenses awarded or reimbursed are to be included in income. In this regard, the technical interpretation, referring to Bill C-28, stated as follows:

> New paragraph 56(1)(l.1) of the Act would require a taxpayer to include in computing income amounts received as an award or reimbursement of legal expenses paid to collect or establish a right to a retiring allowance or benefits under a pension fund or plan in respect of employment. Paragraph 56(1)(l.1) would be applicable to amounts received after 1985 other than amounts received in relation to legal expenses paid before 1986.
>
> New paragraph 60(o.1) would provide for the deductibility of eligible legal expenses paid after 1985 to collect or establish a right to a retiring allowance or pension benefits. Eligible legal expenses would be deductible in a taxation year to the extent that they do not exceed the retiring allowance or pension benefits to

which such expenses relate. The income against which eligible legal expenses may be deducted may be reduced by virtue of a transfer to a registered retirement savings plan or registered pension plan pursuant to paragraph 60(j) or (j.1) of the Act. The non-deductible portion of any such expenses would be eligible for carry forward and deduction in any of the seven subsequent taxation years, to the extent further related income arises.

(e) Liability of Employer for Failure to Withhold

Employers who fail to withhold or remit an amount required by the *Income Tax Act* may be liable for penalties, subject to prosecution, or both.

(i) *Penalties*

Sections 227(8) and 227(9) of the *Income Tax Act* provide a general penalty of 10 per cent of the amount required to be withheld or remitted by an employer. Of course, the employer remains liable for the full amount that has not been withheld or remitted. The penalty is 20 per cent in cases where the failure occurs after an initial penalty had already been assessed and failure to withhold or remit continues. In addition, under section 227(8.3), interest at the prescribed rate is payable on all amounts not withheld or remitted.

(ii) *Offences*

Where an employer fails to comply with the withholding provisions of the *Income Tax Act*, the employer is subject to prosecution under section 238(1) for an offence, punishable on summary conviction by a fine ranging from $1,000 to $25,000, or such a fine and up to 12 months' imprisonment.

(f) Transfer of Retiring Allowance to RPP or RRSP

In general, the full amount of a retiring allowance is included in an employee's taxable income in the year it is received. Section 60(*j*.1) of the *Income Tax Act*, however, permits an employee to make a tax-free transfer of all or a portion of a retiring allowance to a registered pension plan or registered retirement savings plan, in addition to the regular contributions to such plans.

The basic limitation on the portion of a retiring allowance which may be transferred to a RPP or RRSP is that the portion cannot exceed the result obtained by multiplying $2,000 by the number of years the employee was employed by the employer and adding that amount to the amount obtained by multiplying $1,500 by the number of years before 1989 in which the employer did not make contributions to a pension plan for the employee which were vested at the time of the payment of the retiring allowance. For the purposes of this calculation a partial year of employment is considered a full year.

If the portion of the retiring allowance that would qualify under the formula set out is paid directly by the employer into the employee's RPP or RRSP, the employer may obtain a waiver of the withholding tax that would otherwise have to be remitted by completing and filing Form TD2.

8.2 UNEMPLOYMENT INSURANCE ACT

(a) Liability of the Employer for Repayment of Benefits

An employer is liable to remit to the Receiver General a portion of the remuneration an employer is liable to pay to a former employee pursuant to a labour arbitration award, court judgment or otherwise, as set out in sections 37 and 38 of the *Unemployment Insurance Act*, R.S.C. 1985, c. U-1, as amended.

Sections 37 and 38 provide as follows:

> **37.** Where a claimant receives benefit in respect of a period and, pursuant to a labour arbitration award or court judgment or for any other reason, an employer or any other person subsequently becomes liable to pay earnings, including damages for wrongful dismissal, to that claimant in respect of the same period and pays the earnings, that claimant shall pay to the Receiver General as repayment of an overpayment of benefit an amount equal to the benefits that would not have been paid if the earnings had been paid or payable at the time the benefit was paid. [re-en. 1990, c. 40, s. 27]
>
> **38.**–(1) Where pursuant to a labour arbitration award or court judgment, or for any other reason, an employer or other person becomes liable to pay earnings, including damages for wrongful dismissal, to a claimant in respect of a period and has reason to believe that benefit has been paid to the claimant in respect of that period, that employer or other person shall ascertain whether an amount would be repayable under section 37 if such earnings were paid to the claimant and if so shall deduct that amount from the earnings payable to the claimant and remit that amount to the Receiver General as repayment of an overpayment of benefit. [re-en. 1990, c. 40, s. 27]
>
> (2) Where a claimant receives benefit in respect of a period and pursuant to a labour arbitration award or court judgment, or for any other reason, the liability of an employer to pay that claimant earnings, including damages for wrongful dismissal, in respect of the same period is or was reduced by the amount of the benefit or by a portion thereof, the employer shall remit that amount or portion thereof to the Receiver General as repayment of an overpayment of benefit. [re-en. 1990, c. 40, s. 27]

The employer's direct obligation to remit under section 38 is based on the employee's corresponding obligation to remit under section 37. If a dismissed employee has received unemployment insurance benefits for a period, and later the employer becomes liable to pay remuneration to the employee for that same period (for example, under a judgment in a wrongful dismissal action), the employee is liable under section 37 to repay the benefits received.

Under section 38(1) a corresponding obligation is placed on the employer to deduct an amount payable to an employee with respect to an award or judgment "or for any other reason," and remit such amount to the Receiver General as repayment of an overpayment of benefit. The term "or otherwise" (as it existed in an earlier version of the section) was held to encompass out-of-court settlements in *Ferris v. Unemployment Insurance* (1984), 60 N.R. 327

(Fed. C.A.). Note that before the obligation to deduct and remit arises two conditions must be met. First, the employer must be liable to pay remuneration to a claimant in respect of a period in which a benefit has in fact been paid. Second, the employer must have "reason to believe" that a benefit has been paid. If the employer has actual knowledge that a benefit was paid then the obligation to remit is certain. It is not clear from the legislation itself whether or not the employer is under a positive duty to seek information regarding any benefit payments to the employee.

Employment and Immigration Canada was asked to provide clarification with respect to its policies and responded by letter dated June 6, 1989. With respect to the employer's obligation to deduct and remit, Employment and Immigration Canada stated as follows:

> . . . this obligation arises when two conditions are met. First, the employer must have become liable to pay remuneration to a claimant "pursuant to a labour arbitration award, court judgement or otherwise". Secondly, the employer must have "reasons to believe that benefits have been paid to the claimant in respect of that period". When those two conditions are met, the employer must "ascertain whether an amount would be repayable under Section 37 . . . if such remuneration were paid to the claimant and, if so, shall deduct such amount from the remuneration payable by him to the claimant and remit that amount to the Receiver General as payment of an overpayment of benefits."
>
> The obligation for the employer to contact the Commission to "ascertain whether an amount would be repayable under Section 37" arises only when the two conditions referred to above have been met. The employer cannot, however, deduct such amount from the remuneration payable by him to the claimant until it has been ascertained that an amount would be repayable under Section 37.
>
> . . . the mere assumption by an employer that his or her former employee was on claim would not be sufficient to give the employer the power to deduct from the remuneration payable to the claimant any amount pursuant to subsection 38(1).
>
> It is for this reason that a notice is sent to the employer . . . when the claimant files for benefits and it is indicated that the reasons for separation are dismissed or there is any indication that the claimant may seek redress with respect to the separation. This letter advises the employer of the responsibility found in Section 38. . . . [H]owever, . . . the content of this letter is under constant revision . . . .
>
> In determining the extent of this obligation, it must also be remembered that employers should be concerned about the administration of the Program as they do contribute more than 50% of the contributions. This section simply requires that they assume some responsibility to ensure that the integrity of the UI Account is maintained.

A sample of the letter typically sent to employers is as hereinafter set out:

This notice is simply to inform you of your obligations under the law. No action on your part is necessary unless the situation described below takes place.

A former employee of yours, ____________, has established a claim for Unemployment Insurance benefits effective _______.

In cases where an employee does not leave work voluntarily, it's not uncommon for a grievance or similar action to be started under a Federal or Provincial labour code, or in a civil court. If this occurs, and the employee is successful, you as the employer may be required to reinstate and/or pay your former employee wages for the period during which he or she was paid Unemployment Insurance (U.I.) benefits.

If your former employee is successful, or if an out of court settlement is negotiated, you must deduct from any retroactive award or salary settlement, an amount equal to the U.I. benefits paid to the employee, and send that amount to the Receiver General for Canada.

If you're required to reinstate and/or pay retroactive salary or wages to this former employee, please contact this office at ______. We will tell you the amount of U.I. benefits that have been paid. You must then deduct this amount from the wages payable and send it to the Receiver General for Canada in care of this office.

____

Name and Title

Although it is sent at the time of the application for benefits, the letter informs the employer that a claim for benefits has been "established." Such notice may, therefore, provide "reason to believe" that unemployment insurance benefits will be paid to the claimant during the period in question.

Section 38(2) deals with a situation where benefits paid have already been taken into account in determining the amount of an award or judgment. In this situation the employer is again clearly obligated to remit the amount by which the award or judgment was reduced to reflect a benefit already paid.

There is no specific offence in the *Unemployment Insurance Act* for failing to comply with section 38. Section 105(1), however, sets out a general offence for contravening or failing to comply with any provision of the Act or regulations. Section 104 makes an offence under section 105(1) punishable on summary conviction by a fine of up to $5,000 or imprisonment for up to six months, or both. Employment and Immigration Canada advised, with respect to this provision, that:

> Once the two conditions referred to above have been met, the employer is obligated to comply with subsection 38(1) of the *Unemployment Insurance Act*. It is expected that the employer will remit "that portion owing directly to the Commission". A charge could be laid pursuant to subsection 105(1) . . . of the Act for non-compliance. We have no record, however, of cases of employer prosecutions for failure to remit pursuant to subsection 38(1).

9

RIGHTS AND OBLIGATIONS OF DEPARTING EMPLOYEES

9.1 NOTICE OF RESIGNATION

In the absence of an express agreement on point, the employee is obliged to give the employer reasonable advance notice of the resignation of his or her employment. In virtually all cases the notice required of an employee will be substantially less than the notice period that would be required of the employer in the event of the termination of that employee. The reason for this is that the only factor relevant to determining the reasonable period of notice required of an employee is the time it would take the employer to replace the employee or otherwise take steps to adjust to the loss of the employee. In contrast, the reasonable notice of termination required of an employer is largely determined by the age, length of service, and position of the employee. These factors may generate a very long notice period notwithstanding that they do not directly relate to the period of time that the employee will need to find new employment.

In many cases, an employer, presented with advance notice of resignation, will prefer to have the employee leave immediately. A question then arises as to whether the employer is entitled to waive notice of resignation. In the case of *Oxman v. Dustbane Enterprises Ltd.* (1986), 13 C.C.E.L. 209 (Ont. H.C.), varied (1988), 23 C.C.E.L. 157, 32 O.A.C. 154 (C.A.), the notice period offered by the employee was rejected by the employer. The employee, age 42, had been employed for approximately 13 years. His final position before he tendered his resignation was Executive Vice-President, Services, and he was earning approximately $95,000 per year. In the year of his resignation, the company changed hands. This change was fully effective in October. As a result of this new ownership, the compensation scheme was changed from one of salary plus a profit-based bonus to straight salary. The employee was offered a salary of $100,000. The employee contended that he would have earned $105,000 during the year on the previous plan. On November 22, due to his upset over the salary offer, he tendered the following letter to the president of the company. The letter stated:

> This letter will confirm my decision to resign as Executive Vice-President, Modern Building Cleaning for personal reasons so that I may persue [sic] other business opportunities.
>
> I feel as the Senior Officer of the Services Division and the important role this office holds that six months' notice will be sufficient yet necessary to ensure a smooth transaction for the selected candidate to assume this responsibility.
>
> I would be most pleased to assist you in this respect, and provide the necessary guidance to the successful candidate to support the continuity of this office during this change.
>
> I have enjoyed a rewarding career with the Services Division and for this reason I have given my decision a lot of thought before coming to this conclusion.
>
> May I extend to you, my colleagues, and the services Division as a whole, my sincere best wishes for continued success and appreciation for the support and confidence given by all during my tenure as Executive Vice-President. (at pp. 220-221)

The employee presented this letter to his superior. He met to go over the letter and the reasons for his resignation three days later. The employee at that date stated that he was firm in his decision to resign. One week later he met again with his superior. His superior notified him that the company could not accept the six months' notice and instead he presented the employee with a severance package of one month's notice and one month's severance pay. The employee did not accept this counter-offer and left at year end claiming constructive dismissal and wrongful dismissal. The trial Judge, and the Court of Appeal, concluded that the employee was not constructively dismissed. The trial Judge also held that the employer was not bound to accept the six months' notice period and could require the employee to leave earlier. In so doing, Mr. Justice Henry enunciated the following principles:

> (a) An employee may resign from his employment at any time, subject, of course, to the terms of the contract of employment. If he breaches the terms of the contract in so doing, the employer may sue for damages suffered if he can prove them. The employer cannot compel the employee to continue to perform the contract of service.
>
> (b) If there is no contractual term governing the employee's obligation upon resignation, the law requires him to give reasonable notice to the employer. The Court will determine the notice required by reference to similar considerations to those applicable to the dismissal of the employee without cause. The main

purpose of the notice of resignation is to allow the employer a reasonable time to find a replacement.

(c) If the employee resigns voluntarily without giving adequate notice as determined by the Court, the employer may recover damages if proved.

(d) If the employee is found by the Court to have resigned involuntarily, the case should be treated as one of constructive dismissal; the employee is, however, bound by the period of any notice he has given to the employer with his resignation – he cannot claim compensation for the full common law period of notice to which he would be entitled for wrongful dismissal if he has chosen a lesser period for the purposes of his resignation. See *Re Redpath Industries Ltd. and Ison* (1985), 52 O.R. (2d) 770, 9 C.C.E.L. 1, 86 C.L.L.C. 14,029, 11 O.A.C. 371 (sub nom. *Redpath Industries Ltd. v. Ison*) (Ont. Div. Ct.).

(e) If the resignation is voluntary, the notice to which the employer is entitled is a matter of law, not merely a matter of conscience or responsibility on the part of the employee. The employee in giving notice cannot make a virtue of necessity as Mr. Oxman does here.

(f) The requirement that the employee gives notice being in law for the protection of the employer, it can be waived. The employee cannot in law deny that choice to the employer. The risk that he takes if he hopes to gain time to seek other employment is that the employer will waive the notice and release him from his obligations under the contract of employment at once; by so doing the employer also surrenders his right to claim damages. The notice period required is not to give the employee time to find other work.

(g) The resignation of an employee conceptually terminates the relationship with the employer and with it the basis of confidence and trust. Where the parting is amicable, as by mutual agreement, the employer and employee may be expected to negotiate the period of notice and severance terms. These cases are unlikely to come to Court. Where the circumstances of the resignation are in the nature of confrontation, dispute or acrimony, the parties stand on their legal rights. The resignation may take effect immediately and the employee departs at once; the employer may sue for lack of notice or may waive it and accept the employee's conduct. The employee, in these circumstances, cannot claim continued employment (or compensation in lieu thereof) merely because the law requires him to give notice; similarly, if he gives notice he is not entitled to further employment if the employer waives the notice. It is otherwise if the employer accepts the period of notice and in effect extends the contract of employment. In those circumstances I am of opinion that the parties by agreement have put a fixed term on the contract of employment. See *Meyer v. Carstairs (Town)* (1984), 3 C.C.E.L. 258, 52 A.R. 206 (Alta. Q.B.).

(h) In this latter case, once the term has been extended by agreement, in my opinion, the employer who, during that term decides to terminate the employment, must renegotiate that term if he is to avoid a breach.

(i) If the resignation is accompanied by conduct on the part of the employee detrimental to the employer's interest (such as threats to compete, steal confidential information, or seduce other employees) this may be treated as cause for outright severance by the employer.

(j) The resignation may be withdrawn, in which case immediate acceptance of it as if it stood effective, constitutes dismissal. See *Moore v. Univ. of Western Ont.* (1985), 8 C.C.E.L. 157 (Ont. H.C.). (at pp. 232-234)

Mr. Justice Henry concluded that:

> In the case at Bar, the period of notice was waived by the employer as I find. I accept Mr. Perron's evidence that he told Oxman on November 25 that the company did not require the 6 months' notice. Thereafter he confirmed that waiver of the notice on December 6 and followed it up in writing 2 days later and accepted the resignation effective December 31, thus extending the term of employment to that date. Mr. Oxman was paid salary and bonus to that date on the basis of the existing formula; in addition he was paid 1 month's salary based on $100,000, the latter in my opinion being a gratuitous payment. I find the foregoing to be fair dealing in all the circumstances. While that 6 months was properly given by Mr. Oxman as an employee desiring to leave the company, in the circumstances the company was not obliged to retain him as an employee for that 6 months period or to compensate him for it. The 6 months' notice was a term provided by Oxman (and indeed a requirement of the law) for the benefit of the company. The company could waive it and accept his resignation immediately for the reason that the decision to resign was that of Mr. Oxman and unless he negotiated it he was not entitled to force upon the company a period of continued employment while he made other plans. (at p. 234)

The Court of Appeal disagreed, however, with the decision of the trial Judge that an employer can waive the notice given by an employee. The Court of Appeal held that:

> With great respect, I cannot agree with this proposition in the context of the facts of this case. Accepting, as I do, the established principle that an employee is obliged by law to give reasonable notice of the termination of his employment (see *Lazarowicz v. Orenda Engines Ltd.*, [1961] O.R. 141, 26 D.L.R. (2d) 433 (C.A.)), it is clear that, read as a whole, the letter of resignation was notice to Dustbane that Oxman would be leaving his position in 6 months. It makes no sense to read it as an immediate resignation with an offer to remain on in some undefined capacity to ensure "a smooth transition". If his offer to remain for 6 months had been accepted, surely this could only mean that he would continue on as an employee for another 6 months and that his employment would terminate at the end of that period.
>
> The learned trial Judge was of the view that the notice provision was for the benefit of Dustbane and that it was entitled to waive that notice and still accept the resignation. In my opinion, if the offer of resignation is not accepted as offered, which in this case would include a 6-month notice period, its acceptance is not binding on the employee and does not terminate the employment.
>
> The effect then of the proffered severance package by Dustbane was the termination of Oxman's employment on Dustbane's terms. Since Dustbane as employer, had a like duty to terminate on reasonable notice, or pay damages in lieu thereof, the duty of the trial Judge was to determine what would be a reasonable period of notice for Dustbane to give Oxman. Having determined that Oxman's notice to Dustbane of 6 months was more than reasonable, the learned trial Judge should have awarded him damages for wrongful dismissal, the measure of which is the difference between the 1-month period paid by Dustbane and the 6 months offered by Oxman. (at pp. 159-160)

Thus, the Court of Appeal concluded that the stipulated notice period was an integral part of the resignation, such that if the notice period is not accepted, then neither is the resignation. The Court of Appeal did, however, limit the notice period to the reasonable period found by the trial Judge for a resignation of an employee in this position.

The question of what constitutes reasonable notice by an employee to an employer will, of course, depend upon the facts of each case. As might be expected there are few cases to provide guidance. Some assistance, however, is provided by *Engineered Sound Systems Ltd. v. Klampfer* (1994), 3 C.C.E.L. (2d) 105 (Ont. Gen. Div.). In that case the defendant had been employed for 15 years, most recently in a technical sales support and service capacity. The plaintiff was in the business of selling and servicing telecommunications systems. The defendant resigned his employment and provided two weeks notice. The plaintiff took issue with the length of notice and the defendant then offered to provide 30 hours of service to the plaintiff's customers and provide five days of instruction to the plaintiff's employees. The Court concluded that this was reasonable notice in the circumstances.

9.2 NON-COMPETITION

(a) Distinguishing Fiduciary Employees from Non-Fiduciary Employees

In order to discuss the obligations of departing employees in relation to competing with their former employer, it is first necessary to ascertain whether or not the status of the employee is such that the employee owes a fiduciary duty to the employer. In *Can. Aero Service Ltd. v. O'Malley* (1973), [1974] S.C.R. 592, 11 C.P.R. (2d) 206, 40 D.L.R. (3d) 371, Chief Justice Laskin spoke of "top management" and "directors and senior management officials" in describing employees who would have fiduciary duties. In that case, however, the defendants were employed as president and vice-president and as such there was no doubt that their status was that of "top management". Subsequent cases, however, have broadened the class of employees who have fiduciary duties, and also created considerable uncertainty on the point.

In *White Oaks Welding Supplies v. Tapp* (1983), 42 O.R. (2d) 445, 73 C.P.R. (2d) 98, 149 D.L.R. (3d) 159 (H.C.), Mr. Justice Osler found that the sales manager of a welding supply business occupied a fiduciary position stating:

> Nevertheless, the defendant, with his encyclopaedic knowledge of the plaintiff's customers, his unrestricted access to all customer lists and information concerning such customers, and his personal contact with and responsibility for a large proportion of the plaintiff's customers, was a senior employee with a fiduciary relationship to his employer. . . . (at p. 449)

On the other hand, Mr. Justice Barr, in *Genesta Manufacturing Ltd. v. Babey* (1984), 6 C.C.E.L. 291, 48 O.R. (2d) 94, 29 B.L.R. 36, 2 C.P.R. (3d) 32 (H.C.), found that an employee was not "top management" within the meaning of *Can. Aero, supra*, despite the fact that he was "the number two man" in a relatively small company.

Other cases have found a fiduciary duty, not because the individual was "top management" but because the individual was employed in a position of such sensitivity or control that it would be unfair to let the employee compete without being subject to fiduciary duties. *Hudson's Bay Co. v. McClocklin*, [1986] 5 W.W.R. 29, 11 C.P.R. (3d) 523, 42 Man. R. (2d) 283 (Q.B.), provides an example of the extent to which some courts are prepared to expand the scope of the fiduciary obligation. In this case the Court found that the manager of the optical department of a Hudson's Bay store was subject to fiduciary duties, reasoning as follows:

> I have no difficulty in concluding that the plaintiff has demonstrated a strong prima facie case that Mr. McClocklin has been directly soliciting the plaintiff's hearing aid clientele, whom he had come to know and had been serving while he was in the plaintiff's employ. The issue of whether he was thereby in breach of a fiduciary duty to the plaintiff is, perhaps, not quite so easy. Mr. McClocklin hardly represented the "top management" of The Bay. However, The Bay is a department store, and may be viewed, in a sense, as consisting of a large number of separate departments or businesses, of which the hearing aid department, or business, is one. In that limited sphere, Mr. McClocklin was supreme. He managed and controlled the department. He was surely "key" to its functioning. . . .
>
> Some of the principal factors in this case which indicate to me the fiduciary relationship are: the key position occupied by the defendant in the hearing aid department; his long and close personal association with the plaintiff's hearing aid customers; his personal knowledge of them and access to their personal records and needs; the fact that he resigned and was not discharged; and the fact that so soon after leaving he commenced the solicitation complained of. I conclude that there has been at least a prima facie showing of a fiduciary relationship breached by the defendant. (at pp. 33-34)

As can be seen, there is no "bright line" test to apply to distinguish those employees who owe fiduciary duties. As will be seen, however, the mere fact that an employee is, or is not, a fiduciary does not dictate the precise rights and obligations of the employee. As in many areas of the law the courts adopt a practical approach taking into account all of the surrounding circumstances, with the result that rights and obligations of employees may vary somewhat as between different types of fiduciary employees. Thus, a director and officer of a corporation who resigns his employment may be subject to a more exacting fiduciary duty than a person who occupies a subordinate, yet key, position and who is terminated.

(b) Non-Fiduciary Employees

The law favours free competition and to that end there are few restrictions on the right of an employee to compete with a former employer. Thus, in *Edgar T. Alberts Ltd. v. Mountjoy* (1977), 16 O.R. (2d) 682, 2 B.L.R. 178, 36 C.P.R. (2d) 97, 79 D.L.R. (3d) 108 (H.C.), Chief Justice Estey stated as follows:

> It is now beyond argument that a departing servant has the right to compete with his former employer. He may do so by establishing a business in direct or partial competition and he may bring to that business the knowledge and skill which

he acquired while in the former service, including knowledge and skill directly obtained from the previous master in teaching him his business:

> It follows, in my opinion, that the servant may,while in the employment of the master be as agreeable, attentive and skilful as it is in his power to be to others with the ultimate view of obtaining the benefit of the customers' friendly feelings when he calls upon them if and when he sets up business for himself. That is, of course, where there is no valid restrictive clause preventing him doing so.

(*Continued on page 9-7*)

per Maugham, L.J., *Wessex Dairies Ltd. v. Smith*, [1935] 2 K.B. 80 at p. 89.

In an earlier Ontario decision, *Canada Bonded Attorney & Legal Directory Ltd. v. Leonard-Parmiter Ltd.* (1918), 42 O.L.R. 141 at p. 157, 42 D.L.R. 342 at p. 356 (App. Div.), Riddell, J., stated his view of the principle:

> He may, however, make use of knowledge he may have acquired (except in secret formulae etc.,...), or any skill, manual or intellectual – he "is perfectly entitled, when he starts as a rival in business to the plaintiff, to carry it on in the same way as his principal does. He has learnt to do it, and he is entitled to the benefit of that knowledge:" *per* Lindley, L.J., in *Louis v. Smellie* (1895), 73 L.T.R. 226, at p. 228 [C.A.].
>
> . . . .
>
> He may not canvass any customer whose name he has from material obtained or retained in fraud of his employer: S.C.; also *Helmore v. Smith* (1886), 35 Ch.D. 449; but I can find no authority for the proposition that he may not as fair competition canvass those he may remember, even though he first met them when in the previous employ.

This general line of authority has been followed in this Court in *Dominion Al-Chrome Corp. Ltd. v. Stoll et al.* (1974), 14 C.P.R. (2d) 174, wherein Weatherston, J., relied upon the authorities cited above together with a passage from the judgment of Lord Denning, in *Roberts v. Elwells Engineers Ltd.*, [1972] 2 All E.R. 890 at p. 894:

> It is settled law that a servant, having left his master's service, may, without fear of legal consequences, canvass for the custom of his late master's customers, whose names and addresses he has learned during the period of his service, so long as he does not take a list of them away with him: see *Robb v. Green*, [1985] 2 Q.B. 315. (at pp. 686-687)

While more difficult to define, an employee is also subject to a general obligation to not use confidential information for his own benefit. This principle was discussed in *Monarch Messenger Services Ltd. v. Houlding* (1984), 5 C.C.E.L. 219, 56 A.R. 147, 2 C.P.R. (3d) 235 (Q.B.). The defendant had been a driver for a courier service in which capacity he dealt with certain of the larger accounts of the plaintiff. The defendant was terminated and, thereafter, formed a competing business and acquired two large customers who had formerly dealt with the plaintiff. Mr. Justice O'Leary stated the law as follows:

> It is clear from the foregoing that an employee will not be permitted, following termination of his employment, to use for his own benefit confidential information acquired in the course of his employment or information which is "special or peculiar" to his ex-employer. On the other hand, it is equally clear that following termination of the relationship, an employee is free to use for his own benefit or for the benefit of third parties, any skill and general knowledge which he acquires during the course of his employment. The difficult question is to determine what knowledge so acquired is to be considered as confidential or "special or peculiar" and subject to protection for the benefit of the ex-employer. In Batt, The Law of Master and Servant, supra, the type of information which an ex-employee must not use to his own benefit is described as follows at p. 238:

> The information must be of a special or confidential character, since the general information acquired by him in service he may use for his own benefit, and this, even although he is under restrictive covenants. No precise rule or no exhaustive catalogue can be framed. . . .

It is also clear that the information entitled to protection for the benefit of the ex-employer need not be contained in a document or other tangible or physical form. It may include information committed to memory by the ex-employee. (at p. 227)

The Court then concluded that the defendant had breached his obligations, stating:

> I have concluded that in the circumstances of this case, Houlding did in fact make improper use of confidential information acquired by him during the course of his employment with Monarch. In my opinion, certain of the information acquired and used by Houlding must be characterized as confidential and "special or peculiar" to the business of Monarch. Houlding had represented Monarch in dealing with Dome Petroleum and Home Oil for some period of time before his termination. He had become intimately familiar with the special needs of these two companies and had developed a personal relationship with the individuals within those companies who were responsible for employing messenger services. He was familiar with the rates charged by Monarch to these companies. In my opinion, this is the type of information which an employee is prohibited from using for his own benefit during or after his term of employment. I do not believe, on the other hand, that the general knowledge acquired by Houlding during his employment with respect to the operation of a messenger business, can be considered confidential information or as being special or peculiar to Monarch. In the circumstances of this case, however, I am of the view that the specific and intimate knowledge which he acquired concerning Monarch's business dealings with the two large oil companies was of a confidential nature and must be considered as special or peculiar to Monarch's business. This information was, as I have found, improperly used by Houlding following his termination for his own benefit. (at p. 228)

(c) Fiduciary Employees

The starting point in this area is the decision of Chief Justice Laskin in *Can. Aero Service Ltd. v. O'Malley* (1973), [1974] S.C.R. 592, 11 C.P.R. (2d) 206, 40 D.L.R. (3d) 371. The president and vice-president of the plaintiff had been pursuing a lucrative contract on behalf of the plaintiff. When this corporate opportunity had almost reached fruition the president and vice-president resigned their employment, formed a new company, and acquired the contract for themselves. In finding the defendants liable to pay $125,000 in damages for breach of fiduciary duty, Chief Justice Laskin stated:

> . . . They were "top management" and not mere employees whose duty to their employer, unless enlarged by contract, consisted only of respect for trade secrets and for confidentiality of customer lists. Theirs was a larger, more exacting duty which, unless modified by statute or by contract (and there is

nothing of this sort here), was similar to that owed to a corporate employer by its directors. (at p. 606)

. . . .

What these decisions indicate is an updating of the equitable principle whose roots lie in the general standards that I have already mentioned, namely, loyalty, good faith and avoidance of a conflict of duty and self-interest. Strict application against directors and senior management officials is simply recognition of the degree of control which their positions give them in corporate operations, a control which rises above day-to-day accountability to owning shareholders and which comes under some scrutiny only at annual general or at special meetings. It is a necessary supplement, in the public interest, of statutory regulation and accountability which themselves are, at one and the same time, an acknowledgment of the importance of the corporation in the life of the community and of the need to compel obedience by it and by its promoters, directors and managers to norms of exemplary behaviour. (at p. 610)

Edgar T. Alberts Ltd. v. Mountjoy (1977), 16 O.R. (2d) 682, 2 B.L.R. 178, 36 C.P.R. (2d) 97, 79 D.L.R. (3d) 108 (H.C.), deals specifically with the obligations of a departing employee. In this case the plaintiff operated a general insurance agency. The defendant Mountjoy had been employed by the plaintiff as its general manager, and was also a member of its board of directors, until he resigned without notice to start his own insurance agency in competition. A second defendant named Butt had also been employed by the plaintiff, and he resigned his employment to work for Mountjoy in his competing business.

On the facts there was no doubt that Mountjoy's position was such that he was a fiduciary. Further, Chief Justice Estey found that while Butt was a mere employee, by choosing to associate himself with Mountjoy, he was subject to the same fiduciary obligations. Chief Justice Estey then found that there had been a breach of the fiduciary duty, stating:

Thus, the substantial business asset of the plaintiff, namely, its trade attachment with its clients, is a vulnerable asset exposed to the depredations of competition in all forms and particularly competition from ex-employees. Accordingly, it is not surprising to find a fiduciary duty arising in former employees for the protection of the undertaking of the former employer.

In the circumstances with which we are here confronted, a variation of the law relating to corporate opportunity has its application. While the defendant Mountjoy, on the evidence, does not appear to have removed any documents from the premises of the plaintiff, he did leave with a substantial natural advantage which opened up to him the opportunity of taking over for his own profit a substantial trade asset of the plaintiff, that is, its relationship with its insurance clients. (at p. 690)

. . . .

In this case the defendant Mountjoy stood in a fiduciary relationship to the plaintiff and there was accordingly imposed upon him a "larger, more exacting duty" than a duty simply to respect his former employer's trade secrets and the confidentiality of its customer lists. (at p. 692)

. . . .

In my view, the evidence is clear and the inference irresistible, that the defendant Mountjoy set out to establish his own business and to do so by gaining for it the premium income theretofore enjoyed by the plaintiff from its insurance clientele. The defendant Butt participated in this plan at a level commensurate with that which he enjoyed in his employ with the plaintiff. By the end of the first month's operation of the new business established by the defendant Mountjoy, 100% of its commission income came from former clients of the plaintiff. (at p. 693)

In the result the Court awarded the plaintiff damages of $12,500, which was an approximation of the loss of profit the plaintiff would suffer over the two years following Mountjoy's departure.

In *White Oaks Welding Supplies v. Tapp* (1983), 42 O.R. (2d) 445, 73 C.P.R. (2d) 98, 149 D.L.R. (3d) 159 (H.C.), Mr. Justice Osler contrasted the duty of every departing employee from the duty owed by a fiduciary, stating that:

> His obligation was not simply that of every employee to refrain from taking with him material related to his former employer's business and making use of such material. The obligation of Tapp was of an altogether higher nature and was to refrain, not from competition, but from deliberately soliciting customers of the plaintiff, other than as part of the general customer public to whom general solicitation might be made. (at p. 449)

In many types of businesses the legal distinction between impermissible direct solicitation and permissible general solicitation may be of little consequence. First, as a practical matter, direct solicitation is often very difficult to prove, particularly when the departed employee's solicitations are focused on friendly targets. Secondly, in many specialized businesses, a general solicitation such as by a notice in a trade publication will be as effective as a direct solicitation might be in other business contexts. Employers wishing to protect themselves from competition by former employees are, therefore, well advised to secure reasonable restrictive covenants in a written employment contract.

9.3 EMPLOYEE LIABILITY TO EMPLOYER FOR DAMAGES CAUSED BY NEGLIGENCE OR BREACH OF CONTRACT

It is a fact of life that all employees make mistakes from time to time, and in many instances these mistakes cause damage to the employer. Employees who err with frequency will be judged as incompetent and terminated, although usually upon notice or payment in lieu thereof. In rare cases, however, actions have been brought by employers against employees to recover damages caused by negligence or breach of contract on the part of the employee.

In *Overmyer Co. v. Wallace Transfer Ltd.* (1975), [1976] 2 W.W.R. 656, 65 D.L.R. (3d) 717 (B.C.C.A.), the Court considered a case in which Pringle, a 30-year-old high school graduate, had been hired for his first managerial position. Pringle negotiated a lease on behalf of his employer which required 30 days' notice to terminate the tenancy. The employer wanted to terminate the tenancy at a particular time; however, due to the negligence of Pringle notice was not given in a timely fashion. The employer became liable for one extra month's rent, and sued the employee for that amount.

The British Columbia Court of Appeal allowed the employer's claim and its reasoning, in its entirety, is as follows:

> The failure to give the notice in proper time was, in my opinion, negligence. In failing to do what he was clearly required to do he failed to exercise his managerial duties with reasonable care and skill and as a consequence he is liable for the loss suffered by his employer by having to pay the December rent for the leased premises amounting to $4,185. I would allow the appeal and would order that judgment be entered in favour of the appellant, Wallace Transfer Ltd., against the third party, Pringle, in that amount. The case of *Lister v. Romford Ice & Cold Storage Co. Ltd.*, [1957] A.C. 555, [1957] 1 All E.R. 125, followed in this province by *Texada Towing Co. Ltd. v. Minette* (1969), 71 W.W.R. 417, 9 D.L.R. (3d) 286, is clear authority for such a judgment. I respectfully disagree with the learned trial Judge when he indicated that the degree of negligence here falls far short of the degree of negligence that is required. (at p. 657)

Mr. Justice Seaton, in dissent, gave detailed and persuasive reasons in support of dismissing the employer's action. Mr. Justice Seaton distinguished the *Lister* case on the ground that it was concerned with an employer who had been held vicariously liable for the tort of an employee committed in the course of skilled employment. His Lordship then stated:

> In the event of injury to a stranger it is reasonable that the person who caused that injury ought to bear the loss even if his error be only slight. But the same reasoning is not applicable to the employer-employee situation. If by the slightest error the employee causes loss, that is one of the risks of the enterprise that the employer accepts. No employee is infallible and the employer allows for that. He takes it into account when he insures and when he supervises that employee and when he estimates his costs. Losses due to employee error are one of the expenses of the business.
>
> In most cases at the time of the hiring there will be inquiries and undertakings as to the employee's competence. If carefulness is a quality that the job demands there will be inquiries and undertakings with respect to it. What contract is arrived at in that regard is for the parties to decide. If care is important it may be that special insurance will be needed, extra supervision required, or different equipment supplied. In the absence of express agreement as to the degree of care expected I do not think a term ought to be implied that the care will be absolute. (at p. 662)

. . . .

If an employee, by lack of care, causes loss to his employer, I do not think that it should be presumed that the employee will be liable, and I do not think that we should look at decisions on other employment contracts for the answer. We should look at the hiring to see what was said and at the circumstances to see what might properly be implied. It follows that this employment and this error must be looked at to see what terms were in the contract and whether they were breached. (at p. 663)

. . . .

It will be seen at once that this is not a case in which the employer's claim arises out of his vicarious liability for the tort of his employee. Nor is it a case in which there was a failure to perform a skilled job or art or profession for which the employee was hired. It follows that if the answer is to be found by looking at decisions, cases such as *Lister* would not apply but *Pearson v. Black* [(1922), 22 O.W.N. 20 (H.C.)] would. I have already indicated preference for an approach based on each employment having the capacity to include different terms.

There is no express term that can assist the appellant and I do not find an implied one. In his oral reasons dismissing the appellant's claim the trial Judge said:

> As to Pringle's failure to give notice competently, I think that that degree of negligence falls far short of the negligence that is required before a young and inexperienced manager - his first managerial job - 30 years old, who had worked for the company only since May 1972, can be held liable to his own employer.

That makes good sense. I think that it is what the parties would have said had the problem been put to them as a hypothetical one when the employment was agreed upon. It follows that a term to the contrary should not be implied. (at pp. 664-665)

In *Dominion Manufacturers Ltd. v. O'Gorman* (1989), 24 C.C.E.L. 218 (Ont. Dist. Ct.), His Honour Judge Lissaman considered the case of a comptroller who was responsible for the accounting functions of the employer, including responsibility for making the appropriate payroll deductions and remittances. The employee failed to remit the payroll deductions on a timely basis with the result that penalties in the approximate amount of $13,000 were assessed.

While Lissaman D.C.J. commented favourably on the dissenting reasons of Mr. Justice Seaton in *Overmyer*, His Honour found the employee liable, stating:

> Applying Mr. Justice Seaton's reasoning to the case at bar one comes to the conclusion that the defendant Robert O'Gorman should be liable to the plaintiff for the expenses incurred in the nature of penalties, fines and interest charges because of non-payment of payroll remittances, sales remittances and utility bills which total $13,654.60 if I can imply as a term of the contract of hiring that the employer would be indemnified for the losses caused by the acts or non-acts of

> the employee. I do find that the contract contained an implied term of indemnification with respect to such claim. (at p. 223)

It should be noted that in this case the employee was employed in a skilled position and the negligence was gross in that it consisted of a failure to attend to a simple and fundamental function of a comptroller.

In *Ferguson v. Allstate Insurance Co. of Canada* (1991), 35 C.C.E.L. 257 (Ont. Gen. Div.), the plaintiff insurance agent was dismissed for cause which amounted to wilful misconduct and was clearly in breach of his employment contract. The plaintiff failed to ask applicants for insurance the required questions, fabricated their answers and concealed material information from the insurer. The Court had no difficulty in dismissing the claim for wrongful dismissal. It then awarded the employer damages to compensate for the fact it had to pay approximately $124,000.00 in damages pursuant to a policy of insurance which it would not have issued but for the "wilful and deliberate" fabrication of information by the employee.

OTHER LEGISLATION

CONTENTS

EMPLOYERS AND EMPLOYEES ACT

R.S.O. 1990, c. E.12

CONTENTS

Definition

1. In this Act, "wages" means wages or salary whether the employment in respect of which the same is payable is by time or by the job or piece or otherwise. ("salaire") R.S.O. 1980, c. 257, s. 1.

Limitation of voluntary contract of service

2. No voluntary contract of service or indenture is binding for longer than a term of nine years from the date thereof. R.S.O. 1980, c. 257, s. 2.

Agreement for share in profits of business

3.—(1) An agreement entered into by an employee and his or her employer under which a share of the profits of any trade, calling, business or employment is to be paid to the employee in lieu of or in addition to salary, wages or other remuneration, unless the agreement otherwise provides or a contrary intention may be reasonably inferred therefrom, does not,

(*a*) create any relation in the nature of a partnership or the rights or liabilities of partners; or

(*b*) give to the employee the right to examine into the accounts or interfere in the management or affairs of the trade, calling or business.

Employer's statement of profits to be final

(2) Any statement or return by the employer of the net profits of the trade, calling, business or employment on which the employer declares and appropriates the share of profits payable under such agreement is final and conclusive between the parties and all persons claiming under them, and is not impeachable upon any ground, except fraud. R.S.O. 1980, c. 257, s. 3, *revised.*

Complaints by employees for non-payment of wages

4.—(1) Upon the complaint on oath of an employe against his or her employer concerning any non-payment of wages a justice of the peace may summon the employer to appear at a reasonable time to be stated in the summons, and the justice or some other justice upon proof on oath of the personal service of the summons, or of its service as hereinafter authorized, shall examine into the matter of the complaint, whether or not the employer appears, and upon due proof of the cause of complaint the justice may discharge the employee from the service or employment of the employer, and may direct the payment to him or her of any wages found to be due, not exceeding the sum of $500 and the justice shall make such order as to him or her seems just and reasonable for the payment of such wages, with costs, and in case of the non-payment of the same, together with the costs, for the space of eight days after the order has been made the justice shall issue a warrant of distress for the levying of the wages, together with the costs of the order and of the distress.

Warrant for arrest

(2) Where the justice of the peace before whom a complaint is laid under this section is satisfied that the employer is about to leave Ontario, the justice of the peace may issue a warrant in Form 1, in English or French, for the arrest of the employer. R.S.O. 1980, c. 257, s. 4(1, 2), *revised.*

Time within which proceedings may be taken

(3) A proceeding may be taken under this Act within six months after the engagement or employment has ceased, or within six months after the last instalment of wages under the agreement of hiring has become due, whichever last happens.

Work done in Ontario under agreement made out of Ontario

(4) A proceeding may be had for non-payment of wages in respect of service or labour performed in Ontario upon a verbal or written agreement or bargain made out of Ontario.

When master claims set-off

(5) Where the employer claims a set-off or makes a claim for unliquidated damages, the justice of the peace shall investigate the same and give judgment for the balance of wages, if any, due to the claimant after deducting the set-off or claim.

Limit of jurisdiction as to set-off

(6) The justice of the peace does not have jurisdiction to adjudicate upon a set-off or claim exceeding the claim for wages except to the extent of the wages. R.S.O. 1980, c. 257, s. 4(4-7), *revised.*

Additional remedy in cases before provincial judge

5. Where the proceeding is taken before a provincial judge, and payment of wages is ordered by him or her to be made by the employer to the employee, and the same are not paid within the time limited by the order, the same proceeding may be taken by the person claiming the benefit of the order as may be taken by a party having an unsatisfied judgment or order in the Small Claims Court for the payment of any debt, damages or costs, as respects the examination of the judgment debtor touching the judgment debtor's estate and effects and means of discharging the liability, and the disposal the judgment debtor has made of any property, and the provincial judge has the like power and authority to enforce payment of the debt as are possessed by a judge of the Small Claims Court in like cases, and the practice and procedure thereon shall be the same as nearly as may be and have the same effect as in the Small Claims Court. R.S.O. 1980, c. 257, s. 5, *revised.*

Limit of time for payment

6. Subject to section 8, the provincial judge may name in the order for payment of wages such time, not exceeding twenty-one days, as to him or her may seem just and reasonable for the payment of the same and costs, and in case of non-payment within such time the complainant is entitled to take forthwith the proceeding for enforcing payment herein provided. R.S.O. 1980, c. 257, s. 6.

Procedure upon order of provincial judge

7. Where an order is made under this Act by a provincial judge for the payment of money, such order may be proceeded upon and enforced in the manner provided by section 787 of the *Criminal Code* (Canada) and it applies as if it were set out and enacted herein. R.S.O. 1980, c. 257, s. 7.

Jurisdiction of provincial judges

8.—(1) In the case of wages due to any person in respect of services supplied to an improvement within the meaning of the *Construction Lien Act*, the jurisdiction of a provincial judge under this Act extends to wages for thirty days, or for a balance equal to the wages for thirty days, though the same or the balance thereof exceed the sum of $400. R.S.O. 1980, c. 257, s. 8(1), *revised.*

Where no specific rate of wages agreed on

(2) Where no specific rate of wages has been expressly agreed to between the parties, the provincial judge may order payment of the wages, reckoning the amount

thereof according to the current rate of wages in like cases, or according to what may appear to be a just and reasonable allowance. R.S.O. 1980, c. 257, s. 8(2).

Order for payment of wages, enforcing

(3) The order shall direct payment of the wages to be made forthwith, and a warrant of distress shall be issued accordingly, unless the employer takes oath, and the provincial judge believes, that the employer is unable to make the payment forthwith, and expects to be able to pay and intends to pay the same within the time given, and unless also the provincial judge considers the proposed delay to be under the circumstances reasonable, and the provincial judge, if he or she sees fit, may order security to be given as a condition of delay.

Adjournment at instance of employer

(4) In case of an adjournment at the instance of the employer the same shall be on payment for the claimant's time in attending the court, the amount to be fixed by the provincial judge, and such payment shall be made forthwith unless the provincial judge sees reason for dispensing with immediate payment.

Enforcement in Small Claims Court

(5) The order for payment may be filed in the Small Claims Court, and on such filing the order becomes a judgment of the Small Claims Court and may be enforced as a judgment of that court. R.S.O. 1980, c. 257, s. 8(3-5), *revised.*

Service of summons, etc.

9.—(1) Every summons issued under this Act against an individual, firm or corporation, and every subsequent paper or process in the action or proceeding in which the summons has been issued may be served, except in the cases provided for by subsection (2), upon the person to whom it is directed either by delivering it personally or, if the person cannot be found conveniently, by leaving the same for the person at any place where such individual, firm or corporation carries on business with some adult person employed in the office or place of business of such person. R.S.O. 1980, c. 257, s. 9(1), *revised.*

Service on certain public companies

(2) In cases against railway, telegraph, telephone or express companies every such summons and other papers may be served on any agent of the company whose office or place of business as such agent is within Ontario, and for the purposes of this section the word "agent" includes,

- (*a*) in the case of a railway company, a station master having charge of a station belonging to the company;
- (*b*) in the case of a telegraph company, a person having charge of a telegraph office belonging to the company;
- (*c*) in the case of a telephone company, a person having charge of a telephone office belonging to the company; and
- (*d*) in the case of an express company, a person having charge of an express office belonging to the company.

Effect of service under this section

(3) Service as authorized by this section has the same effect as personal service. R.S.O. 1980, c. 257, s. 9(2, 3).

Appeal

10.—(1) An appeal from an order for the payment of wages, or order of dismissal from service or employment, or against any decision of any justice of the peace or provincial judge under this Act shall be made to the Ontario Court (General Division), and in case of dismissal of the appeal, or affirmance of the order or decision, the court appealed to shall enforce the order for payment of wages or of dismisssal, and for the payment of the costs awarded, and shall, if necessary, issue process for carrying such judgment into effect. R.S.O. 1980, c. 257, s. 10(1); 1989, c. 56, s. 28(1).

Idem

(2) The appeal shall be taken within the time and as nearly as may be, in the manner provided by the *Provincial Offences Act* as to appeals to the Ontario Court (General Division), and the proceedings upon and incidental to the appeal and subsequent thereto shall, except as provided by subsection (1) and by section 11, be the same as nearly as may be, as in the case of an appeal under the *Provincial Offences Act.* R.S.O. 1980, c. 257, s. 10(2), *revised.*

Contracts waiving application of Act to be void

11.—(1) Every agreement or bargain, verbal or written, expressed or implied, on the part of any person employed in manual labour whereby it is agreed that this Act shall not apply, or that the remedies hereby provided shall not be available for the benefit of any person entering into such agreement, is void. R.S.O. 1980, c. 257, s. 12(1), *revised.*

Section not to apply to certain persons

(2) This section does not apply to any manager, officer or superintendent. R.S.O. 1980, c. 257, s. 12(2).

FORM 1

Employers and Employees Act

(Section 4(2))

WARRANT TO ARREST

Province of Ontario)
of)

To the Peace Officers in the said ....

Whereas a complaint has been made against ....

of .... under the *Employer and Employees Act*; and whereas I am satisfied that the said .... is about to leave Ontario;

This is therefore to command you, in Her Majesty's name, forthwith to arrest the said .... and bring him or her before .... to be dealt with according to law.

DATED at ...., this .... day of .... 19 ....

....

Justice of the Peace

R.S.O. 1980, c. 257, Form 1, *revised.*

INCOME TAX ACT

S.C. 1970-71-72, c. 63*

CONTENTS

. . . .

Amounts to be included as income from office or employment

6.—(1) There shall be included in computing the income of a taxpayer for a taxation year as income from an office or employment such of the following amounts as are applicable:

value of benefits

(*a*) the value of board, lodging and other benefits of any kind whatever received or enjoyed by him in the year in respect of, in the course of, or by virtue of an office or employment, except any benefit

(i) derived from his employer's contributions to or under a registered pension plan, group sickness or accident insurance plan, private health services plan, supplementary unemployment benefit plan, deferred profit sharing plan or group term life insurance policy,

* As am. to S.C. 1993, c. 24.

(ii) under a retirement compensation arrangement, an employee benefit plan or an employee trust,
(iii) that was a benefit in relation to the use of an automobile, except to the extent that it related to the operation of the automobile,
(iv) derived from counselling services in respect of
(A) the mental or physical health of the taxpayer or an individual related to the taxpayer, other than a benefit attributable to an outlay or expense to which paragraph 18(1)(*l*) applies, or
(B) the re-employment or retirement of the taxpayer, or
(v) under a salary deferral arrangement, except to the extent that the benefit is included under this paragraph by reason of subsection (11);

. . . .

Amounts to be included from business or property

12.—(1) There shall be included in computing the income of a taxpayer for a taxation year as income from a business or property such of the following amounts as are applicable:

. . .

interest

(*c*) any amount received by the taxpayer in the year or receivable by him in the year (depending upon the method regularly followed by the taxpayer in computing his profit) as, on account or in lieu of payment of, or in satisfaction of, interest to the extent that such interest was not included in computing his income for a preceding taxation year;

. . . .

Amounts to be included in income for year

56.—(1) Without restricting the generality of section 3, there shall be included in computing the income of a taxpayer for a taxation year,

. . .

[legal costs]

(*l*.1) amounts received by the taxpayer in the year as an award or a reimbursement in respect of legal expenses (other than those relating to a division or settlement of property arising out of, or on a breakdown of, a marriage) paid to collect or establish a right to a retiring allowance or a benefit under a pension fund or plan (other than a benefit under the *Canada Pension Plan* or a provincial pension plan as defined in section 3 of that Act) in respect of employment;

. . . .

Other deductions

60. There may be deducted in computing a taxpayer's income for a taxation year such of the following amounts as are applicable:

. . .

transfer of superannuation benefits

(*j*) such part of the aggregate of all amounts each of which is

(i) a superannuation or pension benefit (other than any amount in respect of the benefit that is deducted in computing the taxable income of the taxpayer for a taxation year because of subparagraph 110(1)(*f*)(i) or a benefit that is part of a series of periodic payments) payable out of or under a pension plan that is not a registered pension plan, attributable to services rendered by the taxpayer or a spouse or former spouse of the taxpayer in a period throughout which such person was not resident in Canada, and included in computing the income of the taxpayer for the year because of subparagraph 56(1)(*a*)(i), or

(ii) an eligible amount in respect of the taxpayer for the year pursuant to section 60.01, subsection 104(27) or (27.1) or paragraph 147(10.2)(*d*),

as

(iii) is designated by the taxpayer in the taxpayer's return of income under this Part for the year, and

(iv) does not exceed the aggregate of all amounts each of which is an amount paid by the taxpayer in the year or within 60 days after the end of the year

(A) as a contribution to or under a registered pension plan for the taxpayer's benefit, other than the portion thereof deductible under paragraph 8(1)(*m*) in computing the taxpayer's income for the year, or

(B) as a premium (within the meaning assigned by subsection 146(1)) under a registered retirement savings plan under which the taxpayer is the annuitant (within the meaning assigned by subsection 146(1)), other than the portion thereof designated for a taxation year for the purposes of paragraph (*l*),

to the extent that the amount was not deducted in computing the taxpayer's income for a preceding taxation year;

. . .

transfer of surplus

(*j*.01) such part of the aggregate of all amounts each of which is an amount received by the taxpayer before March 28, 1988 that can reasonably be considered to be a payment in respect of the actuarial surplus under a defined benefit provision (within the meaning assigned by subsection 147.1(1)) of a registered pension plan and that is included in computing the income of the taxpayer for the year by virtue of subparagraph 56(1)(*a*)(i) (other than any portion thereof deducted by the taxpayer under subsection 60.2(1) in computing the taxpayer's income for the year) as

(i) is designated by the taxpayer in the taxpayer's return of income under this Part for the year, and

(ii) does not exceed the aggregate of all amounts each of which is an amount paid by the taxpayer in the year or within 60 days after the end of the year

(A) as a contribution to or under a registered pension plan for the taxpayer's benefit, other than the portion thereof deductible under paragraph 8(1)(*m*) or (*m*.1) or 60(*j*) or (*j*.1) in computing the taxpayer's income for the year, or

(B) as a premium (within the meaning assigned by subsection 146(1)) under a registered retirement savings plan under which the taxpayer is the annuitant (within the meaning assigned by subsection 146(1)), other than the portion thereof that has been designated for the purposes of paragraph (*j*), (*j*.1) or (*l*),

to the extent that it was not deducted in computing the taxpayer's income for a preceeding taxation year;

. . .

transfer of retiring allowances

(*j*.1) such part of the aggregate of all amounts each of which is an amount paid to the taxpayer by an employer, or under a retirement compensation arrangement to which the employer has contributed, as a retiring allowance and included in computing his income for the year by virtue of subparagraph 56(1)(*a*)(ii) or paragraph 56(1)(*x*) as

(i) is designated by the taxpayer in his return of income under this Part for the year,

(ii) does not exceed the amount, if any, by which the aggregate of

(A) $2,000 times the number of years during which the employee or former employee in respect of whom the payment was made (in this paragraph referred to as the "retiree") was employed by the employer or a person related to the employer, and

(B) $1,500 times the number by which the number of years before 1989 described in clause (A) exceeds the number that can reasonably be regarded as the equivalent number of years before 1989 in respect of which employer contributions under either a pension plan or a deferred profit sharing plan of the employer or a person related to the employer had vested in the retiree at the time of the payment

exceeds the aggregate of

(C) all amounts deducted under this paragraph in respect of amounts paid before the year in respect of the retiree

(I) by the employer or a person related to the employer, or

(II) under a retirement compensation arrangement to which the employer or a person related to the employer has contributed;

(C.1) all other amounts deducted for the year under this paragraph in respect of amounts paid in the year in respect of the retiree

(I) by a person related to the employer, or

(II) under a retirement compensation arrangement to which a person related to the employer has contributed, and

(D) all amounts deducted under paragraph (*t*) in computing the retiree's income for the year in respect of a retirement compensation arrangement to which the employer or a person related to the employer has contributed, and

(iii) does not exceed the aggregate of all amounts each of which is an amount paid by the taxpayer in the year or within 60 days after the end of the year in respect of the amount so designated

(A) as a contribution to or under a registered pension plan, other than the portion thereof deductible under paragraph (*j*) or 8(1)(*m*) in computing his income for the year, or

(B) as a premium (within the meaning assigned by section 146) under a registered retirement savings plan under which he is the annuitant (within the meaning assigned by section 146), other than the portion thereof that has been designated for the purposes of paragraph (*j*) or (*l*),

to the extent that it was not deducted in computing his income for a preceding taxation year

and for the purposes of this paragraph, "person related to the employer" includes

(iv) any person whose business was acquired or continued by the employer, and

(v) a previous employer of the retiree whose service therewith is recognized in determining the retiree's pension benefits;

. . .

legal expenses

(*o*.1) the amount, if any, by which the lesser of

(i) the total of all legal expenses (other than those relating to a division or settlement of property arising out of, or on a breakdown of, a marriage) paid by the taxpayer in the year or in any of the 7 preceding taxation years to collect or establish a right to an amount of

(A) a benefit under a pension plan (other than a benefit under the *Canada Pension Plan* or a provincial pension plan as defined in section 3 of that Act) in respect of the employment of the taxpayer or a deceased individual of whom the taxpayer was a dependant, relation or legal representative, or

(B) a retiring allowance of the taxpayer or a deceased individual of whom the taxpayer was a dependant, relation or legal representative, and

(ii) the amount, if any, by which the aggregate of all amounts each of which is

(A) an amount described in clause (i)(A) or (B)

(I) that is received after 1985,

(II) in respect of which legal expenses described in subparagraph (i) were paid,

(III) that is included in computing the income of the taxpayer for the year or a preceding taxation year, or

(B) an amount included in computing the income of the taxpayer under paragraph 56(1)(*l*.1) for the year or a preceding taxation year,

exceeds the aggregate of all amounts each of which is an amount deducted under paragraph (*j*), (*j*.01), (*j*.1) or (*j*.2) in computing the income of the taxpayer for the year or a preceding taxation year, to the extent that the amount may reasonably be considered to have been deductible as a consequence of the receipt of an amount referred to in clause (A),

exceeds

(iii) the portion of the aggregate described in subparagraph (i) in respect of the taxpayer that may reasonably be considered to have been deductible under this paragraph in computing the income of the taxpayer for a preceding taxation year;

. . . .

General limitation re expenses

67. In computing income, no deduction shall be made in respect of an outlay or expense in respect of which any amount is otherwise deductible under this Act, except to the extent that the outlay or expense was reasonable in the circumstances.

. . . .

Withholding

153.—(1) Every person paying at any time in a taxation year

. . .

(*c*) a retiring allowance,

. . .

shall deduct or withhold therefrom such amount as may be determined in accordance with prescribed rules and shall, at such time as may be prescribed, remit that amount to the Receiver General on account of the payee's tax for the year under this Part or Part XI.3, as the case may be, and, where at the prescribed time the person is a prescribed person, the remittance shall be made to the account of the Receiver General at a financial institution (within the meaning that would be assigned by the definition "financial institution" in subsection 190(1) if that definition were read without reference to paragraphs (*d*) and (*e*) there of).

. . . .

Tax

212.—(1) Every non-resident person shall pay an income tax of 25% on every amount that a person resident in Canada pays or credits, or is deemed by Part I to pay or credit, to him as, on account or in lieu of payment of, or in satisfaction of,

. . .

retiring allowances

(*j*.1) a payment of any allowance described in subparagraph 56(1)(*a*)(ii), except

(i) such portion, if any, of the payment as may reasonably be regarded as attributable to services rendered by the person, to or in respect of whom the payment is made, in taxation years
(A) at no time during which he was resident in Canada, and
(B) throughout which he was not employed, or was only occasionally employed, in Canada, and
(ii) the portion thereof transferred by the payer on behalf of the non-resident person pursuant to an authorization in prescribed form to a registered pension fund or plan or to a registered retirement savings plan under which the non-resident person is the annuitant (within the meaning assigned by section 146) that would, if the non-resident person had been resident in Canada throughout the year, be deductible in computing his income by virtue of paragraph 60(*j*.1);

. . . .

Penalty

227(8) Subject to subsection (8.5), every person who in a calendar year has failed to deduct or withhold any amount as required by subsection 153(1) or section 215 is liable to a penalty of

(*a*) 10% of the amount that should have been deducted or withheld; or
(*b*) where at the time of the failure a penalty under this subsection was payable by the person in respect of an amount that should have been deducted or withheld during the year and the failure was made knowingly or under circumstances amounting to gross negligence, 20% of the amount.

. . . .

Interest on amounts not deducted or withheld

(8.3) A person who has failed to deduct or withhold any amount as required by subsection 135(3) or 153(1) or section 215 shall pay to the Receiver General interest on the amount at the prescribed rate, computed

(*a*) in the case of an amount required by subsection 153(1) to be deducted or withheld from a payment to another person, from the fifteenth day of the month immediately following the month in which the amount was required to be deducted or withheld, or from such earlier day as may be prescribed for the purposes of subsection 153(1), to,
(i) where that other person is not resident in Canada, the day of payment of the amount to the Receiver General, and
(ii) where that other person is resident in Canada, the earlier of the day of payment of the amount to the Receiver General and April 30 of the year immediately following the year in which the amount was required to be deducted or withheld; and
(*b*) in the case of an amount required by subsection 135(3) or section 215 to be deducted or withheld, from the day on which the amount was required to be deducted or withheld to the day of payment of the amount to the Receiver General.

. . .

Penalty

(9) Subject to subsection (9.5), every person who in a calendar year has failed to remit or pay as and when required by this Act or a regulation an amount deducted or withheld as required by this Act or a regulation or an amount of tax that he is, by section 116 or by a regulation made under subsection 215(4), required to pay is liable to a penalty of

(*a*) 10% of that amount; or
(*b*) where at the time of the failure a penalty under this subsection was payable by the person in respect of an amount that should have been remitted or paid during the year and the failure was made knowingly or under circumstances amounting to gross negligence, 20% of that amount.

. . .

Offences

238.—(1) Every person who has failed to file or make a return as and when required by or under this Act or a regulation or who has failed to comply with subsection 116(3), 127(3.1) or (3.2), 147.1(7) or 153(1), any of sections 230 to 232 or a regulation made under section 147.1(18) or with an order made under subsection (2) is guilty of an offence and, in addition to any penalty otherwise provided, is liable on summary conviction to

(*a*) a fine of not less than $1,000 and not exceeding $25,000; or
(*b*) such a fine and imprisonment for a term not exceeding 12 months.

. . . .

Definitions

248.—(1) In this Act,

. . .

"retiring allowance"

"retiring allowance" means an amount (other than a superannuation or pension benefit, an amount received as a consequence of the death of an employee or a benefit described in subparagraph 6(1)(*a*)(iv)) received

(*a*) upon or after retirement of a taxpayer from an office or employment in recognition of his long service, or
(*b*) in respect of a loss of an office or employment of a taxpayer, whether or not received as, on account or in lieu of payment of, damages or pursuant to an order or judgment of a competent tribunal

by the taxpayer or, after his death, by a dependant or a relation of the taxpayer or by the legal representative of the taxpayer;

. . . .

UNEMPLOYMENT INSURANCE ACT

R.S.C. 1985, c. U-1

[as am. up to 1993, c. 1, s. 2]

. . . .

Return of benefit by employee

37. Where a claimant receives benefit in respect of a period and, pursuant to a labour arbitration award or court judgment, or for any other reason, an employer or any other person subsequently becomes liable to pay earnings, including damages for wrongful dismissal, to that claimant in respect of the same period and pays the earnings, that claimant shall pay to the Receiver General as repayment of an overpayment of benefit an amount equal to the benefits that would not have been paid if the earnings had been paid or payable at the time the benefit was paid.

[re-en. 1990, c. 40, s. 27]

Return of benefit by employer

38.—(1) Where pursuant to a labour arbitration award or court judgment, or for any other reason, an employer or other person becomes liable to pay earnings, including damages for wrongful dismissal, to a claimant in respect of a period and has reason to believe that benefit has been paid to the claimant in respect of that period, that employer or other person shall ascertain whether an amount would be repayable under section 37 if the earnings were paid to the claimant and if so shall deduct that amount from the earnings payable to the claimant and remit that amount to the Receiver General as repayment of an overpayment of benefit. [re-en. 1990, c. 40, s. 27]

Idem

(2) Where a claimant receives benefit in respect of a period and pursuant to a labour arbitration award or court judgment, or for any other reason, the liability of an employer to pay that claimant earnings, including damages for wrongful dismissal, in respect of the same period is or was reduced by the amount of the benefit or by a portion thereof, the employer shall remit that amount or portion thereof to the Receiver General as repayment of an overpayment of benefit. [re-en. 1990, c. 40, s. 27]

[re-en. 1990, c. 40, s. 27]

. . . .

Contravention of Act

105.—(1) Every person who contravenes or fails to comply with any provision of this Act or the regulations is guilty of an offence.

Obstructing officer

(2) Every person who delays or obstructs an officer of the Commission in carrying out his duties or exercising his powers under this Act or the regulations is guilty of an offence.

. . . .

Returns

124. Where a claimant is required to pay a benefit repayment for a taxation year, a return in a form, and containing information, prescribed by order of the Minister shall, without notice or demand therefor, be filed with the Minister as part of the claimant's return of income under Part I of the *Income Tax Act*,

(*a*) in the case of a claimant who has died after October in the year and before May in the immediately following year, by the claimant's legal representative within six months after the day of death;

(*b*) in the case of any other claimant, on or before April 30 in the next year, by that claimant or, if for any reason he is unable to file the return, by his legal guardian, curator, tutor, committee or other legal representative; or

(*c*) in a case where the claimant or his legal representative has not filed the return, by such person as is required by notice in writing from the Minister to file the return, within such reasonable time as the notice specifies.

[am. 1991, c. 49, s. 234]

INDEX

All references are to headings of the text, unless a page reference to an Appendix is given.